Sixth Edition

Harmonic Materials in Tonal Music

A PROGRAMED COURSE

Part II

Paul O. Harder

Greg A. Steinke The University of Arizona

Allyn and Bacon Boston London Sydney Toronto

Library of Congress Cataloging-in-Publication Data

Harder, Paul O.

Harmonic materials in tonal music: a programed course / Paul O. Harder, Greg A. Steinke.—6th ed.

p. cm.

Includes bibliographical references.

ISBN 0–205–12317–1 (v. 1). — ISBN 0–205–12319–8 (v. 2)

1. Harmony—Programmed instruction. I. Steinke, Greg A., 1942– II. Title.

MT50.H26 1990

781.2'5'077—dc20 89-18154

CIP

MN

Series Editor: Stephen P. Hull
Editorial-Production Services: Helyn Pultz
Manufacturing Buyer: Tamara Johnson

Printed in the United States of America

10 9 8 7 6 5 4 3 2 1 95 94 93 92 91 90

Contents

Preface to the Sixth Edition

It is a challenging task to revise a book that has already enjoyed many years of success and has been through five editions over more than twenty years. It has indeed been an honor to be asked to undertake the revision of this edition, and it was with some trepidation that I approached the task. However, I have had a deep belief in these books ever since I first used them as a very young theory teacher back in 1967, when they were first available. With a lot of history behind me, the highest respect and regard for all of Paul Harder's diligent efforts over the years on these books, I now offer various revisions and enhancements to the books, which I believe keep to the original spirit of Dr. Harder's programmed concept, and which I hope all users will find helpful as they work through these pages.

In making the revisions, I have tried to respond to comments that were made available to me from Dr. Harder's estate, reviewers, and current users of the books. The revisions are most apparent in additions made to the supplementary exercises, dropping the use of the d^7 in favor of the circle and slashed circle in conjunction with diminished seventh chords, and some additions to the appendix material. In selected places throughout the book I tried to clarify definitions or soften them to allow a broader interpretation, or to demonstrate to the reader that there are always alternatives to those ideas presented in the book, and that the reader should explore them on his or her own or in class with the instructor. In making these changes in tone, I hope that the differences in theoretical and analytical approaches (which I know will always be there) can work comfortably with these books and also provide many interesting points of discussion in class. I'm quite sure that Dr. Harder never intended these volumes to be the final definitive answer, but rather to provide an informed point of departure to explore the many anomalies that are always to be found in musics everywhere.

The exposition of the material is presented via a four-part, step-by-step process, which, to some, may seem mechanical, but it does ensure, in general, a good understanding of the basic tenets of the harmonic materials of the so-called common practice period in music. I would emphasize that this approach does not preclude presenting alternatives nor the exploration of other possibilities of how composers may work with various cause and effect relationships as they write rather than following any set of rules. A very rich learning experience can be created for all concerned, instructor as well as student, by exploring together all the many exceptions to the so-called rules or principles. In so doing, it becomes possible to link all that is studied to actual musical literature, or to create many varieties of creative assignments to solidify the understanding of the basic harmonic framework presented within these pages.

I am grateful both to Mildred Harder, who recommended me to undertake these revisions, and to Allyn and Bacon, for accepting the recommendation and providing helpful comments and support throughout the revision process. I also wish to thank Mrs. Harder for providing me with access to all notes and support materials Dr. Harder used in the original creation of these books and for her ever-helpful comments and moral support to complete this project. I would also thank long-time colleagues David Steck and Gary White for their comments, encouragement, and assistance on revision ideas; also my new colleagues here at The University of Arizona, J. Timothy Kolosick and Timothy Kloth for similar help and encouragement; and the reviewers who also provided a number of valuable comments and feedback in the revision process: Moonyeen Albrecht, Central Michigan University, Robert Dickow, University of Idaho, Tom Durham, Brigham Young University, Jerome Laszloffy, University of Connecticut, Alex Lubet, University of Minnesota, Minneapolis, Lynn Roginske, Wisconsin Conservatory of Music, Howard Slenk, Calvin College, and David Stech, University of Alaska, Fairbanks. I am grateful to all concerned and am most appreciative of the help they have all provided. And finally, special thanks go to my wife, Kari, and my two boys, Carl and Kyle, for being patient and quiet while I worked and always offering moral support. I hope users of these volumes will find many hours of rich musical learning to enhance their developing musicianship.

G.A.S.

Preface to the Fifth Edition

This book is the second of a two-part study of tonal harmony. The first volume concerns the concepts and techniques associated with harmonic tonality, triads, phrase structure, harmonic progression, and nonharmonic tones. The material covered in this volume includes seventh, ninth, eleventh, and thirteenth chords; various types of altered nonharmonic tones and chords; and modulation.

The refinements incorporated into this edition are designed to make the book an even more useful aid for learning the materials and practices of tonal harmony. One change concerns the summaries that follow the expository section of each chapter. For a more complete overview of the main points covered, many of the summaries have been expanded. The summaries, plus all new mastery frames, help the learners assess their comprehension of the information before proceeding. Another change involves the supplementary assignments, which are also all new. In addition, they are now organized so that each may be removed separately from the book to submit to the instructor for evaluation.

The chief emphasis in this two-part study of tonal harmony is on the basic elements of harmony that have retained their validity throughout the period from about 1600 to 1900. Music from this period is still very much a part of our musical life. Not only does a large part of the current repertoire consist of eighteenth- and nineteenth-century music, but tonal harmony is the basis of practically all commercial music. All composers, no matter what style they generally employ, turn to tonal harmony when such material is appropriate to their expressive purpose. This book is not devoted to the study of any one composer's works, nor is it limited to four-part writing; various applications of harmonic principles are shown in musical examples drawn from a variety of periods and compositional types.

Since most of the music we hear and perform is based on tonal harmony, it is essential that serious students become familiar with this system. For the composer, competence in writing requires thorough understanding of techniques practiced by composers of previous generations. For the performer, the ability to convey delicate nuances and subtleties of phrasing often stems from a cultivated sensitivity to harmonic processes.

Experience has shown that the type of programed instruction used in this book can lead to rapid, yet thorough mastery of musical concepts and techniques. Also, it has proved to be versatile in that it can be used not only by a single student working independently, but also by students in large classes. Still more important is the flexibility that programed material brings to the instructor. The core of knowledge contained in this book may be expanded by emphasis upon creative writing, analysis, or the study of music literature. Because students evaluate their own exercises, the instructor is free to prepare more vital and creative supplementary learning experiences.

The development of this course was supported by the Educational Development Program at Michigan State University. The author is grateful to Dr. John Dietrich, Assistant Provost, and Dr. Robert Davis, Director of the Educational Development Program, for their assistance; also to Drs. Jere Hutcheson, Clifford Pfeil, and Gary White, who helped develop practical classroom methods. Particular tribute, though, must be paid to the many students who, over a period of several years, assisted in proving out the approaches incorporated in this book. Thanks also go to Rita Fuszek, Professor of Music at California State University, Fullerton, the diligent pianist who recorded the examples contained in the cassettes that accompany this book. And finally, special thanks go to my wife Mildred, who has not only typed countless pages over the years, but provided helpful comment and moral support.

How to Use This Book

This book features the use of programed instruction to convey conceptual information and provide drills to develop techniques for handling harmonic materials. In programed instruction, information is presented in small, carefully sequenced parcels which combine in cumulative fashion to give students mastery of the subject. The parcels into which the material is divided are called *frames.* Most frames require a written response, which may be a word or two, or consist of the solution of a musical problem. Since correct answers are provided by the book itself, this type of material is self-correcting; thus students may work entirely alone and proceed at their own pace. When used in class, supplementary examples and lessons may be supplied by the instructor as he or she sees fit.

The principal part of each frame is located on the right-hand side of the page. The answers, which appear on the left-hand side, should be covered with a slip of paper or a ruler (merely the hand will do). After the response is written, the appropriate answer is uncovered so the response may be checked immediately. Since each step in this process is small, few mistakes are made. Because of this, learning is reinforced and misconceptions have little chance to become part of the student's thinking.

To the Student

Do not begin this study of tonal harmony without thorough knowledge and/or review of the fundamentals of music including scales, key signatures, intervals, and triads. You are strongly urged to review the author's *Basic Materials in Music Theory,* also published by Allyn and Bacon.

This book features the use of programed instruction to convey conceptual information and provide drills to develop techniques for handling harmonic materials. In programed instruction, information is presented in small, carefully sequenced parcels that combine in cumulative fashion to help you master the subject. The parcels into which the material is divided are called *frames.* Most frames require a written response, which may be a word or two, or perhaps the solution to a musical problem.

The principal part of each frame is located to the right-hand side of the page. The answers, which appear on the left-hand side, should be covered with a slip of paper or a ruler (or merely the hand will do). After you write your response, uncover the answer and check your work immediately. There are many cases in which your answer need not be exactly the same as that supplied by the text. You should consider your response correct if it conveys the same meaning as the one given. Use common sense to decide whether or not you comprehend a particular item. Because each step is small, you should make few mistakes.

Each chapter ends with a series of "mastery" frames. These frames allow you to evaluate your mastery of key points—concepts and skills essential to coping with matters that lie ahead. *Do not proceed unless your handling of the mastery frames assures you that you are ready to continue.*

Mastery frames are identified with double numbers to prevent confusion with the frames that constitute the body of the text. References to the frames that cover the subject of each question are provided along with the correct answers. Avail yourself of these references in order to focus remedial study precisely upon the points missed.

Many musical examples are given in the text to acquaint you with the way various composers use harmonic devices. You should play these at the piano, or program them in a computer for playback, so that they are actually *heard.* It is not sufficient to approach this study on an intellectual level alone; you must have command of the harmonic vocabulary as an aural phenomenon as well. The purpose of conceptualizing musical processes is to render more understandable the responses elicited by the auditory stimuli of music. Remember, music is an *aural* art; it is apprehended better by the ear than by the eye.

A ■ beside a frame indicates that the music in that frame is reproduced on the cassettes.

An Important Perspective for the Study of Harmony

One would suppose that, by now, the study of tonal harmony would be passé. After all, traditional harmonic tonality, with its wide, attendant vocabulary of chords, has become more diffused and of a broader scope through the compositions of the impressionists of the late nineteenth century and the atonalists of the early twentieth century. The impressionists—Debussy in particular—created an expression of the conception of tonality through the use of non-tertian chords and nonfunctional streams of chords, as well as by the expansion of tonal frontiers. By the end of the first decade of the twentieth century, Arnold Schönberg had shown in works such as *Pierrot Lunaire* that expressive music could indeed be created without resorting to either traditional tonality or tertian harmony. The dodecaphonic, or twelve-tone, system was designed to effectively negate any lingering influences of traditional harmonic practices. This system, as employed by members of the second Viennese School (Webern and Berg, in addition to Schönberg), as well as by countless others during the succeeding decades, led to a large body of music, including many highly expressive works.

Harmonic music, however, is still with us. Far from being dead, it is alive and well. Most of the music heard through mass media, and practically all commercial music, is based on traditional harmonic practices. This is true, also, of music performed in churches and studied in schools. Even concert and recital programs reveal a stubborn adherence to the standard repertoire, with the inclusion of only an occasional nontonal work. There is, of course, the all-too-rare program devoted exclusively to advanced music. Unfortunately, such programs have little impact, considering the overwhelming amount of more traditional music heard.

What accounts for the persistence of traditional music? Reasons can only be stated as speculation. A few follow:

1. There are those who would point to the "natural" basis of harmonic music. Because the natural harmonic series is a phenomenon of nature, the generation of chords by thirds and the relation of roots to the tonic according to precepts derived from the series can be seen not only as being ordained by nature, but also as possessing special moral sanction.
2. Perhaps because most people in our society, from birth, have heard little other than harmonic music, preference is given to the familiar; choice is made on the basis of conditioning, which produces an inertia of values.
3. Music in which tones bear relatively simple acoustical relations to one another is easier both to sing and to apprehend. Much folk music, for example, displays preference for limited range and relatively small intervals, as well as emphasis on the perfect fourth and fifth—intervals which have special tonal significance.
4. It is apparent that the expressive resources of tonal music have not been exhausted. The rapidly changing styles of commercial music demonstrate that fresh draughts of musical expression still remain to be drawn from the well of harmonic resources.

Rationale aside, harmonic music clearly constitutes the bulk of what is heard by our society at large. It also dominates the music studied and performed by students in our schools of music. These realities justify the continued study of tonal harmony. And the time is not yet in sight when this study will be without meaning and thus disappear from the standard music curriculum.

The two basic parameters of music are *temporal* and *sonic* (time and sound). With respect to the sonic parameter, two principal methods of organization have evolved in Western music: counterpoint (linear) and harmony (chordal). The technique of counterpoint developed much earlier than the concept of harmony as an independent musical principle. From about the beginning of the tenth century to nearly 1600, the chief organizing principles were related to counterpoint. But from the beginning, the effect of voices sounding together was recognized as an important factor. This is evidenced by the changing preferences for intervals during the course of musical evolution.

Early in the development of counterpoint, the chief consonances were perfect unisons, octaves, fourths, and fifths. Open sonorities such as 1-5-8 were the main consonant sonorities, with complete triads (1-3-5) appearing as passing occurrences. The frequency of triads gradually increased after 1300, occurring even at cadence points, except for the final cadence where perfect consonances (1-5-8) were still preferred. From about the middle of the fifteenth century, complete triads in both root position and first inversion predominated, but music from this period displays no systematic approach to harmonic progression, except at the cadences, where plagal, authentic, and Phrygian cadences are used.

After 1600, the preeminence of the first, fourth, and fifth scale degrees began to be established, and greater consistency of root movement developed. This led to the establishment of major/minor tonality, which supplanted the modal system of the medieval and Renaissance periods. During the baroque period, the vocabulary of chords was enlarged to include various altered chords such as the Neapolitan sixth and secondary dominants. Chromaticism and systematic modulation also developed at this time. In response to the classical ideals of clarity, lightness, and balance, harmonic action tended to be simpler and more formula driven. The form-defining function of contrasting tonalities, however, became even more important. Also, there was more frequent modulation to distant keys.

Harmony received its fullest development during the romantic period (1825–1900), during which time the tonal horizon was pushed back to the very limits of equal temperament, and the repertoire of chords was expanded by the use of the complete chromatic scale. Frequent use of altered chords, coupled with modulations to distant keys, led to the eventual disintegration of tonality, and the fall of tonality brought down the whole structure of tonal relations and chord structures associated with tertian harmony. But, as we have seen, harmonic music refuses to die; its emotive power is still strong. And, although it appears that the evolution of harmony was complete by 1900, harmonic materials may still be exploited for new ends.

The evolution of harmony may also be traced through the writings of various theorists. For this purpose we shall review briefly some of the major contributions to the field of harmonic theory. It is surprising that recognition of harmony as an independent musical parameter occurred so late. After all, several contrapuntal lines produce simultaneous sounds, and for several centuries prior to 1600, many of these sounds resulted in chords. But pre-baroque technique exploited the interval as the basic constructive unit—the concept of chord did not exist. What we recognize as chords were viewed then as conglomerations of intervals. The first recognition of the chord as an entity occurred in Gioseffo Zarlino's *Istituzioni armoniche* of 1558. In this work Zarlino refers to the *harmonia perfetta,* which results from the first six tones of the natural harmonic series. It is, in effect, the major triad. Being the first to recognize the triad as a harmonic entity, Zarlino is the father of modern harmonic theory.

A still greater contribution to harmonic theory was made by Jean-Philippe Rameau, whose treatise *Traité de l'Harmonie* was published in 1722. Many of the principles set forth by Rameau are still employed today to explain harmonic processes. Rameau's writings are extensive and involved. His chief contributions, however, are threefold:

1. He postulated that the lowest note of the triad in 1-3-5 position is the root and is the generator of the 3rd and 5th. Also, this note (1) remains the root when the chord is inverted to either 3-5-8 (first inversion) or 5-8-10 (second inversion).
2. The roots of chords, as opposed to the actual bass line, constitute the "fundamental bass," and the fundamental bass is the true motivator of the harmony. The result of this principle is to reduce the number of harmonic entities and provide a simple method for relating chords to one another and to the tonal center.
3. The symmetrical structure of harmonic tonality was identified by Rameau, who, recognizing the fundamental accoustical nature of the perfect fifth, also saw the subdominant and dominant as straddling the tonic (IV-I-V), the dominant a fifth higher, the subdominant a fifth lower. It was Rameau who first used the term *sous-dominante* to designate the "lower" dominant.

Rameau, like Zarlino, based his theories on the natural harmonic series and mathematics. Most later harmonic theorists did likewise. Some, however, chose other bases for their speculations. For example, in 1754 Guiseppe Tartini published his treatise *Trattato di musica,* in which reference is made not only to the natural harmonic series and mathematics, but also to geometry. In 1853, Moritz Hauptmann published his *Die Natur der Harmonik und Metrik,* in which a philosophical approach based on Hegel's dialectical metaphysics is employed.

The theorists reviewed here, plus many others,* felt that they were dealing with harmony as a science, that basic principles which would explain music phenomena, and more, lay hidden, waiting only to be discovered and proved. But this has proved to be a chimera; for no harmonic theory, including Rameau's, is free of inner contradictions. There have been many near misses; but nature has not cooperated by providing a closed system to tone relations, at least in terms of the kinds of music with which people have to date been concerned.

*Please see the Bibliography for Further Study for sources on other theorists.

chapter one

SAT 3:15 –

Introduction to Seventh Chords: The Dominant Seventh

The harmonic materials presented in this study thus far have been limited to triads. Most dissonance has been incidental to the harmony—the result of nonharmonic tones. Seventh chords, on the other hand, introduce dissonance as an integral part of the harmony. Seventh chords consist of four tones; thus they are more complex than triads. Whereas triads are limited to four types (major, minor, diminished, and augmented), there are seven types of seventh chords. Seventh chords are used not only for their tonal variety, but also for the tension supplied by their dissonance. Urgency of resolution is a feature of seventh chords, and this feature contributes to the sense of harmonic motivation so much a part of more advanced harmonic idioms.

1. A SEVENTH CHORD consists of four tones and is written by adding a note the interval of a third above the fifth of a triad.

TRIAD SEVENTH CHORD

7th

Seventh chords may be regarded as extended triads. Like triads, they consist of superimposed 3rds.

thirds

---

2. A chord consisting of a triad plus a fourth note which is the interval of a third above the fifth is called a Seventh chord.

seventh chord

---

3. Write seventh chords by adding a fourth note the interval of a third above the fifth of each triad.

(1) (2) (3)

(1) (2) (3)

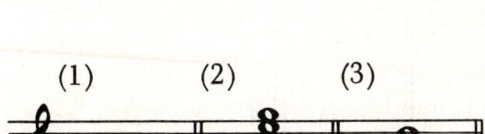

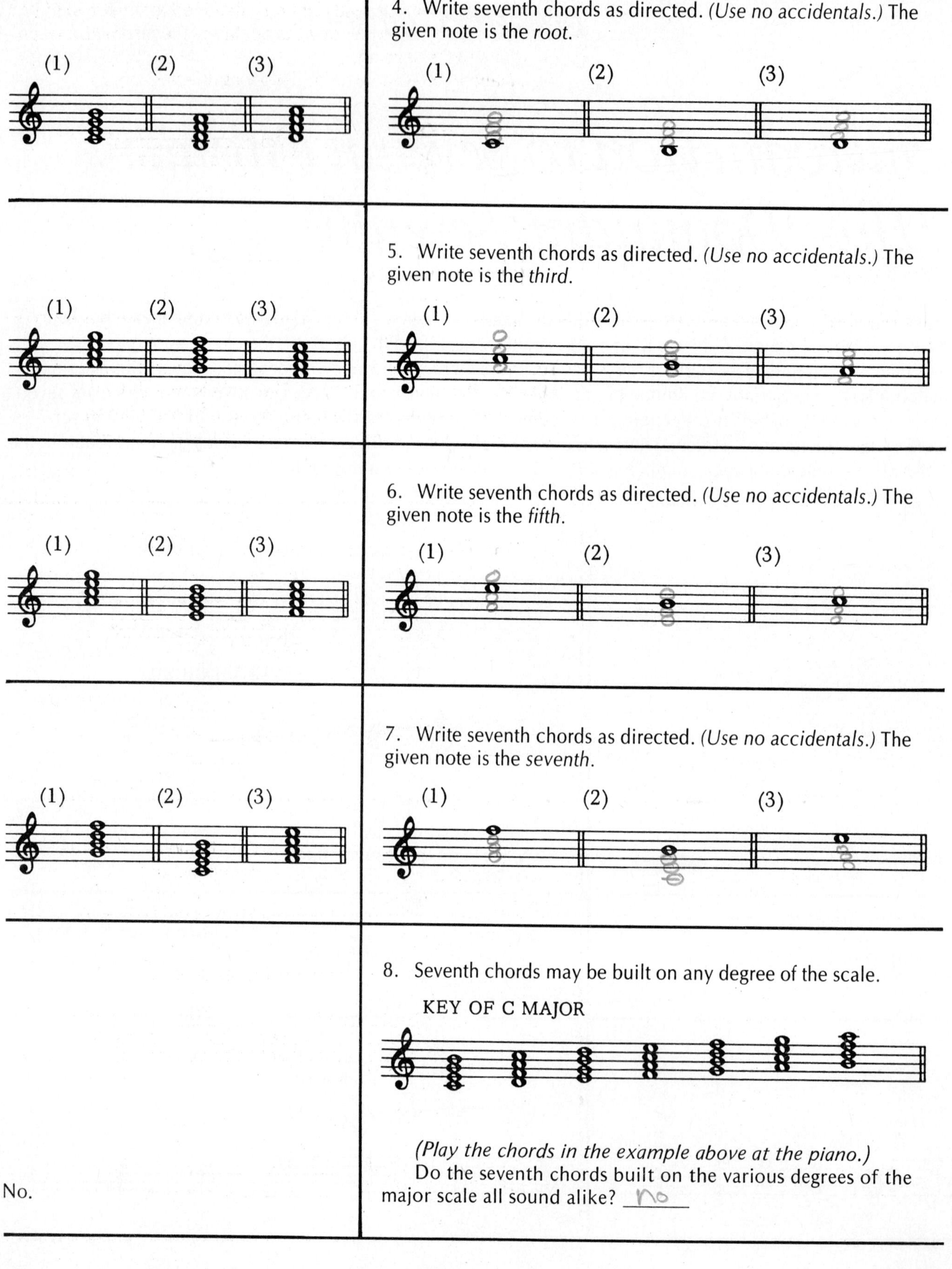

(1)
(2)
(3)
4. Write seventh chords as directed. *(Use no accidentals.)* The given note is the *root*.
5. Write seventh chords as directed. *(Use no accidentals.)* The given note is the *third*.
6. Write seventh chords as directed. *(Use no accidentals.)* The given note is the *fifth*.
7. Write seventh chords as directed. *(Use no accidentals.)* The given note is the *seventh*.
8. Seventh chords may be built on any degree of the scale.
KEY OF C MAJOR
(Play the chords in the example above at the piano.)
Do the seventh chords built on the various degrees of the major scale all sound alike? no
No.

9. The quality of a seventh chord is identified through two of its features: the type of triad, and the quality of the interval between the root and the seventh.

Analyze the seventh chord below as directed.

7th

Triad

(1) Type of triad: ____________
(2) Quality of 7th: ____________

(1) Major
(2) Minor

---

10. The chord shown in the preceding frame is called a MAJOR-MINOR seventh chord. The first part of this term (major) refers to the type of triad; the second part (minor) refers to the quality of the interval between the root and the ____________.

seventh

---

11. Analyze the seventh chord below as directed.

7th

Triad

(1) Type of triad: ____________
(2) Quality of triad: ____________

(1) Diminished
(2) Minor

---

12. The chord shown in the preceding frame is called a ____________-____________ seventh chord.

diminished-minor

---

13. Analyze the seventh chord below as directed.

7th

Triad

(1) Type of triad: ____________
(2) Quality of 7th: ____________

(1) Minor
(2) Minor

minor-minor

14. The chord shown in the preceding frame may be called a MINOR-MINOR seventh chord. It is customary, however, to eliminate one part of the term when the quality of the interval between the root and the seventh is identical to the type of triad. Thus, the term *minor seventh chord* means the same as ______-______ seventh chord.

---

diminished

15. A seventh chord which consists of a diminished triad plus the interval of a diminished seventh above the root is called a ______ seventh chord.

---

(1) Major-minor
(2) Major
(3) Minor

16. Indicate the name of each chord.

(1) (2) (3)

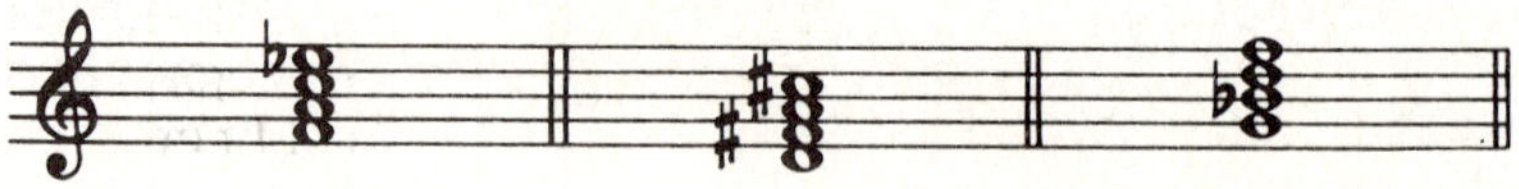

(1) ______ seventh chord
(2) ______ seventh chord
(3) ______ seventh chord

---

diminished

17. If you called the second chord in the preceding frame a major-major seventh chord, or the third chord a minor-minor seventh chord, you were not wrong, as this nomenclature is sometimes used. It is simpler, however, to avoid unnecessary repetition of terms.

The term *diminished seventh chord* indicates a chord consisting of a diminished triad plus the interval of a ______ seventh above the root.

---

(1) Diminished-minor
(2) Minor-major
(3) Minor

18. Indicate the name of each chord.

(1) (2) (3)

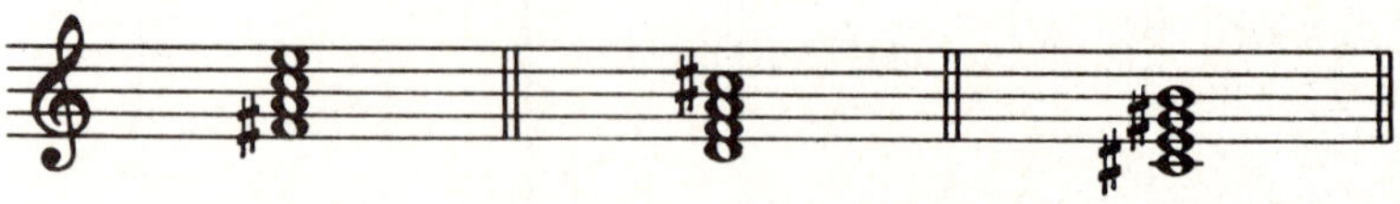

(1) ______ seventh chord
(2) ______ seventh chord
(3) ______ seventh chord

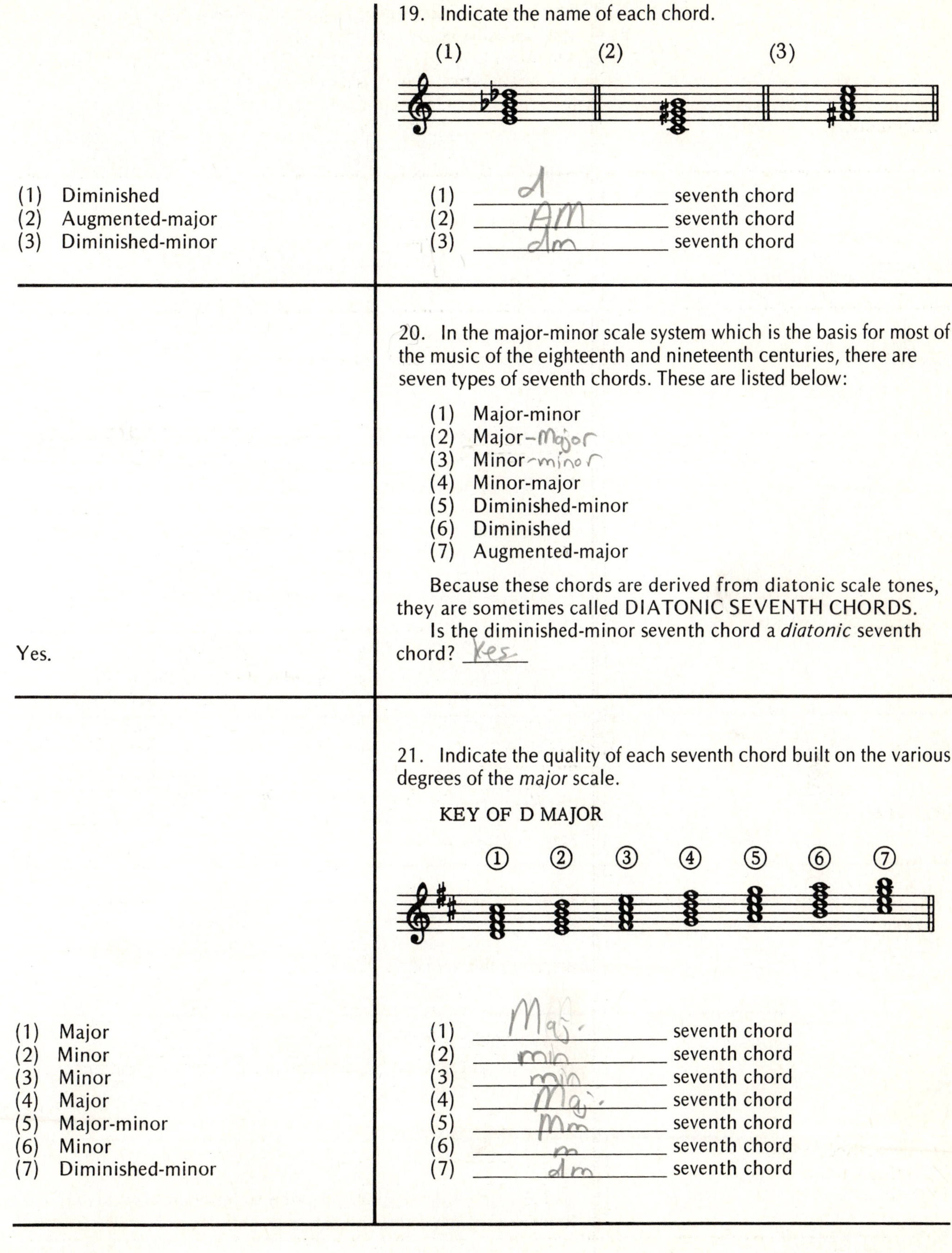

19. Indicate the name of each chord.

(1) (2) (3)

(1) ___d___ seventh chord
(2) ___AM___ seventh chord
(3) ___dm___ seventh chord

(1) Diminished
(2) Augmented-major
(3) Diminished-minor

---

20. In the major-minor scale system which is the basis for most of the music of the eighteenth and nineteenth centuries, there are seven types of seventh chords. These are listed below:

(1) Major-minor
(2) Major-Major
(3) Minor-minor
(4) Minor-major
(5) Diminished-minor
(6) Diminished
(7) Augmented-major

Because these chords are derived from diatonic scale tones, they are sometimes called DIATONIC SEVENTH CHORDS.

Is the diminished-minor seventh chord a *diatonic* seventh chord? ___Yes___

Yes.

---

21. Indicate the quality of each seventh chord built on the various degrees of the *major* scale.

KEY OF D MAJOR

① ② ③ ④ ⑤ ⑥ ⑦

(1) ___Maj.___ seventh chord
(2) ___min___ seventh chord
(3) ___min___ seventh chord
(4) ___Maj.___ seventh chord
(5) ___Mm___ seventh chord
(6) ___m___ seventh chord
(7) ___dm___ seventh chord

(1) Major
(2) Minor
(3) Minor
(4) Major
(5) Major-minor
(6) Minor
(7) Diminished-minor

22. Indicate the quality of each seventh chord built on the various degrees of the *harmonic minor* scale.

KEY OF D HARMONIC MINOR

① ② ③ ④ ⑤ ⑥ ⑦

(1) ________ seventh chord
(2) ________ seventh chord
(3) ________ seventh chord
(4) ________ seventh chord
(5) ________ seventh chord
(6) ________ seventh chord
(7) ________ seventh chord

(1) Minor-major
(2) Diminished-minor
(3) Augmented-major
(4) Minor
(5) Major-minor
(6) Major
(7) Diminished

---

23. Before proceeding, you should learn the quality of the seventh chord on the various degrees of major and minor scales. You should know, for example, that the major-minor seventh chord occurs as a diatonic seventh chord only on the fifth scale degree in either major or (harmonic) minor. Also, play the chords in the preceding two frames at the piano to become familiar with their sounds.

The minor-major seventh chord occurs as a diatonic chord only in harmonic minor on the ________ scale degree.

first

---

24. In the *major* scale, the minor seventh chord appears on the ________, ________, and ________ degrees.

2nd, 3rd, (and) 6th
(Any order.)

---

25. The diminished-minor seventh chord appears on the ________ degree of the *major* scale, and on the ________ degree of the *harmonic minor* scale.

7th 2nd

---

26. Does the diminished seventh chord occur as a diatonic chord in the major scale? ________

No.

---

27. Except for the diminished seventh chord (discussed later), the Roman numeral used to indicate a seventh chord is the

same as for a triad on the same root plus the number seven (7) placed at the upper right-hand corner.

Notice that the quality of the triad is shown by the form of the Roman numeral. The quality of the seventh, however, is not identified. It is assumed that the seventh is a tone of the diatonic scale unless an alteration is shown.

Spell the chord indicated by the Roman numeral.

A♭: ii7 Bb – Db – F – Ab

B♭ D♭ F A♭

---

28. Spell the chords indicated by the Roman numerals:

(1) D: V7 A – C# – E – G
(2) B♭: vi7 G – Bb – D – F
(3) E: viiø7 D# – F# – A – C#

(1) AC♯EG
(2) GB♭DF
(3) D♯F♯AC♯

---

29. Write the appropriate chord symbol for each chord. (*Indicate quality carefully.*)

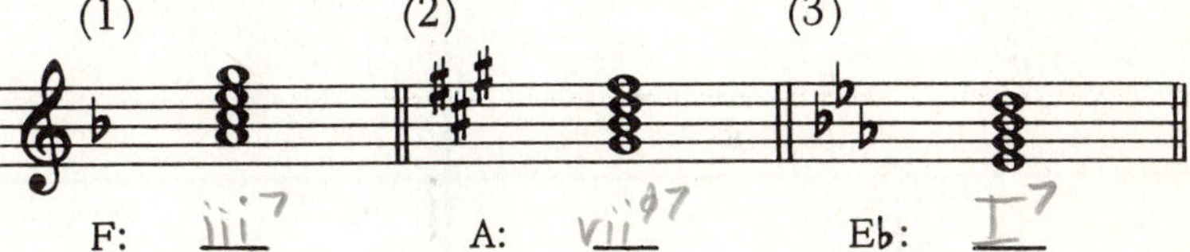

(1) iii7
(2) viiø7
(3) I7

---

30. The example below shows the chord symbols used to indicate the diatonic seventh chords in D harmonic minor:

Three of the chord symbols above need to be explained. These are i7̸, iiø7, and viio7. In the first case the figure 7̸ indicates that the seventh of the chord is raised a half-step. The slash drawn through the seven distinguishes between this chord (DFAC♯) and the tonic seventh chord in natural minor which would consist of the following notes: D F A C .

DFAC

31. The quality of the triad is shown by the form of the Roman numeral, thus the symbol V^7 is sufficient to indicate the dominant seventh chord in the preceding frame. But when the seventh is an altered tone it is necessary to show the alteration by the actual accidental used (or by a slash if the note is raised a half-step).

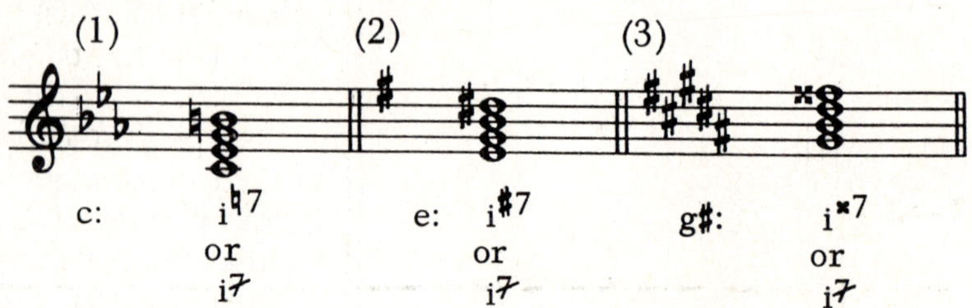

The chord symbol varies slightly according to the accidental (unless the slash is used).

What is the quality of each chord above? ____________ - ____________ seventh chord.

Minor-major

---

32. Write the appropriate chord symbol for each chord.

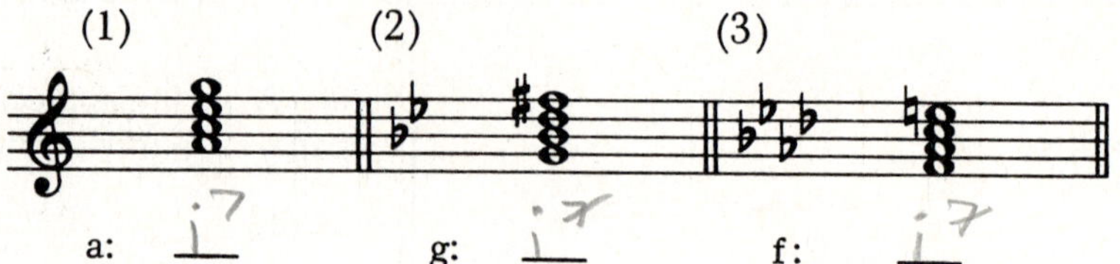

(1) i^7
(2) $i^{\not{7}}$ or $i^{\sharp 7}$
(3) $i^{\not{7}}$ or $i^{\natural 7}$

---

33. Chord (1) in the preceding frame is a minor seventh chord. The fact that no accidental is used in the chord symbol shows that the ____________ minor scale is used.

natural
(or pure)

---

34. Notes of the natural minor scale are considered "diatonic" and require no special figure in the chord symbol. Alterations (usually the raised sixth or seventh degrees) are shown either by the form of the Roman numeral or by a sign indicating the alteration of the seventh.

A note raised in pitch a half-step always calls for a sharp in the chord symbol. (True/False) ____________

False.
(If you answered incorrectly, review Frames 30-33).

F♯ACE♭

35. The second and third chord symbols in Frame 30 which need explanation are those used to indicate the supertonic ($\mathrm{ii}^{\varnothing 7}$) and leading tone ($\mathrm{vii}^{\varnothing 7}$ or $\mathrm{vii}^{\circ 7}$) seventh chords. Diminished seventh chords appear frequently and perform a variety of harmonic functions. In this book, for the diminished-minor seventh chord (e.g., $\mathrm{ii}^{\varnothing 7}$, $\mathrm{vii}^{\varnothing 7}$), a circle with a slash denotes a diminished triad with a minor seventh, a so-called "half-diminished" seventh chord; for the fully diminished, or so-called "diminished" seventh chord ($\mathrm{vii}^{\circ 7}$), a circle denotes both the quality of the triad and of the seventh.

Spell the chord indicated by the symbol.

g: $\mathrm{vii}^{\circ 7}$ F#-A-C-Eb

---

(1) B(♮)DFA♭
(2) E♯G♯BD
(3) A(♮)CE♭G♭

36. Spell the chords indicated by the symbols.

(1) c: $\mathrm{vii}^{\circ 7}$ B-D-F-Ab
(2) f♯: $\mathrm{vii}^{\circ 7}$ E#-G#-B-D
(3) b♭: $\mathrm{vii}^{\circ 7}$ A-C-Eb-Gb

---

(1) Diminished-minor
(2) Diminished

37. Note the difference between the two chords below:

(1) (2)

G: $\mathrm{vii}^{\varnothing 7}$ g: $\mathrm{vii}^{\circ 7}$

Identify the quality of each chord.

(1) dm seventh chord
(2) d seventh chord

(fully) diminished

38. The example in the preceding frame shows that the circle with slash is used in the case of a diminished-minor seventh chord. The small circle is used only for fully dim. seventh chords.

---

(1) $\mathrm{ii}^{\varnothing 7}$
(2) $\mathrm{vii}^{\circ 7}$
(3) $\mathrm{vii}^{\varnothing 7}$

39. Write the proper symbol for each chord. (*Be sure to check the quality before writing.*)

(1) (2) (3)

d: $\mathrm{ii}^{\varnothing 7}$ b: $\mathrm{vii}^{\circ 7}$ B♭: $\mathrm{vii}^{\varnothing 7}$

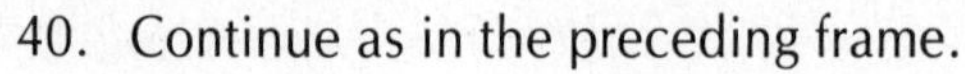

40. Continue as in the preceding frame.

(1) (2) (3)

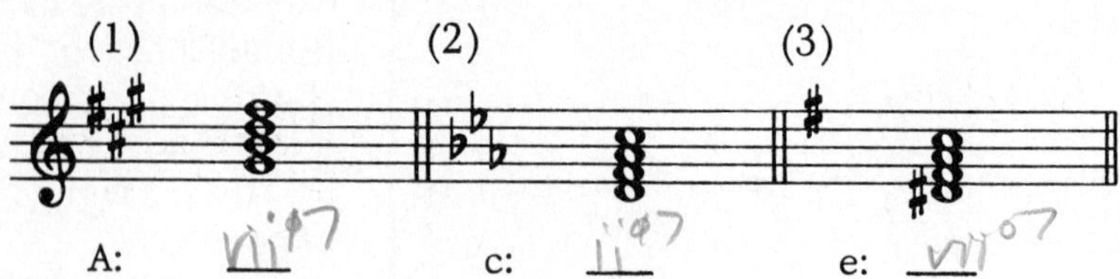

A: ___ c: ___ e: ___

(1) vii^{ø7}
(2) ii^{ø7}
(3) vii^{o7}

---

41. Spell the chords indicated by the symbols. (*Use the notes of the harmonic minor scale.*)

(1) c♯: vii^{o7} ___
(2) f: ii^{ø7} ___
(3) a: VI^{7} ___

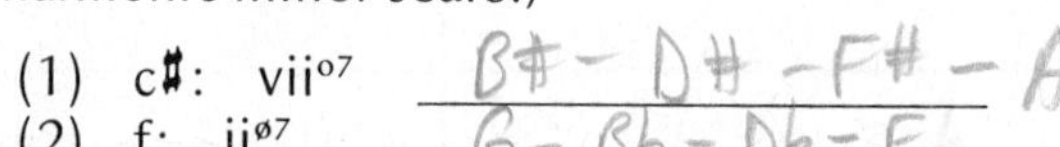

(1) B♯D♯F♯A
(2) GB♭D♭F
(3) FACE

---

42. Spell the chords indicated by the symbols. (*Note that some keys are major and some are minor. In the case of minor keys, use the notes of the harmonic minor scale.*)

(1) B: IV^{7} ___
(2) f♯: i^{7} ___
(3) c: ii^{ø7} ___
(4) D♭: iii^{7} ___
(5) A: vii^{ø7} ___
(6) e♭: V^{7} ___

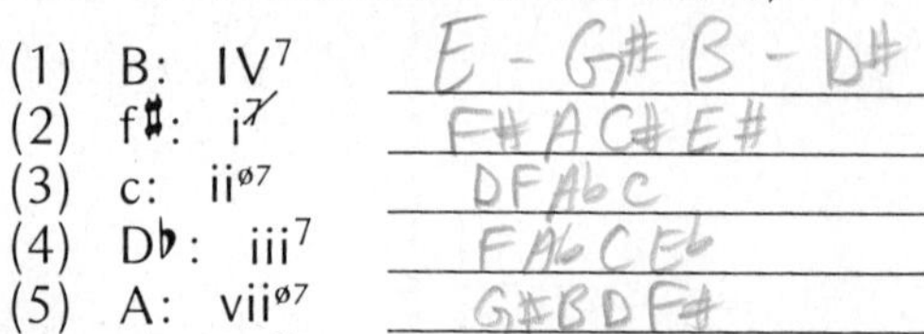

(1) EG♯BD♯
(2) F♯AC♯E♯
(3) DFA♭C
(4) FA♭CE♭
(5) G♯BDF♯
(6) B♭D(♮)FA♭

---

43. Supply the appropriate symbol for each chord.

(1) (2) (3)

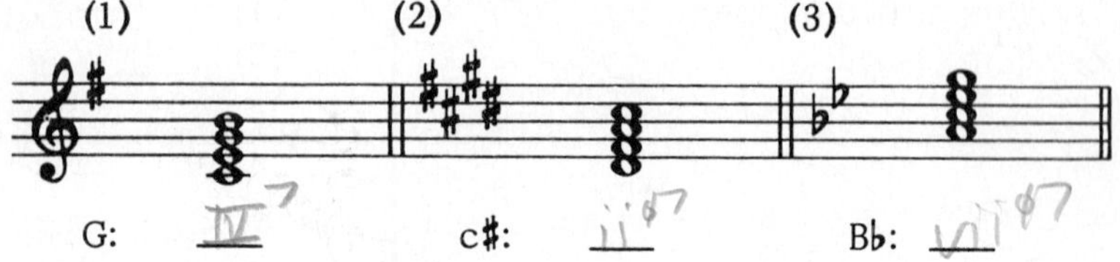

G: ___ c♯: ___ B♭: ___

(1) IV^{7}
(2) ii^{ø7}
(3) vii^{ø7}

---

44. Continue as in the preceding frame.

(1) (2) (3)

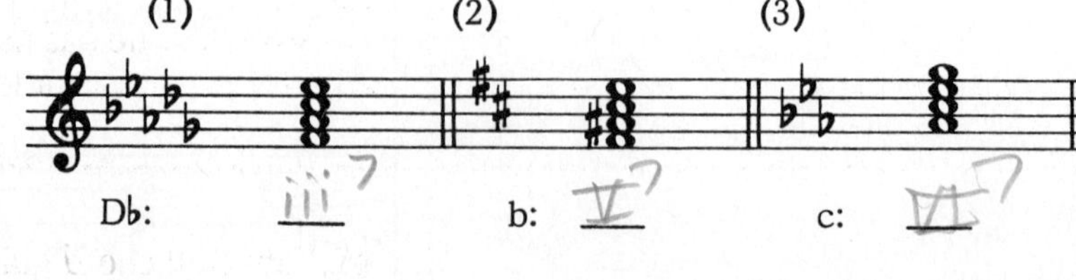

D♭: ___ b: ___ c: ___

(1) iii^{7}
(2) V^{7}
(3) VI^{7}

(1) III^{+7}
(2) ii^{7}
(3) $i^{\not 7}$ or $i^{\natural 7}$

45. Continue as in the preceding frame.

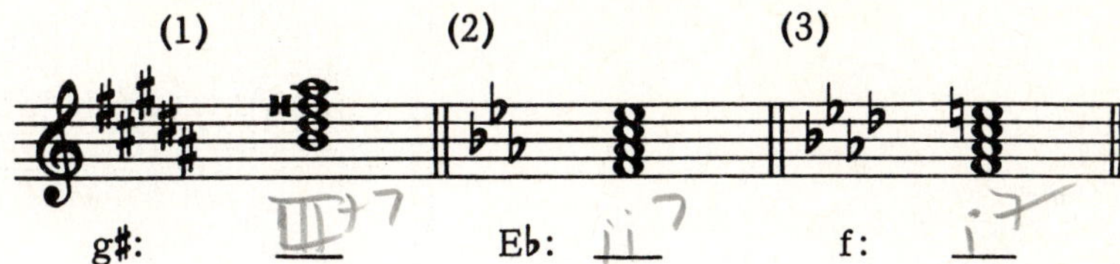

---

(1) $vii^{ø7}$
(2) vii^{o7}
(3) III^{+7}

46. Continue as in the preceding frame.

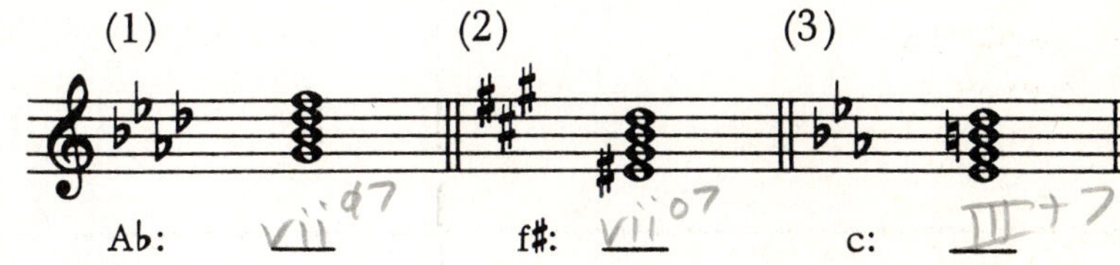

(b) melodic minor.

47. The alternate sixth and seventh degrees of the melodic minor scale (ascending and descending forms) produce a large number of seventh chords.

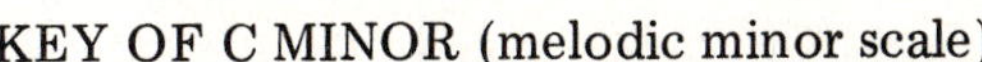

Although all of these chords are available to the composer, several of them are seldom used and infrequently found in musical literature. These have been marked with asterisks in the above example.

Which scale has the most tonal variety (a) harmonic minor, (b) melodic minor, or (c) major? ______________

---

48. Seventh chord qualities and their corresponding chord symbols in major and minor keys are partially summarized on the following page.

Quality	*Major*	*Minor*
Mm^7	V^7	V^7
M^7	I^7, IV^7	VI^7
m^7	ii^7, iii^7, vi^7	iv^7
mM^7	—	i^7
dm^7	$vii^{ø7}$	$ii^{ø7}$
d^7	—	vii^{o7}
AM^7	—	III^+

(No response.)

49. Seventh chords, like triads, are used in various inversions. The figured bass symbols used to indicate seventh chords in *root* position are shown below:

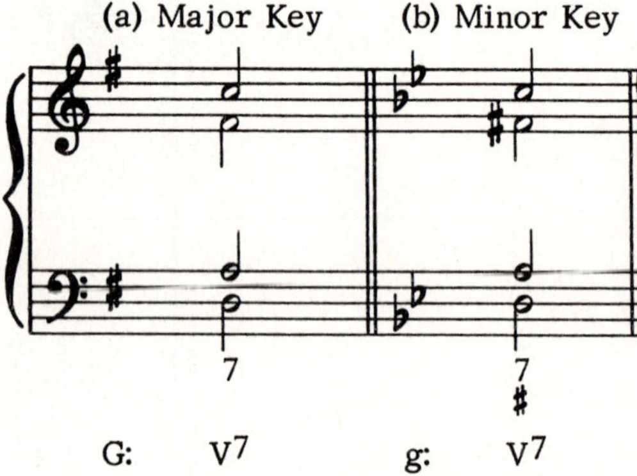

The figured bass symbol for a seventh chord in root position is simply the number seven (7) unless either the third or fifth of the chord is altered, in which case the alteration is shown by the appropriate symbol. The figured bass symbol 7 indicates a seventh chord in ________ position.

root

50. The figured bass symbol used to indicate seventh chords in *first inversion* is shown below:

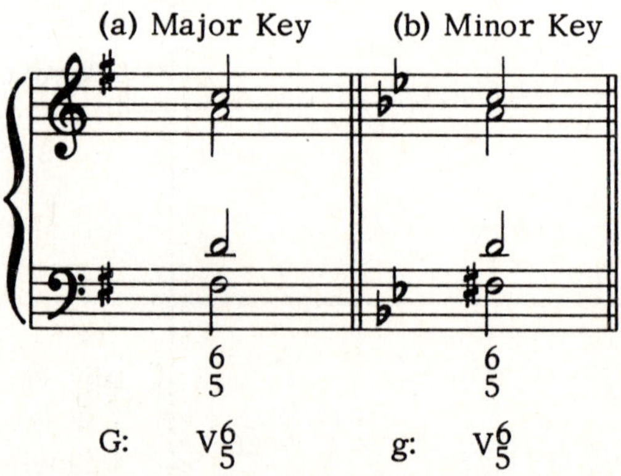

3rd	Notice that the numbers 6 and 5 are incorporated into the chord symbol. Thus the chord symbol itself shows the inversion of the chord. The figured bass symbol $^6_5$ beneath a bass note indicates a seventh chord in first inversion. Therefore, the note in the bass is the (root/3rd/5th/7th) ______________ of the chord.
5th	51. The chords below are in *second inversion.* 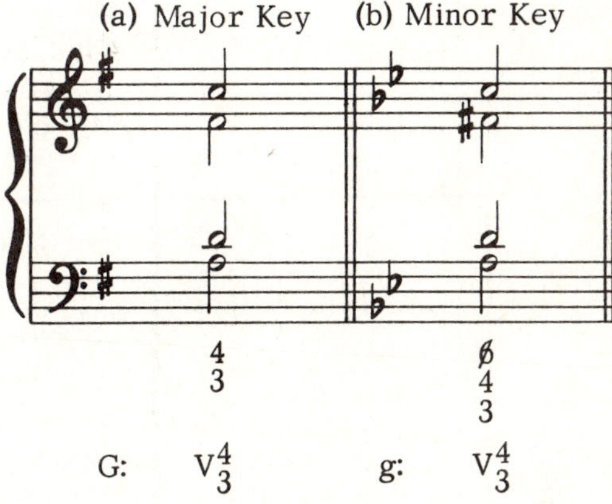 The symbol $^4_3$ suffices to indicate a seventh chord in second inversion unless the sixth above the bass is altered as in (b) above. The root of the seventh chord in second inversion is located a (interval) ______________ below the bass note.
7th	52. The chords below are in *third inversion.* 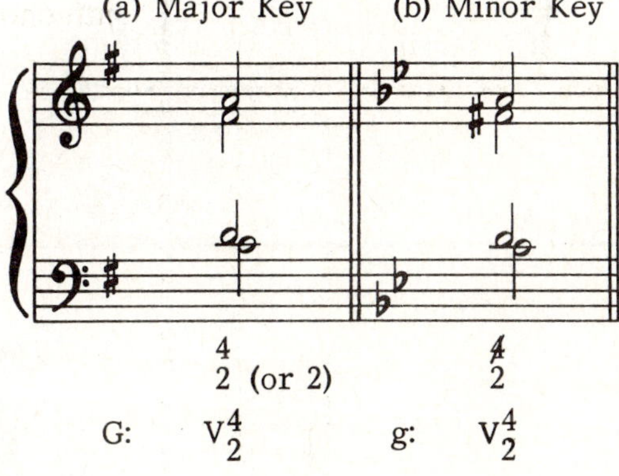 Usually the symbol $^4_2$ is used to indicate a seventh chord in third inversion, but sometimes this is reduced to merely 2. The figured bass symbol cannot be abbreviated in (b) because the figure 4̸ is needed to show the alteration of F to F-sharp. When the symbol $^4_2$ (or 2) appears beneath a bass note, that note is the (root/3rd/5th/7th) ______________ of the chord.

53. The previous few frames have shown that figured bass symbols are combined with Roman numerals to show the various inversions of seventh chords.

Root position: I^7, ii^7, etc.

First inversion: I^6_5, ii^6_5, etc.

Second inversion: I^4_3, ii^4_3, etc.

Third inversion: I^4_2, ii^4_2, etc.

These symbols are used consistently throughout this study except when it is of no importance to identify specific inversions.

The figure $^4_3$ signifies that the (root/3rd/5th/7th) _______ of a chord is in the bass.

5th

---

54. Check (√) the correct option:

1. Chord symbols show not only the scale degrees on which chords are built, but also the inversions.
2. The symbol V^6_5 indicates that the third of the dominant seventh chord is in the bass.

True statements:
(1) _____ (2) _____ Both _____ Neither _____

Both √

---

55. Supply the chord symbol for each chord.

(1) (2) (3)

Bb: _____ d: _____ Ab: _____

(1) V^4_2
(2) V^4_3
(3) V^6_5

---

56. Continue as in the preceding frame.

(1) (2) (3)

e: _____ Eb: _____ g: _____

(1) $ii^{ø6}_5$
(2) I^4_2
(3) V^4_3

(1) G

(2) F

(3) A

57. Indicate the bass note for each chord.

Bass Note

(1) A♭: V^6_5 G

(2) c: V^4_2 F

(3) E: $vii^{ø4}_3$ A

58. Slightly more complicated symbols are required to show the inversions of diminished seventh chords.

Indicate the bass note for each chord.

Bass Note

(1) f: vii^{o4}_2 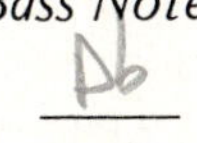

(2) b: vii^{o6}_5 

(3) c♯: vii^{o4}_3 

(1) D♭

(2) C♯

(3) F♯

59. Supply the chord symbol for each chord.

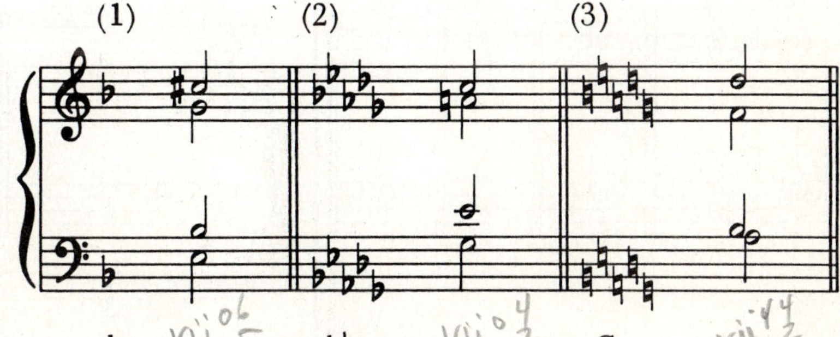

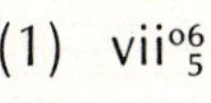

(1) vii^{o6}_5

(2) vii^{o4}_2

(3) $vii^{ø4}_2$

(1) vii$^{ø6}_{5}$

(2) vii$^{o6}_{5}$

60. Chord (3) in the preceding frame is a diminished-minor seventh chord, not a diminished seventh chord. The symbol for the former is vii$^{ø4}_{2}$; the latter is vii$^{o4}_{2}$.

Write the appropriate chord symbol for each chord.

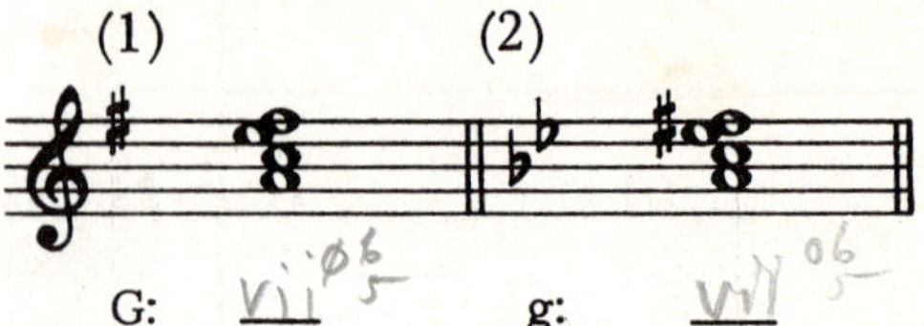

61. All four tones of a seventh chord are usually present in simple four-part writing. This means that no doubling is necessary; each of the four voices takes one of the chord tones. Observe this practice in the frames which follow.

Complete the chords as indicated by the figured bass *(Use close structure.)*

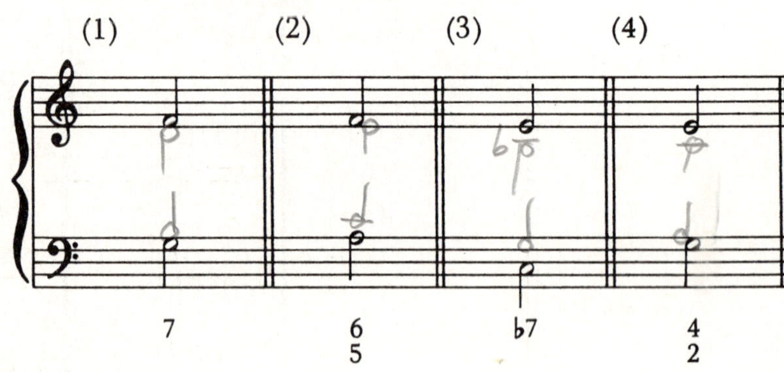

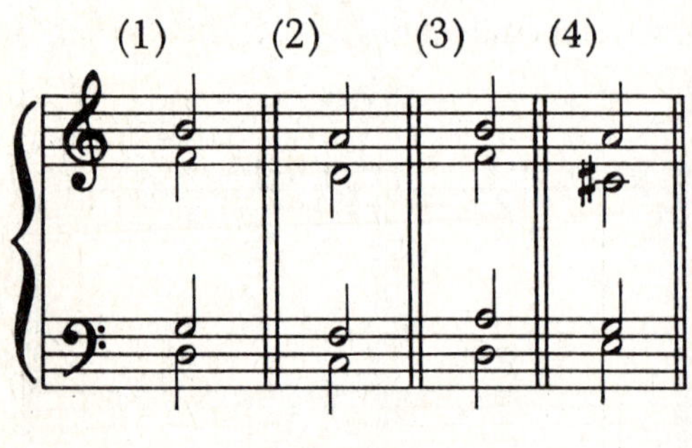

62. Complete the chords as indicated by the figured bass. (*Use open structure.*)

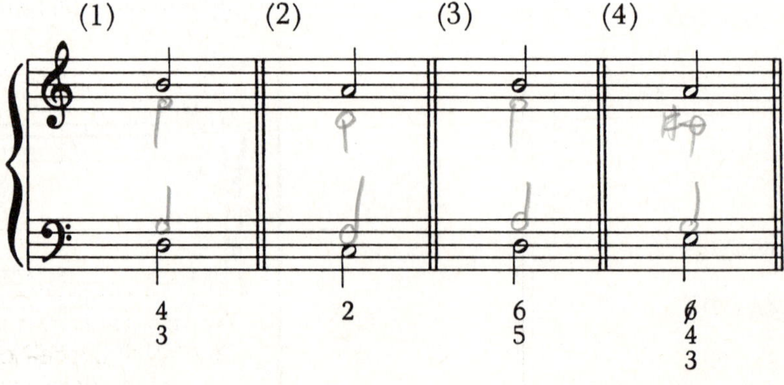

(1) (2) (3) (4)

63. Complete the chords as indicated by the figured bass. (*Use open structure.*)

(1) $^{6}_{5}$

(2) 7

(3) $^{4}_{3}$

(4) $^{6}_{5}$

64. Write the proper figured bass symbol beneath each chord.

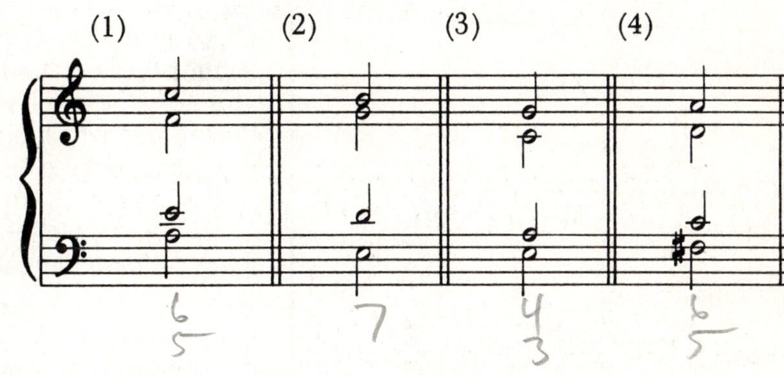

(1) $^{4}_{2}$ or 2

(2) $^{7}_{♯3}$ or $^{7}_{♯}$

(3) $^{6}_{4}{}_{3}$

(4) $^{6}_{5}$

65. Continue as in the preceding frame. (*Don't forget to indicate altered notes.*)

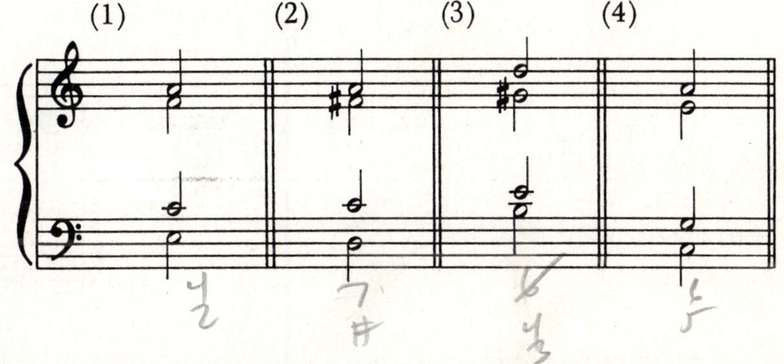

■

66. The V^7 chord is known as the DOMINANT SEVENTH CHORD. This chord is by far the most prevalent of all seventh chords. For this reason, its use will be examined in detail.

Like the dominant triad, the dominant seventh chord usually progresses to the tonic or submediant triads.

Supply the Roman numeral analysis for the last four chords.

Brahms, *Ein deutsches Requiem,* Op. 45, I

Ziemlich langsam und mit Ausdruck

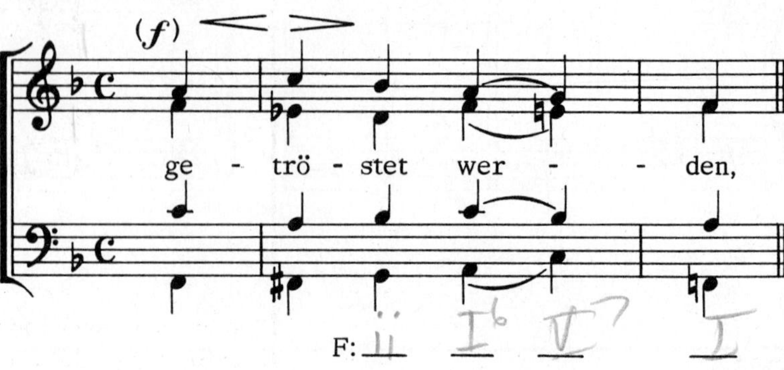

ii - I^6 - V^7 - I

---

67. The dominant seventh chord is a major-minor seventh chord. It consists of a major triad plus a minor seventh above the root. This type of chord has two dissonant elements: the seventh, and the tritone,* which occurs between the third and seventh. It is the resolution of these dissonant elements which governs the part writing.

Refer again to the example in the preceding frame. Which two notes comprise the tritone in the dominant seventh chord? ______ and ______.

*The term tritone means three (whole) tones. It is the same as the augmented fourth, or diminished fifth.

B♭ (and) E

---

68. The tritone and its resolution (from the example in Frame 66) are shown below:

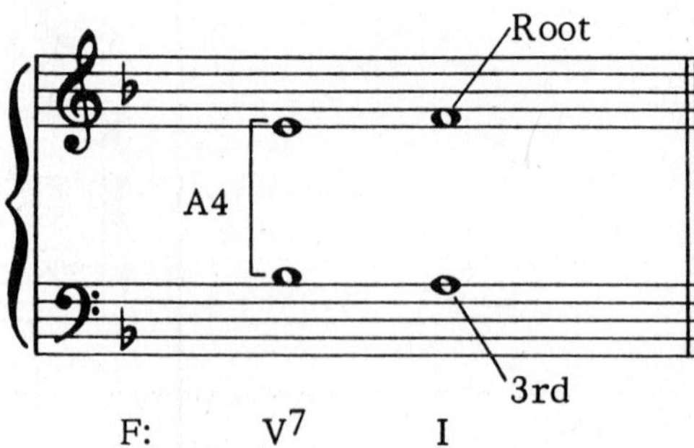

Notice that each of the notes of the tritone (B♭ and E) moves by a half-step to the note of resolution. Could the voices find a place in the same chord (F major) with equal smoothness by moving in the opposite direction? ______

No.

inward

69. The inversion of the example in Frame 68 produces the interval of a diminished fifth.

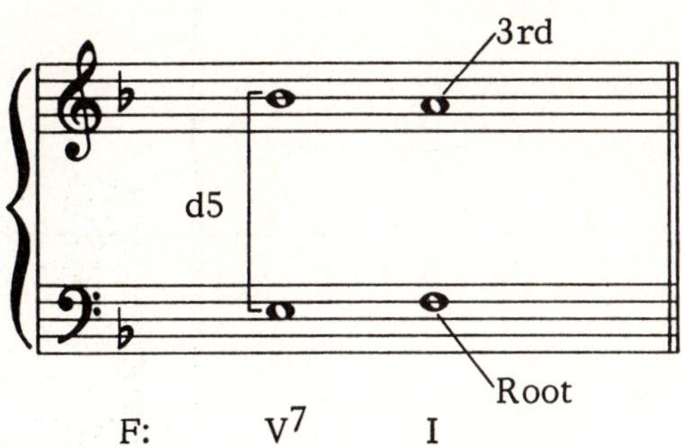

Whereas the tones which constitute the interval of an augmented fourth resolve *outward* to the root and third of the tonic triad, the tones of a diminished fifth resolve inward.

4 (and) 7

70. The tendency for the tones of the augmented fourth to resolve outward and those of the diminished fifth to resolve inward is the result of the melodic attraction of active tones to inactive ones.

The inactive tones of the major scale are the tones of the tonic triad. The remaining tones are active, and are attracted to the inactive ones primarily in the direction of the arrows.

KEY OF F MAJOR

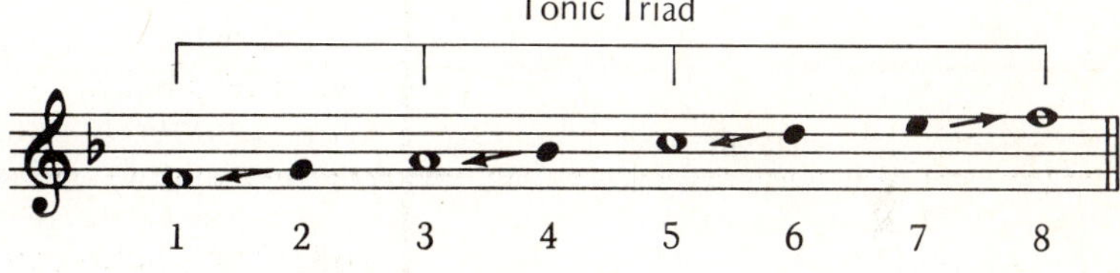

In each case active tones move to the *nearest* member of the tonic triad. The second scale degree is a whole-step removed from both the first and third; but, since the attraction of the keynote (F) is stronger than the third (A), the downward tendency predominates.

Which two of the active scale degrees are only a half-step removed from the notes to which they are attracted?
4 and 7.

71. Because of their close proximity to tones of the tonic triad, the fourth and seventh are the most active degrees of the major scale. This melodic activity is intensified when they are combined to form a tritone. For this reason, the effective resolution of the dominant seventh chord depends upon resolving the fourth and seventh scale degrees in accordance with their natural tendency.

(1) (2)

Resolve each tritone to notes of the tonic triad in the smoothest possible manner.

■

72. The overriding importance of resolving the tritone according to the melodic activity of its constituent tones often leads to irregular doubling in the chord which follows.

Mozart, *Symphony No.* 41, K. 551

There are three roots, one third, but no 5th.

Describe the irregular doubling in the chord at the asterisk. triple root, no 5th ______________________________.

Yes.
(The note D in the soprano is an embellishment.)

73. Another dominant seventh chord occurs in the third measure of the example in the preceding frame. In this case the tritone occurs between the soprano and bass voices. Does this tritone resolve normally? yes

74. Write the second chord in each case. (*Be sure to resolve the tritone normally even though irregularities of doubling may occur.*)

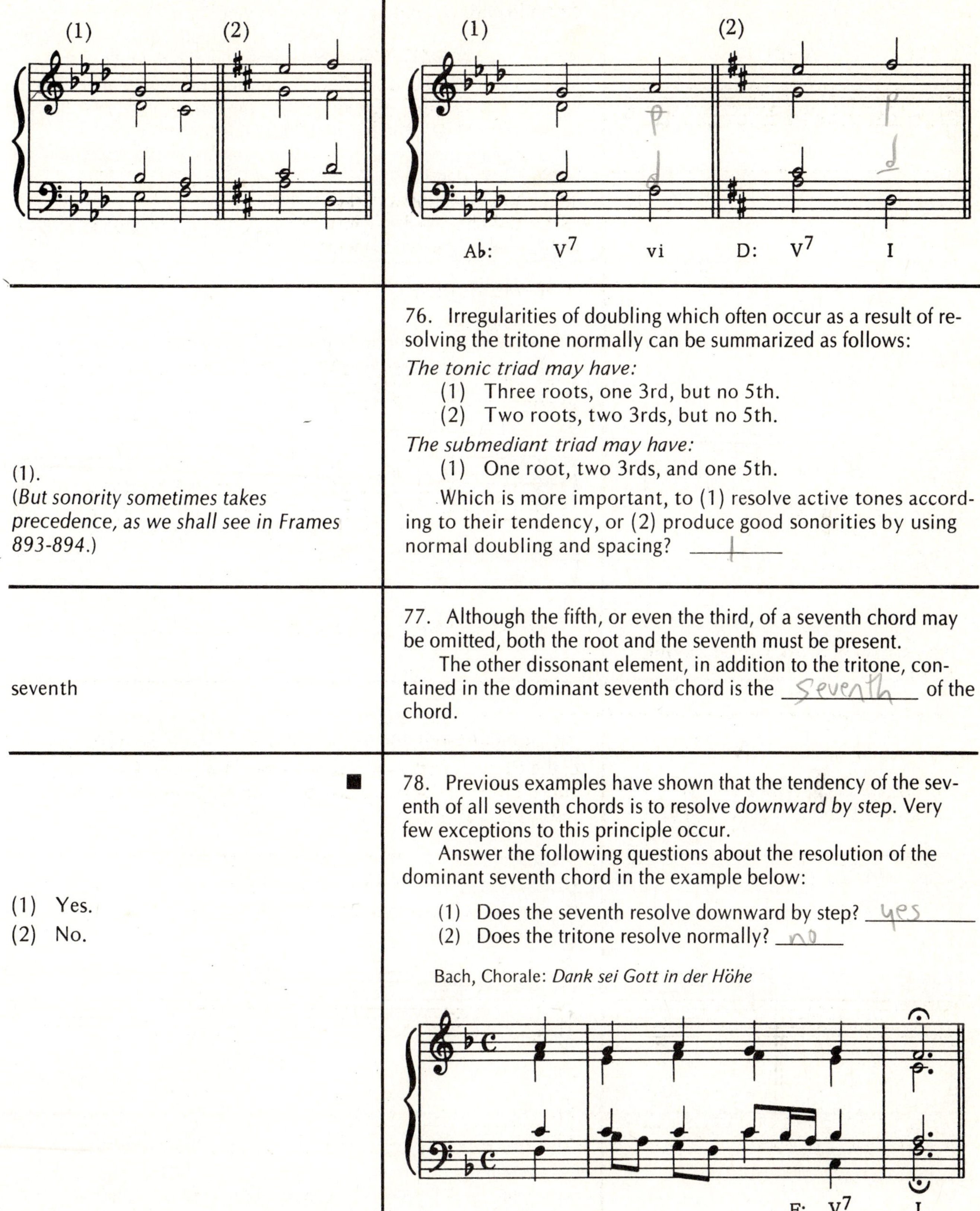

75. Continue as in the preceding frame.

(1).
(*But sonority sometimes takes precedence, as we shall see in Frames 893-894.*)

76. Irregularities of doubling which often occur as a result of resolving the tritone normally can be summarized as follows:

The tonic triad may have:

(1) Three roots, one 3rd, but no 5th.
(2) Two roots, two 3rds, but no 5th.

The submediant triad may have:

(1) One root, two 3rds, and one 5th.

Which is more important, to (1) resolve active tones according to their tendency, or (2) produce good sonorities by using normal doubling and spacing? ________

seventh

77. Although the fifth, or even the third, of a seventh chord may be omitted, both the root and the seventh must be present.

The other dissonant element, in addition to the tritone, contained in the dominant seventh chord is the ________ of the chord.

■

(1) Yes.
(2) No.

78. Previous examples have shown that the tendency of the seventh of all seventh chords is to resolve *downward by step*. Very few exceptions to this principle occur.

Answer the following questions about the resolution of the dominant seventh chord in the example below:

(1) Does the seventh resolve downward by step? ________
(2) Does the tritone resolve normally? ________

Bach, Chorale: *Dank sei Gott in der Höhe*

79. The example in the preceding frame shows that, due to the desire to end with the stronger sonority provided by a complete triad, the tritone (B♭-E) is not resolved normally. Specifically, the leading tone (E in the alto voice) drops down to the fifth of the tonic triad instead of obeying its melodic tendency to ascend to the keynote (F). This occurs frequently in the inner voices, but rarely in the soprano, where the weak melodic effect is more evident.

Although the tritone in this case does not resolve normally, the seventh (B♭ in the tenor voice) moves according to its natural tendency which is ____________ by step.

downward

80. Complete the second chord in each case so that a *complete* triad with regular doubling (two roots, one third, and one fifth) results. (*Be sure to resolve the seventh downward by step.*)

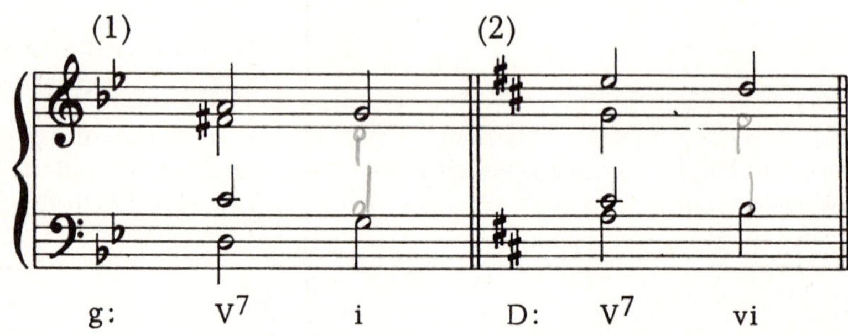

---

(1) (2)

81. Continue as in the preceding frame. (*Use no irregular doubling.*)

■

82. When the dominant seventh chord is in first inversion, the seventh scale degree is in the bass. Because of its prominent position, the natural tendency of the leading tone to move upward to the keynote is intensified. *This tendency should rarely be violated.*

Mozart, *Fantasia in C Minor,* K. 475

Is there any irregularity in the resolution of the dominant seventh chord in the above example? ________

No.

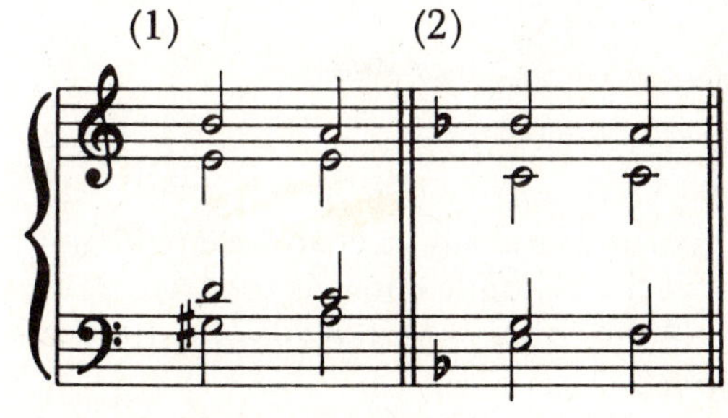

83. Write the second chord in each case, in such a way that no irregularity of doubling or resolution of active tones results.

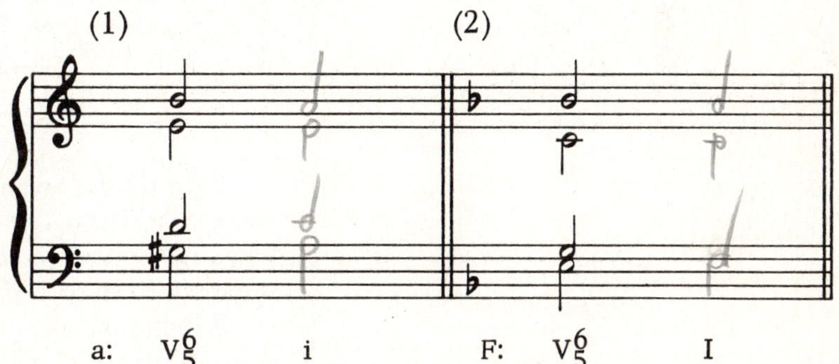

■

84. Analyze with Roman numerals the phrase below. (*Don't be misled by nonharmonic tones.*)

Bach, Chorale: *Jesu, Deine tiefen Wunden*

No.

85. The chord at the asterisk in the preceding frame is a dominant seventh chord. Aside from the 9-8 suspension in the tenor (in the following chord), are there any irregularities of doubling or resolution? ___no___

■

86. A dominant seventh chord in second inversion is shown below:

Schumann, *Papillons*, Op. 2

Like triads, seventh chords in second inversion are relatively weak sonorities. The one in the example above is used as a "passing chord" to connect the tonic in first inversion with the same chord in root position.

Which note is in the lowest voice when a seventh chord is in second inversion? (Root/3rd/5th/7th) ___5___

5th.

■

87. Supply the Roman numeral analysis for the phrase below:

Haydn, *Quartet*, Op. 76, No. 4

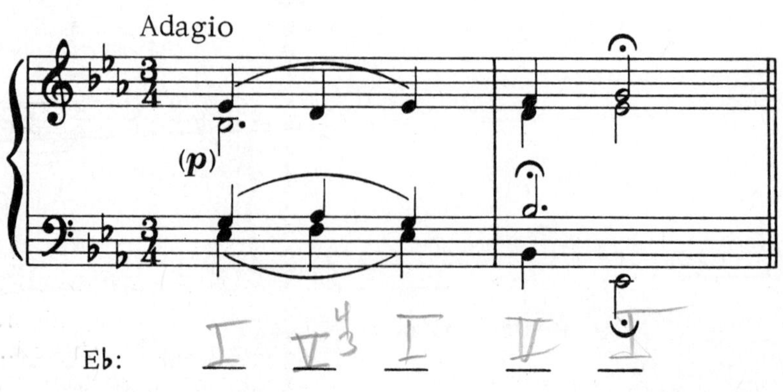

(1) (2)

88. Complete the part writing in such a way that no irregularities of doubling occur.

■

89. Supply the Roman numeral analysis for the phrase below:

Bach, Chorale: *Gott lebet noch*

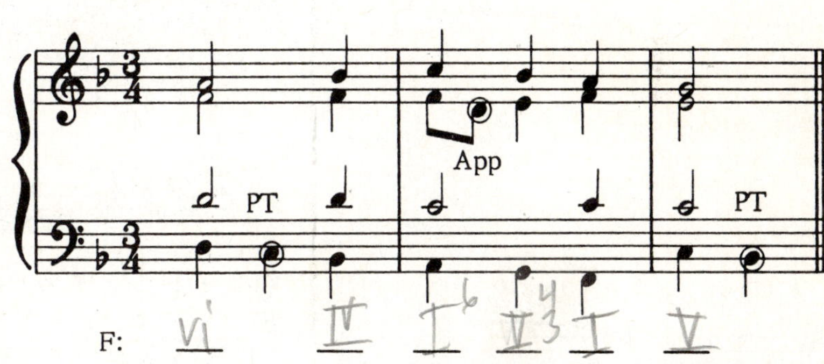

90. The third inversion has the seventh in the bass.

By being in the bass voice, the natural tendency of the seventh to resolve downward (by step) is emphasized. The dominant seventh chord in third inversion almost always resolves (as above) to the tonic triad in ____________ inversion.

first

91. Write the second chord in such a way that no irregularities of doubling occur.

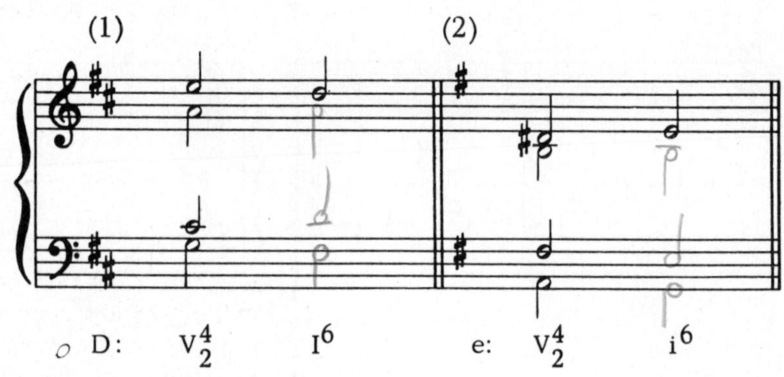

■

92. Supply the Roman numeral analysis for the fragment below:

Beethoven, *Sonata,* Op. 13

93. In all of the examples shown thus far, the seventh resolves downward by step. Exceptional resolutions of the seventh are extremely rare. Two examples are shown below:

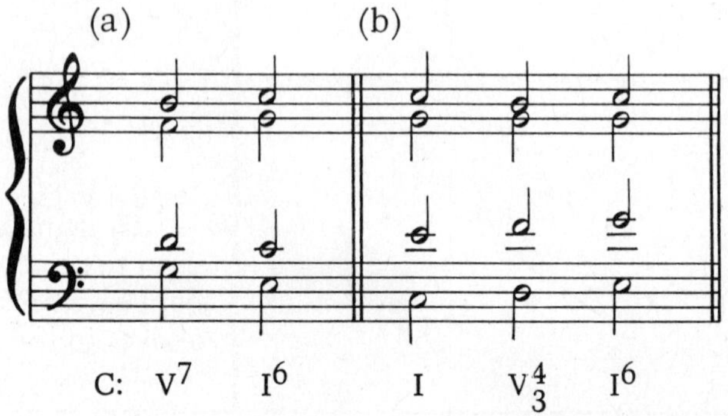

Notice that in both cases the bass voice takes the note to which the seventh would normally have resolved (the third of the tonic triad).

Learn this principle: *If the bass takes the note of resolution, the seventh may rise to the nearest chord tone.*

What is the *normal* resolution of the seventh?

____

Downward by step.

---

94. The tendency for the seventh of a seventh chord to resolve downward by step is seldom ignored. The *approach* to the seventh, on the other hand, is made in a variety of ways. Actually, it may be approached in any way that produces an effective melodic contour, taking into account its tendency to resolve downward.

Greater freedom may be exercised in the approach to the seventh than in its resolution. (True/False) __________

True.

---

95. Whereas the seventh may be approached in any way that results in a good melodic line and satisfactory part writing, several patterns are encountered more frequently than others. These are by preparation, by step, and by leap (from below).

(a) Preparation (b) Step (c) Leap

G: ii V^7 I I V^7 I V V^6_5 I

The seventh in each of the above examples may be likened to a nonharmonic tone. In (a), for example, the pattern of approach and resolution suggests a suspension. The pattern in (b) is like that of a passing tone, while the pattern in (c) suggests a(n) ______________.

appoggiatura

---

96. Like (b) in the preceding frame, the example on the following page shows a seventh approached and left by step. What nonharmonic tone is suggested by this pattern? The ______________ ______________.

neighboring tone

SUMMARY

Seven types of seventh chords are generated by the major/minor system. The various types are named according to two features: (1) the quality of the triad; and (2) the quality of the interval between the root and the seventh. The term "major-minor" seventh chord, for example, means that the chord consists of a major triad with a minor seventh above the root.

The figured bass symbols commonly used to indicate the various positions of seventh chords are shown below:

Root Position	*1st Inversion*	*2nd Inversion*	*3rd Inversion*
7	6 5	4 3	4 or 2 2

The dominant seventh chord is used more frequently than any other. The addition of the seventh to the dominant triad does not change its function. In fact, the introduction of a dissonant element (the seventh) serves to increase the activity of the dominant triad and makes more imperative its usual resolution to the tonic or submediant triads.

Two dissonant elements are contained in the dominant seventh chord: the seventh, and the interval of a tritone between the third and seventh. The proper resolution of the tritone, which is dictated by the melodic tendencies of the various scale degrees (the seventh tends to resolve upward while the fourth degree tends to resolve downward), is one of the factors which affects the part writing of passages containing dominant seventh chords. The second factor is the desirability of obeying the tendency of the chord seventh to resolve downward by step.

Greater freedom is exercised in the approach to the seventh than in its resolution. Nevertheless, the majority of sevenths occur in patterns which suggest nonharmonic tones. The approach by preparation is like the suspension; the approach by step is like the passing tone or the neighboring tone; and the approach by leap is like the appoggiatura.

Dominant seventh chords are used in root position and in all inversions. When the more active tones (the seventh and third) are placed in the bass or soprano, their melodic tendencies are more apparent. You must take care in such cases that these tendencies are not violated.

Mastery Frames

Four. (1-2)	1-1. How many tones are required to produce a complete seventh chord? ________
(1) Quality of triad (2) Quality of 7th (9-22)	1-2. The quality of a seventh chord is represented by a term such as below. Indicate to what feature of the chord each part of the term applies. (1) ________ **Diminished** — **Minor** (2) ________
Seven. (20)	1-3. How many diatonic seventh chords occur in the major-minor scale system? ________
(1) Major (2) Minor (3) Minor (4) Major (5) Major-minor (6) Minor (7) Diminished-minor (21)	1-4. Indicate the quality of each of the seventh chords based on the major scale. (1) (2) (3) (4) (5) (6) (7) C: (1)________ (2)________ (3)________ (4)________ (5)________ (6)________ (7)________

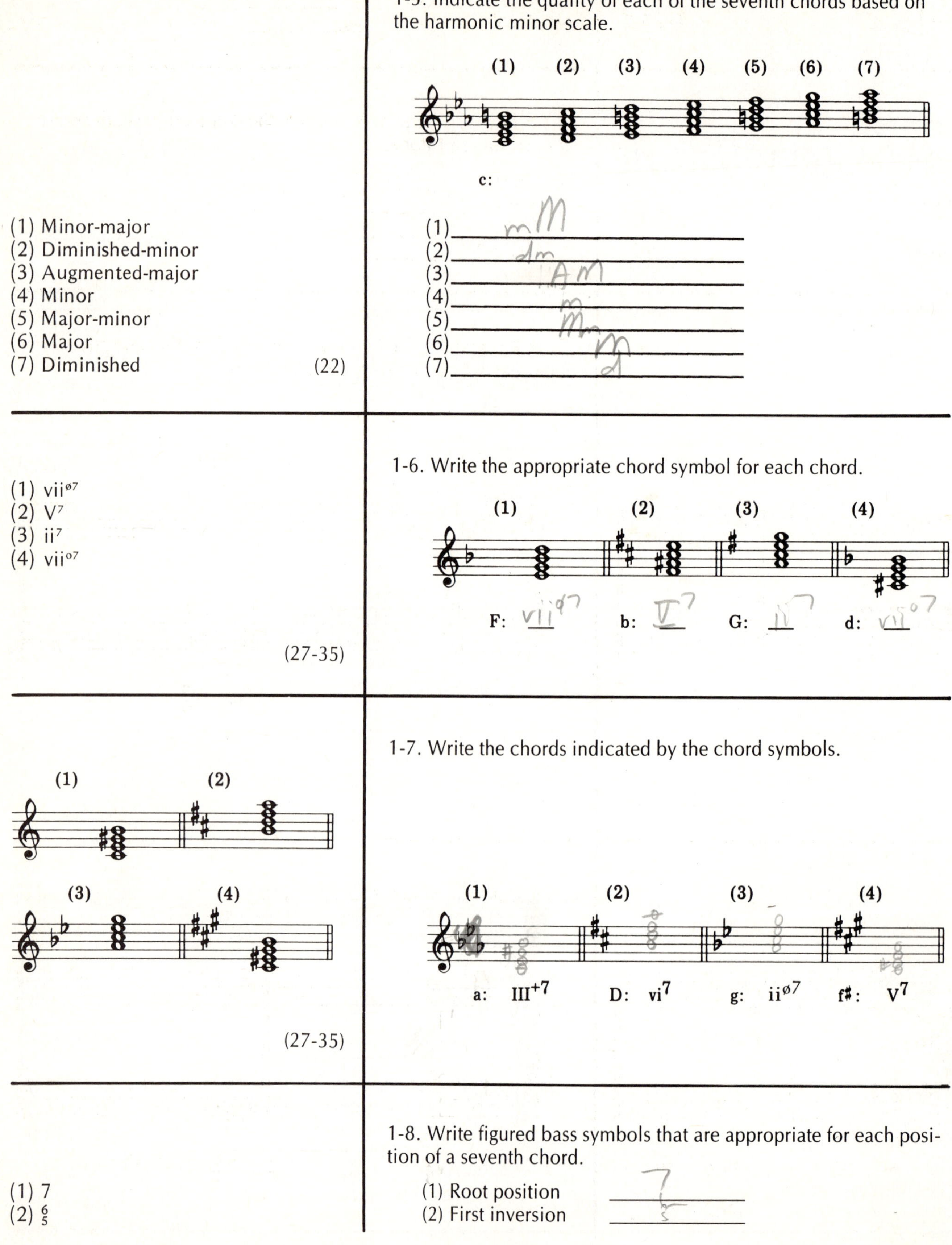

(1) Minor-major
(2) Diminished-minor
(3) Augmented-major
(4) Minor
(5) Major-minor
(6) Major
(7) Diminished (22)

1-5. Indicate the quality of each of the seventh chords based on the harmonic minor scale.

(1)________________
(2)________________
(3)________________
(4)________________
(5)________________
(6)________________
(7)________________

---

(1) $vii^{ø7}$
(2) V^7
(3) ii^7
(4) vii^{o7}

(27-35)

1-6. Write the appropriate chord symbol for each chord.

(27-35)

1-7. Write the chords indicated by the chord symbols.

---

(1) 7
(2) $^6_5$

1-8. Write figured bass symbols that are appropriate for each position of a seventh chord.

(1) Root position ____________
(2) First inversion ____________

(3) $^{4}_{3}$
(4) $^{4}_{2}$ or 2 (49-52)

(3) Second inversion ______
(4) Third inversion ______

Third √

Seventh √ (67

1-9. Check (√) the two elements of the dominant seventh chord that produce a tritone.

Root ______
Third ______
Fifth ______
Seventh ______

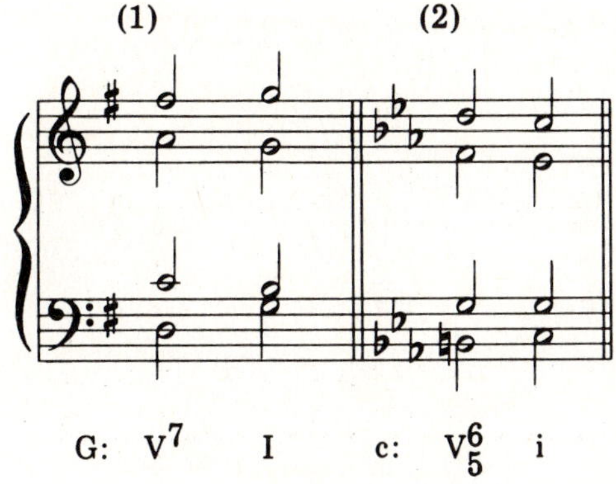

(67-81; 82-84)

1-10. Resolve the dominant seventh chords so that all active tones move according to their normal tendency.

(86-89, 90-92)

1-11. Continue as in the preceding frame.

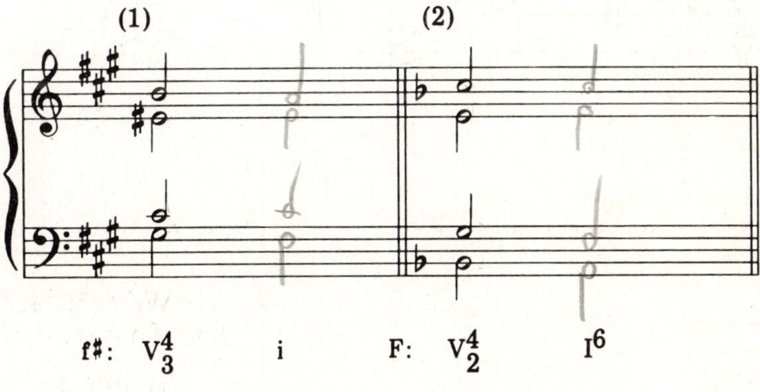

Supplementary Assignments

ASSIGNMENT 1-1 Name________________________________

1. Write seventh chords as indicated. *(The given note is the root.)*

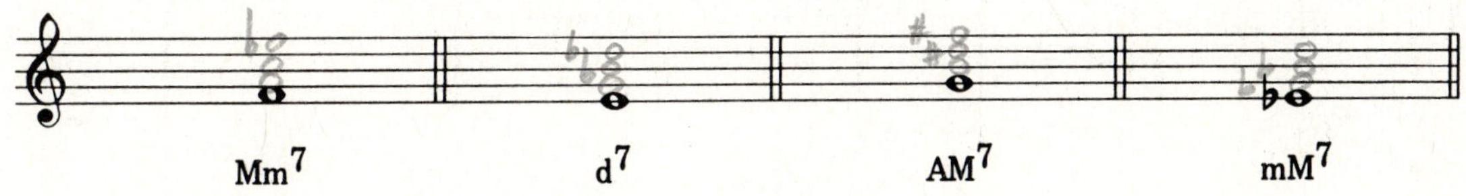

2. Write seventh chords as indicated. *(The given note is the third.)*

3. Write seventh chords as indicated. *(The given note is the fifth.)*

4. Write seventh chords as indicated. *(The given note is the seventh.)*

5. Write chords as indicated.

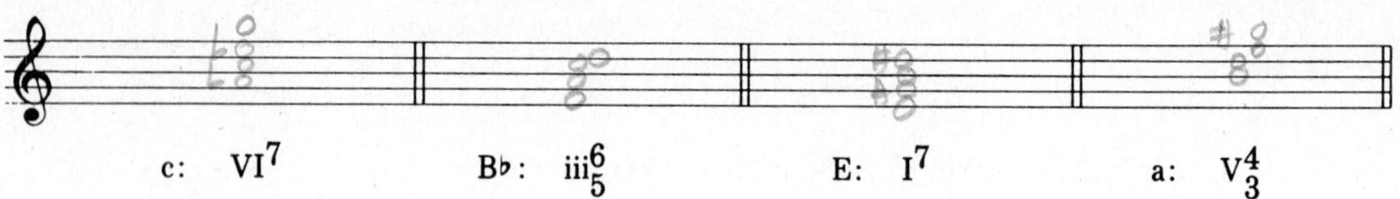

6. In which example is the dominant seventh chord correctly resolved?______

7. In which example is the dominant seventh chord both correctly written and resolved?______

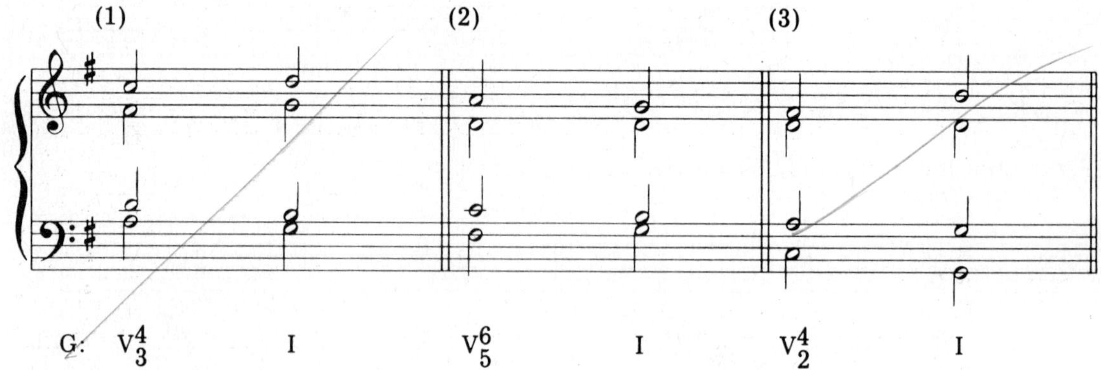

8. Resolve each dominant seventh chord so that all active tones resolve in the direction of their activity.

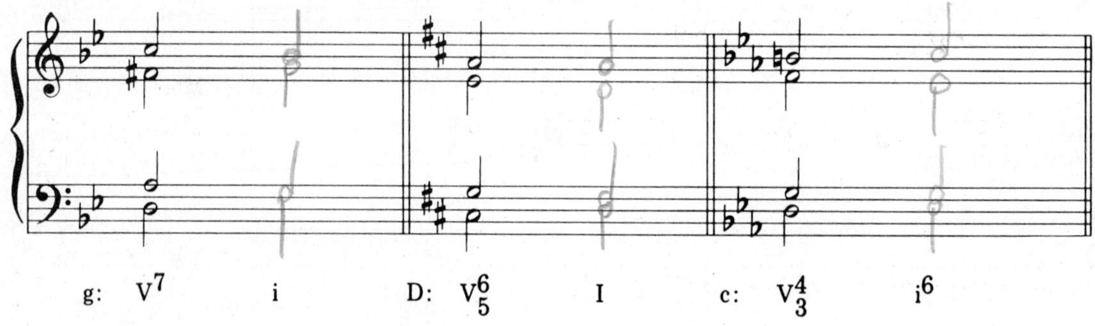

ASSIGNMENT 1-2 Name ____________________

1. Indicate the quality of each chord. Use symbols such as Mm⁷, m⁷, etc.

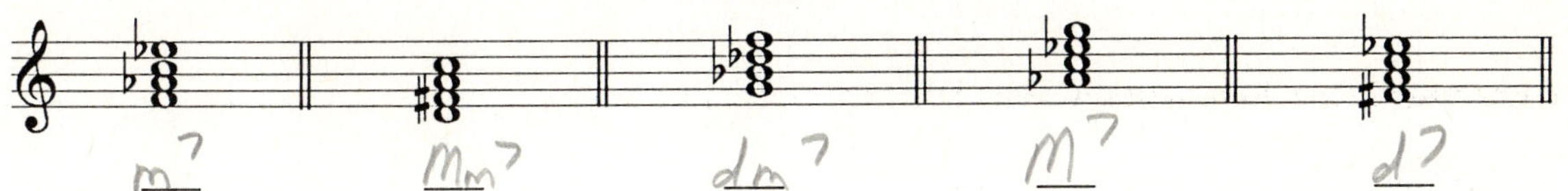

2. Write chords as indicated. (Given note is the root.)

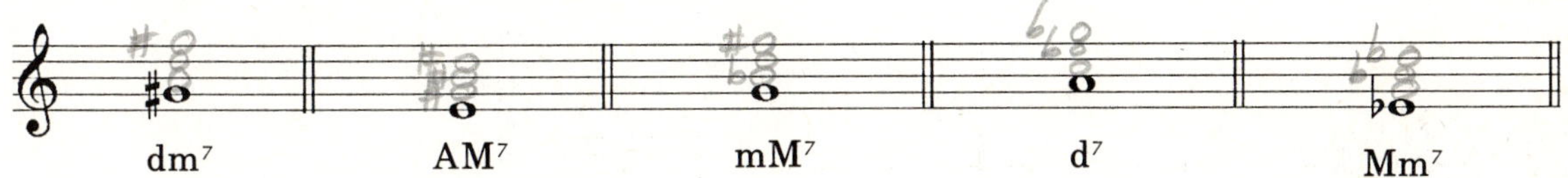

3. Supply the chord symbol for each chord. (*Indicate inversions.*)

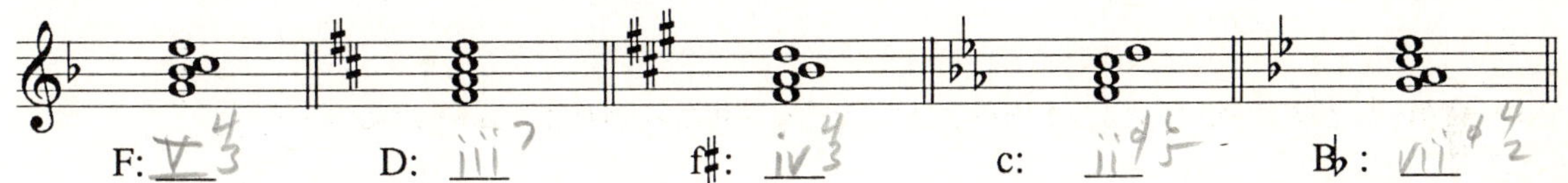

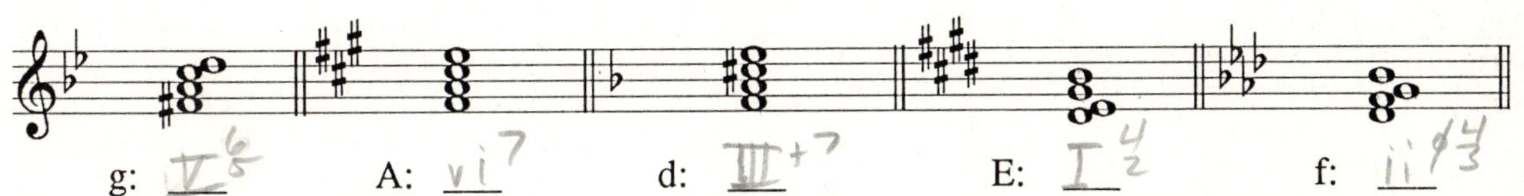

4. Write chords as indicated.

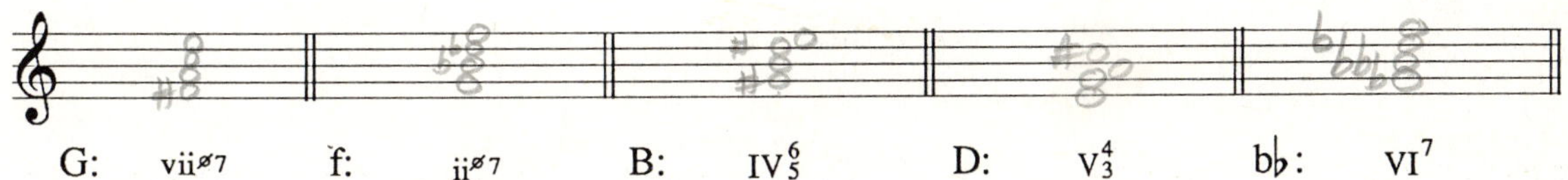

5. Which chord agrees with the chord symbol? ________

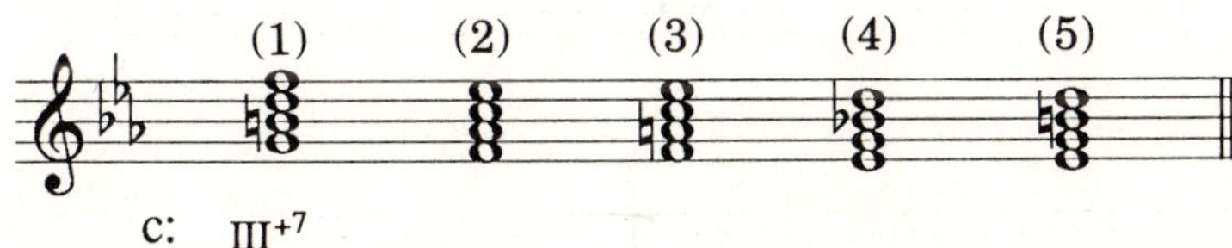

6. Which chord agrees with the chord symbol? ________

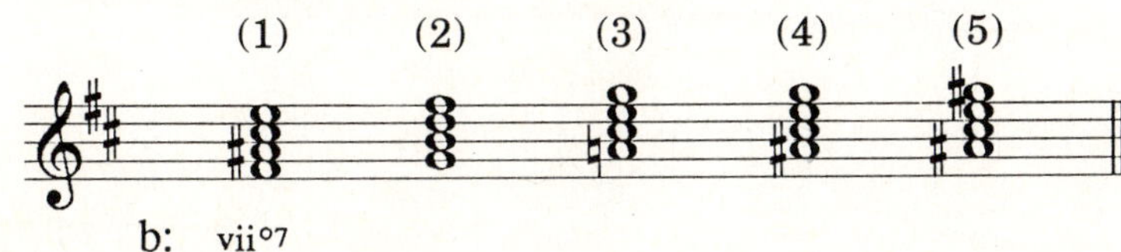

7. Which chord agrees with the chord symbol? ________

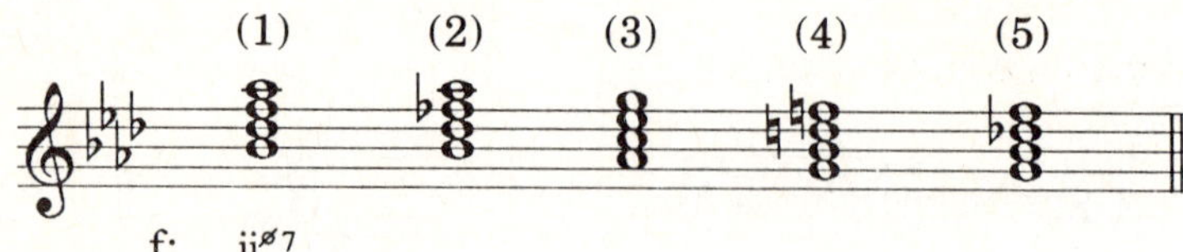

8. In which case is the seventh chord correctly written and resolved? ________

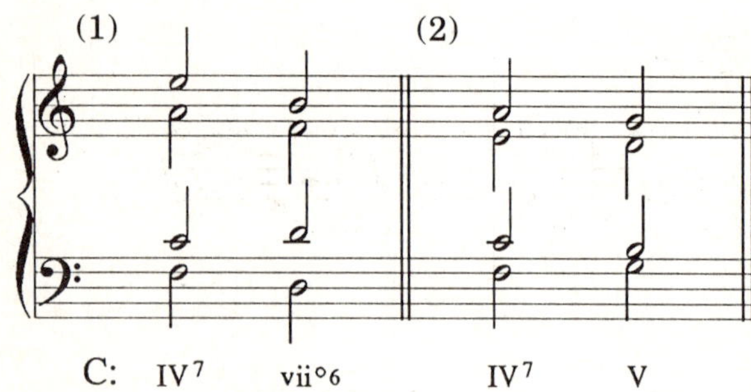

9. In which case is the seventh chord correctly written and resolved? ________

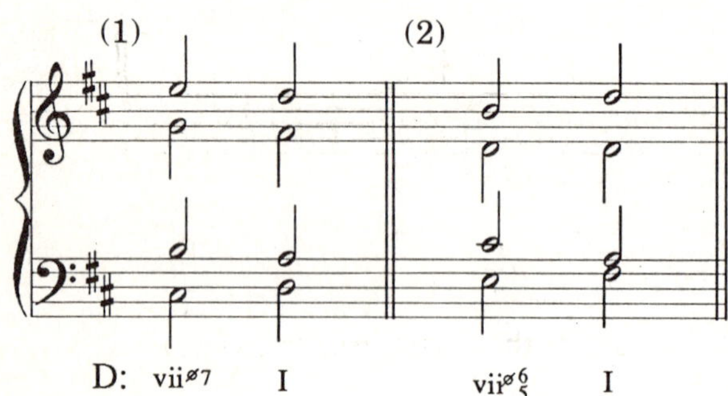

10. Write the second chord in each case so that *all* active tones are resolved in the direction of their activity.

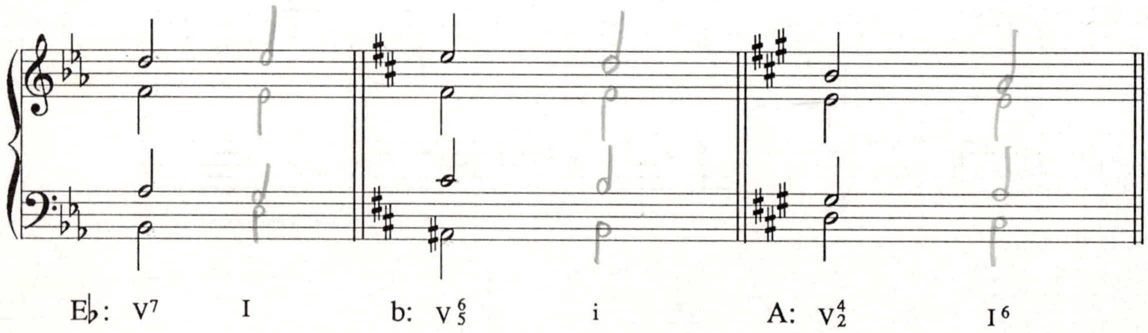

ASSIGNMENT 1-3 Name______________________

1. Supply chord symbols for the six chords in the example below.

Kuhlau: *Sonatina*

2. Analyze with Roman numerals the examples below. Also indicate the nonharmonic tones.

Beethoven: *Sonata,* Op. 31, No. 3

Mozart: *Fantasia in D minor*, K. 397

3. Use chord symbols to indicate a progression which would permit the seventh to resolve down by step in each case.

Major Key	*Minor Key*
ii^7 - ______	$ii^{ø7}$ - ______
iii^7 - ______	III^{+7} - ______
IV^7 - ______	iv^7 - ______
vi^7 - ______	VI^7 - ______
$vii^{ø7}$ - ______	vii^{o7} - ______

4. Add the alto and tenor to the given figured basses. Circle each chord seventh and draw a line from the circle to the note of resolution. Analyze with Roman numerals.

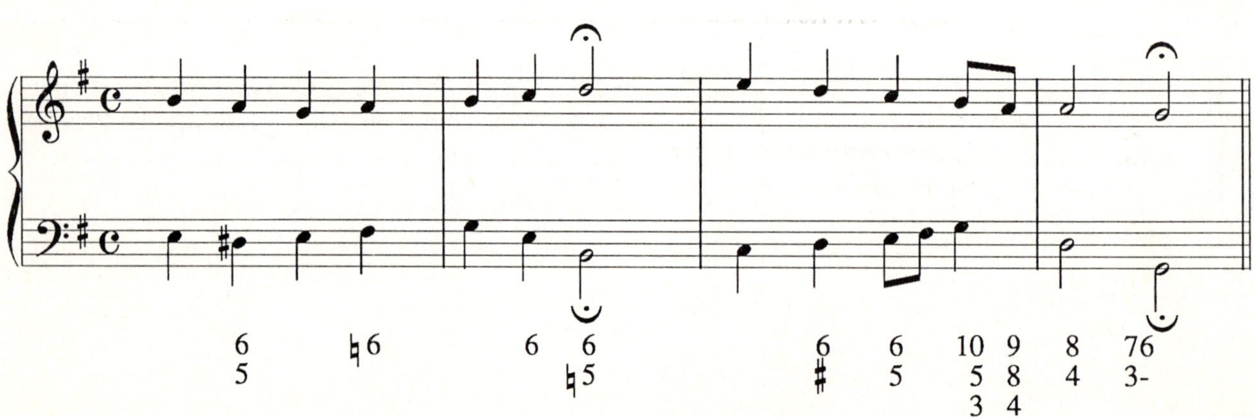

chapter two

Nondominant Seventh Chords

Seventh chords occur on all degrees of the diatonic scale. Compared with the dominant seventh chord, however, the remainder are of low frequency. This is due to the fact that, in most music, dominant harmony possesses structural importance next to that of the tonic. Thus, dominant chords occur relatively frequently in comparison to other chords. Also, harmonic variety depends upon the interplay of sonorities possessing various degrees of activity. Excessive use of similar sonorities—seventh chords, for example—leads to bland effects. Harmonic vitality is achieved by exploiting a wide variety of chords, including the ever useful triads.

No. *(Seventh chords are more active.)*	97. Except for the tonic, seventh chords have the same harmonic function as their corresponding triads. Do seventh chords and triads possess the same degree of activity? __NO.__
nonharmonic	98. The desire for melodic and rhythmic activity causes many chord sevenths to appear as nonharmonic tones rather than chord tones. This is particularly true of nondominant harmony.* It is often difficult to decide whether or not a particular dissonant tone is actually a member of the chord or merely the result of melodic (nonharmonic) activity. Such decisions are made by assessing the importance of the dissonance as a harmonic effect, and duration is often the deciding factor. To be an integral part of the chord a seventh must not be heard as a __nonharmonic__ tone. *The term *secondary seventh chords* is used by some writers to refer to all seventh chords other than the dominant seventh.
■ *(There may be some difference of opinion, but most analysts will classify this note as a passing tone.)*	99. Would you classify the note circled in the example on the following page as a nonharmonic tone, or as part of a seventh chord? __passing tone__

Mendelssohn, *Andante con Variazioni,* Op. 82

■ 100. In the preceding frame, the circled note (A-flat) occupies merely the last half of the beat and occurs in a pattern characteristic of the passing tone. This note is, of course, the chord seventh, and may be analyzed as such if you wish; but, in any case, its function is more melodic than harmonic.

Supply the Roman numeral analysis for the example below. (*Analyze one chord per measure.*)

Schubert, *Waltz,* Op. 9, No. 13

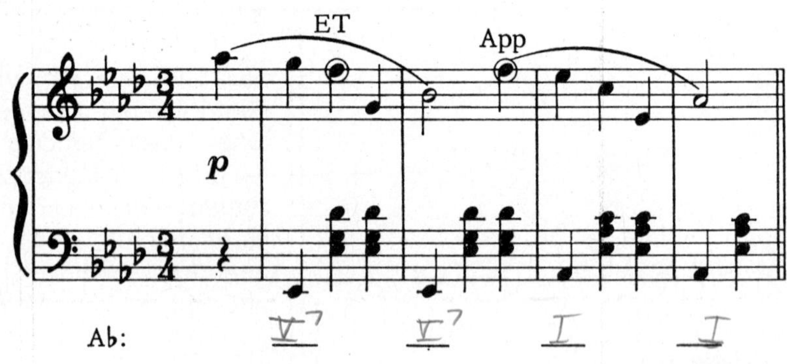

A♭: V^7 - V^7 - I - I

101. Does the seventh of the dominant seventh chord in the preceding frame (first and second measures) have a harmonic or melodic function? ______________

Harmonic.

102. Check (√) the correct option:

1. The harmonic function of the seventh varies according to its duration and melodic status.
2. Many seventh chords can be "explained away" as the result of nonharmonic tones.

True statements:

(1) _____ (2) _____ Both _____ Neither _____

Both √

103. Check (√) the correct option:

1. All seventh chords are the result of nonharmonic usage.
2. The seventh of a seventh chord must be an integral part of the chord.

True statements:

(1) _____ (2) _____ Both _____ Neither _____

(2) √

■ 104. The SUPERTONIC SEVENTH CHORD occurs frequently as part of a cadence formula.

Mozart, *Quartet,* K. 465

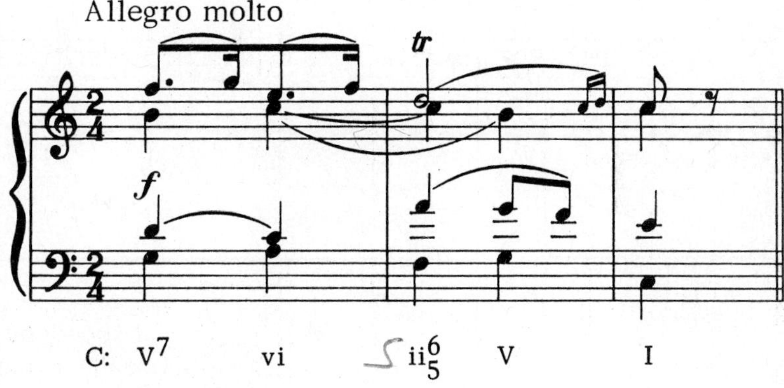

The supertonic seventh chord in the above example is in _____ inversion.

first

■ 105. The same cadence formula as that in the preceding frame is shown in a minor key below:

Beethoven, *Sonata,* Op. 2, No. 1

diminished-minor

The supertonic seventh chord in a major key is a minor seventh chord. In a minor key the supertonic seventh chord is a ________________ seventh chord.

■ 106. The supertonic seventh chord in root position occurs more frequently in major than in minor. Supply the Roman numeral analysis for the example below:

Bach, Chorale: *Herr Christ, der ein'ge Gott's-Sohn*

■ 107. The supertonic seventh chord in root position is used much less frequently in a minor key because of the diminished fifth which occurs above the bass. The $ii^{ø7}$ in root position in the example below is part of a sequential pattern.

Chopin, *Prelude*, Op. 28, No. 22

■ 108. The supertonic seventh chord is rarely used in second inversion. Third inversion, however, is more common. An example is shown at the asterisk on the following page.

Bach, Chorale: *Was willst du dich, o meine Seele*

The seventh of the supertonic seventh chord in the example above occurs in a pattern which resembles the (nonharmonic tone) ___sus___ .

suspension

■ 109. The MEDIANT SEVENTH CHORD is rarely used. It occurs more frequently in major than in minor, and often is part of a harmonic sequence. It usually resolves to the submediant.

Bach, Chorale: *O Ewigkeit, du Donnerwort*

What irregularity of doubling occurs in the mediant seventh chord (at the asterisk) above?

___2 3rds, no 5th___

____

There are two 3rds, and the 5th is omitted.

■ 110. Supply the Roman numeral analysis for the example on the following page.

Chopin, *Etude*, Op. 10, No. 1

■ 111. The mediant seventh chord in minor is extremely rare. Because of the alternate seventh degrees of the melodic minor scale there are two forms.

The resolution of each chord is to the submediant triad, but in (b) the leading tone (B-natural) necessitates a doubled third in the second chord. What part writing error would result if the submediant triad had been written as in (a)? ______________

An augmented second in the tenor voice.

■ 112. Most seventh chords resolve to a chord whose root is a fifth below, but the SUBDOMINANT SEVENTH CHORD does not usually resolve in this way, except when part of a harmonic sequence. This is due to the weak sonority of the leading tone triad. A common resolution is to the dominant triad or seventh chord. Supply the Roman numeral analysis for the example on the following page.

Bach, Chorale: *Vater unser im Himmelreich*

third

■ 113. Another common resolution of the subdominant seventh chord is to the supertonic triad or seventh chord.

Bach, *Well-Tempered Clavier,* Vol. 1, Prelude I

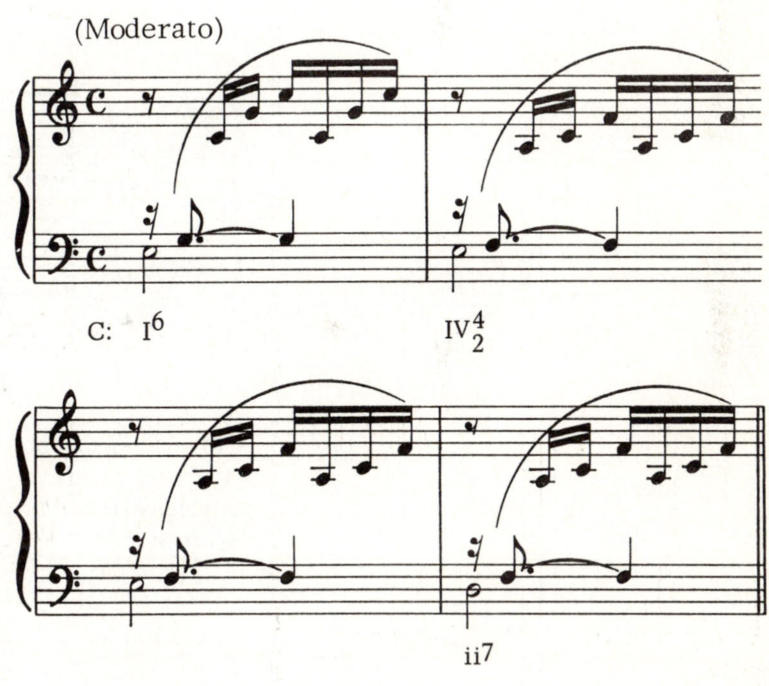

As analyzed in the above example, the subdominant seventh chord is in ____3rd____ inversion. (Alternative analyses are certainly possible for this example.)

■ 114. In minor, there are two forms of the subdominant seventh chord, both of which usually resolve to the dominant triad or seventh chord.

first

The irregularly doubled dominant chord in (a) is necessary to avoid parallel perfect fifths between the soprano and alto voices. In (b) both the subdominant seventh and dominant seventh chords are in ______________ inversion.

■ 115. Supply the Roman numeral analysis for the example below:

Bach, Chorale: *Erhalt' uns, Herr, bei deinem Wort*

Note: From this point on you may perhaps determine alternative analyses; please feel free to explore an alternative even if not explicitly stated in the text. Alternative solutions could be reviewed with an instructor in class or with a tutor.

---

minor

116. What is the quality of the subdominant seventh chord in the preceding frame? A ______________ seventh chord.

■ 117. Supply the Roman numeral analysis for the example on the following page.

d: III i IV^6_5 V^6_5 i V

Bach, Chorale: *Herr, straf mich nicht in deinem Zorn*

d: ______ ______ ______ ______ ______ ______

False.
(It is a major-minor seventh chord.)

118. The chord at the asterisk in the preceding frame is a minor seventh chord. (True/False) ____________

---

dominant

119. In a minor key the subdominant seventh chord may be either a minor seventh chord or a major-minor seventh chord, depending upon which of the alternate sixth scale degrees is used. Each of these types of subdominant seventh chords commonly progresses to the ____________ triad or seventh chord.

---

minor

120. The SUBMEDIANT SEVENTH CHORD occurs most frequently in root position. It may resolve to the subdominant, supertonic, dominant, or leading tone triads or seventh chords.

(a) (b)

C: vi^7 ii^7 vi^7 V^6

What is the quality of the submediant seventh chord in a major key? A ____________ seventh chord.

(No response.)

121. The seventh of the submediant seventh chord in (b) of the preceding frame is retained in the alto to become a part of the following chord. This is called a PASSIVE RESOLUTION. In spite of the smooth voice leading, passive resolutions occur rarely. This is because the tension of the dissonant seventh is best resolved by normal resolution, which is downward by step.

■ 122. Supply the Roman numeral analysis for the example below:

Bach, Chorale: *Schmücke dich, o liebe Seele*

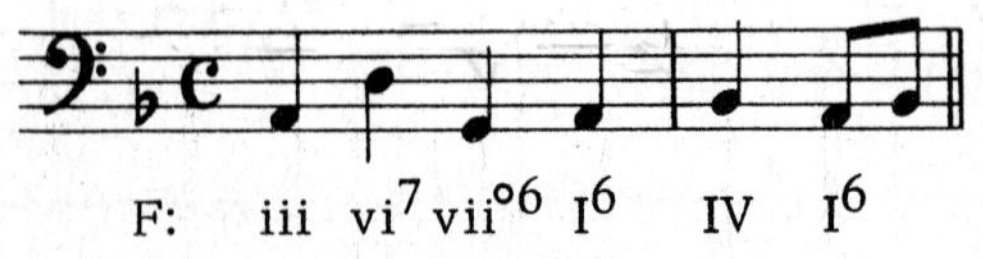

---

123. In a minor key the submediant seventh chord has two forms.

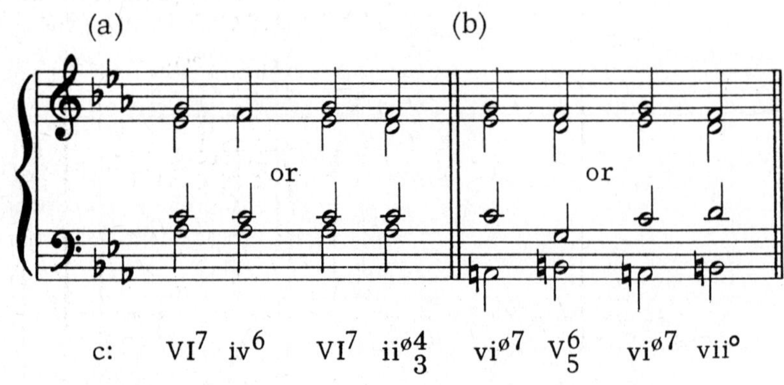

Identify the quality of the two types of submediant seventh chords used in a minor key (as shown above).

(a) ______________ seventh chord

(b) ______________ seventh chord

(a) Major

(b) Diminished-minor

■ 124. Complete the harmonic analysis for the example on the following page.

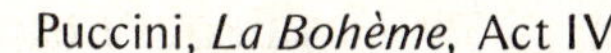

125. Supply the Roman numeral analysis for the example below:

Bach, Chorale: *Warum betrübst du dich, mein Herz*

126. The LEADING TONE SEVENTH CHORD performs the same function as the dominant seventh chord. It is generally used in root position, first and second inversions.

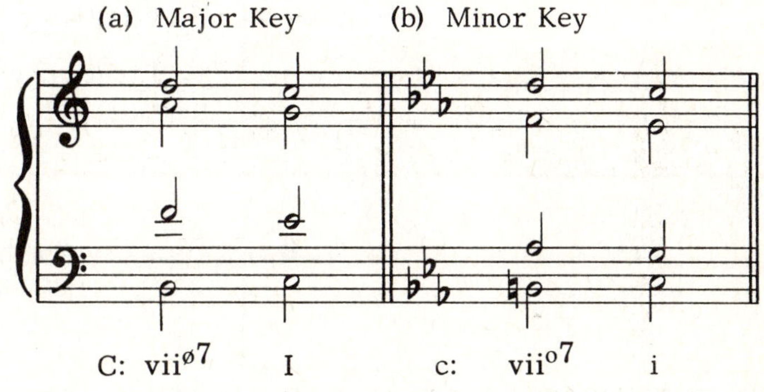

diminished-minor

What is the quality of the leading tone seventh chord in major? A ________________ seventh chord.

Bb: vii^{ø7} I -

■ 127. The leading tone seventh chord is used less frequently in major than in minor. Supply the Roman numeral analysis for the first two chords in the example below:

Mozart, *Quartet,* K. 458

Moderato

Ant

Ant

sf

sf

Bb: _____ _____ vii^{o7}/vi vi

■ 128. In a minor key the leading tone seventh chord is a fully diminished seventh chord.

Beethoven, *Sonata,* Op. 13

Allegro

p

c: vii$^{o}{}^{4}_{3}$ - i

second

The leading tone seventh chord above is in ____________ inversion.

■ 129. Supply the Roman numeral analysis for the example on the following page.

b: V IV^{6} V$^{6}_{5}$ i - vii^{o7}i V

Bach, Chorale: *Herzliebster Jesu, was hast du verbrochen*

■

130. The leading tone seventh chord is often used to produce a cadence effect which is somewhat less positive than that of the dominant seventh chord.

Mozart, *Sonata,* K. 333

tonic

The leading tone seventh chord almost always progresses to the __tonic__ triad.

131. The TONIC SEVENTH CHORD progresses to the subdominant triad, or occasionally to the supertonic triad or seventh chord.

(a) Major

(b) Minor

In minor, the lowered seventh scale degree is used in order to descend smoothly to the third of the subdominant triad.

Identify the quality of the tonic seventh chord in major and minor keys (as shown above).

(a) ___Maj.___ seventh chord

(b) ___Minor___ seventh chord

C: V^4_2 I^6 I^7 IV I

■ 132. Supply the Roman numeral analysis for the example below:

Bach, Chorale: *Puer natus in Bethlehem*

Yes.

■ 133. The example below shows the tonic seventh chord in minor.

Brahms, *Intermezzo,* Op. 117, No. 2

Andante non troppo . . .

Does the seventh of the tonic seventh chord in the example above resolve normally? ___yes___

134. Seventh chords often appear in sequence patterns. The harmonic activity generated by a chain of active chords gives such passages a strong sense of forward motion.

Mozart, *Sonata,* K. 332

No.

Do any of the sevenths resolve irregularly in the example above? No

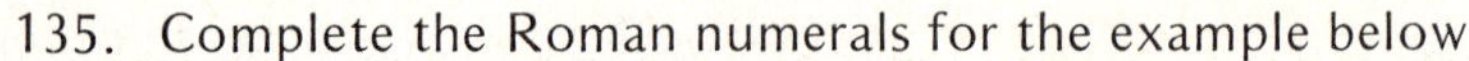

135. Complete the Roman numerals for the example below:

Kuhlau, *Sonatina,* Op. 88, No. 3

136. In general, a seventh chord can be used at any place where the corresponding triad can be used.

Rewrite the alto and tenor voices in such a way that by changing *one note* the supertonic triad becomes a seventh chord.

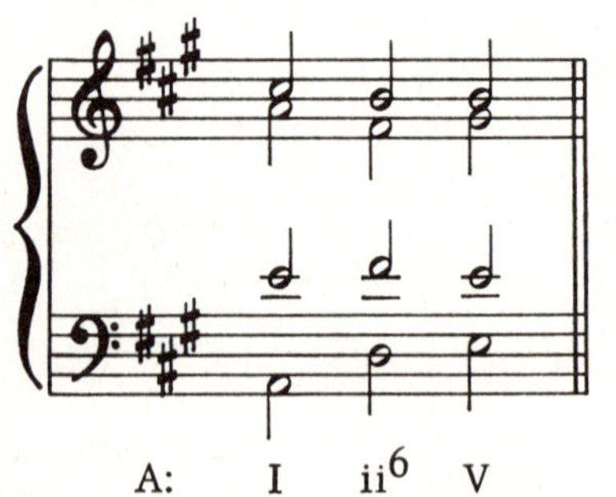

137. Rewrite the alto and tenor voices in such a way that by changing *three notes* the submediant, supertonic, and dominant triads become seventh chords.

138. Rewrite the alto, tenor, and bass voices in such a way that by changing *two notes* the subdominant and dominant triads become seventh chords.

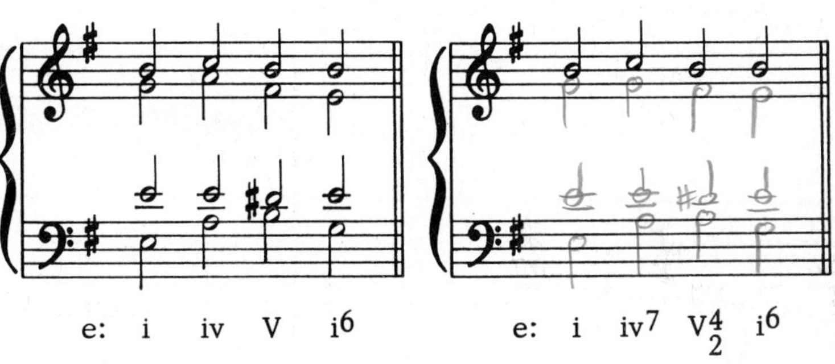

139. When harmonizing a melody each note can now be considered the root, third, fifth, or *seventh* of a chord. In the key of C major, for example, the first scale degree may be harmonized by any one of four chords.

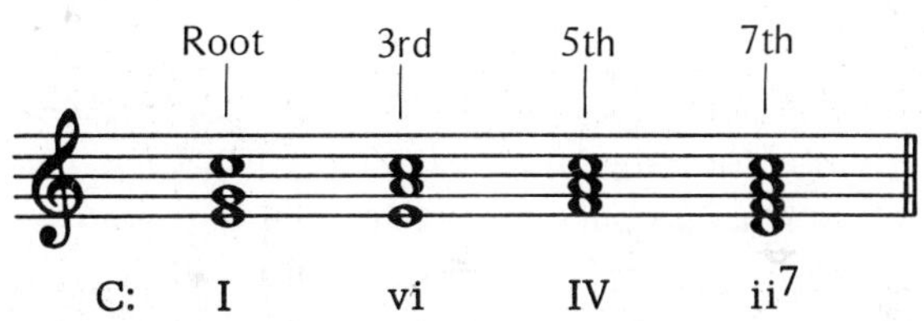

Indicate with Roman numerals the four chords which may be used to harmonize the *fourth* scale degree in a major key.

IV, ii, vii°, V7

140. When harmonizing a melody, the necessity of resolving the seventh downward by step must be considered. For a particular note to be harmonized as the seventh of a seventh chord, *the note which follows must be a second lower to allow for proper resolution.*

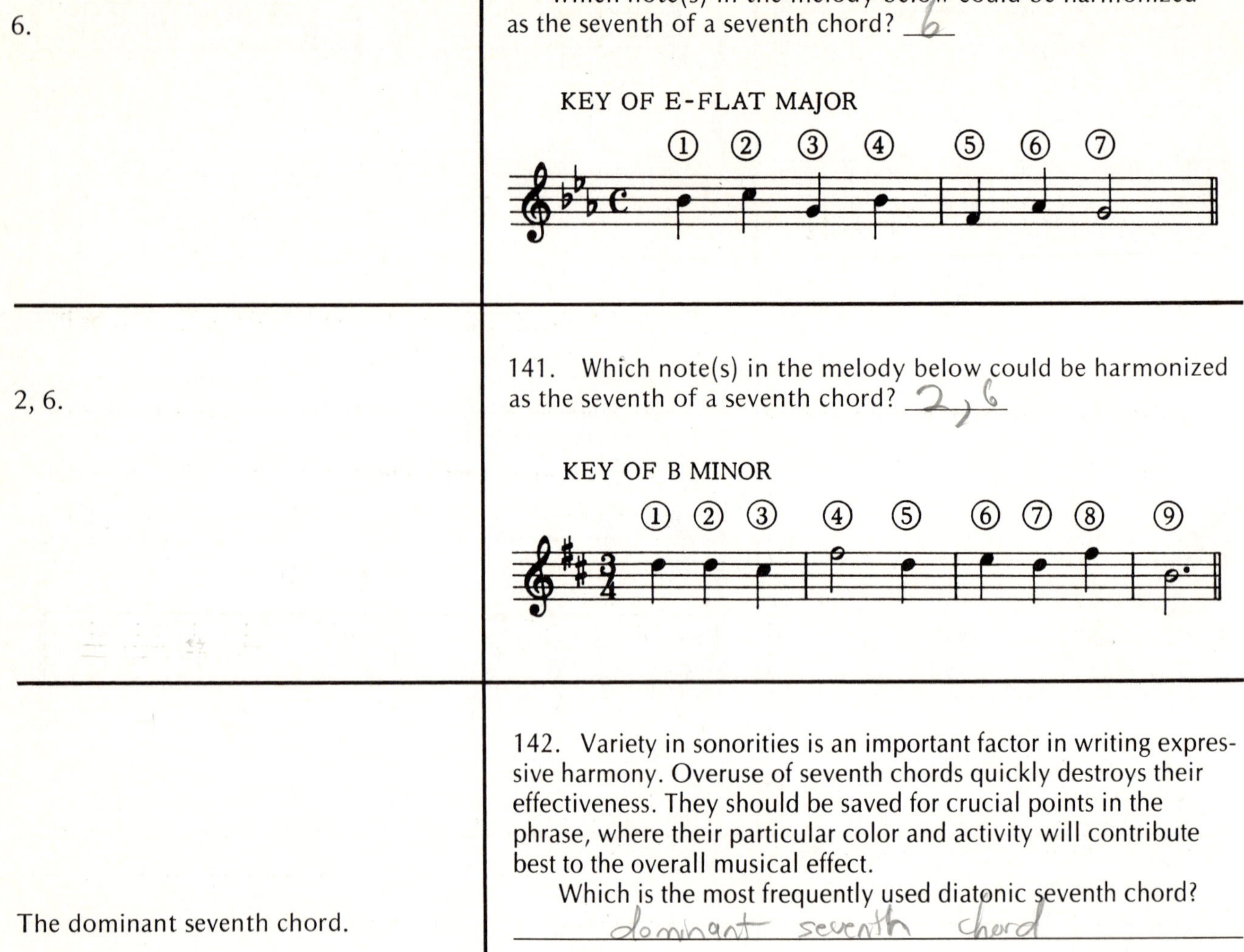

6.	Which note(s) in the melody below could be harmonized as the seventh of a seventh chord? 6 KEY OF E-FLAT MAJOR ① ② ③ ④ ⑤ ⑥ ⑦
2, 6.	141. Which note(s) in the melody below could be harmonized as the seventh of a seventh chord? 2, 6 KEY OF B MINOR ① ② ③ ④ ⑤ ⑥ ⑦ ⑧ ⑨
The dominant seventh chord.	142. Variety in sonorities is an important factor in writing expressive harmony. Overuse of seventh chords quickly destroys their effectiveness. They should be saved for crucial points in the phrase, where their particular color and activity will contribute best to the overall musical effect. Which is the most frequently used diatonic seventh chord? dominant seventh chord

SUMMARY

A seventh chord may be built on any degree of the scale. The harmonic function of a seventh chord is the same as the corresponding triad except for the tonic. In this case the addition of a seventh causes the inactive tonic triad to become active.

The seventh of a seventh chord introduces essential (harmonic) dissonance into music in contrast to the unessential dissonance of a nonharmonic tone. Since the seventh is the active element it should not be doubled. Also, the tension of this tone is resolved most satisfactorily if it proceeds *downward by step.* The seventh should rarely be resolved otherwise.

Mastery Frames

False. (97)	2-1. A seventh chord possesses the same degree of activity as its corresponding triad. (True/False) ________
(1) Diminished-minor seventh chord (2) Diminished seventh chord (126-128)	2-2. The leading tone seventh chord is shown in both a major and minor key below. (1) G: (2) g: Identify the quality of each chord. (1)________ (2)________
(1) Minor seventh chord (2) Diminished-minor seventh chord (105)	2-3. The supertonic seventh chord is shown in both a major and minor key below. (1) B♭: (2) b♭: Identify the quality of each chord. (1)________ (2)________
Subdominant (IV) or supertonic (ii). (131)	2-4. The harmonic function of a seventh chord is the same as its corresponding triad with the exception of the tonic. To what chord(s) would the tonic seventh chord likely resolve? ________ ________

Root vi^7

3rd IV^7

5th ii^7

7th $vii^{ø7}$

(139)

2-5. Any note is potentially the root, third, fifth, or seventh of a seventh chord. Indicate with chord symbols the seventh chords that include the given note in the manner indicated.

KEY OF D MAJOR

Root ______

3rd ______

5th ______

7th ______

---

lower (140-141)

2-6. To be harmonized as the seventh of a seventh chord, a note generally should be followed by a note that is the interval of a second (lower/higher) ______.

---

i

VI

iv

(Any order.)

(140-141)

2-7. Indicate with chord symbols three triads to which the chord below could progress with normal resolution of the seventh.

KEY OF F MINOR

f: III^7

Resolutions
______
______
______

Supplementary Assignments

ASSIGNMENT 2-1 Name________________________________

1. Write the soprano, alto, and tenor voices in accordance with the chord symbols.

2. Supply the Roman numeral analysis. Also indicate the nonharmonic tones.

Chopin: *Scherzo*, Op. 39

3. Write soprano, alto, tenor, and bass voices to conform to the chord symbols.

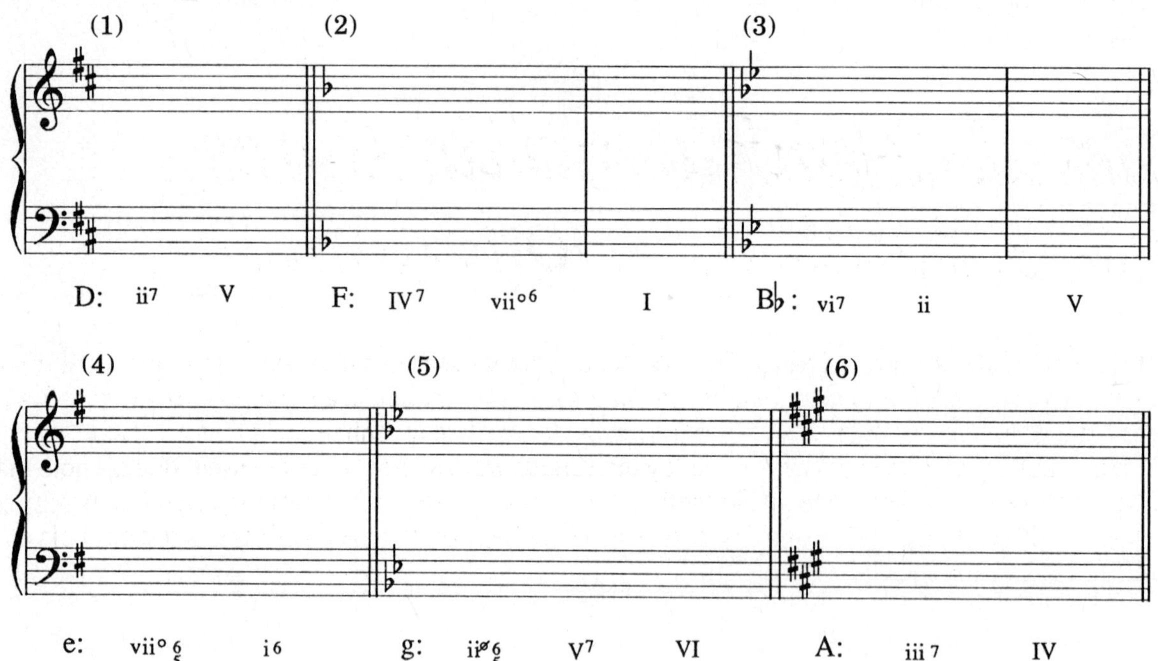

4. Compose a two-phrase period based on the harmonic progression indicated by the Roman numerals. (Consult Appendix B, *Piano Styles*. For this assignment, styles 19-20 are recommended.)

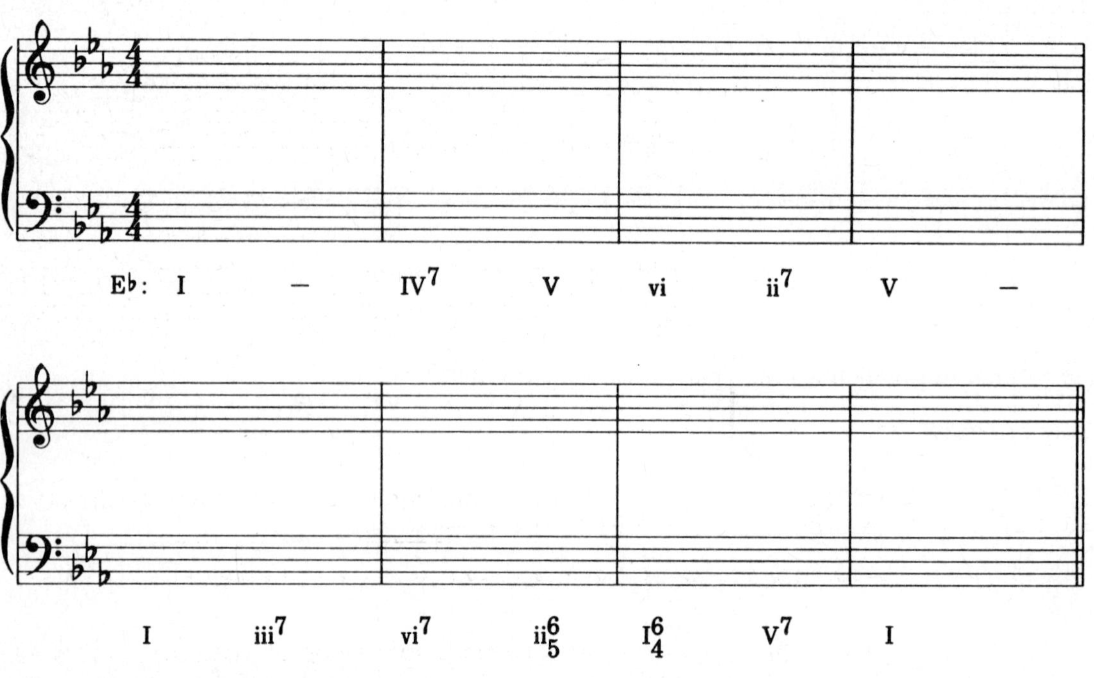

5. Compose one or more periods of music generally based on the harmonic progression indicated by the Roman numerals and suggested meter below. Suggest a minor key.

$\frac{6}{8}$ i - V^6_5 - i - $ii^{ø6}_5$ - V - i - III^7 - iv - V^7 - i - etc.

chapter three

Altered Nonharmonic Tones and Secondary Dominants

For greater color and variety than is available from the tonal material of diatonic scales, composers sometimes use tones which are not included in the prevailing tonality. These are chromatic alterations of diatonic tones and are called "altered" or "foreign" tones. Such tones occur either as altered nonharmonic tones or as members of altered chords. In this chapter we shall begin to study the various ways altered tones are used. (Please note that there may be times when you determine an alternative analysis in a given musical example. Feel free to explore an alternative even if not explicitly stated in the text. It could perhaps be reviewed with an instructor in class or with a tutor.)

■ 143. Tones which are foreign to the prevailing tonality often appear as ALTERED NONHARMONIC TONES. In the example below, the circled notes are *not* included in the G major scale.

Beethoven, *Trio*, for two oboes and English horn, Op. 87

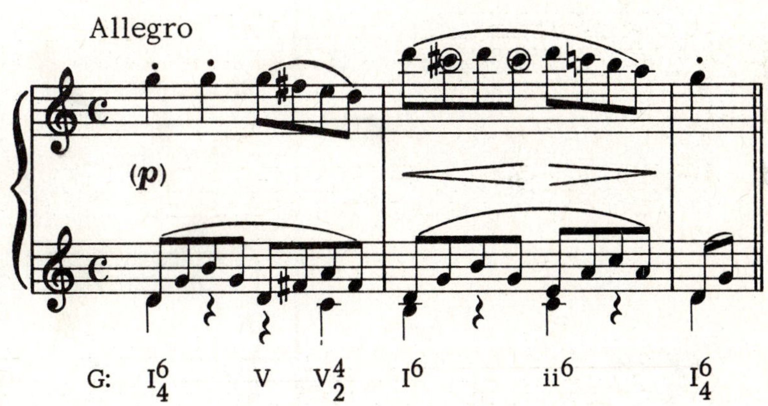

The type of nonharmonic tone illustrated by the circled notes is the ______________ ______________.

neighboring tone

■ 144. Altered nonharmonic tones are used to supply tonal color and variety. They are also used to bring attention to particular harmonies. A tone which is foreign to the tonality naturally attracts attention to itself and to the chord with which it is associated. In the example on the following page, the altered tones (D-sharps) occur with the tonic triad in second inversion.

Beethoven, *Sonata,* Op. 31, No. 2

fourth

The altered tones in this case are the raised fourth scale degree.

seventh

■ 145. The altered passing tone in the bass (at the asterisk) in the example below is the lowered 7th scale degree.

Bach, Chorale: *Schaut, ihr Sünder*

146. The two most frequent alterations of diatonic scale degrees in major are shown in the previous two frames. These are the *raised fourth* and the *lowered seventh* degrees. Each of these provides a gesture toward an important structural triad as shown on the following page.

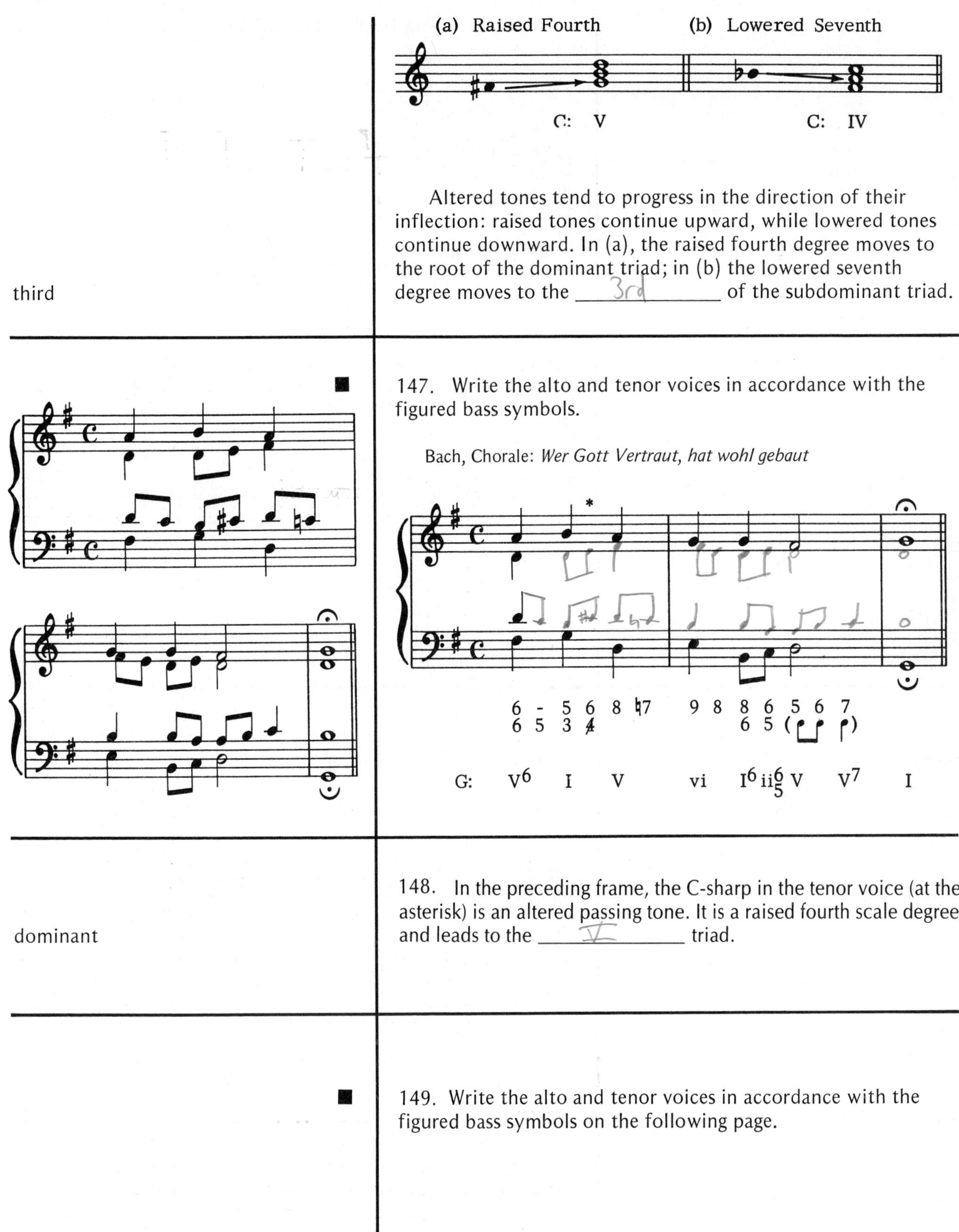

Altered tones tend to progress in the direction of their inflection: raised tones continue upward, while lowered tones continue downward. In (a), the raised fourth degree moves to the root of the dominant triad; in (b) the lowered seventh degree moves to the ______ of the subdominant triad.

third

---

147. Write the alto and tenor voices in accordance with the figured bass symbols.

---

148. In the preceding frame, the C-sharp in the tenor voice (at the asterisk) is an altered passing tone. It is a raised fourth scale degree and leads to the ______ triad.

dominant

---

149. Write the alto and tenor voices in accordance with the figured bass symbols on the following page.

Bach, Chorale: *Ach Gott und Herr, wie gross und schwer*

lowered

150. In the preceding frame, the B-flat in the tenor (at the asterisk) is an altered passing tone which provides a gesture toward the subdominant triad. It is a ______ seventh scale degree.

151. Altered nonharmonic tones other than the raised fourth or lowered seventh scale degrees are comparatively rare. The more likely alterations of the various scale degrees in major are shown below. *(The white notes indicate the tone to which each usually progresses.)*

KEY OF C MAJOR

True.

Altered tones tend to continue in the same direction as their inflection. (True/False) ______

152. The more likely alterations of the various scale degrees in minor are shown below. (The white notes indicate the tone to which each usually progresses.)

KEY OF C MINOR

Fewer tones are considered altered in minor than in major because of the wealth of tonal variety provided by the alternate sixth and seventh degrees of the melodic minor scale.

The altered tone which occurs most frequently *in both major and minor* is the raised fourth scale degree. The *lowered* seventh scale degree is encountered frequently in major. Is this also an altered tone in minor? ______

No.
(The lowered seventh is a diatonic tone in melodic minor and natural minor.)

■ 153. Both of the tones indicated by asterisks in the example below are *chromatic* passing tones.

Chopin, *Mazurka,* Op. 33, No. 3

Do both of these altered tones resolve in the direction of their inflection? ______

Yes.

154. Chromatic alterations sometimes cause two or more passing tones to occur in succession.

Liszt, *Du bist wie eine Blume*

The two passing tones (B and B-sharp) fill in the melodic interval of a ________ between A and C-sharp.

third

---

155. Chromatic alterations sometimes cause simultaneous false relations.*

Chopin, *Valse*, Op. 64, No. 1

The G-natural at the asterisk clashes with the chord seventh G-flat in the left hand. What type of nonharmonic tone is demonstrated here? ______________________

____

*The term FALSE RELATION applies to chromaticism which occurs between two **different** voices. See Frame 602 for a written music example.

Neighboring tone.

■ 156. Double neighboring tones are shown below.*

Brahms, *Waltz,* Op. 39, No. 14

dolce

C: I V⁷ I

The notes at the asterisk are the raised ________ and ________ scale degrees.

*For another example of double altered nonharmonic tones see Frame 203.

2nd (and)
4th

---

157. Melodic activity generated by nonharmonic tones is increased by chromatic alteration. Altered tones tend to continue in the direction they are inflected. The two most common alterations are the raised fourth and the lowered seventh scale degrees. The raised fourth degree usually continues up to the fifth, thus providing a tonal gesture towards the dominant. The lowered seventh degree resolves to the sixth, which often is set as the third of the subdominant chord.

In addition to motivation, altered tones provide color. They do not necessarily weaken the influence of the tonal center, but a chromatic melodic style often is associated with an abundance of altered chords.

(No response.)

---

158. In addition to their nonharmonic function, tones which are foreign to the prevailing tonality often are absorbed into the harmony to produce ALTERED CHORDS. Such chords perform a role similar to that of altered nonharmonic tones: they produce more colorful harmony, and, in some cases, help stress the structural function of the diatonic chords to which they resolve.

A chord which contains a tone foreign to the prevailing tonality is called a(n) ________ chord.

altered

---

159. Altered chords appear frequently in the works of eighteenth-century composers. The evolving chromatic harmonic idiom of the nineteenth century, however, caused them to occur with ever-increasing abundance during this period.

The profuse use of altered chords is associated with a ______ harmonic idiom.

chromatic

■ 160. Much nineteenth-century music contains what seems to be a bewildering array of altered chords. Study of altered chords is simplified, however, by the fact that most fall into but four classes: SECONDARY DOMINANTS, BORROWED CHORDS, CHROMATIC MEDIANTS, and AUGMENTED SIXTH CHORDS. Further, most altered chords belong to the first of these groups (secondary dominants). Because of this, we shall begin our study of altered chords with secondary dominants.

Which chord in the example below is an *altered chord*? ______

Bach, Chorale: *Ach Gott, wie manches Herzeleid*

⑦

---

161. Chord number seven in the example of the preceding frame contains a note (F-sharp) which is foreign to the key of C major. Therefore, it is an altered chord. This chord (DF♯AC) relates to the one which follows as a dominant seventh to a tonic. *It is as if for a brief moment the key of G major had been established.*

But if you will play this phrase at the piano, it will be clear that the key of G major is NOT established. The altered chord does no more than provide a dominant-like reinforcement of the dominant triad (GBD) in the key of ______ major.

C

major-minor

162. The reinforcement of a diatonic triad in the manner shown in Frame 160 accomplishes several things: the dominant triad is elevated in status, additional color is introduced by the alteration, and greater harmonic motion is produced by changing the nondominant supertonic seventh chord (DFAC) to the more active dominant seventh chord-type (DF♯AC).

The nondominant supertonic seventh chord (DFAC) is a minor seventh chord. What is the quality of the chord in its altered form (DF♯AC)? A ______________ seventh chord.

---

tonicization

163. The term *tonicization* refers to the concept of emphasizing a particular diatonic chord by embellishing it with an altered chord which bears a dominant relation to it. This concept is used by some theorists to account for much more extended nontonic tonal orientations than merely a single chord. There is a close relation between secondary dominants and modulation, as will be shown later.

Altered chords of the secondary dominant type are a simple manifestation of the principle of ______________.

---

dominant

■ 164. The actual analysis of the example in Frame 160 remains to be shown. Since we have determined that all of the chords in this example are in the key of C major, a symbol must be used for the altered chord (DF♯AC) which not only makes this clear, but also expresses the *function* of the chord.

Bach, Chorale: *Ach Gott, wie manches Herzeleid*

C: I^6 vii^{o6} I ii^6_5 V vi V^6_5/V V - I

The oral expression of the symbol V^6_5/V is either "dominant six-five of the dominant," or, more simply, "five six-five of five." This chord is the dominant seventh of the ______________ in the key of C major.

165. The altered chord (at the asterisk) in the preceding frame is called a SECONDARY DOMINANT. It results in a tonicization of the dominant (GBD) in C major. This chord can be used in any inversion, but root position and first inversion occur more frequently.

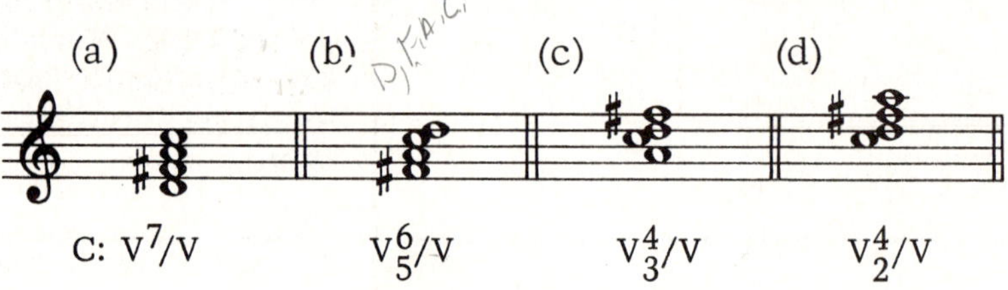

In (d), the seventh is in the lowest voice. Thus, the following chord would likely be the dominant in __________ inversion.

first

■

166. Supply the Roman numeral analysis.

Bach, Chorale: *Herzliebster Jesu, was hast du verbrochen*

---

167. Only one type of secondary dominant has been shown thus far: the major-minor seventh chord (dominant seventh) whose root is a perfect fifth above the root of the chord to which it relates. Actually, there are several types of chords which perform a "dominant" function similar to the dominant seventh chord. These are shown below with the appropriate symbol for each:

GBD.

Spell the chord to which each of the secondary dominants in the preceding example normally resolves. ________

---

168. The diminished seventh chord (e) in the preceding frame is used to embellish either major or minor triads, whereas the diminished-minor seventh chord (d) relates to major triads only.

(Compare the effect of the two examples below by playing them at the piano.)

(a) Undesirable — Tritone — a: vii^{ø7}/iv iv

(b) Desirable — a: vii^{o7}/iv iv

The effect in (a) is unpleasant due to the tritone which occurs between the two chords. Diminished-minor seventh chords should progress to ________ triads.

major

---

169. A tritone is not produced by relating a diminished-minor seventh chord to a *major* triad.

P4

G: ____ ____

Supply the chord symbol for each chord.

G: vii^{ø7}/V-V

---

170. Supply the chord symbol for each chord. *(Take care to show the precise quality of each chord.)*

(1) Bb: ____ (2) e: ____ (3) Ab: ____

(1) B♭: vii^{o}/V

(2) e: V^{7}/V

(3) A♭: vii^{ø7}/V

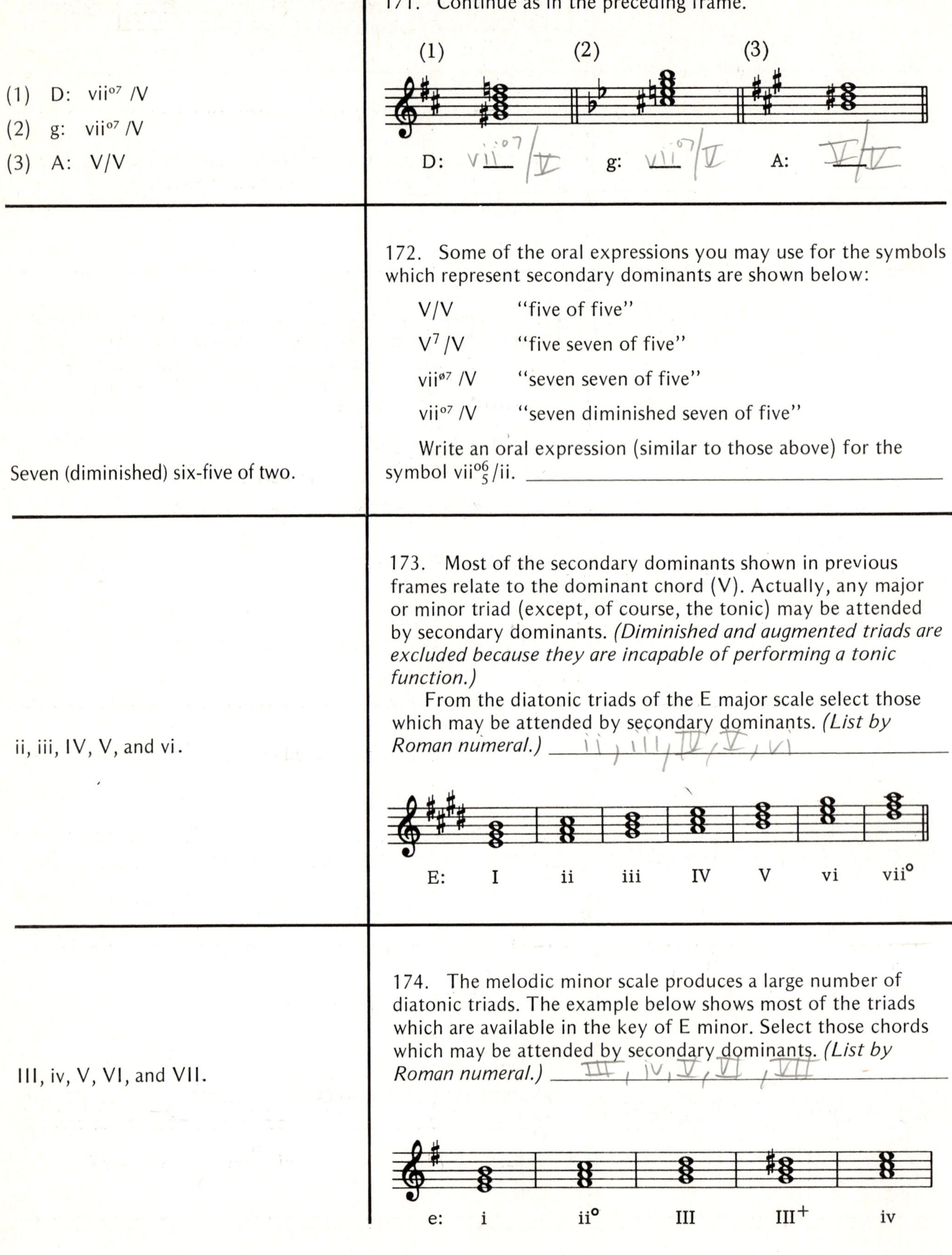

171. Continue as in the preceding frame.

(1) (2) (3)

D: ___ g: ___ A: ___

(1) D: vii°⁷ /V
(2) g: vii°⁷ /V
(3) A: V/V

---

172. Some of the oral expressions you may use for the symbols which represent secondary dominants are shown below:

V/V	"five of five"
V⁷ /V	"five seven of five"
viiø⁷ /V	"seven seven of five"
vii°⁷ /V	"seven diminished seven of five"

Write an oral expression (similar to those above) for the symbol $\text{vii}^{\circ 6}_{5}$/ii. ______________________________

Seven (diminished) six-five of two.

---

173. Most of the secondary dominants shown in previous frames relate to the dominant chord (V). Actually, any major or minor triad (except, of course, the tonic) may be attended by secondary dominants. *(Diminished and augmented triads are excluded because they are incapable of performing a tonic function.)*

From the diatonic triads of the E major scale select those which may be attended by secondary dominants. *(List by Roman numeral.)* ______________________________

E: I ii iii IV V vi vii°

ii, iii, IV, V, and vi.

---

174. The melodic minor scale produces a large number of diatonic triads. The example below shows most of the triads which are available in the key of E minor. Select those chords which may be attended by secondary dominants. *(List by Roman numeral.)* ______________________________

e: i ii° III III+ iv

III, iv, V, VI, and VII.

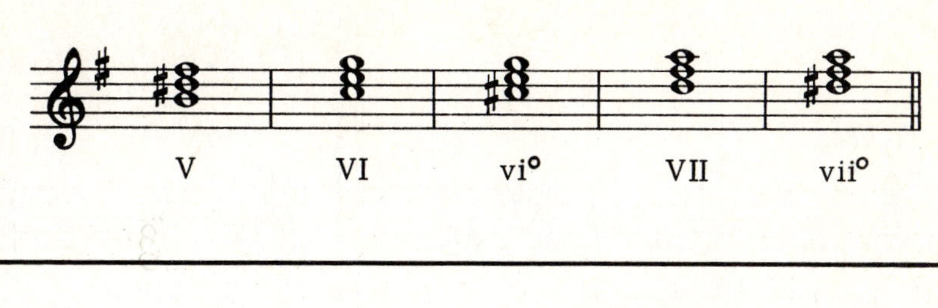

False.
(Secondary dominants can relate only to major or minor triads.)

175. Any diatonic triad in either a major or minor key may be attended by a secondary dominant. (True/False) ________

(No response.)

176. There are two types of secondary dominants: (1) chords which bear a *dominant* relation to the following chord; (2) chords which bear a *leading tone* relation to the following chord. Both types perform the same harmonic function, but root relations are different.

Dominant relation

V/x V^7/x	root is a *perfect fifth above* root of tonicized chord

Leading tone relation

vii°/x $vii^{ø7}$/x vii^{o7}/x	root is a *half-step below* root of tonicized chord

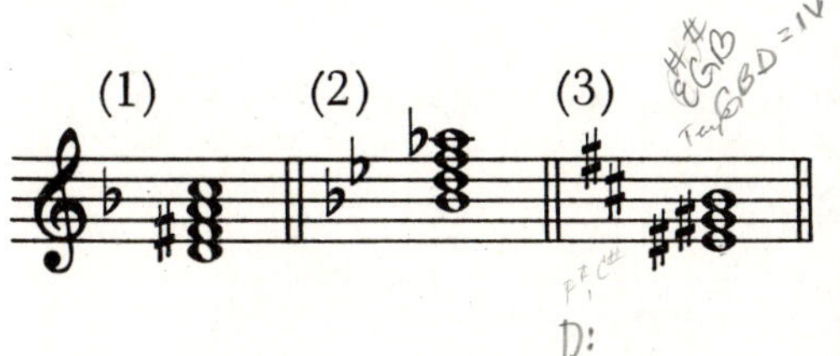

177. Write the chords indicated by the Roman numerals.

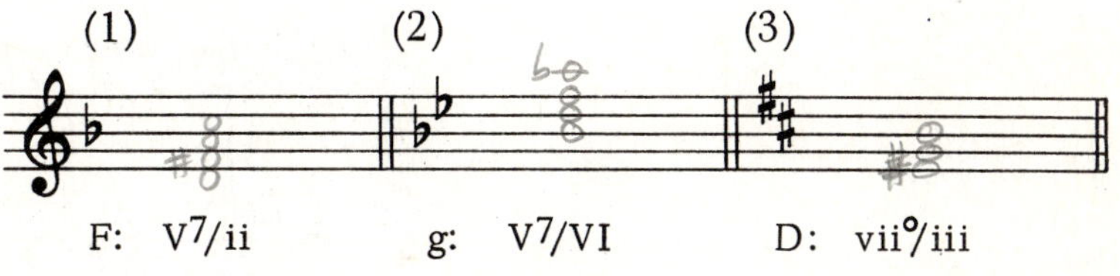

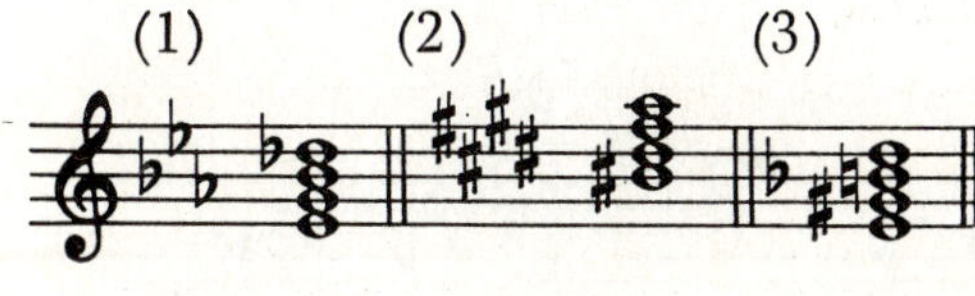

178. Continue as in the preceding frame.

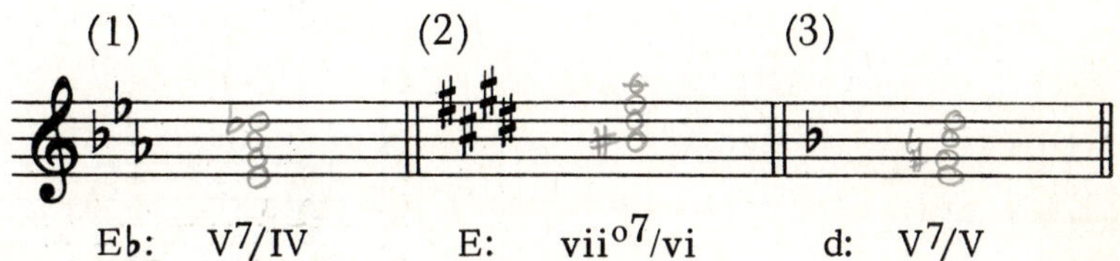

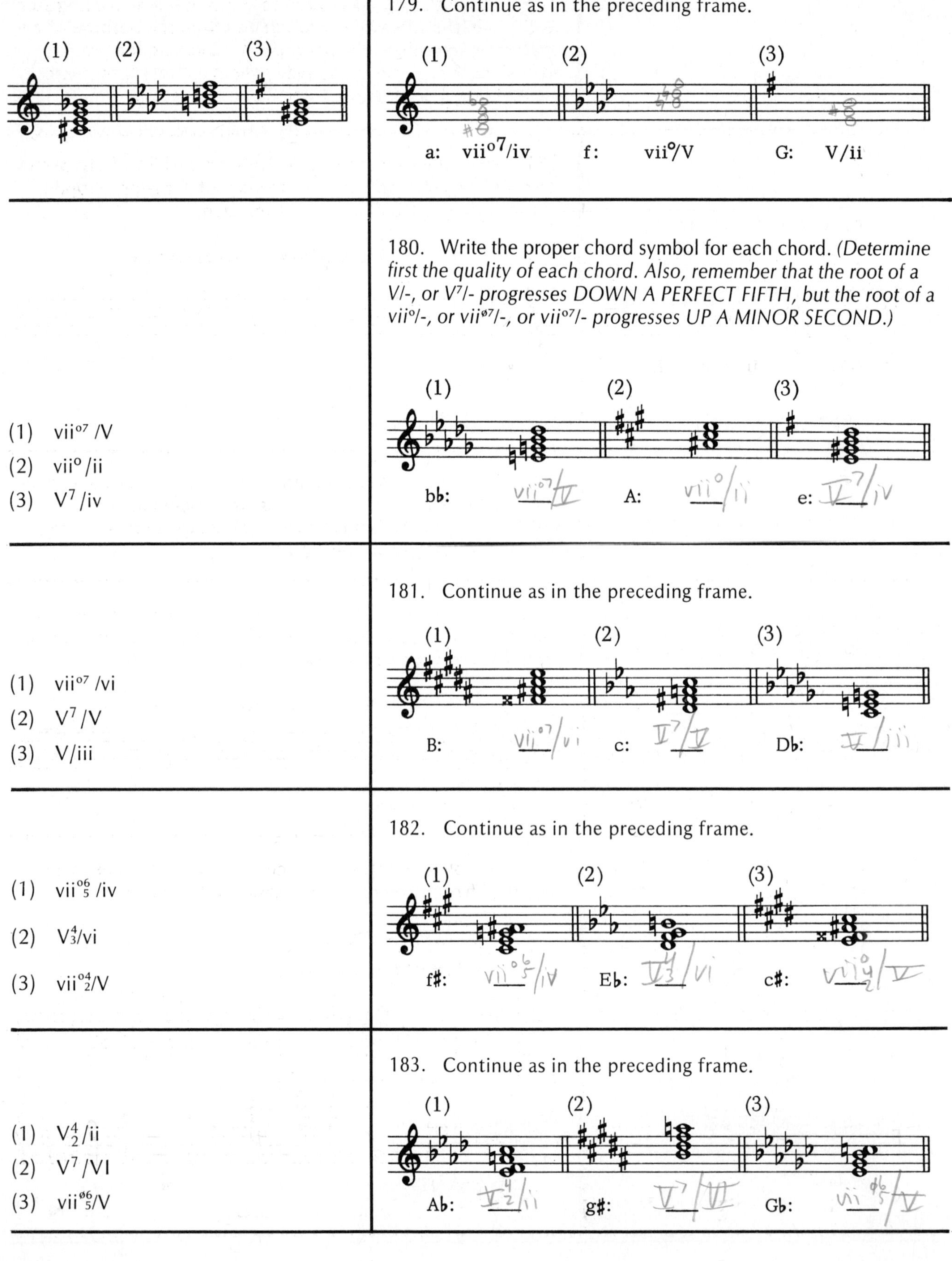
(1)
(2)
(3)
179. Continue as in the preceding frame.
(1)
(2)
(3)
a: vii°7/iv
f: vii°/V
G: V/ii
180. Write the proper chord symbol for each chord. (Determine first the quality of each chord. Also, remember that the root of a V/-, or V7/- progresses DOWN A PERFECT FIFTH, but the root of a vii°/-, or viiø7/-, or vii°7/- progresses UP A MINOR SECOND.)
(1) vii°7 /V
(2) vii° /ii
(3) V7 /iv
(1)
(2)
(3)
bb:
A:
e:
181. Continue as in the preceding frame.
(1) vii°7 /vi
(2) V7 /V
(3) V/iii
(1)
(2)
(3)
B:
c:
Db:
182. Continue as in the preceding frame.
(1) vii°6/5 /iv
(2) V4/3/vi
(3) vii°4/2/V
(1)
(2)
(3)
f#:
Eb:
c#:
183. Continue as in the preceding frame.
(1) V4/2/ii
(2) V7 /VI
(3) viiø6/5/V
(1)
(2)
(3)
Ab:
g#:
Gb:

(No response.)

184. It is not always necessary to use symbols as complicated as those in the preceding two frames. Often the purpose of an analysis is served equally well by not indicating the precise inversion. In such cases you may simplify symbols by representing chords as if they all were in root position.

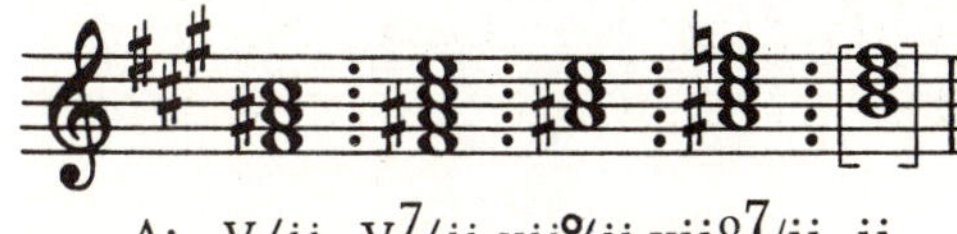

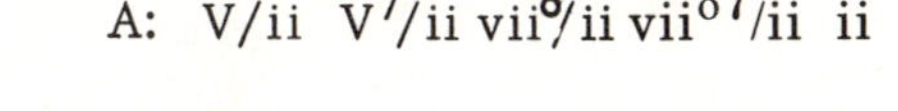

(See next frame.)

185. Write the *four* secondary dominants which likely would precede the supertonic triad in the key of A major. Supply, also, the proper Roman numeral for each.

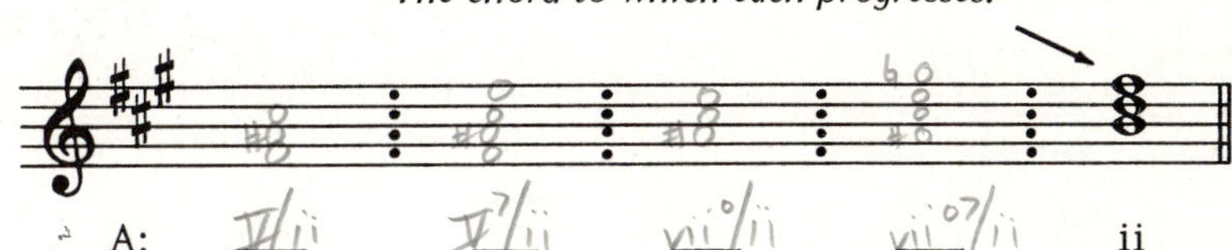

(No response.)

186. The vii^ø7/ii was omitted from the possible secondary dominants in the preceding frame because the resolution of a diminished-minor seventh chord to a minor triad produces an undesirable effect. *(See Frame 168.)*

187. Write the *five* secondary dominants which may precede the dominant triad in the key of D-flat major. Supply, also, the proper Roman numeral for each.

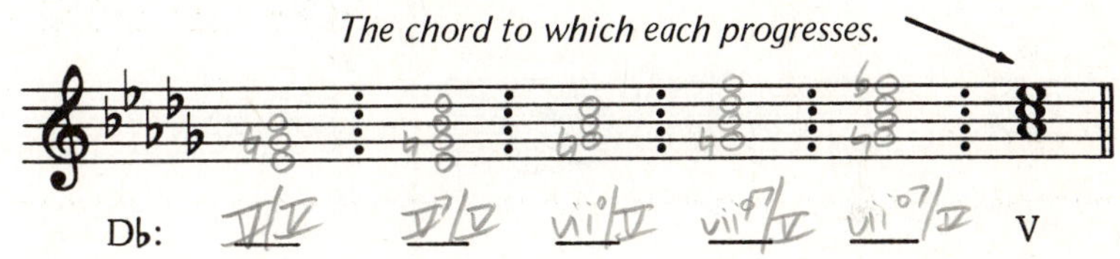

■

A: I V7/ii

188. Complete the Roman numeral analysis for the example below. *(The circled notes are nonharmonic tones.)*

■

D: $\text{vii}^{\circ 6}_{5}$/ii ii^{6}

V^{7} I

189. Supply the Roman numeral analysis for the example below:

Beethoven, *Sonata,* Op. 28

■

190. Complete the Roman numeral analysis for the example below:

Schubert, *Symphony No. 8,* in B minor

■

191. Supply the Roman numeral analysis for the example below:

Schumann, *Album for the Young,* Op. 68, No. 31

192. Complete the alto and tenor voices and analyze with Roman numerals.

Bach, Chorale: *Wenn ich in Angst und Not*

193. Supply the Roman numeral analysis for the example below:

Schubert, *Erlkönig,* Op. 1

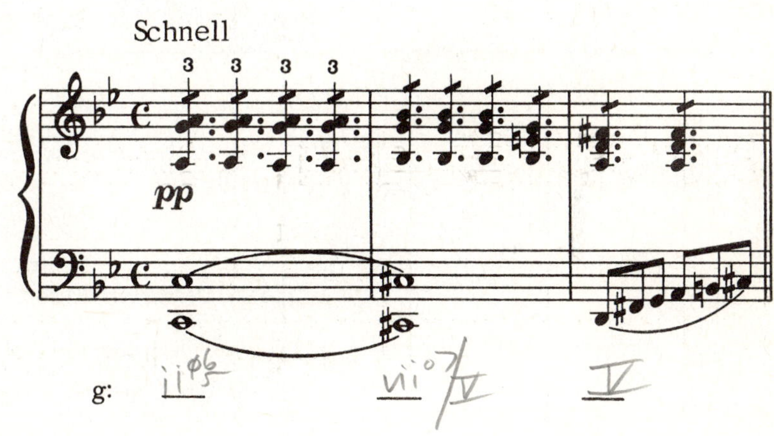

194. Complete the alto and tenor voices and analyze with Roman numerals on the following page.

Bach, Chorale: *Befiehl du deine Wege*

altered

195. The E-flat in the alto voice of the example in the preceding frame does not prevent the phrase from being entirely in the key of F-major. This device is called an ______________ nonharmonic tone.

■

196. Supply the Roman numeral analysis for the example below:

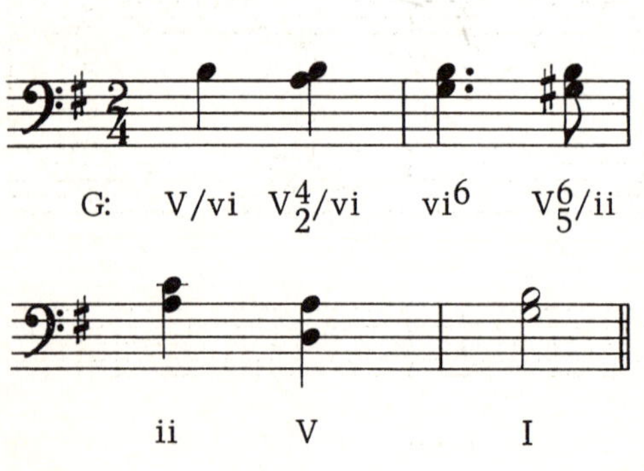

Beethoven, *Piano Concerto No. 4,* Op. 58

Andante con moto

■ 197. Supply the Roman numeral analysis for the example below:

Mozart, *Fantasia in C Minor,* K. 475

---

198. The example in the preceding frame shows a typical use of the vii^{o7}/vi chord. When used in this way, it provides additional color and impetus to the ______________ cadence.

deceptive

■ 199. Since the leading tone triad is diminished, it is not capable of performing a tonic function. Secondary dominants, therefore, may not be used in connection with it. The triad on the *lowered* seventh degree of the melodic minor scale, however, is a major triad and sometimes is embellished by a secondary dominant.

Supply the Roman numeral analysis for the example below:

Bach, *Toccata in D Minor,* for organ

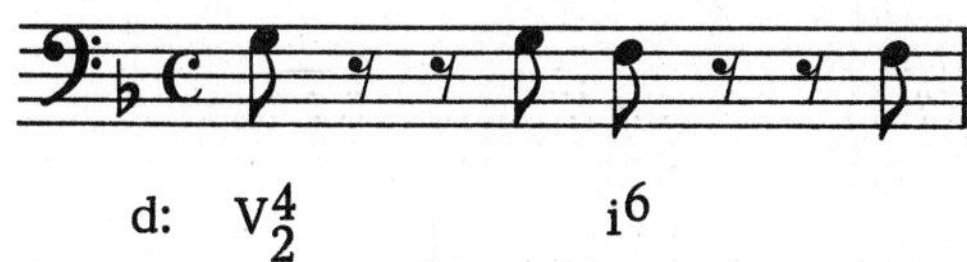

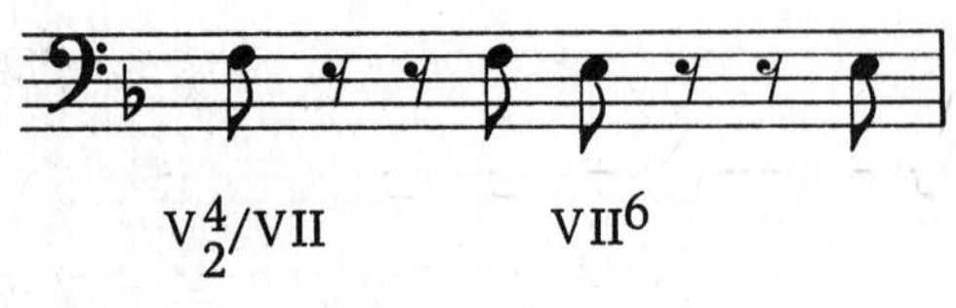

■ 200. Supply the Roman numeral analysis for the example below. *(The circled notes are nonharmonic tones.)*

Beethoven, *Sonata,* Op. 53

Allegro con brio

201. The example in the preceding frame shows that secondary dominants do not always resolve as expected. The V^7/vi does not progress to the submediant (vi), but to the subdominant (IV). This is comparable to the resolution of the V^7 to VI instead of to the tonic as occurs in the deceptive cadence.

Resolve the secondary dominant two ways as indicated by the Roman numerals. *(Avoid writing an augmented second in one of the voices.)*

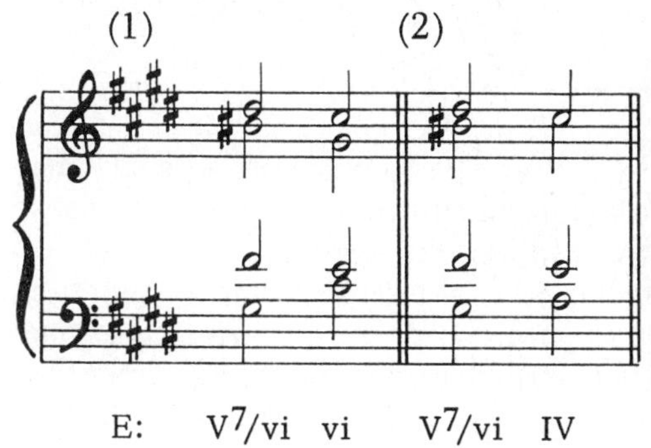

202. Resolve the secondary dominant as indicated by the Roman numerals.

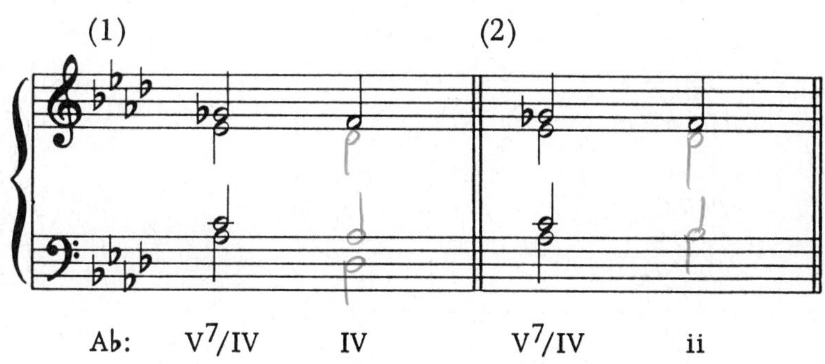

■

203. Another unexpected resolution of a secondary dominant is shown below:

Chopin, *Mazurka,* Op. 67, No. 3

The reiterated notes (C) in the bass constitute a pedal. The V^7/V resolves neither to the dominant nor deceptively to the mediant, but to an altered leading tone seventh chord. Since the leading tone seventh chord has the same harmonic function as the dominant triad or seventh chord, the substitution of one for the other does not change the basic harmonic movement. Chord choice in such a case is made at the discretion of the composer to achieve the desired color effect.

The leading tone triad is a secondary triad of the dominant. (True/False) __________

True.

■ 204. The example below shows still another unexpected resolution of a secondary dominant:

Brahms, *An die Nachtigall,* Op. 46, No. 4

In this case the root of the secondary dominant (G-sharp) progresses neither down a fifth, nor up a second, but down a ______________.

second

(No response.)

205. A secondary dominant's chief function is to tonicize the chord which follows. Thus, the normal resolution of a V^7/V is as in (a); the resolution in (b) is merely a deceptive resolution of the secondary dominant.

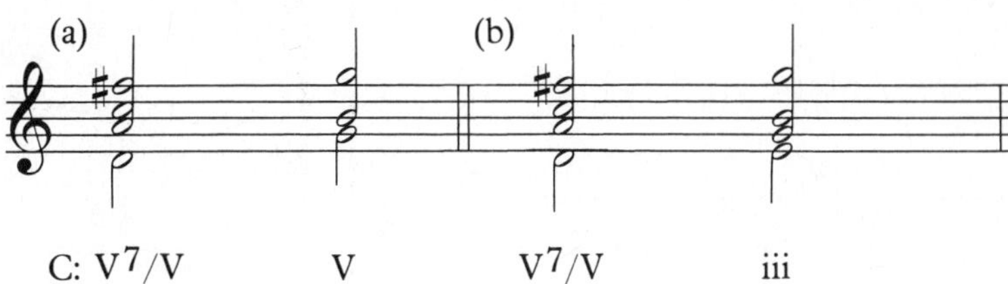

But still more unusual resolutions occur, and sometimes a potential secondary dominant may be analyzed better as another type of altered chord. You must be prepared for the fact that, in some cases, alternate interpretations are acceptable.

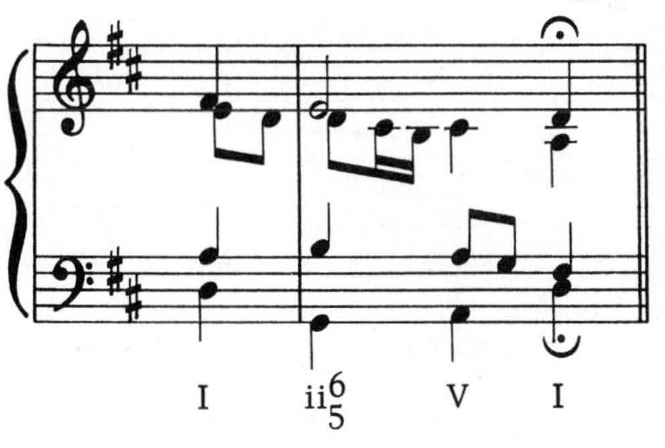

206. Complete the alto and tenor voices. Supply, also, the Roman numeral analysis.

Bach, Chorale: *Wie schön leuchtet der Morgenstern*

It is an altered passing tone. *(In your own words.)*

207. On the first beat of the example in the preceding frame the G-sharp appears in the tenor. This note is not included in the D-major scale. How can you account for its presence? ________
____

e: vii°6/IV vii°$^4_3$/IV IV^6 vii°^{7}

i V$^6_5$/V V I

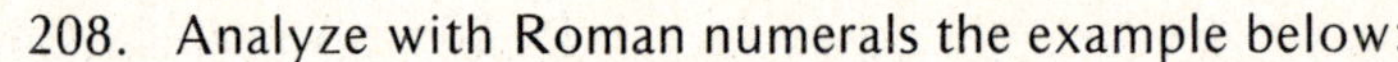

208. Analyze with Roman numerals the example below:

Bach, Chorale: *Jesu, meine Freude*

e: ___ ___ ___ ___ ___ ___ ___ ___ ___

209. A sequence of dominant seventh chords results when one secondary dominant resolves to another.

Chopin, *Mazurka*, Op. 33, No. 3

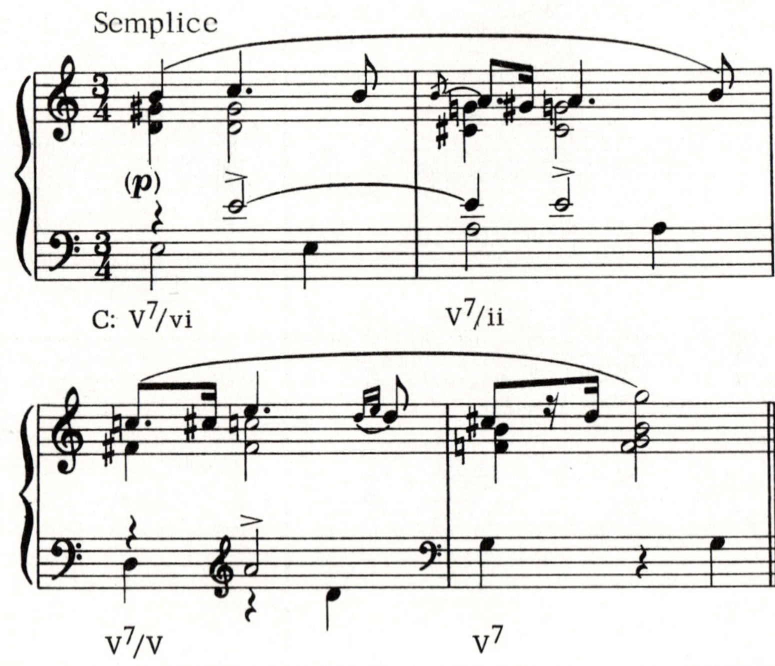

Each of the secondary dominants resolves, not to a simple triad, but to another secondary dominant. The progression of roots from each chord to the next is consistently down in (interval) _______________.

fifths

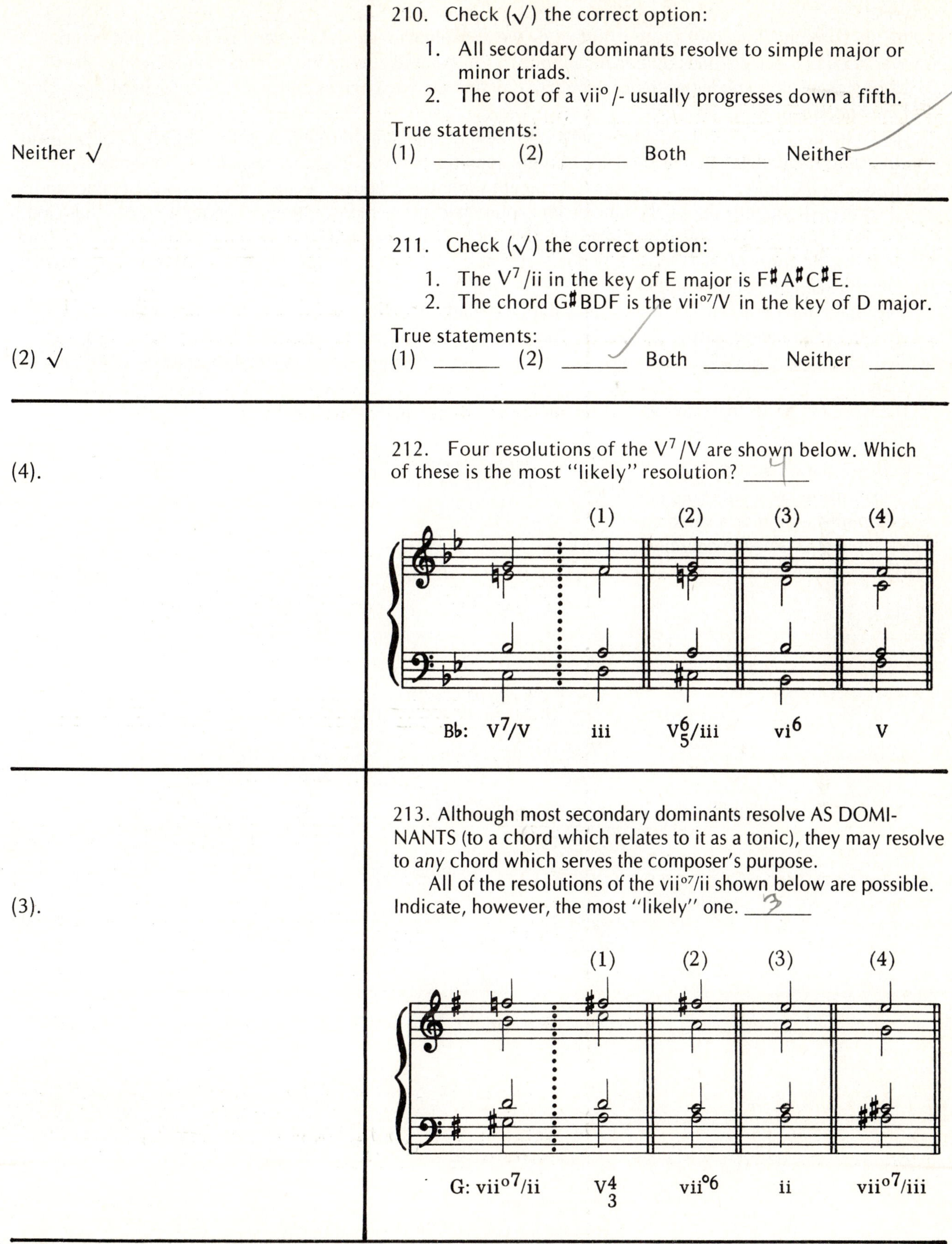

Neither √

210. Check (√) the correct option:

1. All secondary dominants resolve to simple major or minor triads.
2. The root of a vii° /- usually progresses down a fifth.

True statements:
(1) ______ (2) ______ Both ______ Neither ______

---

(2) √

211. Check (√) the correct option:

1. The V^7/ii in the key of E major is F♯A♯C♯E.
2. The chord G♯BDF is the vii^{o7}/V in the key of D major.

True statements:
(1) ______ (2) ______ Both ______ Neither ______

---

(4).

212. Four resolutions of the V^7/V are shown below. Which of these is the most "likely" resolution? ______

---

(3).

213. Although most secondary dominants resolve AS DOMINANTS (to a chord which relates to it as a tonic), they may resolve to *any* chord which serves the composer's purpose.

All of the resolutions of the vii^{o7}/ii shown below are possible. Indicate, however, the most "likely" one. ______

SUMMARY

Altered nonharmonic tones are easily absorbed by the prevailing tonality. As integral parts of altered chords, however, altered tones provide additional harmonic resources and expand the boundaries of tonality. Many altered chords result from the transfer of dominant function to other degrees of the scale. Such chords are called *secondary dominants.*

The chief function of secondary dominants is to increase the harmonic motion within the phrase. Dominant sonorities possess an inherent tension. This, plus the conditioned expectation for resolution to their tonic, is responsible for the unique motivation which dominant sonorities produce. Secondary dominants are encountered ever more frequently during the nineteenth century because composers grew to prefer dominant function to more stable sonorities. It is as if dominant function, once associated primarily with the cadence, is spread out over virtually the entire phrase. Secondary dominants also produce greater tonal variety, and often the effect of their unexpected color is most striking.

Secondary dominants elevate the status of diatonic triads to which they resolve. The reinforcement which they give to such triads is called *tonicization.* Any diatonic triad (other than the tonic) which is major or minor may be embellished by a secondary dominant. The triad which is most frequently embellished, however, is the dominant.

The types of chords that may serve as secondary dominants are listed below:

1. Major triad (V of X)
2. Major-minor seventh chord (V^7 of X)
3. Diminished seventh chord (vii° of X)
4. Diminished-minor seventh chord ($vii^{ø7}$ of X)
5. Diminished seventh chord ($vii^{\circ 7}$ of X)

Mastery Frames

True. (143)

3-1. Altered nonharmonic tones not only are extraneous to the harmony, but are not included in the prevailing tonality. (True/False)__________

Raised fourth and lowered seventh. (146)

3-2. Name the two most frequent alterations of diatonic scale degrees in major. ____________________

PT NT APP NT

CPT

(151-154)

3-3. Use accidentals to convert each of the notes with an asterisk to an *altered* nonharmonic tone. Label each nonharmonic tone.

* * * * *

C: V$^6_5$ I^6 V$^6_5$ I

---

(1) Major triad
(2) Minor triad
(Any order.) (173-175)

3-4. In order to be tonicized, a chord must be capable of serving as a tonic. Name the two chord types that qualify.

(1)____________________
(2)____________________

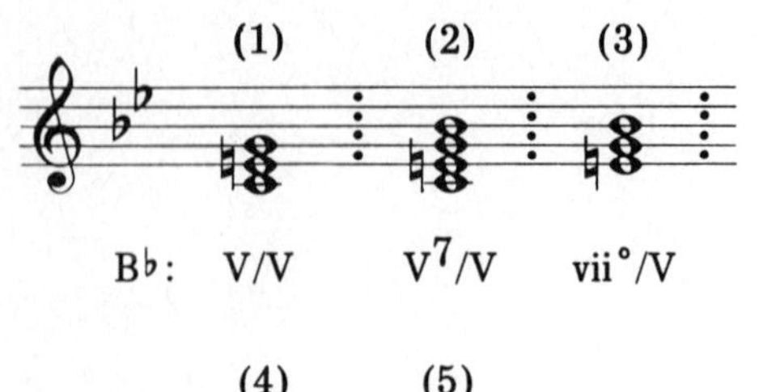

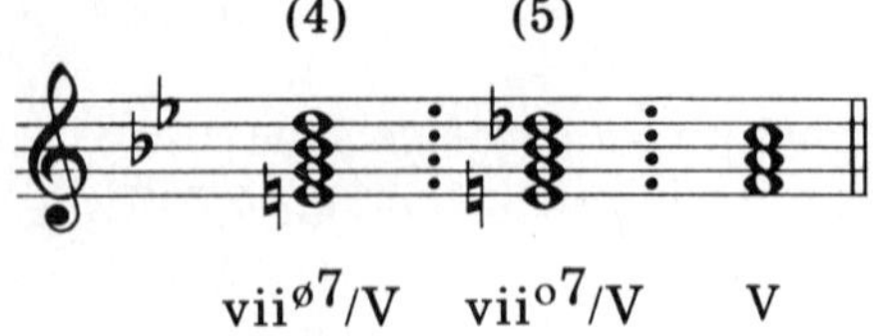

(Any order.) (167, 176)

3-5. Write each of the five chords that may serve as secondary dominants to the dominant in the key of B-flat major. Provide the proper chord symbols.

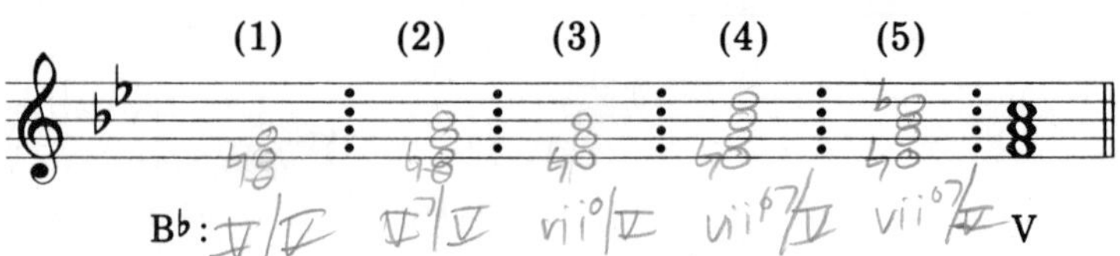

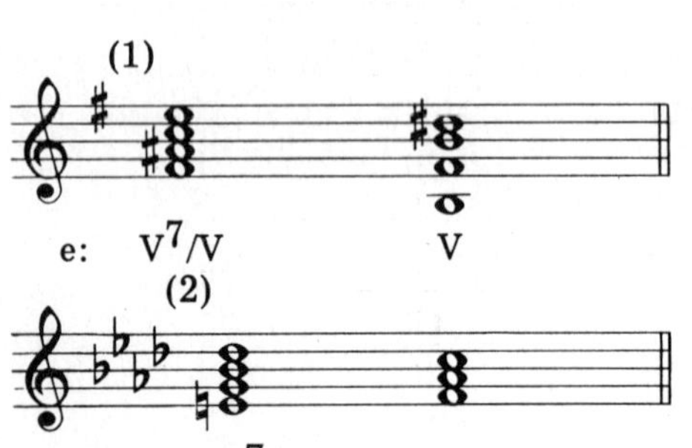

(180-184)

3-6. Provide the proper chord symbols.

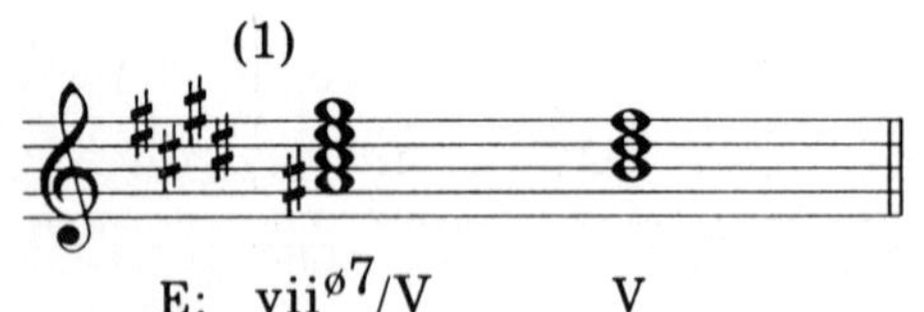

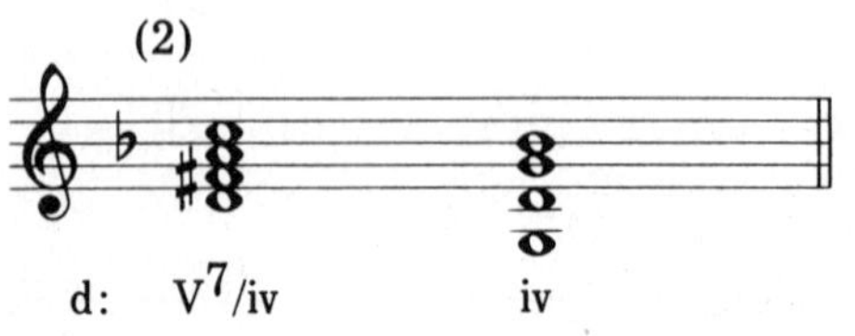

(180-184)

3-7. Provide the proper chord symbols.

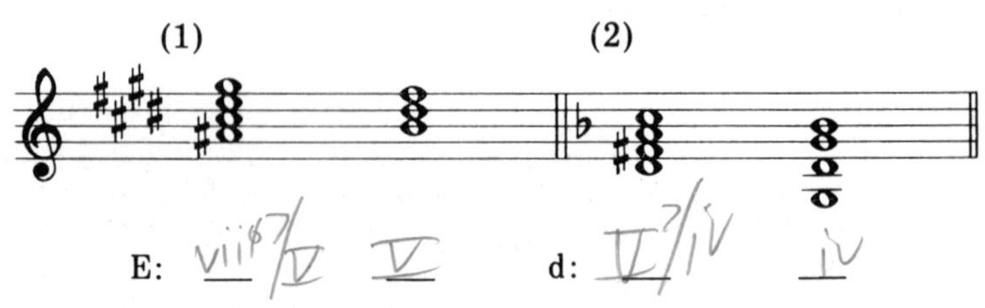

Supplementary Assignments

ASSIGNMENT 3-1 Name______________________________

1. Circle each *altered* nonharmonic tone and indicate its type (use abbreviations such as P.T., N.T., App., etc.).

Schumann: *Carnival* ("Eusebius")

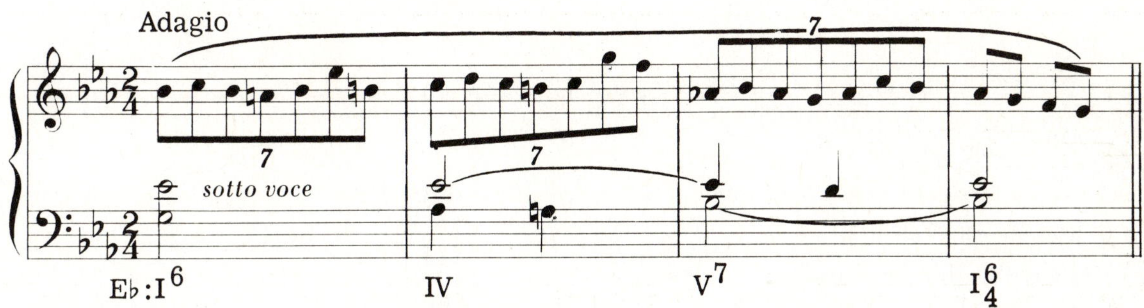

2. Provide the harmonic analysis and label each *altered* nonharmonic tone.

Schumann: *Carnival* ("Valse Noble")

3. Circle each nonharmonic tone in the example below; indicate its type and whether it is diatonic or altered.

Haydn: *Quartet*, Op. 76, No. 4 ("The Sunrise")

4. Analyze with Roman numerals.
Beethoven: *Sonata,* Op. 49. No. 1

5. Analyze with Roman numerals. This example contains several types of secondary dominants. Take care to indicate precisely the quality of each.
Schumann: *Nachtstücke,* Op. 23, No. 2

ASSIGNMENT 3-2 Name________________________________

1. Indicate the quality (major triad, diminished seventh chord, etc.) of each secondary dominant represented below:

vii°/V ____________________
V/iii ____________________
vii^{o7}/vi ____________________
V^{7}/ii ____________________
vii^{ø7}/v ____________________

2. Provide the chord symbol for each chord.

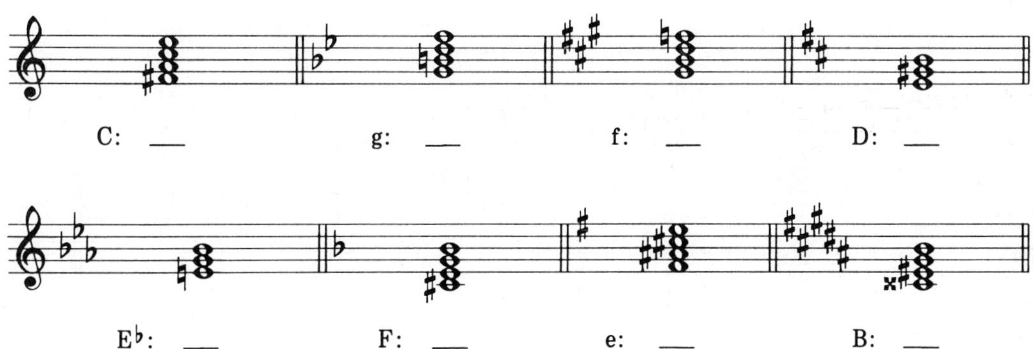

3. Write the chords indicated by the chord symbols.

4. Write the chord to which the secondary dominants below would normally resolve. Provide, also, the chord symbols.

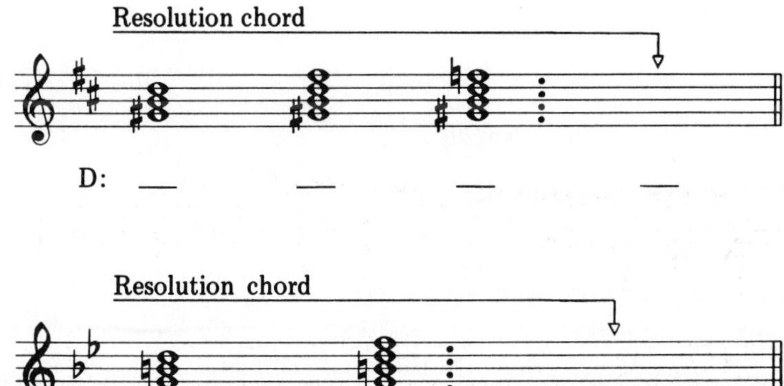

5. Write the alto and tenor voices and provide the Roman numeral analysis.

(Begin in close structure.)

B♭: ___ ___ ___ ___ ___ ___ ___ ___

(Begin in open structure.)

A: ___ ___ ___ ___ ___ ___ ___ ___

6. Compose a small composition (at least four phrases long) which exploits both altered nonharmonic tones and secondary dominants.

Suggested working method:

A. For each phrase construct a simple harmonic background consisting of diatonic chords as below:

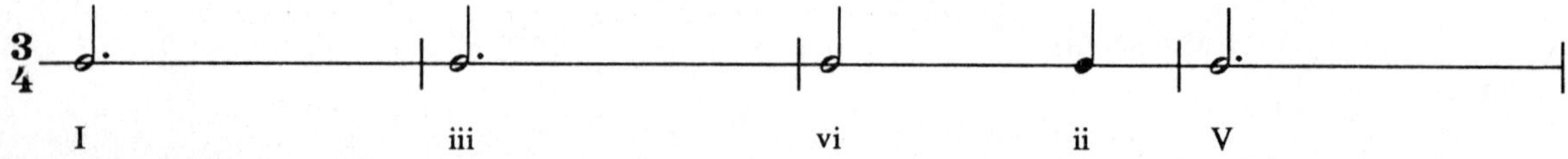

B. Embellish some chords with secondary dominants.

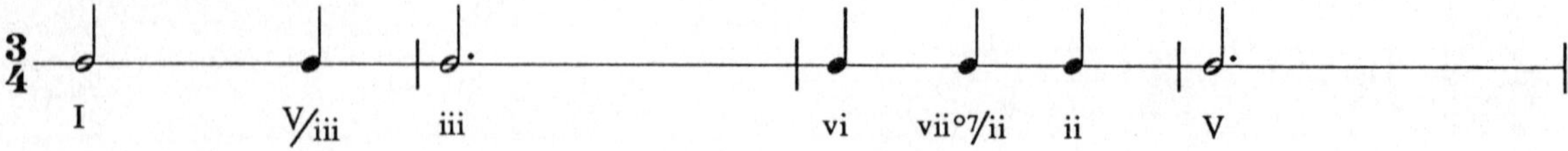

C. Write a melody which conforms to the harmonic background.

D. Supply an appropriate accompaniment configuration.

E. Complete your composition, paying particular attention to these points:

(1) Refine the doubling and voice leading.

(2) Provide complete and correct notation, including tempo, dynamic, and phrasing indications.

(3) Make a final copy suitable for performance.

chapter four

Modulation to Closely Related Keys

Secondary dominants provide harmonic motivation and enlarge color resources. The gesture towards another tonality made by a secondary dominant is too fleeting to undermine the established key, but more extensive tonicization, involving several chords which function in the new key, causes the ear to be attracted to the new tonal center. This is particularly so if the new key is confirmed by a cadence. The process of establishing a new tonality is called *modulation.* Used not only for additional tonal resources, modulation builds form by juxtaposing tonalities in various intervallic relations to one another.

214. Secondary dominants are used to reinforce diatonic triads through the dominant (or leading tone) relationship that they bear to them. This is the process of *tonicization.* For a brief instant the triad which has been preceded by a secondary dominant assumes a tonic role.

Supply the Roman numeral analysis for the example below:

Bach, Chorale: *Ach Gott, wie manches Herzeleid*

215. Compare the example in the preceding frame with the one on the following page, which is taken from the same chorale. *(Play each of these examples at the piano.)*

Bach, Chorale: *Ach Gott, wie manches Herzeleid*

half

The example in the preceding frame ends with an authentic cadence in A major. What type of cadence is used above? *(Listen carefully before answering.)* It is a ____________ cadence.

E major.

216. There is a similarity between the chords over which brackets have been placed in Frames 214 and 215. Notice, in particular, the chords at the asterisks. The crucial difference between these two examples is that whereas in Frame 214 the chord at the asterisk is a secondary dominant (V^6_5/V) which leads to an authentic cadence (V^7-I) in the key of A major, in Frame 215 the chord at the asterisk is followed by chords which produce a half cadence not in the tonic key of A major, but the key of the dominant. Name the key in which this phrase ends. ____________

The chords following the secondary dominant must function in the original key.

217. The phrase following that shown in Frame 215 continues in the key of E major, thus confirming the change of key.

When followed by chords which do not function in the original key, secondary dominants may cause a shift from one tonal center to another. Whether or not a change of key occurs depends upon what happens after the secondary dominant. Actually, any secondary dominant is capable of propelling the music into a new key. Explain how secondary dominants may be held to the original key. ____________________________________

---

218. Secondary dominants introduce a volatile element into music. They may function entirely within the original key, or the tonicization which they produce may be confirmed to the extent that a new key is established. *A change from one key to another is usually accomplished by introducing the dominant of the new key.* Thus, a close relationship exists

dominant

between secondary dominants and some of the processes by which music moves from one key to another. The act of establishing a new tonal center is called MODULATION.

Modulation occurs when the influence of one tonal center is supplanted by another. This implies that a new key must be established firmly enough and endure long enough to cause the ear to reorient itself to the new tonal center. The ear is often directed toward the new tonal center by the _________ chord of the new key.

(*No response.*)

219. Except for very short compositions, the effect of a single key tends to be monotonous. Modulations from the principal tonal center to other keys help to satisfy the need for greater tonal variety than can be supplied by a single key. Modulations may also contribute to the formal design of a composition. The sense of departure from, and return to a principal tonality often is instrumental in giving "shape" to the music.

In addition to contributing to formal design, modulations are necessary (especially in larger works) for the sake of tonal variety.

---

tonic (*or key center*)

220. In modulation, one tonal center is replaced by another. An understanding of how a new tonality is established is important. This is not a simple matter, and several points must be discussed in this connection before we proceed to the actual processes of modulation. Except when modulating from a minor key to its relative major, the new key contains one or more tones which are not included as diatonic tones in the original key. The influence of the original key is undermined by the appearance of these new tones, which are instrumental in directing the ear toward the new tonal center.

Modulation causes the ear to accept a new tone as the _______________.

■

221. Circle the notes in the example below which are not included in the original key (D major).

Mozart, *Sonata,* K. 284

f

D:

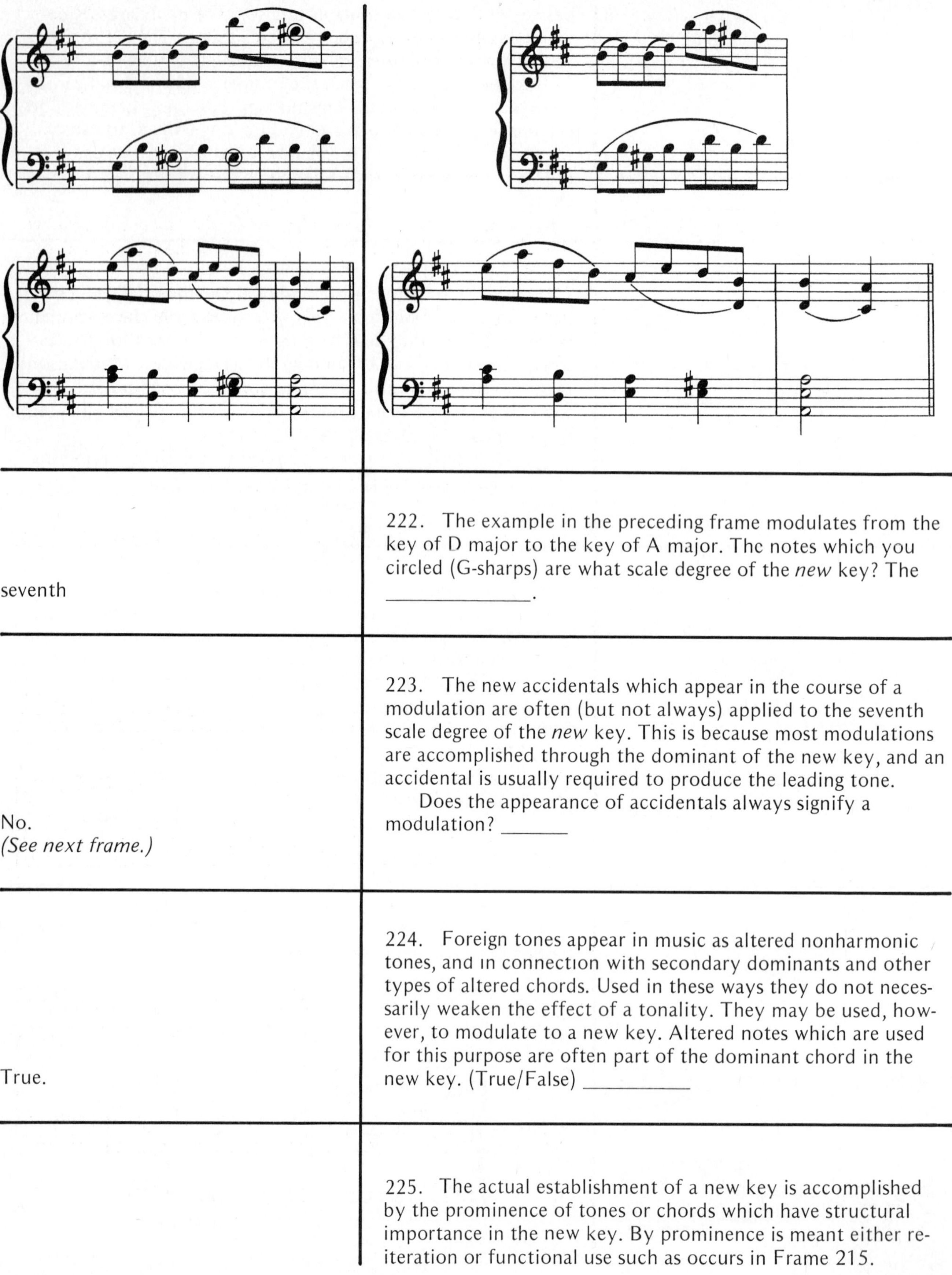

seventh

222. The example in the preceding frame modulates from the key of D major to the key of A major. The notes which you circled (G-sharps) are what scale degree of the *new* key? The ______________.

No.
(See next frame.)

223. The new accidentals which appear in the course of a modulation are often (but not always) applied to the seventh scale degree of the *new* key. This is because most modulations are accomplished through the dominant of the new key, and an accidental is usually required to produce the leading tone.

Does the appearance of accidentals always signify a modulation? ______

True.

224. Foreign tones appear in music as altered nonharmonic tones, and in connection with secondary dominants and other types of altered chords. Used in these ways they do not necessarily weaken the effect of a tonality. They may be used, however, to modulate to a new key. Altered notes which are used for this purpose are often part of the dominant chord in the new key. (True/False) __________

225. The actual establishment of a new key is accomplished by the prominence of tones or chords which have structural importance in the new key. By prominence is meant either reiteration or functional use such as occurs in Frame 215.

Refer once again to the example in Frame 215. Is the new key (E major) established through reiteration of functional chords (notice that there are two dominant chords), or by the cadence used? ______________________________

____

(*See next frame.*)

---

226. Whatever opinion you expressed in the preceding frame you were correct. But, although the reiteration of the dominant chord is a factor in establishing the new key, the structural use of this chord in the cadence formula is even more important. The example in Frame 215 shows the importance of the dominant chord in establishing a new key.

(*No response.*)

■

227. Both the dominant and tonic chords are usually involved in the process of modulation, but the dominant is more important, and does not require resolution to the tonic to give a convincing impression of the new key.

The ability of the dominant chord to establish a key without *resolution to the tonic* is shown in the example below:

Brahms, *Waltz*, Op. 39, No. 9

half

The first section (at the double bar) closes with a ________ cadence in the key of G minor.

---

228. Modulation can be likened to secondary dominants. But whereas secondary dominants produce merely momentary tonicizations, modulation causes a new tonal center to be established. Not all theorists are in agreement about the degree of emphasis needed to produce a modulation. All secondary dominants can be regarded as producing extremely brief modulations; many modulations, on the other hand, can be analyzed as extended tonicizations. In any case, you must judge whether or not a new key is actually established. The term "transient" modulation is sometimes used to refer to cases where the new key is established, but endures for only a short time.

Most modulations are made through the dominant chord of the *new* key. It is, in fact, difficult to establish a key without prominent use of dominant harmony. Once introduced, a new key is confirmed through the reiteration of chords which are functional in that key, or by a cadence. Cadences, remember, are usually not ambiguous as to tonality. In situations where the tonality is vague, *cadences often serve as the chief points of tonal reference.*

(No response.)

---

229. In modulation, the relation of keys to one another is vital. Some keys are more remote to a given tonal center than others. The subject of this chapter is modulation to *closely related keys,* so we shall now define what is meant by this term.

Closely related keys are those whose signatures differ from one another by not more than one sharp or flat.

The closely related keys of C major are shown below:

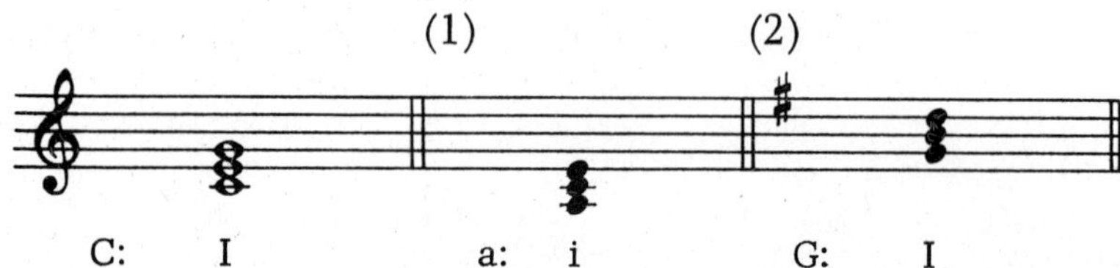

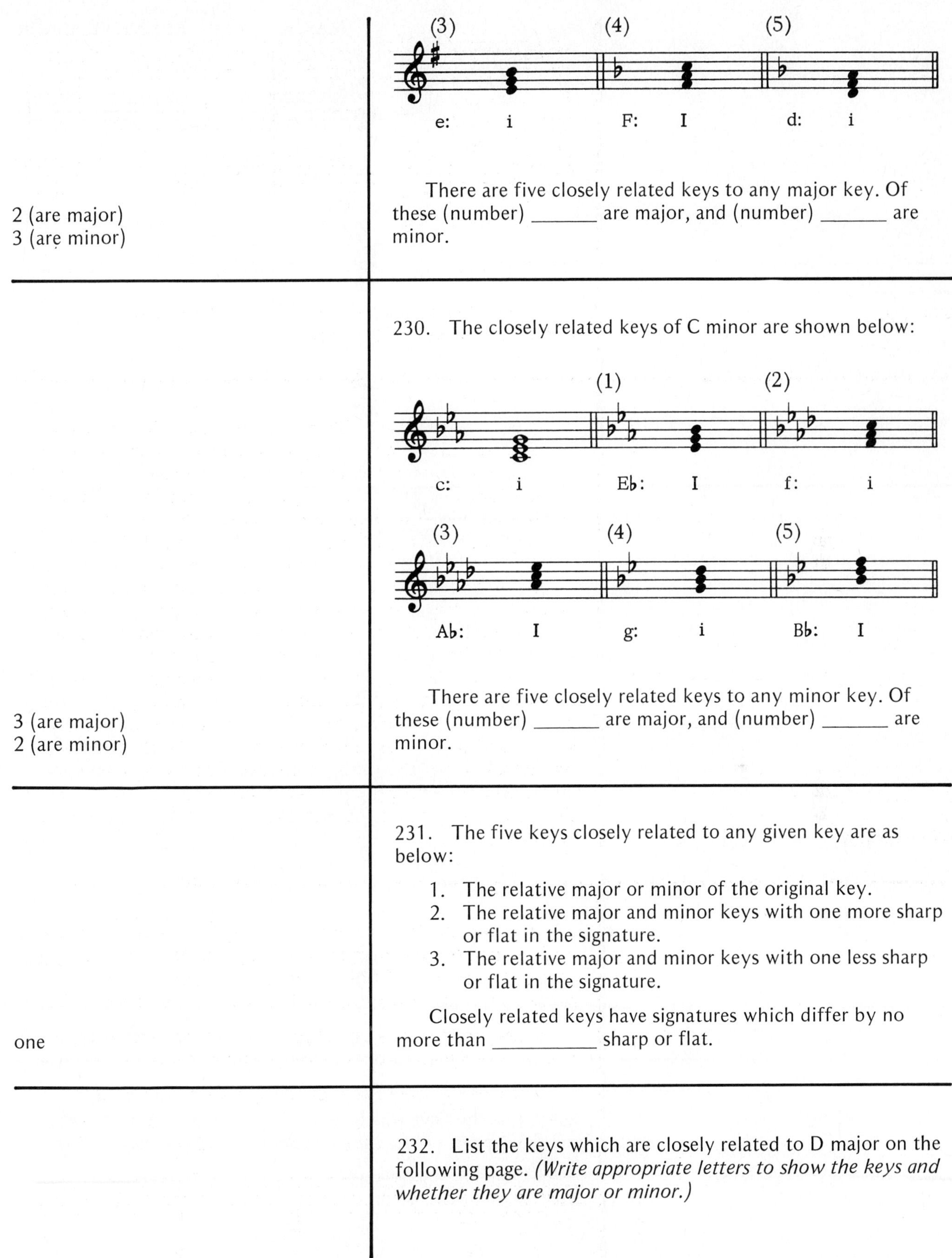

2 (are major)
3 (are minor)

There are five closely related keys to any major key. Of these (number) ______ are major, and (number) ______ are minor.

---

230. The closely related keys of C minor are shown below:

3 (are major)
2 (are minor)

There are five closely related keys to any minor key. Of these (number) ______ are major, and (number) ______ are minor.

---

231. The five keys closely related to any given key are as below:

1. The relative major or minor of the original key.
2. The relative major and minor keys with one more sharp or flat in the signature.
3. The relative major and minor keys with one less sharp or flat in the signature.

one

Closely related keys have signatures which differ by no more than __________ sharp or flat.

---

232. List the keys which are closely related to D major on the following page. *(Write appropriate letters to show the keys and whether they are major or minor.)*

(1) b
(2) A
(3) f♯
(4) G
(5) e

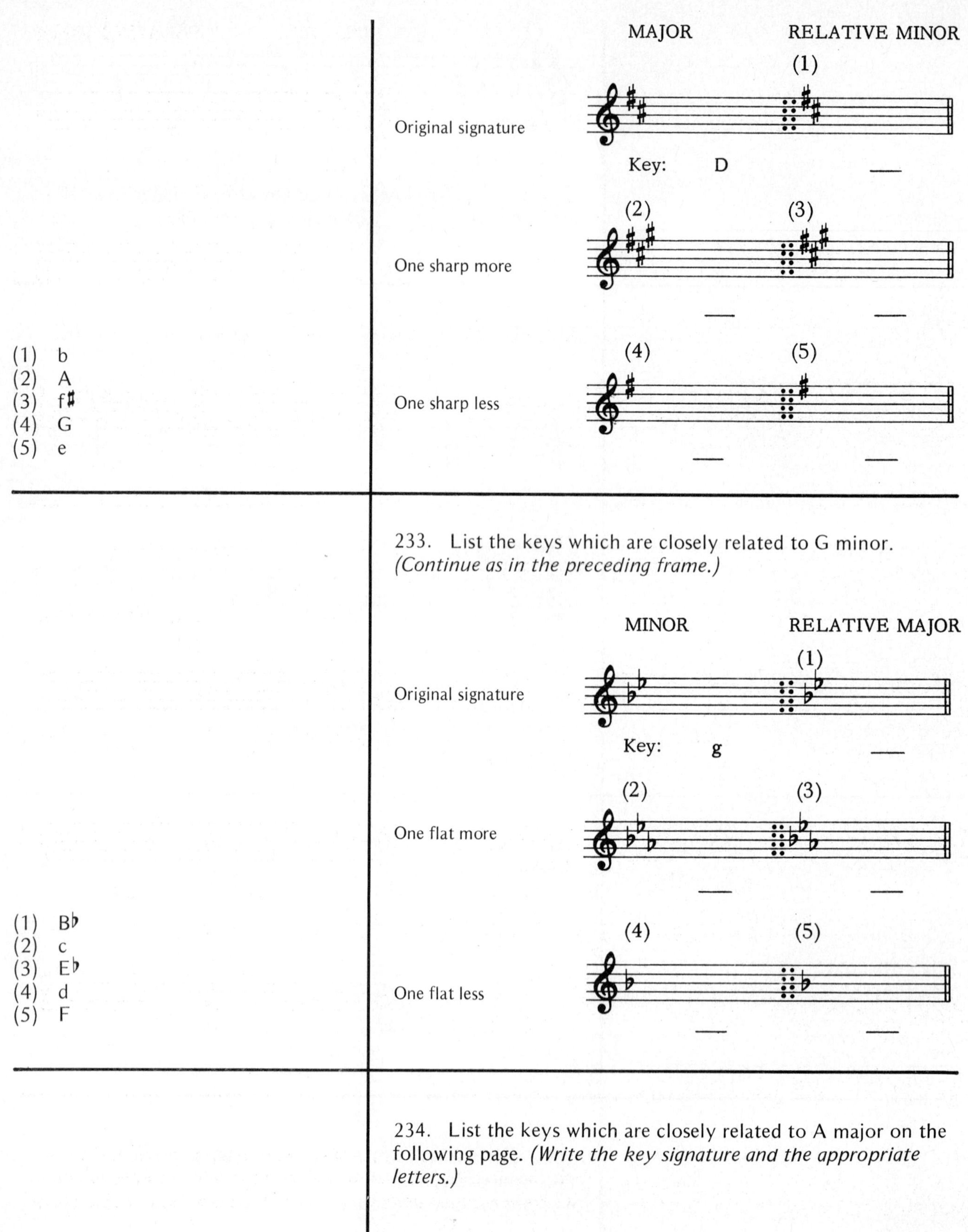

233. List the keys which are closely related to G minor. *(Continue as in the preceding frame.)*

(1) B♭
(2) c
(3) E♭
(4) d
(5) F

234. List the keys which are closely related to A major on the following page. *(Write the key signature and the appropriate letters.)*

235. List the keys which are closely related to F minor. *(Continue as in the preceding frame.)*

236. There is another practical way to identify the five keys which are closely related to a given key: *find the keys of the subdominant and dominant, and the relative keys of these plus that of the tonic.*

	Major	Relative Minor
Original key	C	a
Subdominant key	F	d
Dominant key	G	e

Do the signatures of the keys listed above differ from the original key (C major) by more than one accidental? ______

No.

M.	R.M.
B♭	g
E♭	c
F	d

237. Complete the list of keys which are closely related to B-flat major.

	Major	Relative Minor
Original key	B♭	____
Subdominant key	____	____
Dominant key	____	____

M.	R.M.
E	c♯
A	f♯
B	g♯

238. Complete the list of keys which are closely related to E major.

	Major	Relative Minor
Original key	E	____
Subdominant key	____	____
Dominant key	____	____

M.	R.M.
A♭	f
D♭	b♭
E♭	c

239. Complete the list of keys which are closely related to A-flat major.

	Major	Relative Minor
Original key	A♭	____
Subdominant key	____	____
Dominant key	____	____

---

minor

240. When the original kev is minor, the notes of the *pure* minor scale must be used.

	Minor	Relative Major
Original key	c	E♭
Subdominant key	f	A♭
Dominant key	g	B♭

The keys which are closely related to a *minor* key include the subdominant and dominant keys plus the relative *major* keys of the tonic, subdominant, and dominant. In minor keys, the key of the dominant is a (major/minor) ____________ key.

M.	*R.M.*
b	D
e	G
f♯	A

241. Complete the list of keys which are closely related to B minor.

	Minor	*Relative Major*
Original key	b	____
Subdominant key	____	____
Dominant key	____	____

M.	*R.M.*
g	B♭
c	E♭
d	F

242. Complete the list of keys which are closely related to G minor.

	Minor	*Relative Major*
Original key	g	____
Subdominant key	____	____
Dominant key	____	____

M.	*R.M.*
e♭	G♭
a♭	C♭
b♭	D♭

243. Complete the list of keys which are closely related to E-flat minor.

	Minor	*Relative Major*
Original key	e♭	____
Subdominant key	____	____
Dominant key	____	____

(No response.)

244. You now have two methods for determining which keys are closely related to a given key. The first of these is to find the relative major or minor of the original key, the relative major and minor keys with one more sharp or flat in the signature, and the relative major and minor keys with one less sharp or flat in the signature.

The second method is to find the keys of the subdominant and dominant, and the relative keys of these plus that of the tonic.

Use whichever method works best for you.

---

(2) and (5).

245. Which of the keys listed below are NOT closely related to B major? ____________________

(1) C♯ minor
(2) D major
(3) F♯ major
(4) G♯ minor
(5) A major

(1), (3), and (4).	246. Which of the keys listed below are NOT closely related to F minor? ______ (1) G minor (2) B♭ minor (3) C major (4) D♭ minor (5) E♭ major
(2) and (5).	247. Which of the keys listed below are NOT closely related to E-flat major? ______ (1) C minor (2) A♭ minor (3) B♭ major (4) F minor (5) D minor
(3) and (5).	248. Which of the keys listed below are NOT closely related to C-sharp minor? ______ (1) B major (2) G♯ minor (3) F♯ major (4) A major (5) C♯ major
(No response.)	249. It was brought out in the preceding frame that the key of C-sharp major is *not* a closely related key of C-sharp minor. This is surprising because there is undoubtedly a close affinity between parallel major and minor keys as they have the same structural tones (the first, fourth, and fifth scale degrees). One cannot even refer to a change of key from C-sharp major to C-sharp minor as a modulation since the tonal center is the same. "Change of mode" is the expression usually used in such cases. Change of mode is an important device in modulation because parallel major and minor keys each have their own set of closely related keys. This fact facilitates modulations to more remote keys, as will be seen in Chapter Nine. Parallel keys have the same key center but are not closely related due to the difference of more than one sharp or flat between their signatures.
	250. In music of the eighteenth century most modulations are to closely related keys. Such modulations do not seriously threaten the influence of the central tonality. Since modulations to closely related keys are, in fact, modulations to the various

fifth *(See next frame.)*	diatonic major and minor triads, they perform on a larger scale the same function as secondary dominants, namely the raising in status of diatonic triads through the process of tonicization. Modulations to closely related keys even tend to emphasize the structure of tonality. With this in mind, to what degree of the scale would you expect many modulations to be directed? To the ______________.
False. *(Not necessarily—they may even strengthen tonal structure.)*	251. Modulations to the fifth scale degree (the dominant) occur frequently in order to emphasize the tonic-dominant axis which is the basis of tonal harmonic structure. This is especially true in major keys. In minor keys, the strong influence of the relative major results in a high proportion of modulations to the mediant. Modulations result in a weakening of the tonal structure. (True/False) __________
True.	252. The tonic triads of closely related keys are all diatonic triads in the original key. (True/False) __________
■	253. We shall now examine the various means by which modulations are produced. Three basic types of modulation will be presented: PHRASE MODULATION, COMMON CHORD MODULATION, and CHROMATIC MODULATION. Phrase modulation occurs at the beginning of a new phrase.

Mozart, *Sonata,* K. 331

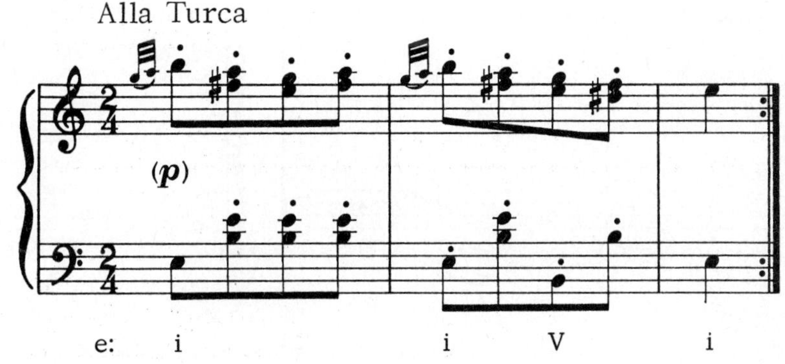

Are the two keys (as analyzed above) closely related? _____

Yes.

---

254. The ear readily accepts a change of key at the beginning of a phrase because of the pause provided by the cadence. Phrase modulation is shown in the example below. Identify the key of the second phrase and complete the Roman numeral analysis.

Bach, Chorale: *Es ist das Heil uns kommen her*

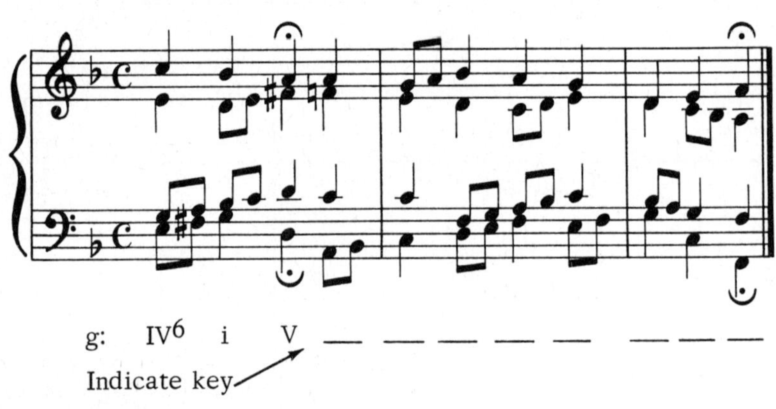

---

255. A modulation occurs between the two phrases in the example below. Indicate the key of each phrase and supply the Roman numeral analysis.

Beethoven, *Für Elise*

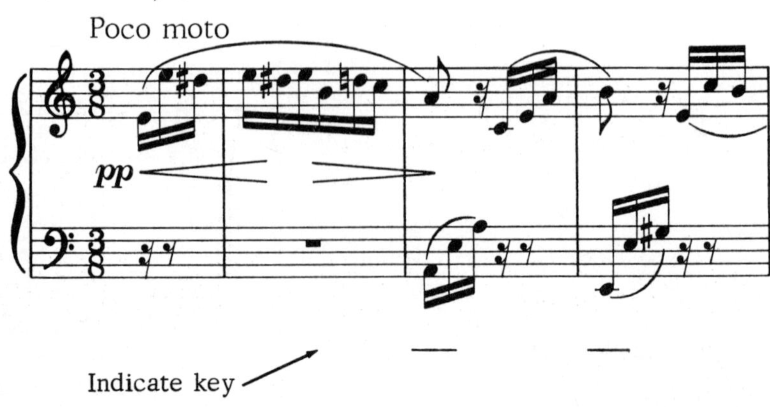

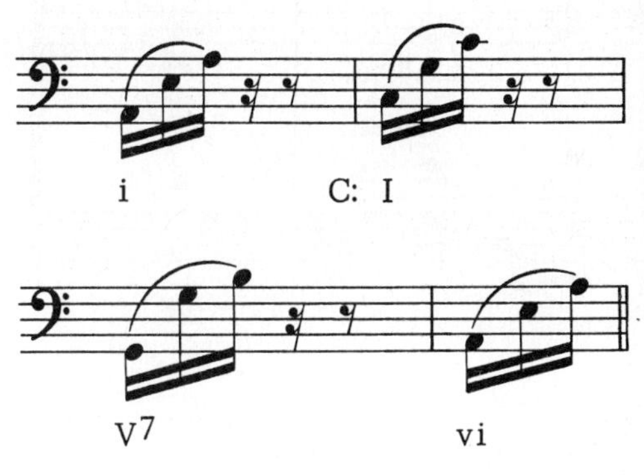

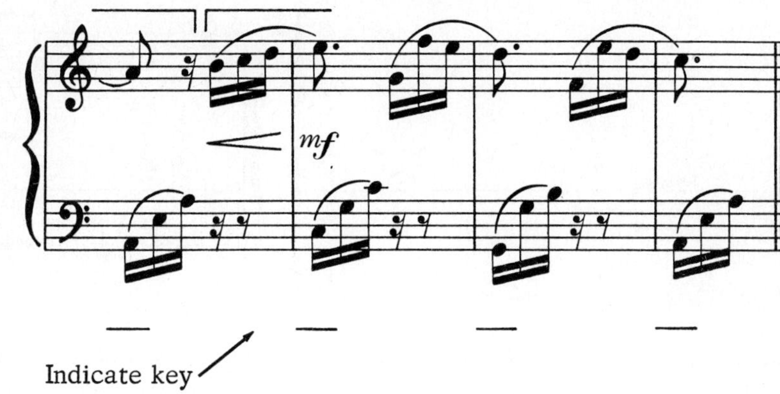

256. Supply the Roman numeral analysis for the example below. *(Remember to indicate the new key at the beginning of the second phrase.)*

Bach, Chorale: *Allein zu dir, Herr Jesu Christ*

257. Supply the Roman numeral analysis for the example below. *(Remember to indicate the new key at the beginning of the second phrase.)*

Bach, Chorale: *Christe, du Beistand deiner Kreuzgemeine*

■

258. Supply the Roman numeral analysis for the example below.

Beethoven, *Sonata,* Op. 10, No. 1

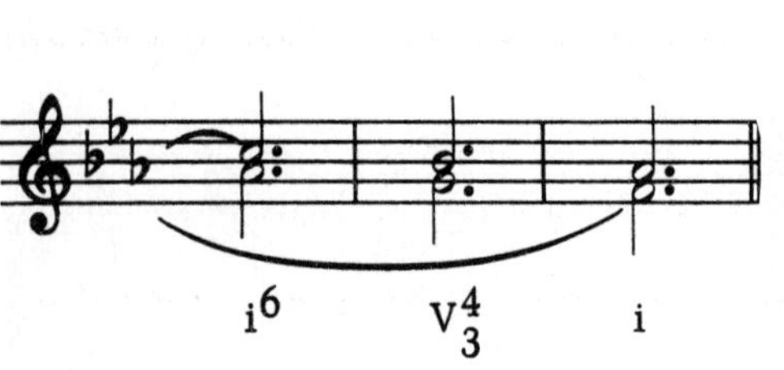

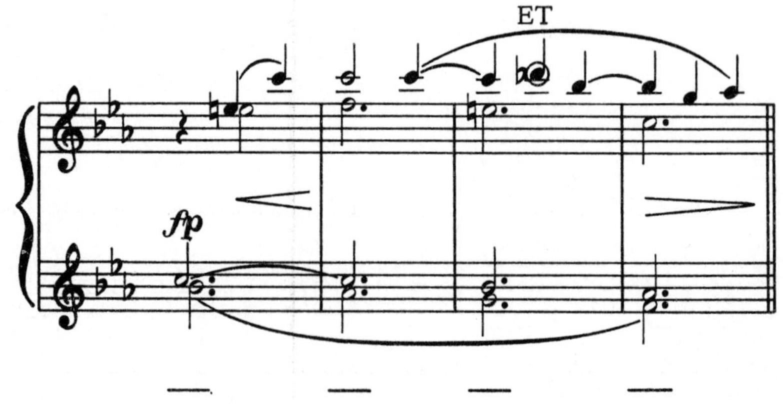

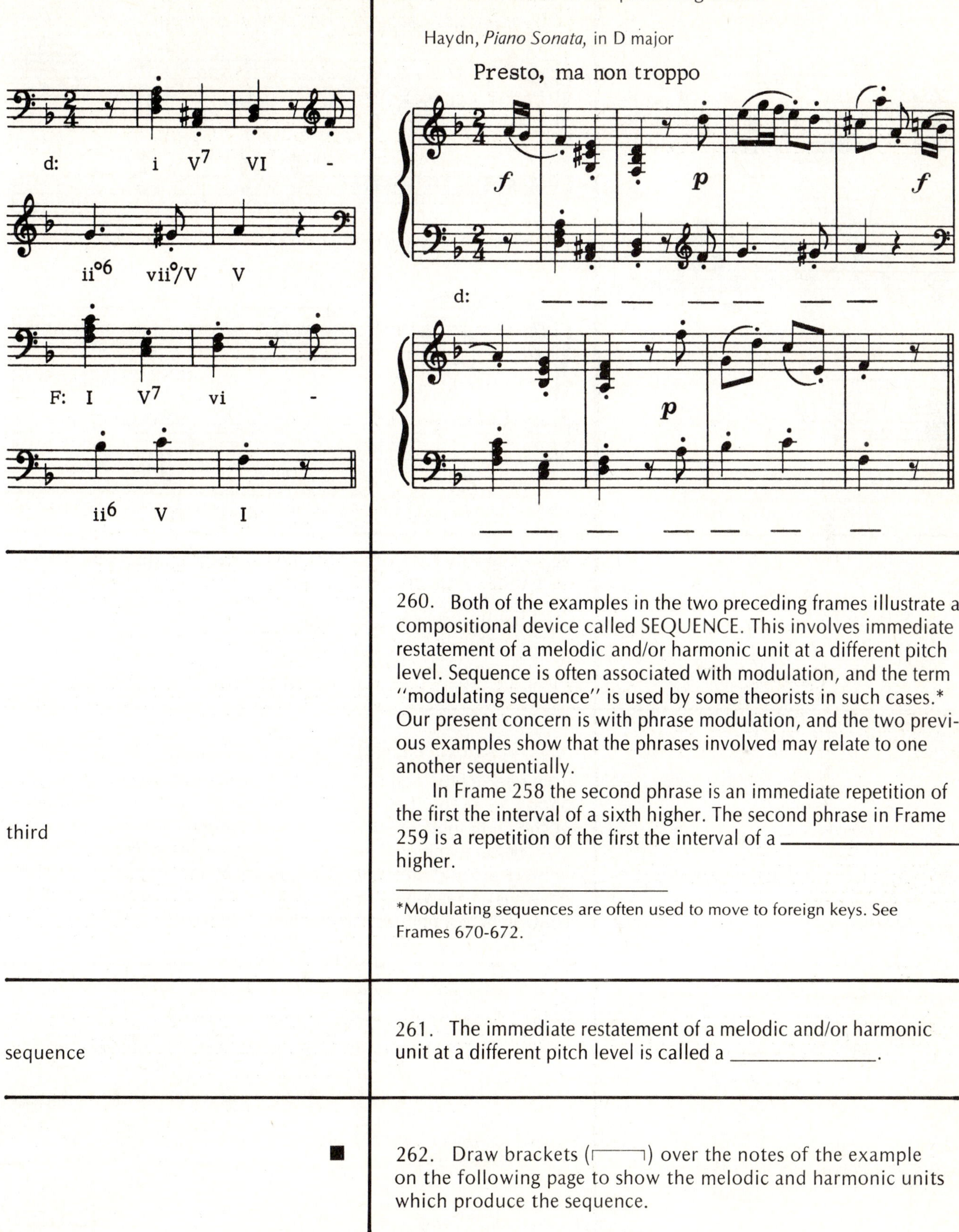

■

259. Continue as in the preceding frame.

Haydn, *Piano Sonata,* in D major

---

260. Both of the examples in the two preceding frames illustrate a compositional device called SEQUENCE. This involves immediate restatement of a melodic and/or harmonic unit at a different pitch level. Sequence is often associated with modulation, and the term "modulating sequence" is used by some theorists in such cases.* Our present concern is with phrase modulation, and the two previous examples show that the phrases involved may relate to one another sequentially.

In Frame 258 the second phrase is an immediate repetition of the first the interval of a sixth higher. The second phrase in Frame 259 is a repetition of the first the interval of a ____________ higher.

third

*Modulating sequences are often used to move to foreign keys. See Frames 670-672.

---

sequence

261. The immediate restatement of a melodic and/or harmonic unit at a different pitch level is called a ____________.

■

262. Draw brackets (⌐¬) over the notes of the example on the following page to show the melodic and harmonic units which produce the sequence.

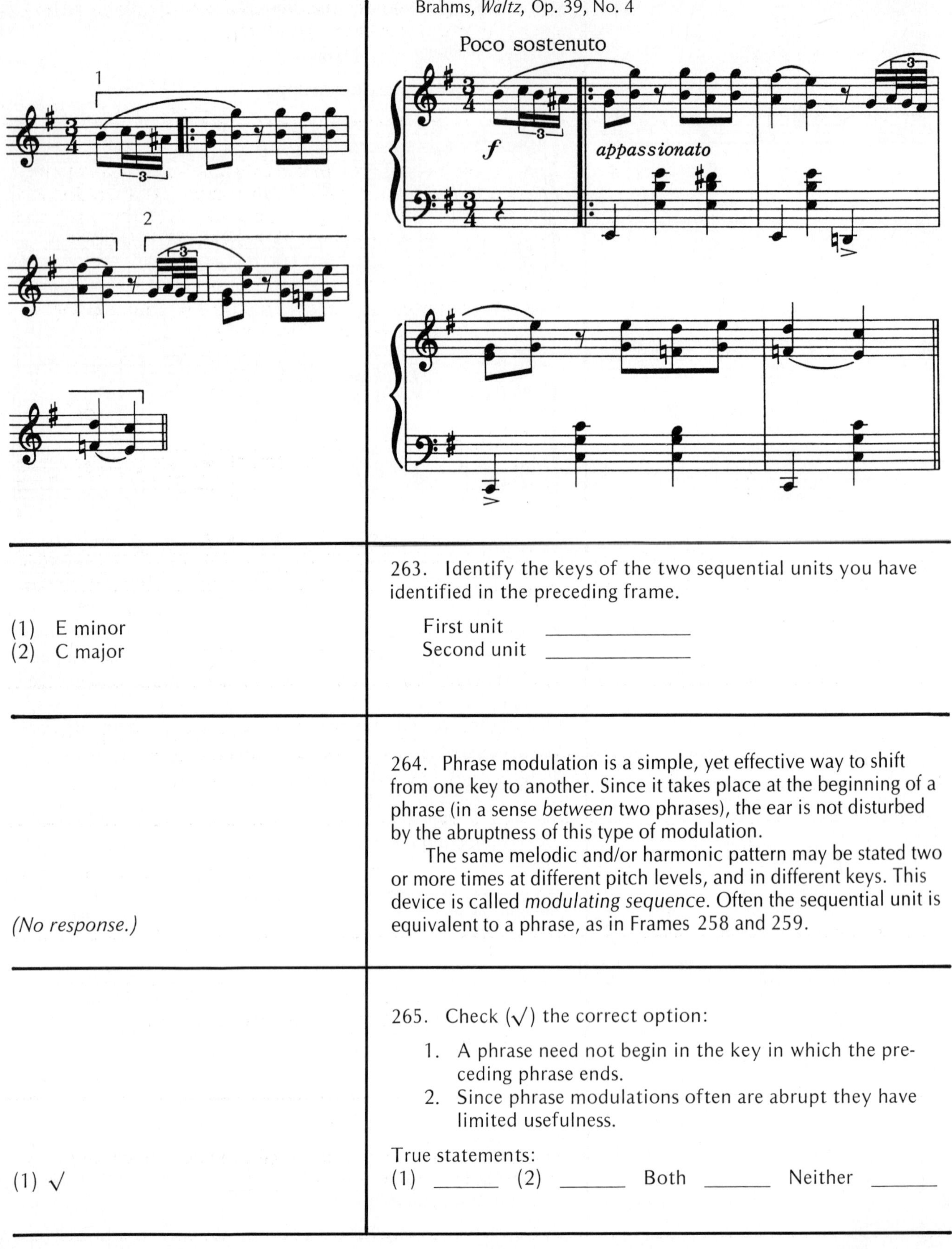

(1) E minor
(2) C major

263. Identify the keys of the two sequential units you have identified in the preceding frame.

First unit ______________
Second unit ______________

(No response.)

264. Phrase modulation is a simple, yet effective way to shift from one key to another. Since it takes place at the beginning of a phrase (in a sense *between* two phrases), the ear is not disturbed by the abruptness of this type of modulation.

The same melodic and/or harmonic pattern may be stated two or more times at different pitch levels, and in different keys. This device is called *modulating sequence.* Often the sequential unit is equivalent to a phrase, as in Frames 258 and 259.

(1) √

265. Check (√) the correct option:

1. A phrase need not begin in the key in which the preceding phrase ends.
2. Since phrase modulations often are abrupt they have limited usefulness.

True statements:
(1) ______ (2) ______ Both ______ Neither ______

False.
(The repetition must be at a different pitch.)

266. The repetition of a melodic and/or harmonic pattern is a device called sequence. (True/False) __________

■

A: I V I⁶ V I

267. In addition to occurring between phrases, modulations also take place within phrases. In such cases it is often desirable that the ear be led smoothly from one key to another, and one way to accomplish this is by COMMON CHORD MODULATION.

After playing at the piano the example below, supply the Roman numeral analysis, *to and including* the chord at the asterisk. *(Do not go beyond this chord.)*

Bach, Chorale: *Jesu Leiden, Pein und Tod*

A: __ __ __ __ __

No.

268. Referring again to the example in the preceding frame, is the chord immediately following the one at the asterisk (BD♯F♯) a diatonic chord in the key of A major? ______

E

269. The final two chords in Frame 267 produce an authentic cadence in the key of ______ major.

Yes.

270. In Frame 267, the chord at the asterisk is a tonic triad (I) in the key of A major. Is this chord also a diatonic chord in the key of E major? ______

IV.

271. What Roman numeral is used to analyze this chord (AC♯E) in the key of E major? ______

■

272. Since the chord at the asterisk in Frame 267 (and below) is diatonic in both A major and E major, it is called a COMMON CHORD.*

Complete the analysis by supplying the proper Roman numerals *in the key of E major.*

Bach, Chorale: *Jesu Leiden, Pein und Tod*

*The term *pivot* chord is sometimes used.

A: [I
E: [IV V I

---

273. Notice in the preceding frame that the common chord (at the asterisk) is analyzed twice, in both the "old" key of A major, and the "new" key of E major. The two Roman numerals are bracketed ([ ) to show the multiple function of the common chord, and the analysis continues at a different level as a visual representation of the "new" key.

A chord which is diatonic in two keys is called a __________ __________.

common chord

■

274. We shall analyze with Roman numerals the phrase below. *(Follow instructions carefully.)*

Start with the first chord and proceed until you reach a chord which is NOT diatonic in the key of C major; *do not analyze this chord or any which follow.*

Bach, Chorale: *Ach Gott, wie manches Herzeleid*

G major
(The phrase ends with a half cadence.)

275. Now determine the key in which the phrase in the preceding frame ends. This example modulates from the key of C major to the key of ______________.

Yes.

276. The last chord analyzed in Frame 274 is the tonic triad (I) in C major. Is this chord (CEG) diatonic in the key of G major? _______

---

common chord

277. Since the chord CEG is diatonic in both C major and G major, it is called a _______________ ___________.

■

C: I I^6 I IV V^4_2 [I^6
G: [IV^6

V^6 $(^6_5)$ I V

278. Now complete the Roman numeral analysis. *(Observe the form established in Frame 272.)*

Bach, Chorale: *Ach Gott, wie manches Herzeleid*

C: I I^6 I IV V^4_2 I^6

■

D: iii vi^7 V^6_5

I IV [$vii^{ø6}_5$
b: [$ii^{ø6}_5$ V^7 i

279. The example below contains a common chord modulation. Supply the Roman numeral analysis by applying the methods presented in the preceding frames.

Bach, Chorale: *Wer nur den lieben Gott lässt*

PT

D:

280. Supply the Roman numeral analysis for the example below:

Mozart, *Sonata,* K. 284

D:

281. We shall pause now to make a few general observations regarding common chord modulation. It should be clear from the examples presented thus far that it is the dominant chord (in the new key) which propels the music out of the originally established key. The leading tone triad or seventh chord, of course, accomplishes the same purpose. The common chord provides a stepping-stone to the dominant, and is usually the first chord preceding it. Thus, as a rule, *the common chord immediately precedes the first chord encountered which is not diatonic in the old key.*

Which chord actually produces a modulation, the common chord or the dominant which follows? The ______________.

dominant

282. Another point which has an influence on the selection of an appropriate common chord is the fact that since the common chord usually precedes a dominant chord, it is likely to be either a subdominant or supertonic chord (in the new key). Other possibilities include the tonic or submediant chords. Is this principle borne out by all of the examples of common chord modulation presented thus far (Frames 272, 278, 279, 280)? ______

Yes.

283. The chords which are comon to the key of C major and each of its closely related keys are shown below. *Only the chords which occur in harmonic minor are shown here, but the chords derived from melodic minor are also available.* These chords increase the number of common chords where minor keys are concerned.

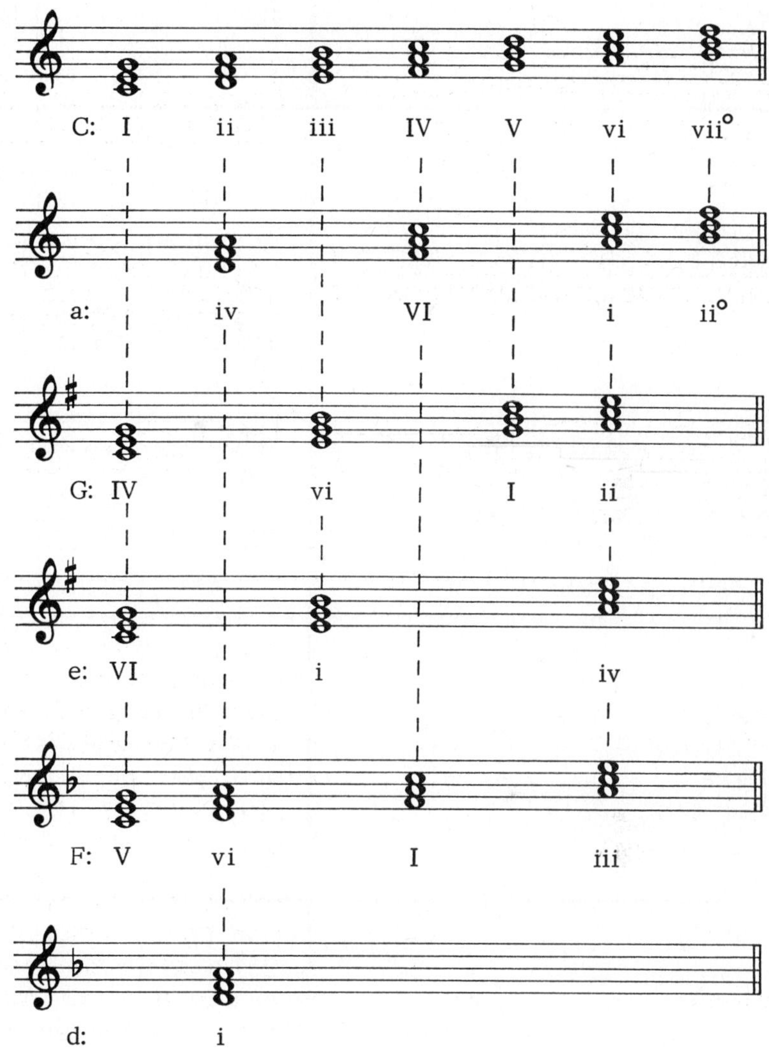

In a common chord modulation, the common chord often is either a subdominant or supertonic chord in the NEW key. According to the chart above, there are two keys in which neither the subdominant nor supertonic chord is available. Name these keys. ____________________

F major; D minor.

DFA.
(C: ii = d: i or C: IV = d: III)

284. If neither the subdominant nor the supertonic chord (in the key to which a modulation is to be made) is available as a common chord, the tonic or submediant chords in the new key are acceptable. Actually, any chord which is common to two keys may be used in a common chord modulation, but it is desirable that your attention be directed first to the more useful possibilities.

Spell the chord which would *most likely* be used in a common chord modulation from C major to D minor. ______

---

285. On the lower staff write all of the triads which are common to the keys of D-flat and A-flat major. Indicate also the appropriate Roman numerals.

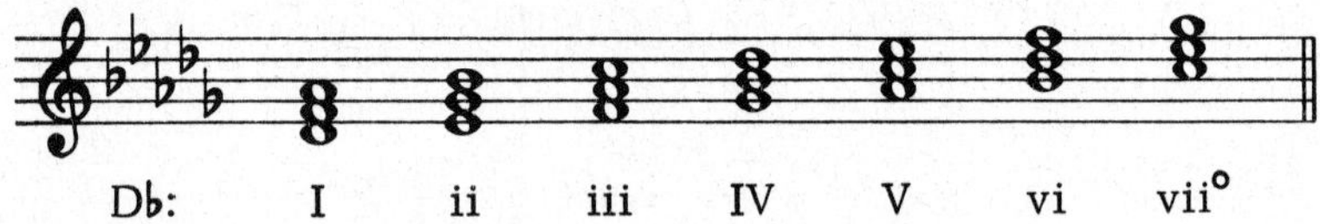

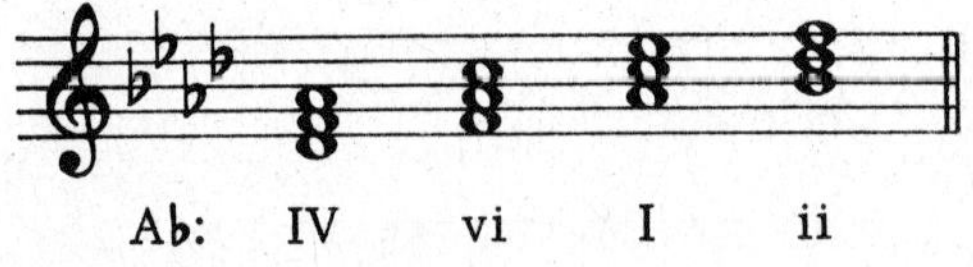

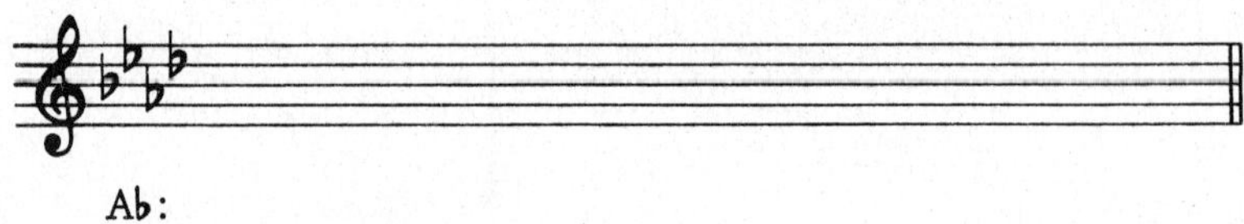

D♭FA♭.
(D♭: I = A♭: IV)
B♭D♭F.
(D♭: vi = A♭: ii)

286. Which two chords that are common to the keys of D-flat and A-flat major (as identified in the preceding frame) would *most likely* be used as a common chord in a modulation?

____

---

287. On the lower staff write all of the triads which are common to the keys of A major and C-sharp (harmonic) minor. Supply also the appropriate Roman numerals.

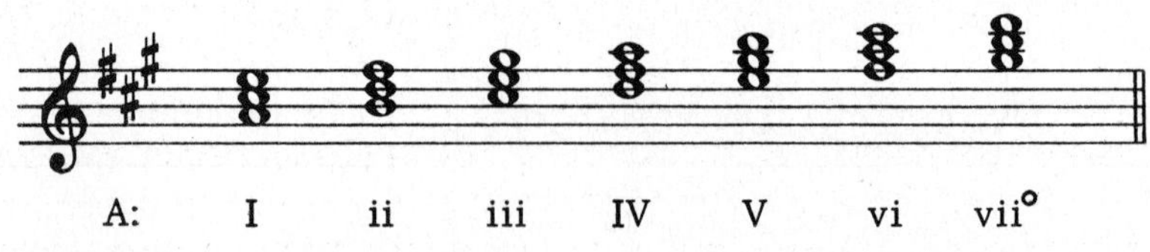

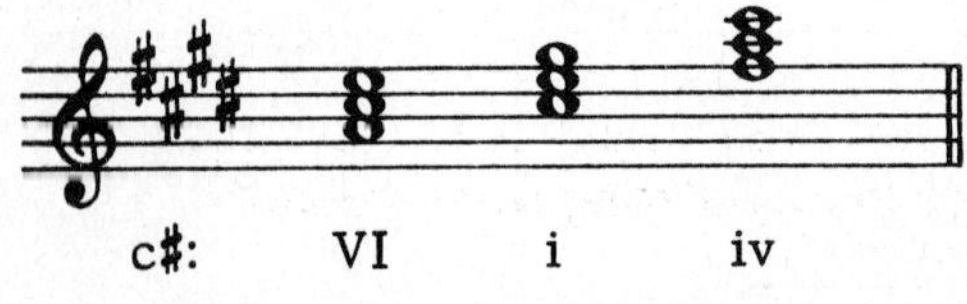

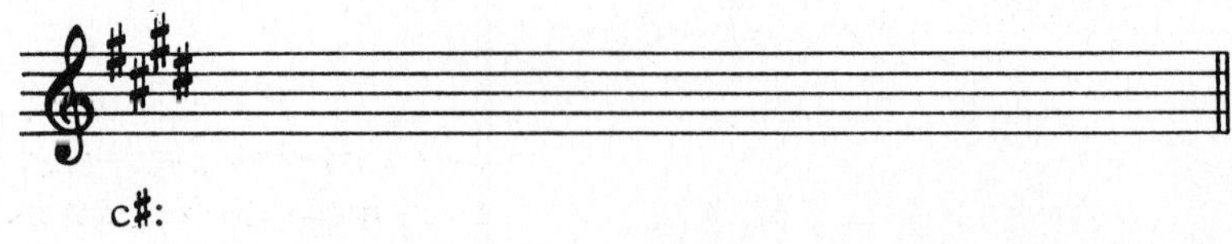

F♯AC♯.
(A: vi=c♯:iv)

288. Spell the chord which would most likely be used as a common chord in modulating from the key of A major to C-sharp minor. __________

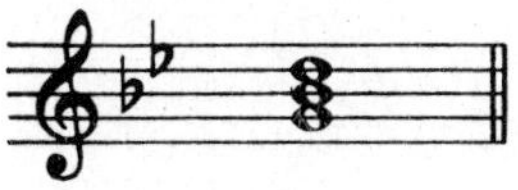

g: i

289. On the lower staff write all of the triads which are common to the keys of F major and G (harmonic) minor. Supply also the appropriate Roman numerals.

F: I ii iii IV V vi vii°

g:

GB♭D
(F:ii=g:i)

290. Spell the chord which would most likely be used as a common chord in modulating from the key of F major to G minor. __________

(c).
(E♭:vi=g:iv)
(See next frame.)

291. Which chord below would most likely be used as a common chord in modulating from the key of E-flat major to G minor? ______

(a) (b) (c) (d)

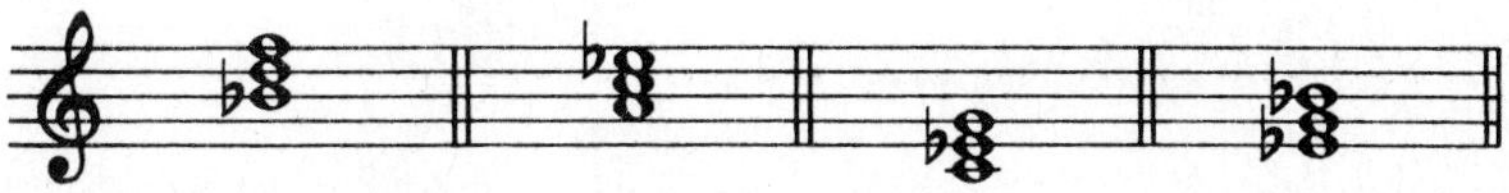

(No response.)

292. Both (a) and (d) in the preceding frame are common chords, but do not lead to the dominant in G minor as effectively as the subdominant. Choice (b) is not appropriate at this time because this chord is not a diatonic chord in the original key of E-flat major.

(b).
(B: vi=F♯:ii)

293. Which chord on the following page would most likely be used as a common chord in modulating from the key of B major to F-sharp major? ______

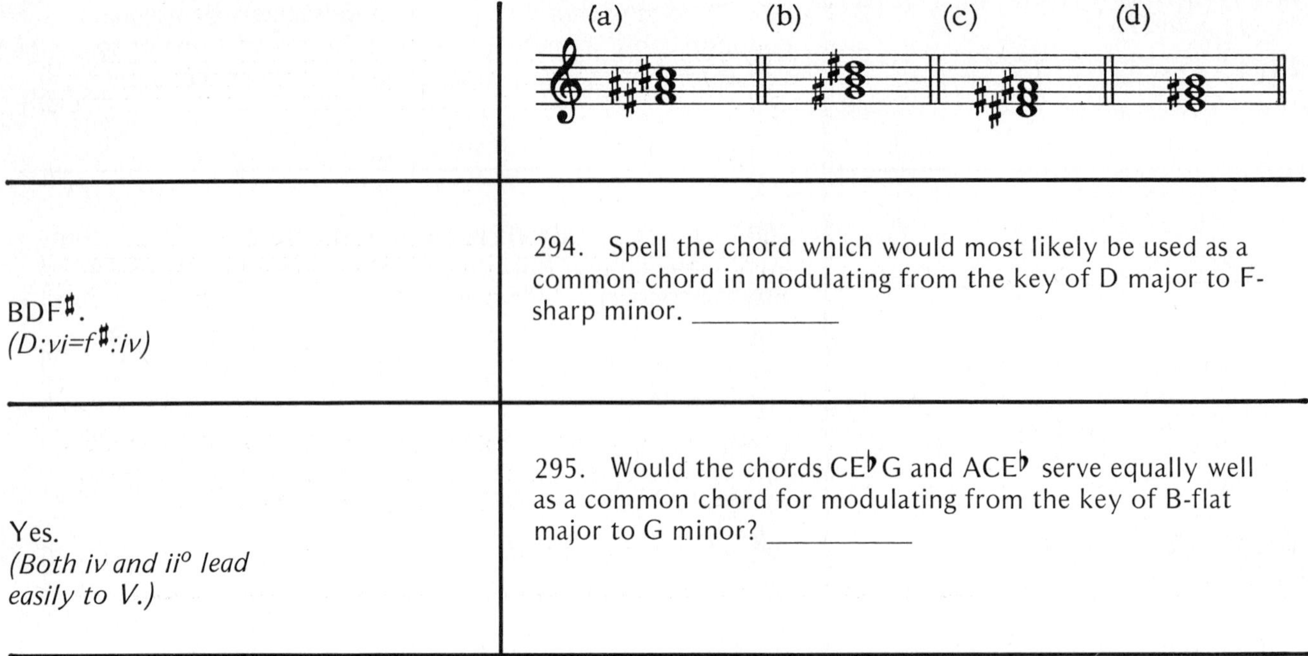

BDF♯.
(D:vi=f♯:iv)

294. Spell the chord which would most likely be used as a common chord in modulating from the key of D major to F-sharp minor. __________

Yes.
(Both iv and ii° lead easily to V.)

295. Would the chords CE♭G and ACE♭ serve equally well as a common chord for modulating from the key of B-flat major to G minor? __________

296. The chords which are common to the key of C minor (harmonic form) and each of its closely related keys are shown below:

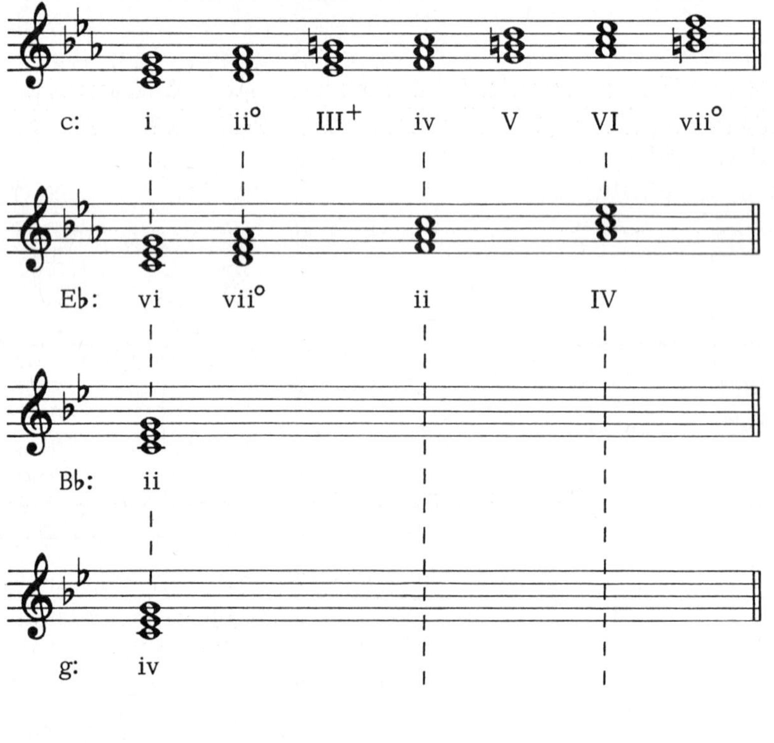

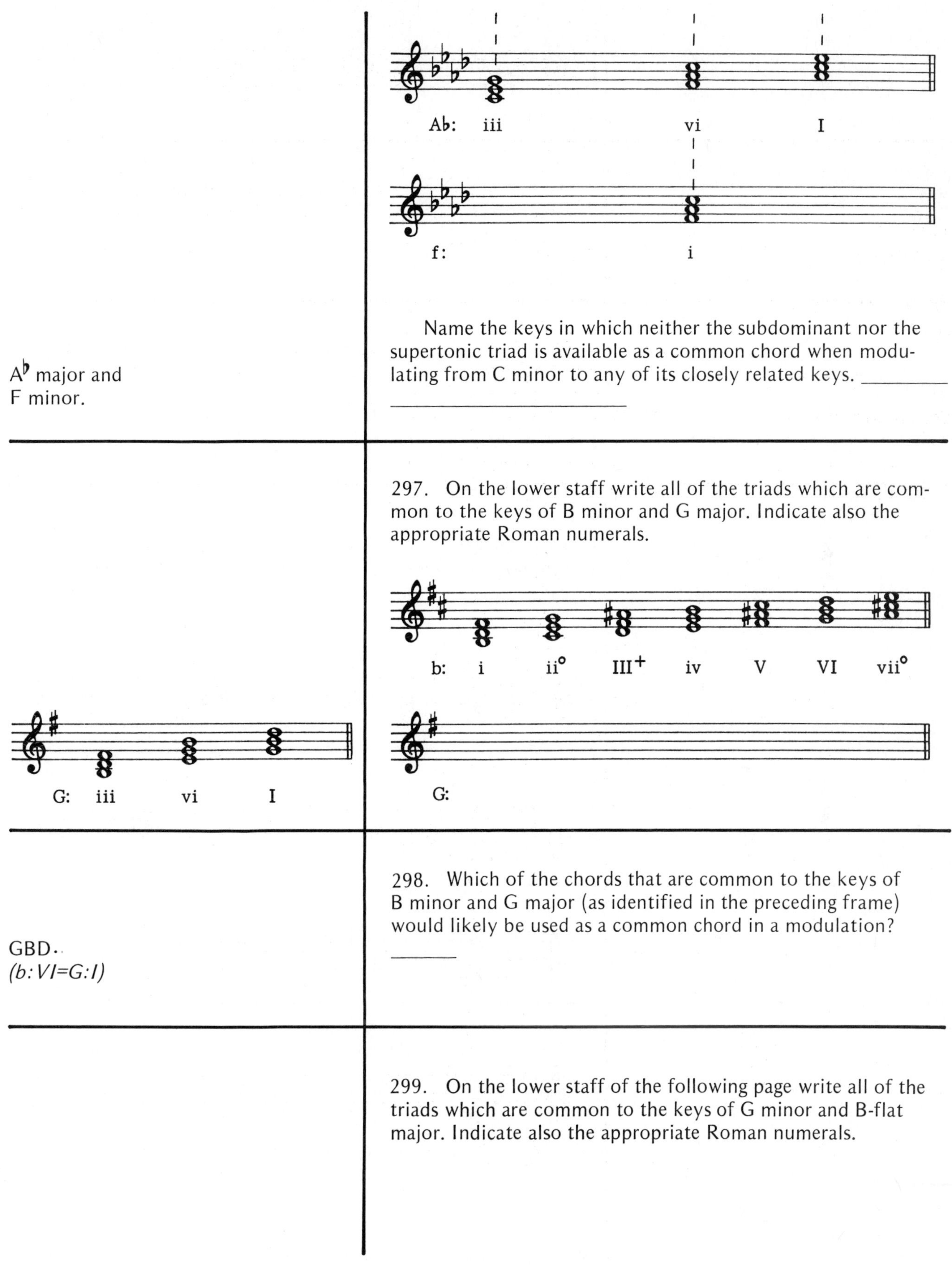

Name the keys in which neither the subdominant nor the supertonic triad is available as a common chord when modulating from C minor to any of its closely related keys. ________ ____________________

A♭ major and F minor.

297. On the lower staff write all of the triads which are common to the keys of B minor and G major. Indicate also the appropriate Roman numerals.

298. Which of the chords that are common to the keys of B minor and G major (as identified in the preceding frame) would likely be used as a common chord in a modulation? ______

GBD.
(b: VI=G: I)

299. On the lower staff of the following page write all of the triads which are common to the keys of G minor and B-flat major. Indicate also the appropriate Roman numerals.

CE♭ G.
(g:iv=B♭:ii)
E♭GB♭.
(g: VI=B♭:IV)

300. Which two chords that are common to the keys of G minor and B-flat major (as identified in the preceding frame) would most likely be used as a common chord in a modulation? __________ __________

(b).
(f:iv=b♭:i)

301. Which chord below would most likely be used as a common chord in modulating from the key of F minor to B-flat minor? ________

(d).
(c♯:i=g♯:iv)

302. Which chord below would most likely be used as a common chord in modulating from the key of C-sharp minor to G-sharp minor? ______

EGB.
(e:i=D:ii)

303. Spell the chord which would most likely be used as a common chord in modulating from the key of E minor to D major. __________

GB♭ D
(d:iv=F:ii)
B♭ DF
(d:VI=F:IV)

304. Spell the two chords which would most likely be used as a common chord in modulating from the key of D minor to F major. __________ and __________.

---

305. To this point, in order to reduce the number of choices, chords have been limited to those which are derived from the harmonic minor scale. The melodic minor scale produces additional chords which may be used as common chords. On the lower staff write all of the triads which are common to the keys of C minor and G minor and supply the appropriate Roman numeral for each. *(Include all of the triads derived from the G melodic minor scale. There are seven common chords; try to find all of them.)*

(Triads derived from the C melodic minor scale.)

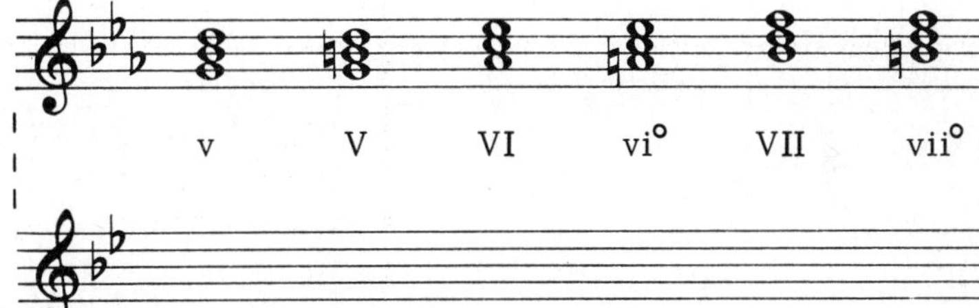

(No response.)

306. The preceding frame shows that the melodic minor scale produces a large number of diatonic triads, which increases greatly the number of possible common chords (especially when both keys involved are minor keys). Although any chord which is common to two keys may serve as a common chord, those most often exploited are the subdominant or supertonic chords in the new key. If neither of these is available, either the tonic or submediant may be used. Most common chord modulations involve one of these chords; but you must be alert for other, less usual, practices. In any case, regardless of what chord is used, common chord modulations produce a relatively smooth transition from one key to another. The common chord itself, since it functions in both keys, serves as a bridge between them.

*This is a modulation to the relative minor key.

307. Write the alto and tenor voices and supply the Roman numeral analysis.

Bach, Chorale: *Herr Christ, der ein'ge Gott's-Sohn*

*This is a modulation to the subdominant major key.

308. Write the alto and tenor voices and supply the Roman numeral analysis.

Bach Chorale: *Uns ist ein Kindlein heut' gebor'n*

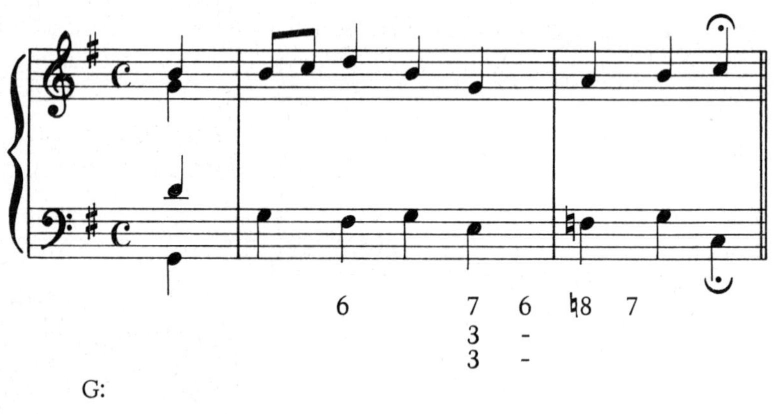

■

*This is a modulation to the relative minor key.

309. Complete the alto and tenor voices and supply the Roman numeral analysis.

Bach, Chorale: *Auf meinen lieben Gott*

■

*This is a modulation to the mediant minor key.

310. Supply the Roman numeral analysis.

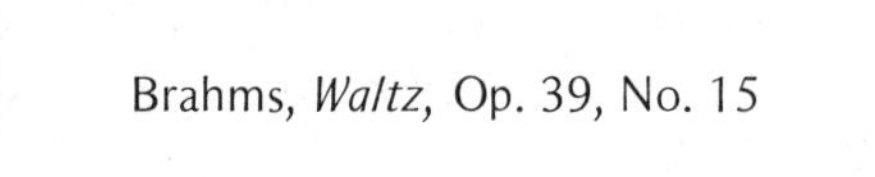

Brahms, *Waltz,* Op. 39, No. 15

*This is a modulation to the dominant major key.

311. Supply the Roman numeral analysis.

Beethoven, *Sonata,* Op. 2, No. 3

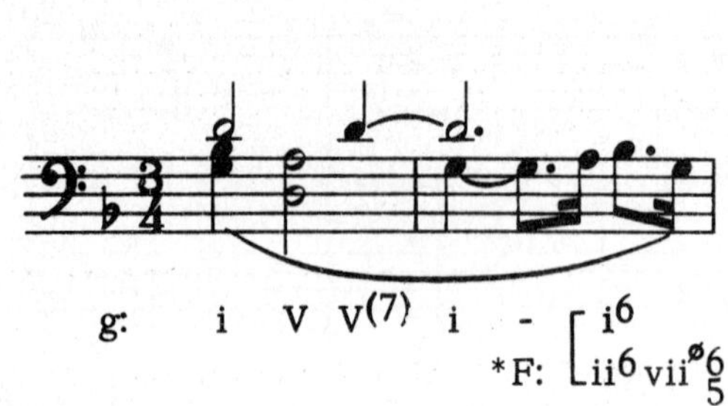

*This is a modulation to the subtonic major key.

312. Supply the Roman numeral analysis. *(In the second measure analyze a chord at each of the two asterisks.)*

D. Scarlatti, *Sonata,* in G minor

■

g: i V6 i iv6 V^6_5/iv

iv [i

d:* [iv $V^7(i^6_4)$ V I

**This is a modulation to the dominant minor key.*

313. Supply the Roman numeral analysis. *(Analyze the chord at the asterisk as a secondary dominant.)*

Bach, Chorale: *Ach Gott, vom Himmel sieh' darein*

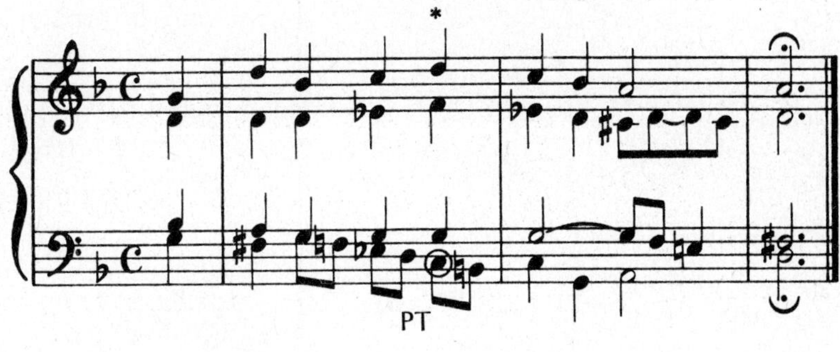

g:

Note: The preceeding frames have demonstrated modulations to the five closely related keys mentioned previously.

314. In the common chord modulations presented thus far, the melodic movement preceding and following the common chord has been diatonic (by step first in the old key, then in the new). To make this clear, the alto voice of the preceding example is shown below at the point of modulation. The numbers above the staff indicate the scale degrees in the old key (G minor). In like manner, write numbers below the staff to represent the scale degrees in the new key (D minor).

No.
(See next frame.)

315. Does the fragment in the preceding frame contain chromatic movement in either of the two keys? ______

(No response.)

316. Distinction is made between a half-step which involves *two* basic notes, and a half-step which involves only *one.*

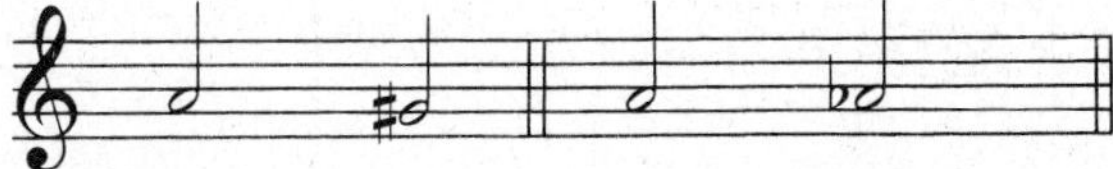

The term "chromatic movement" refers to the half-step as notated in (2).

Yes.

317. A modulation which involves diatonic melodic movement in all voices, and in which the common chord is diatonic (not altered) in both the old and the new keys, is called a DIATONIC MODULATION. Stated simply, a diatonic modulation makes use only of tonal material which is diatonic—first in the old key, then in the new.

Does the modulation below qualify as a diatonic modulation? ______

Beethoven, *Quartet,* Op. 18, No. 3

No.
(See next frame.)

318. One of the features of a diatonic modulation is the absence of chromatic movement in any of the voices immediately preceding and following the common chord. With this in mind, does the modulation from the key of F major to G minor in the phrase below qualify as a diatonic modulation? ______

Bach, Chorale: *O Ewigkeit, du Donnerwort*

319. We shall look closely at the example in the preceding frame. The chromatic movement in the bass at chord 3 (E-E♭) prevents the modulation from being diatonic. The change of key occurs suddenly, and the chromatic movement is the most striking feature.

(Play this example at the piano, and listen carefully to the effect of the modulation.)

(You may have chosen 2, 3, or 4. Continue with the next frame for explanation.)

Indicate (by number) the first chord you feel functions more strongly in the new key (G minor) than in the old (F major).______

(No response.)

320. You may have had difficulty deciding between chords 2, 3, and 4 in answering the question posed in the preceding frame. Chord 2 is actually a common chord (F: vii°=g: vi°), but its function in F major as a leading tone triad is stronger than its function in G minor as a submediant triad on the raised sixth degree. The problem, remember, was to identify the first chord which functions *more strongly* in the new key than the old.

Whereas chord 4 (B♭ DF♯) clearly functions as III⁺ in G minor, chord 3 (ACE♭ G) could be heard as either $ii^{ø7}$ in G minor or $vii^{ø7}$/IV in F major. *The choice between these two chords is based on aural impression.* Does the ear anticipate resolution of chord 3 in one key more strongly than the other, and if so, which key? There is no absolute answer to this question; but since the supertonic seventh chord occurs so frequently in key-defining cadence patterns—much more frequently than does the $vii^{ø7}$/IV—most of you probably hear the third chord in Frame 318 as $ii^{ø7}$ in G minor. Thus, it is Chord 3 which first asserts the new key.

---

chromatic

321. Care has been taken to identify the first chord in Frame 318 which functions in the new key to show that it coincides with the chromatic movement. Although chord 2 is a common chord, its function in the new key is weak, and *it is the chromatic bass line which actually pulls the ear away from the old key*. For these reasons the common chord is ignored, and the process is called a CHROMATIC MODULATION.

A modulation in which not all voices move diatonically is often called a ______________ modulation.

■

322. On the following page, the harmonic analysis is shown to the point of modulation. Supply the remaining chord symbols.

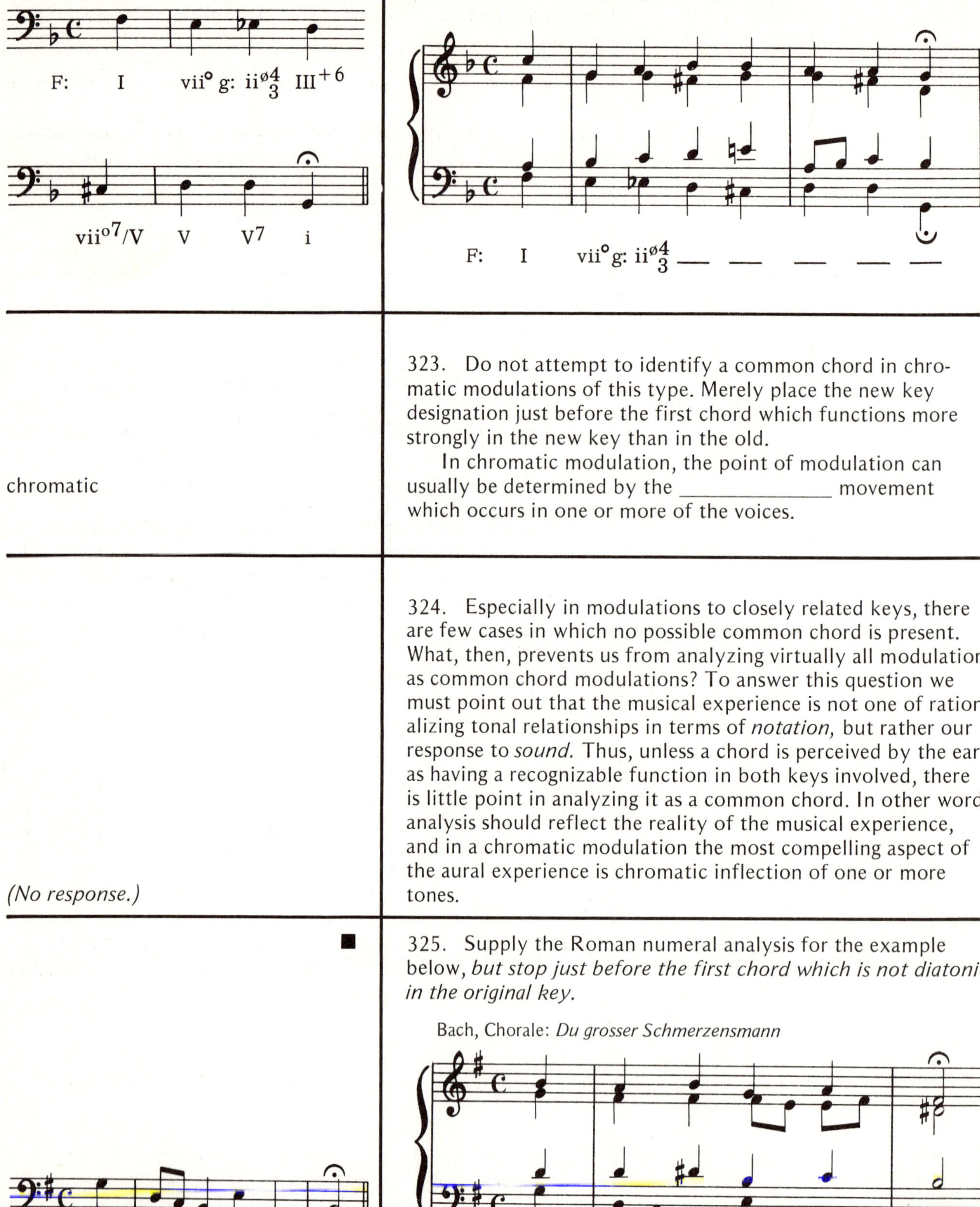

323. Do not attempt to identify a common chord in chromatic modulations of this type. Merely place the new key designation just before the first chord which functions more strongly in the new key than in the old.

In chromatic modulation, the point of modulation can usually be determined by the ______________ movement which occurs in one or more of the voices.

chromatic

324. Especially in modulations to closely related keys, there are few cases in which no possible common chord is present. What, then, prevents us from analyzing virtually all modulations as common chord modulations? To answer this question we must point out that the musical experience is not one of rationalizing tonal relationships in terms of *notation,* but rather our response to *sound.* Thus, unless a chord is perceived by the ear as having a recognizable function in both keys involved, there is little point in analyzing it as a common chord. In other words, analysis should reflect the reality of the musical experience, and in a chromatic modulation the most compelling aspect of the aural experience is chromatic inflection of one or more tones.

(No response.)

■

325. Supply the Roman numeral analysis for the example below, *but stop just before the first chord which is not diatonic in the original key.*

E minor

326. The example in the preceding frame begins in the key of G major, but ends with a half cadence in the key of ______ __________.

Yes.
(See next frame.)

327. Refer again to the example in Frame 325. The last chord which could be analyzed as diatonic in the key of G major is the dominant (DF♯A). Can this chord be analyzed in the key of E minor? ______

■

328. The chord DF♯A is the dominant triad in the key of G major and the subtonic triad (VII) in the key of E minor. Thus, there actually is a common chord in the example of Frame 325. In spite of this, however, we shall call this progression a chromatic modulation. Here are the reasons: First of all, while the chord DF♯A has a strong function in the key of G major, its function in E minor is very weak; secondly, the chromatic movement in the tenor voice (D-D♯) is the feature which actually thrusts the music into the new key. Chromatic movement, then, is often the most compelling reason for deciding in favor of a chromatic modulation. So, we shall ignore the common chord for the two reasons stated above.

Complete the analysis.

Bach, Chorale: *Du grosser Schmerzensmann*

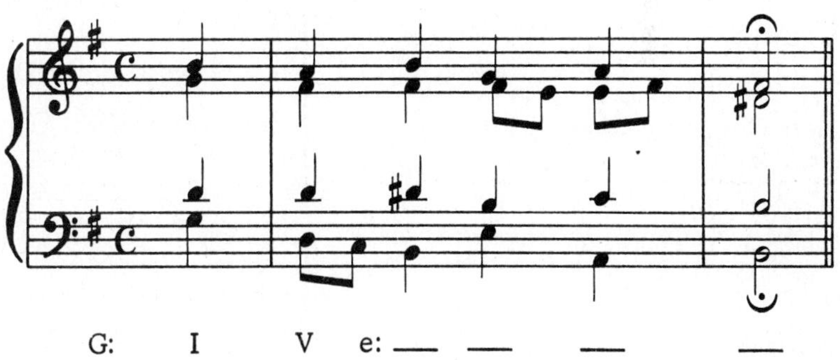

■

329. Supply the Roman numeral analysis on the following page. *(Analyze the chord at the asterisk as a secondary dominant.)*

Bach, Chorale: *Allein Gott in der Höh' sei Ehr'*

G:

■

330. Supply the Roman numeral analysis.

Bach, Chorale: *Das neugeborne Kindelein*

Bb:

■

331. Supply the Roman numeral analysis.

Schubert, *Waltz,* Op. 127, No. 17

g:

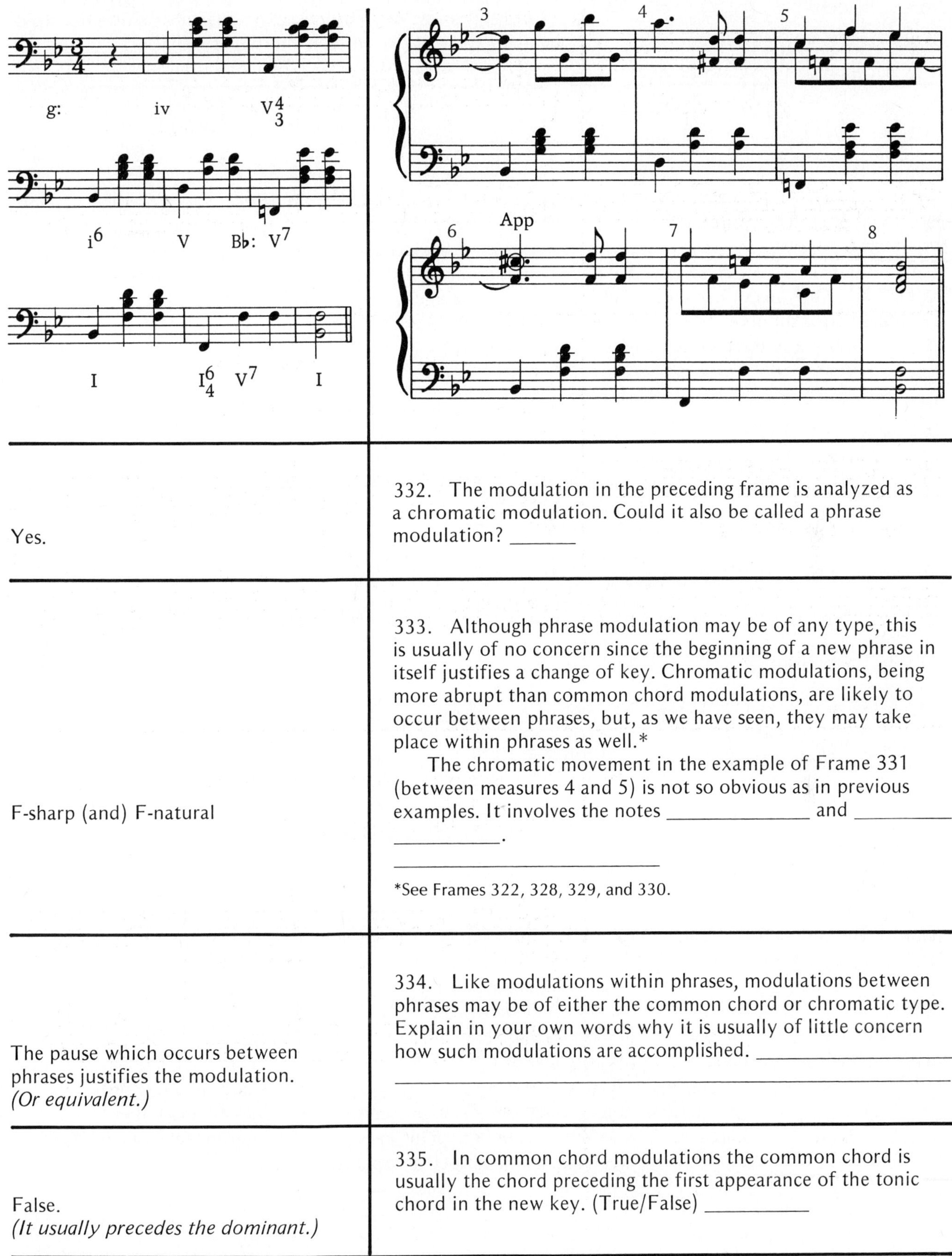

Yes.

332. The modulation in the preceding frame is analyzed as a chromatic modulation. Could it also be called a phrase modulation? ______

F-sharp (and) F-natural

333. Although phrase modulation may be of any type, this is usually of no concern since the beginning of a new phrase in itself justifies a change of key. Chromatic modulations, being more abrupt than common chord modulations, are likely to occur between phrases, but, as we have seen, they may take place within phrases as well.*

The chromatic movement in the example of Frame 331 (between measures 4 and 5) is not so obvious as in previous examples. It involves the notes ____________ and ____________.

____

*See Frames 322, 328, 329, and 330.

The pause which occurs between phrases justifies the modulation. *(Or equivalent.)*

334. Like modulations within phrases, modulations between phrases may be of either the common chord or chromatic type. Explain in your own words why it is usually of little concern how such modulations are accomplished. ______________________

____

False. *(It usually precedes the dominant.)*

335. In common chord modulations the common chord is usually the chord preceding the first appearance of the tonic chord in the new key. (True/False) __________

True.

336. In the case of a chromatic modulation, no attempt need be made to locate a common chord. (True/False) __________

SUMMARY

Closely related keys have signatures that differ by not more than one sharp or flat. The preceding statement is correct; but another approach, one that underscores the special relationship of closely related keys, may be stated as follows: *The tonic triad of a closely related key occurs as a diatonic triad in the original key.* Thus a modulation to a closely related key involves the establishment of a diatonic triad in the old key as a new tonic. Only major or minor triads may serve as a tonic, so diminished triads are ruled out. The examples below show the five closely related keys to the keys of D major and D minor. (Note that in the case of a minor key the natural form of the scale is used.)

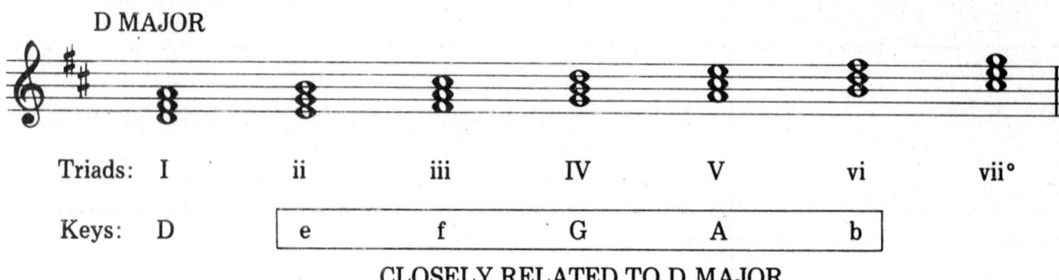

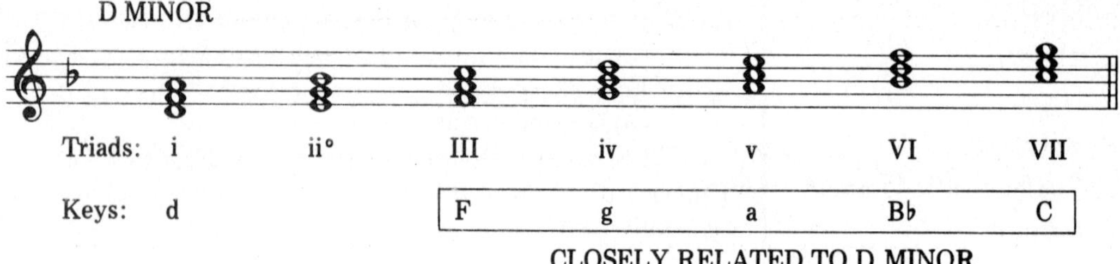

The term phrase modulation does not refer to a *process,* but to the fact that the modulation occurs between phrases. The ear readily accepts a change of key at such points because of the momentary pause produced by structural divisions of music. The two actual processes presented in this chapter are common chord and chromatic modulation. Of these, common chord modulation ordinarily achieves smoother transition to a new key because of the "pivot" chord which functions simultaneously in both keys.

Diatonic common chord modulation results in diatonic melodic movement in all voices both preceding and following the common chord. Chromatic modulation, on the other hand, involves chromatic movement in one or more voices. This causes the new key to appear more suddenly than in the case of common chord modulation. Hardly a modulation can be written in which some kind of common chord does not exist. But if the common chord's harmonic function is weak in one or both of the keys, chromatic movement—often the most distinctive aural feature—causes the modulation to be classed as chromatic.

Mastery Frames

Answer	Frames	Question
modulation	(218-220)	4-1. The act of establishing a new key during the course of a composition is called ________________.
closely related	(229-230)	4-2. Keys whose signatures differ by no more than one accidental are called ________________ keys.
No.	(249)	4-3. Are parallel keys (C major and C minor, for example) closely related keys?______
(1) E minor (2) D major (3) B minor (4) C major (5) A minor *(Any order.)*	(231-244)	4-4. Name the five keys that are closely related to the key of G major. (1)________________ (2)________________ (3)________________ (4)________________ (5)________________
(1) F major (2) C major (3) A minor (4) B-flat major (5) G minor *(Any order.)*	(231-244)	4-5. Name the five keys that are closely related to the key of D minor. (1)________________ (2)________________ (3)________________ (4)________________ (5)________________
phrase	(253-259)	4-6. Change of key at the beginning of a phrase is called ________________ modulation.

modulating (260-264)	4-7. When stages of a sequence are in different keys, the term ________________ sequence is used.
(1) (A: ii = f♯: iv) (3) (A: vii° = f♯: ii°) (281-306)	4-8. Which two chords would most likely serve as common chords when modulating from the key of A major to F-sharp minor?________________ (1) (2) (3) (4) A: ii V vii° iii
(2) (c: III = B♭: IV) (3) (c: i = B♭: ii) (281-206)	4-9. Which two chords would most likely serve as common chords when modulating from the key of C minor to B-flat major?________________ (1) (2) (3) (4) c: ii° III V^7 i
chromatic (317-323)	4-10. The example below contains a modulation from D major to F-sharp minor. This is an example of a (diatonic/chromatic)____________ modulation.

Supplementary Assignments

ASSIGNMENT 4-1 Name________________________________

1. The signatures of closely related keys differ by not more than ________ accidental(s).
2. List the keys which are closely related to A major.

____

____

3. List the keys which are closely related to B-flat minor.

____

____

4. The keys of D major and D minor are called ________________ keys.
5. Circle the keys that are NOT closely related to A-flat major.

   D♭ G♭ C f c E♭ b♭ a♭
6. Circle the keys that are NOT closely related to F-sharp minor.

   C♯ A F♯ b g♯ D E c♯
7. Write the signature and identify the key that is parallel to each of the specified keys.

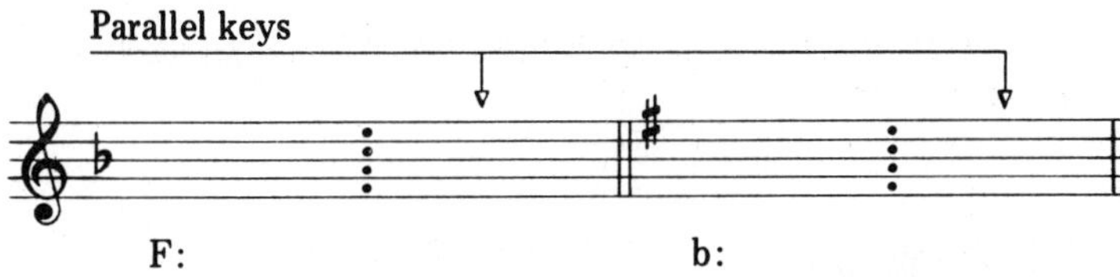

8. The example below contains a common chord modulation. Complete the statements regarding this example.

Bach, *Chorale:* "Wachet auf, ruft uns die Stimme"

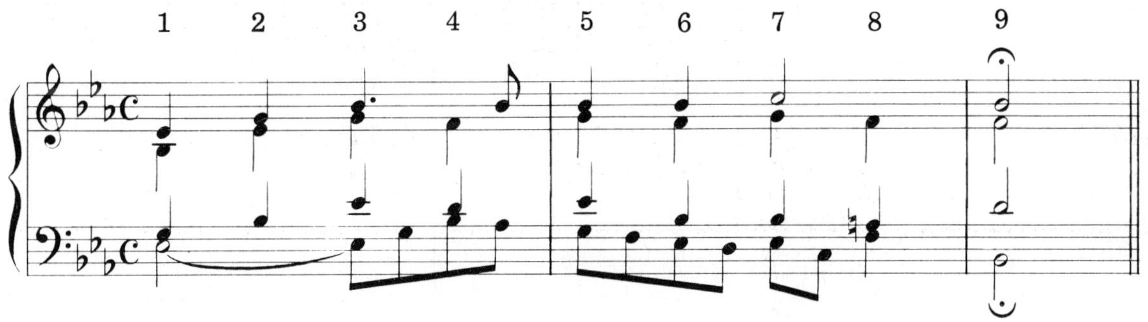

(a) The phrase modulates from the key of ______________ to the key of ______________.
(b) The common chord is chord number ______________.
(c) The harmonic function of the common chord is ______________ in the old key and ______________ in the new key.

9. Provide the missing information below regarding the following example.

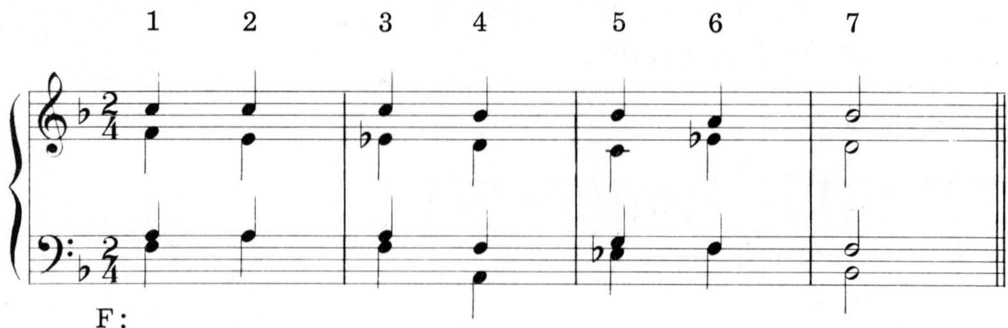

(a) This example shows a modulation from the key of F major to the key of ________________.
(b) At which chord is the music first pulled away from the original tonality? Chord number __________.
(c) Is the modulation by common chord or is it chromatic? ________________

10. Provide the harmonic analysis for the example below.

11. What type of modulation is illustrated in the previous example? ________________________

12. The example below shows a modulation from G major to E minor. Which chord is the common chord? _______

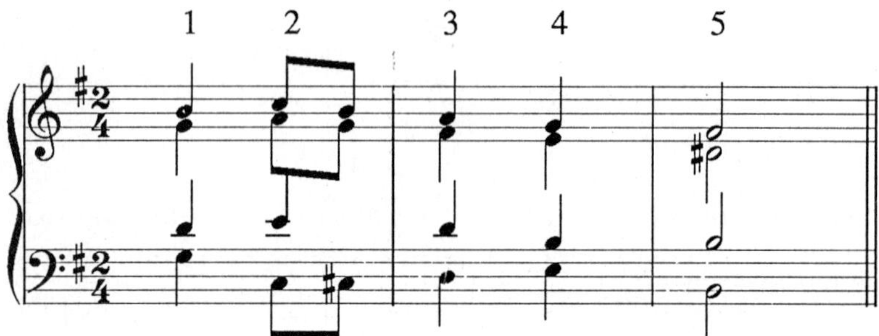

13. The example below shows a modulation from C minor to B-flat major. Which chord is the common chord? _______

ASSIGNMENT 4-2 Name______________________

1. Provide the harmonic analysis for the example below.

Beethoven: *Sonata*, Op. 2, No. 1

2. What type of modulation is illustrated in the above example?______________________

3. Harmonize the melodies that follow in four-voice chorale style. Modulate as directed.

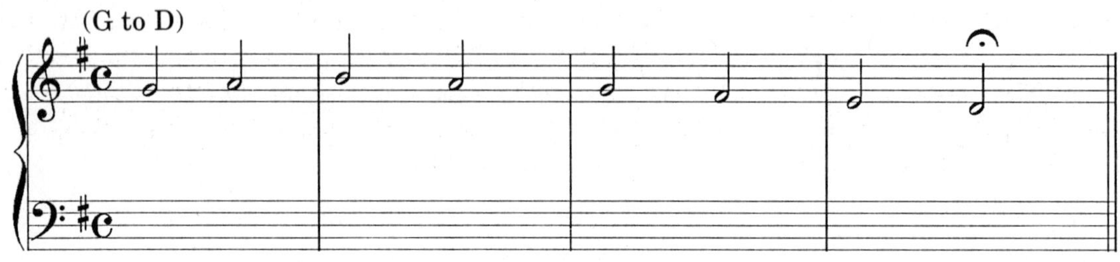

4. A modulation in which the common chord has little functional value in one or both of the keys involved is often called a ______________ modulation.

5. Phrase modulation may occur any place in the phrase. (True/False) ______

6. A compositional device which involves the immediate restatement of a melodic and/or harmonic unit is called a ______________________.

7. Compose small compositions in either a piano or instrumental style (at least four measures long) which illustrate the following types of modulation (one composition combining illustrations of all three modulations could be done as well):

   A. Phrase modulation
   B. Common chord modulation
   C. Chromatic modulation

Complete your composition(s) following the same general procedures outlined in Assignment 3-2, exercise 6.

8. Complete an analysis of a short composition (supplied by your instructor or tutor) which comments on the following:

   A. A complete harmonic (Roman numeral) and non-harmonic tone analysis of the score.
   B. A short commentary discussing the form and rhythm used and their relationship to the meter, modulations, and/or any chromatic alterations and any other significant items you discover.

chapter five

Borrowed Chords

Harmonic resources are expanded by exchanging diatonic chords between parallel major and minor keys. Chords which normally belong in one key but are used in a parallel key are called borrowed chords. Due to the alternate sixth and seventh degrees of the melodic minor scale, there are more diatonic chords available in minor keys than in major. Thus, most borrowed chords occur in major keys to supplement the comparatively limited array of chords provided by the major scale.

G B♭ D♭ F.

■ 337. The fourth chord in the example below is an altered chord. Spell this chord. ______________

Bach, Chorale: *Christus, der ist mein Leben*

$ii^{ø6}_{5}$

338. Although the chord GB♭ D♭ F is an *altered* chord in the key of F major, it is a *diatonic* chord in the key of F minor. Write the Roman numeral which is appropriate for this chord in F minor.

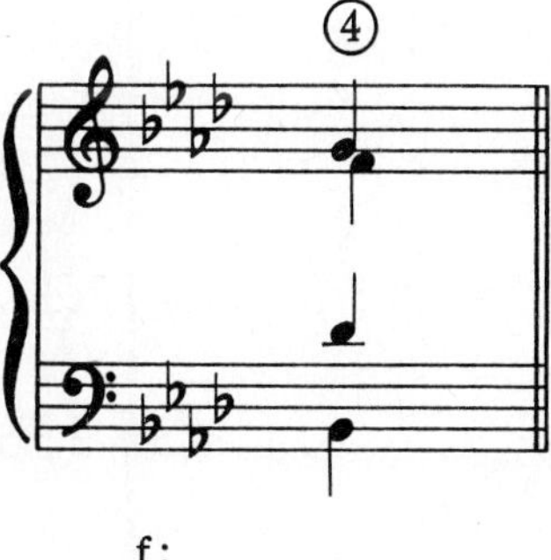

f: ___

■

339. Now supply the complete Roman numeral analysis using the symbol for the altered chord (4) which is appropriate for the key of F minor.

Bach, Chorale: *Christus, der ist mein Leben*

F: I vii^{o6} I^6 ii$^{ø6}_{5}$ V I

---

340. In the preceding frame the supertonic seventh chord (G B♭ D♭ F) is a diatonic chord in F minor. Used in F major it is called a BORROWED CHORD.

Most borrowed chords occur in major keys; they are "borrowed" from parallel _____________ keys.

minor

---

341. The exchange of diatonic chords between parallel major and minor keys through the use of borrowed chords is sometimes called MODAL MIXTURE, MODAL EXCHANGE, or CHANGE OF MODE.

Most borrowed chords occur in major since the major scale provides considerably less tonal variety than the minor scale.

Select from the chords below those which are *borrowed chords* in the key of F major. *(Remember that while altered in one key, borrowed chords are diatonic in the parallel key.)*

(List by number.) ________________________________

(2), (3), and (5).
(See next frame.)

secondary dominants

342. All of the chords in the preceding frame are altered chords in the key of F major, but only (2), (3), and (5) are borrowed chords. The remainder are all examples of another type of altered chord. These are called ________________ ________________.

---

diminished

343. The most common borrowed chords in major are shown below:

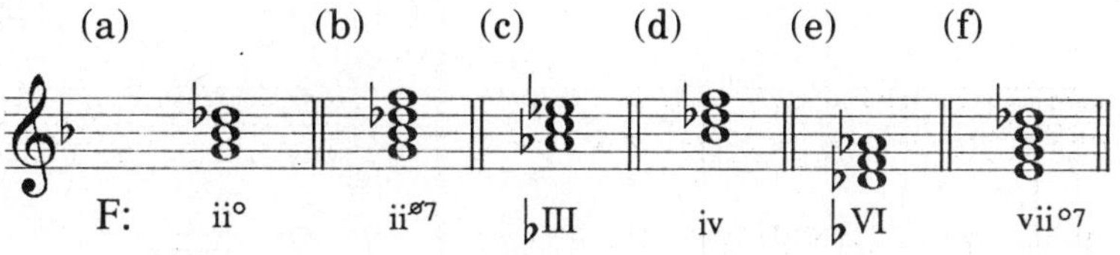

(a) (b) (c) (d) (e) (f)

F: ii° ii^{ø7} ♭III iv ♭VI vii^{o7}

The symbols reflect the quality of the chords. In (c) and (e), the flat placed at the lower left-hand corner of the Roman numeral indicates that the *root* of the chord is flatted (it is a half-step lower than in its unaltered form). In (f), the symbol shows that the chord is a ____________seventh chord.

---

root

344. When a chord is built on an altered tone, the actual accidental used is included as part of the chord symbol.

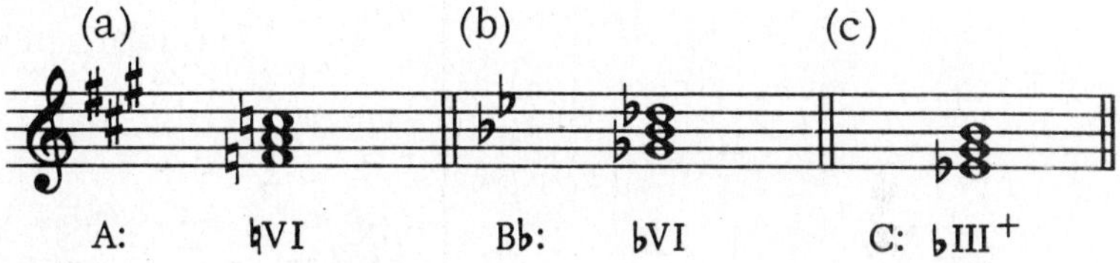

(a) (b) (c)

A: ♮VI Bb: ♭VI C: ♭III^{+}

An accidental placed at the lower left-hand corner of a Roman numeral refers to the ____________ of the chord.

---

(2), (3), (6), (10), and (12).

345. Some of the diatonic triads and seventh chords in the key of B minor are shown in the example below and on the following page. Select from these chords those which most likely would occur as *borrowed chords* in the key of B major. (You may refer to Frame 343. Also, take care not to include chords which are *diatonic* in both keys.)

List by number. ________________________________

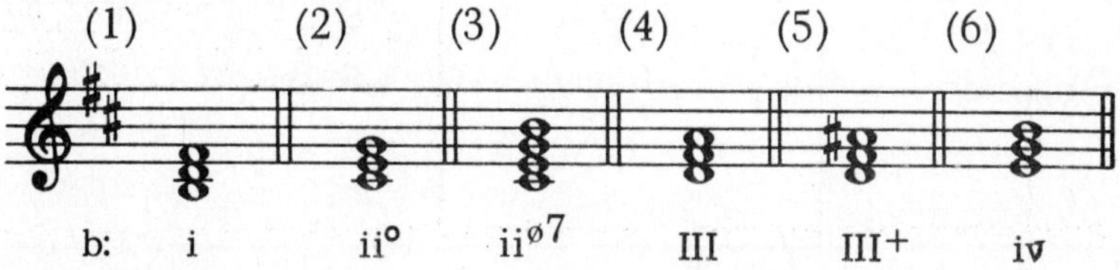

(1) (2) (3) (4) (5) (6)

b: i ii° ii^{ø7} III III^{+} iv

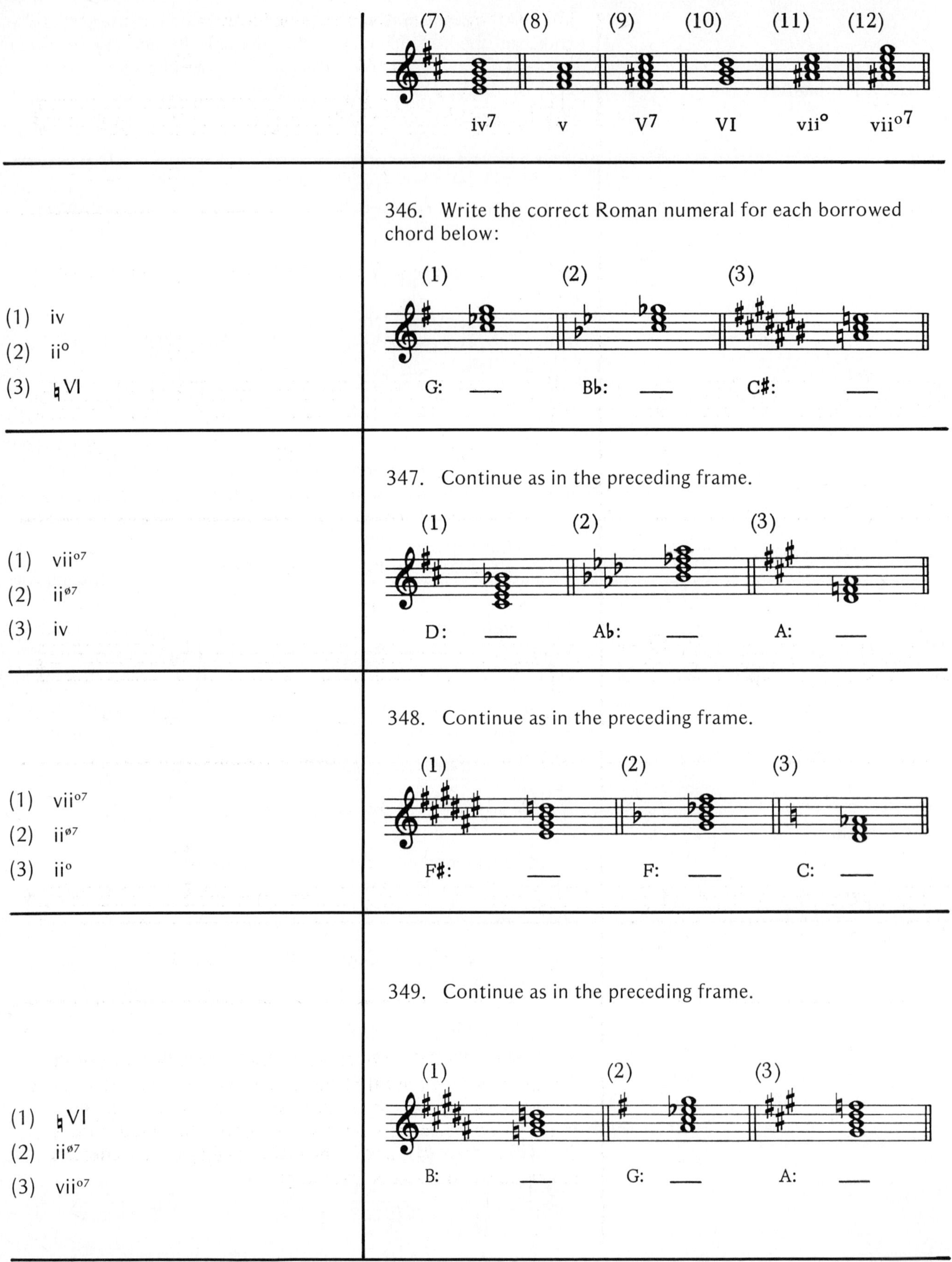

(1) iv
(2) ii°
(3) ♮VI

346. Write the correct Roman numeral for each borrowed chord below:

(1) vii°7
(2) iiø7
(3) iv

347. Continue as in the preceding frame.

(1) vii°7
(2) iiø7
(3) ii°

348. Continue as in the preceding frame.

(1) ♮VI
(2) iiø7
(3) vii°7

349. Continue as in the preceding frame.

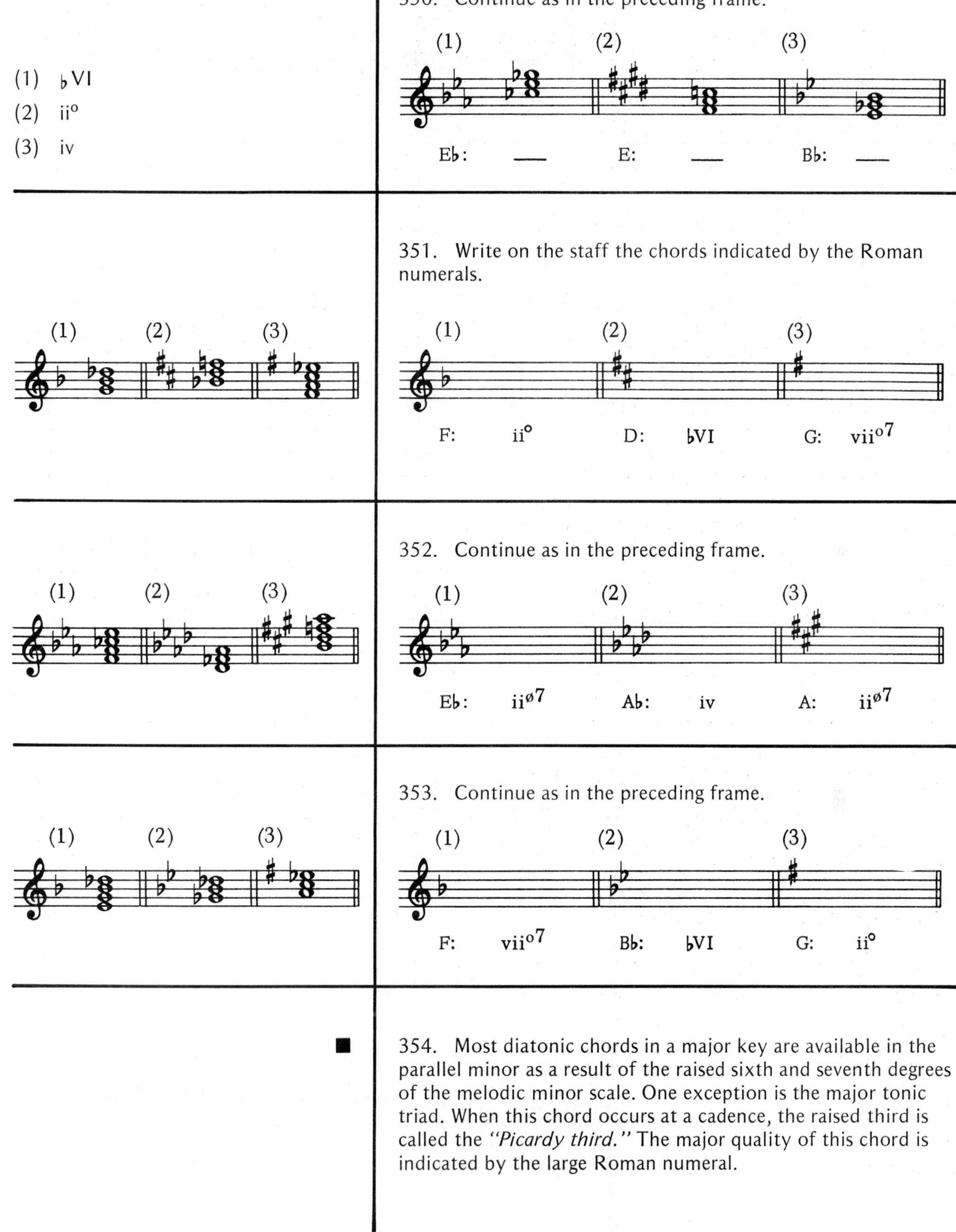

(1) ♭VI
(2) ii°
(3) iv

350. Continue as in the preceding frame.

(1) E♭: ___ (2) E: ___ (3) B♭: ___

351. Write on the staff the chords indicated by the Roman numerals.

(1) F: ii° (2) D: ♭VI (3) G: vii°7

352. Continue as in the preceding frame.

(1) E♭: iiø7 (2) A♭: iv (3) A: iiø7

353. Continue as in the preceding frame.

(1) F: vii°7 (2) B♭: ♭VI (3) G: ii°

■

354. Most diatonic chords in a major key are available in the parallel minor as a result of the raised sixth and seventh degrees of the melodic minor scale. One exception is the major tonic triad. When this chord occurs at a cadence, the raised third is called the *"Picardy third."* The major quality of this chord is indicated by the large Roman numeral.

Bach, *Well-Tempered Clavier,* Vol. 2, Fugue XVI

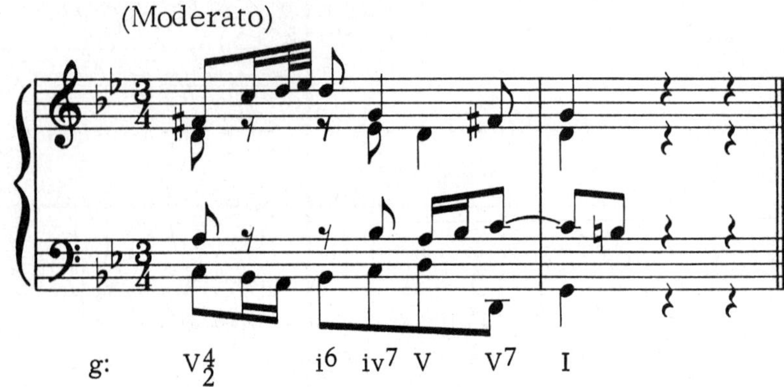

borrowed

The major tonic is the chief ______________ chord which appears in a minor key.

---

355. Two other possible borrowed chords in minor are shown below:

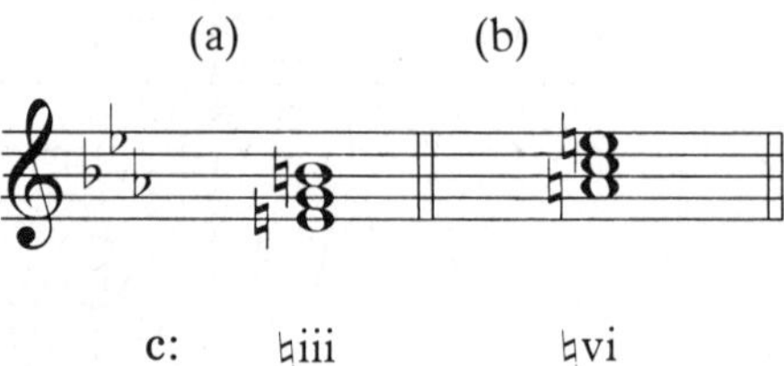

These chords are little used, but are available if an extreme mixture of modality is desired.

(No response.)

---

356. Borrowed chords are used primarily to introduce greater tonal variety into major keys. Few occur in minor due to the greater tonal resources of the melodic minor scale. The most common borrowed chord in minor is the major tonic. This chord occurs most frequently at the cadence where the major quality is often preferred to the minor. The third of this chord is called the *Picardy third.*

The most common borrowed chords in major are the diminished supertonic, the diminished-minor supertonic seventh chord, the minor subdominant, the major submediant (on the lowered sixth scale degree), and the diminished seventh chord on the leading tone.

The use of borrowed chords results in an exchange in quality between major and minor which is referred to as *modal mixture.*

(No response.)

■

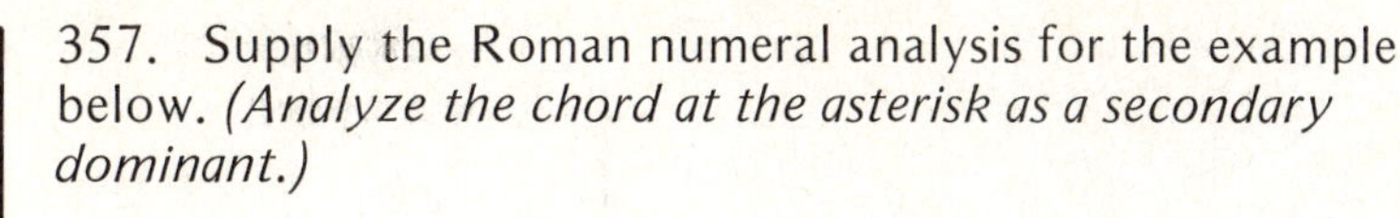
357. Supply the Roman numeral analysis for the example below. *(Analyze the chord at the asterisk as a secondary dominant.)*

Bach, Chorale: *Herzliebster Jesu, was hast du verbrochen*

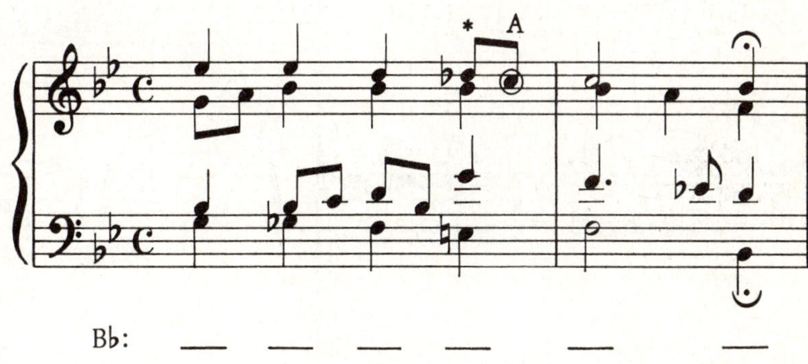

---

borrowed

358. The second chord in the preceding frame is not diatonic in the key of B-flat major. It is called a ____________ chord.

■

359. Supply the Roman numeral analysis for the example below:

Schubert, *Das Wirtshaus*

360. Complete the Roman numeral analysis for the example below:

Mozart, *Sonata,* K. 330

361. Supply the Roman numeral analysis for the example below:

Schubert, *Symphony No. 5,* in B-flat major

Deceptive.

362. What type of cadence is illustrated in the preceding frame? ______________

363. The altered submediant triad (♭VI) produces an especially colorful effect when used in a deceptive cadence. Another example is shown below:

Bach, Chorale: *Vater unser im Himmelreich*

Why is it necessary to double the third in the altered submediant triad (at the asterisk)? ______________________

____

To avoid an augmented 2nd (E-D♭) in the alto.

364. The borrowed submediant and subdominant triads produce colorful effects in the example below:

Brahms, *Symphony No. 3,* Op. 90

Supply the Roman numeral analysis for the above example.

■ 365. Supply the Roman numeral analysis for the example below:

Brahms, *Ballade,* Op. 10, No. 4

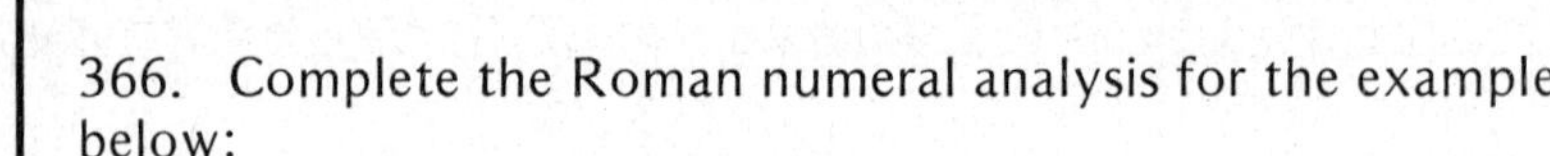

■ 366. Complete the Roman numeral analysis for the example below:

Chopin, *Ballade,* Op. 52

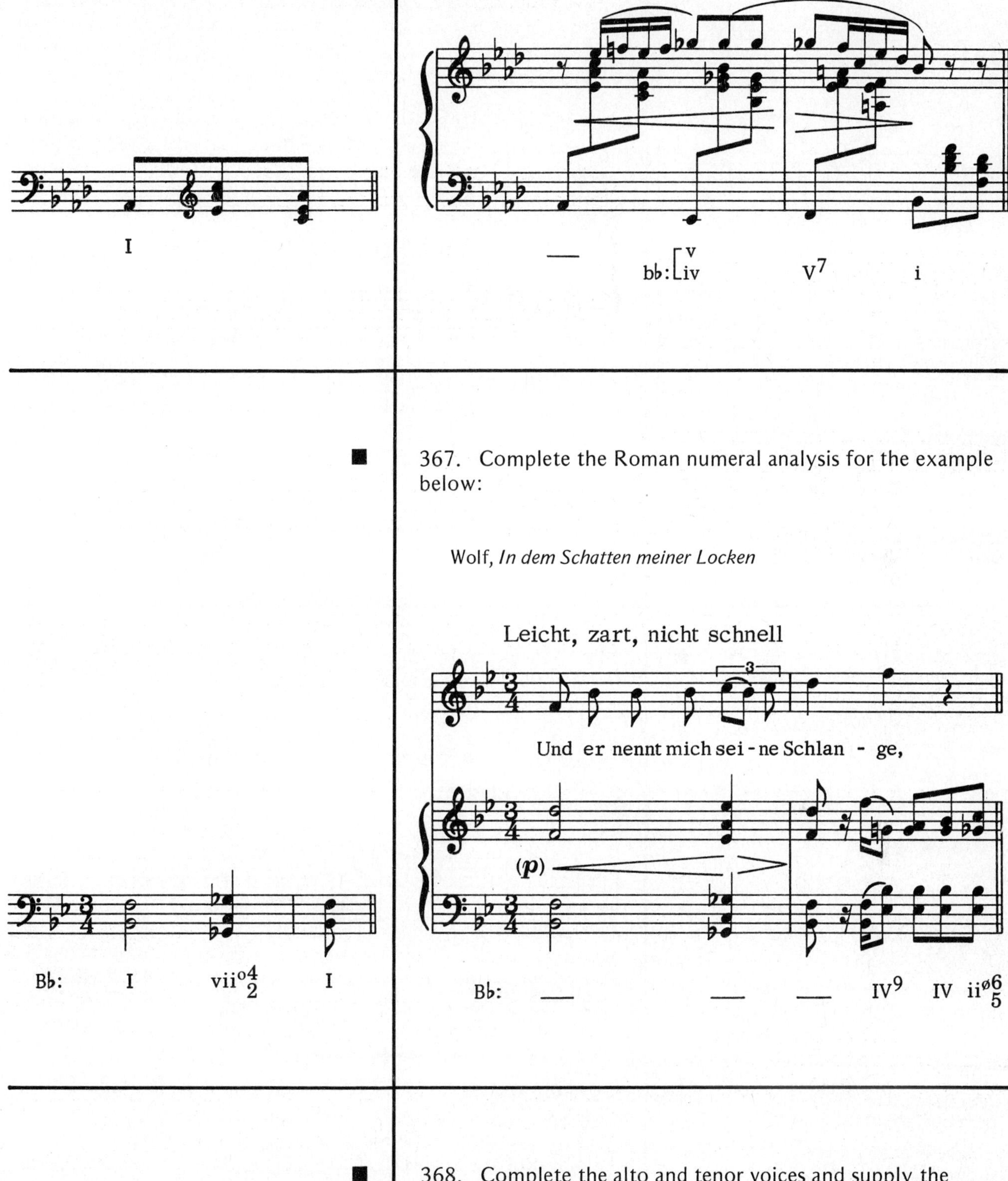

■ 367. Complete the Roman numeral analysis for the example below:

Wolf, *In dem Schatten meiner Locken*

■ 368. Complete the alto and tenor voices and supply the Roman numeral analysis on the following page. *(Analyze two chords at the asterisk.)*

Bach, Chorale: *Herr, ich habe missgehandelt*

(1) 1
(2) 3

■ 369. The example below contains two altered chords. Indicate (by number) which chord is a secondary dominant and which is a borrowed chord.

Mozart, *Sonata,* K. 576

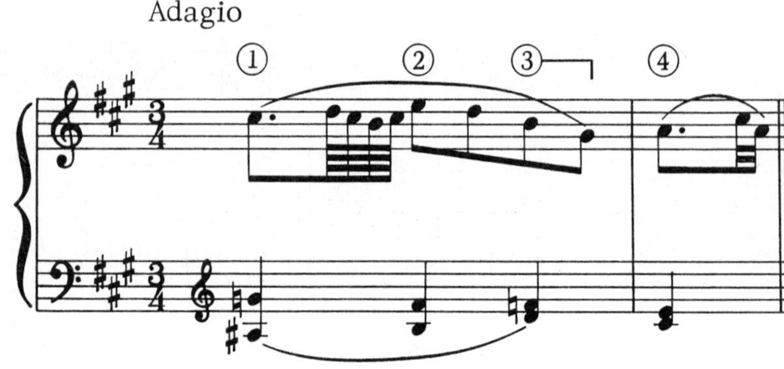

(1) Secondary dominant ______
(2) Borrowed chord ______

Chord 1: $vii^{\circ 7}/ii$

Chord 3: $vii^{\circ 4}_{3}$

370. Write the proper Roman numeral for each of the altered chords in the preceding frame.

Chord 1: ____________________

Chord 3: ____________________

5th.

371. Chord 1 in Frame 369 is an incomplete seventh chord. Which member of the chord is omitted? (Root/3rd/5th/7th)

____

True.

372. Chords 1 and 3 in Frame 369 are both diminished seventh chords. (True/False) __________

---

second

373. Chord 1 in Frame 369 is in root position; chord 3 is in ______________ inversion.

■

C: I IV I

♭VII I iv I

374. Complete the Roman numeral analysis for the example below:

Brahms, *Symphony No. 1,* Op. 68

Allegro

① ② ③ ④ ⑤ ⑥ ⑦

ff

ff

ff

C: ___ ___ ___ ♭VII ___ ___ ___

4 and 6.

375. List (by number) the chords in the preceding frame which are not diatonic in the key of C major. ________________

---

natural *(or pure)*

376. Chord 4 in Frame 374 is called the *subtonic* triad. It uses tones of the ____________ minor scale.

C: I $\quad$ V^6_5

V^4_2/iv $\quad$ iv^6 $\quad$ i^6_4

V^6_5/V $\quad$ V

■ 377. An occasional borrowed chord in major results in only a fleeting sensation of the minor mode. Several used in succession, however, cause a more definite change of mode.

Supply the Roman numeral analysis for the example below:

Mozart, *Mass in C Major,* K. 317

Andante maestoso

f p Ky-ri-e, *f p* Ky-ri-e, *f p* Ky-ri-e,

C: ___ ___ ___

f Ky - ri - e e - le - i - son.

___ ___ ___ ___

---

change (of) mode

378. Change of mode must not be confused with modulation. Whereas modulation involves a change of key center from one pitch to another, change of mode is merely a change from major to minor (or the reverse) *with the same tonal center retained.*

Change from a major key to its *relative minor* is a modulation because a new key center is established; but change from a major key to its *parallel minor* is called ____________ of ____________.

---

379. The frequent use of borrowed chords and change of mode sometimes results in passages which are ambiguous as to mode.

Nielsen, *Sinfonia Espansiva,* Op. 27

The first part of this passage contains chords of both A major and minor. The key of D minor established in the fourth measure is less ambiguous, but notice the use of F-sharp in the next-to-the-last measure. Such blending together of the major and minor modes is an important feature of much late nineteenth-century music.

Does the frequent use of borrowed chords result in ambiguity of tonality? ______

(Ambiguity of modality, yes; but not necessarily tonality.)

For greater tonal variety or color.

380. Borrowed chords have the same harmonic function as their unaltered counterparts. A subdominant triad, for example, tends to progress to the dominant, tonic, or supertonic chords regardless of whether it is major or minor in quality. Since the use of borrowed chords does not affect harmonic function, what is the reason for using them? ______________________

____

(c).

381. Which is the *least likely* chord (a, b, or c) to follow the altered supertonic seventh chord below? ______

(a) (b) (c)

A: $ii^{\o}{}^{6}_{5}$ V I^{6}_{4} IV

(b).

382. Which is the *most likely* chord (a, b, or c) to follow the altered leading tone seventh chord below? ______

(a) (b) (c)

B: $vii^{o}{}^{4}_{3}$ ii I^{6} iii

(a).
(Choice (b) produces a retrogression; choice (c) produces poor voice leading.)

383. Which is the *most likely* chord (a, b, or c) to precede the altered submediant chord below? ______

(a) (b) (c)

E♭: V^7 ii^6 V^6 ♭VI

(b).
(vii^{o7}-iv is a retrogression.)

384. Which is the *least likely* chord (a, b, or c) to precede the altered subdominant chord below? ______

(a) (b) (c)

G: IV vii^{o6}_{5} I^6 iv

(1) √

385. Check (√) the correct option:

1. Most borrowed chords occur in major keys.
2. Borrowed chords are taken from the relative minor (or major) key.

True statements:
(1) ______ (2) ______ Both ______ Neither ______

Both √

386. Check (√) the correct option:

1. Borrowed chords sometimes result in modal ambiguity.
2. Borrowed chords have the same harmonic function as their unaltered counterparts.

True statements:
(1) ______ (2) ______ Both ______ Neither ______

SUMMARY

Altered chords result from the use of tones which are not included in the diatonic scale. Whereas alterations which produce secondary dominants often change or intensify the function of a chord, those which produce borrowed chords do not. Borrowed chords tend to progress in the same way as their unaltered counterparts. They are used to introduce greater tonal variety than is contained solely in the diatonic scale.

Borrowed chords are "borrowed" from the *parallel* major or minor key. The result is a mixture of major and minor modes. Most borrowed chords occur in major. Few occur in minor because ample chord variety is provided by the alternate notes of the melodic minor scale. Only one borrowed chord occurs prominently in minor: the major tonic (by use of the Picardy third), mostly at cadences.

The chief (or commonly utilized) borrowed chords which occur in major are as follows (other borrowed chords could be found in music literature but would probably be considered rare occurances):

BORROWED CHORDS IN MAJOR

Mastery Frames

C minor (340)

5-1. Borrowed chords that appear in the key of C major are taken from the key of ______________.

---

first (354, 356)

5-2. The Picardy third produces a major triad on the ______________ scale degree in a minor key.

---

(1) (2) (3)

g: I D: ♭VI A: i

(4) (5) (6)

a: ♯vi F: vii^{o7} G: ♭III^{+}

(343-353)

5-3. Supply the chord symbol for each chord below.

(1) (2) (3)

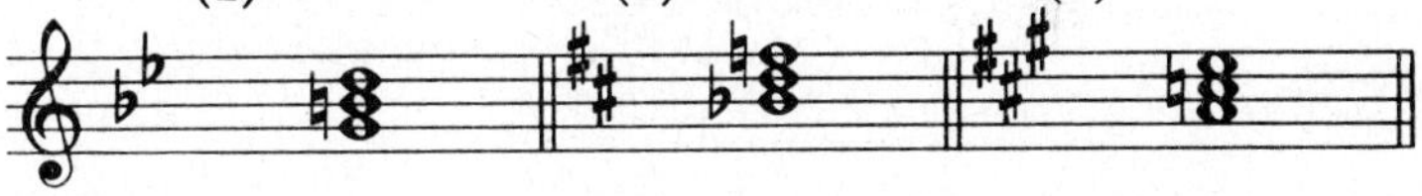

g: __ D: __ A: __

(4) (5) (6)

a: __ F: __ G: __

---

(1) (2) (3)

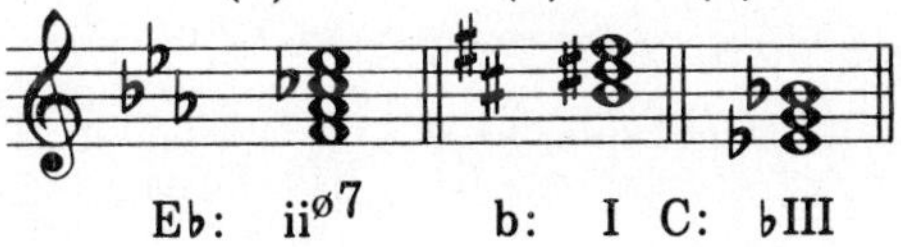

E♭: ii^{ø7} b: I C: ♭III

(4) (5) (6)

E: iv^{7} F: vii^{o7} B♭: ♭VI

(343-353)

5-4. Supply the chord symbol for each chord.

(1) (2) (3)

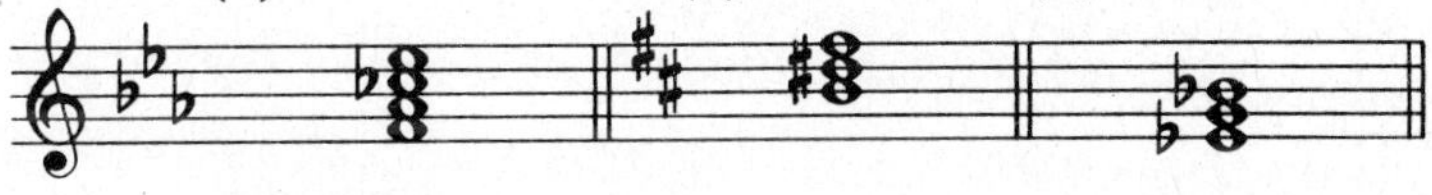

E♭: __ b: __ C: __

(4) (5) (6)

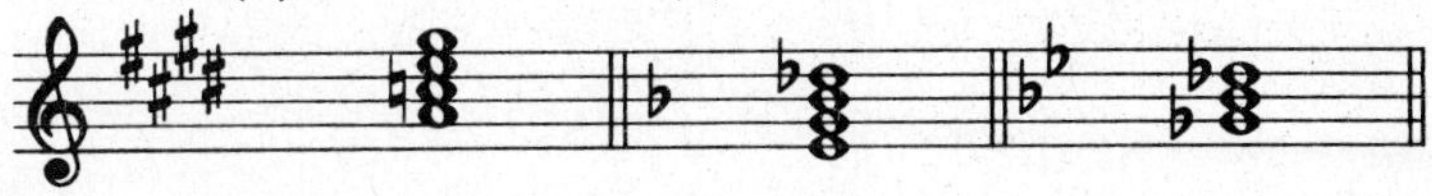

E: __ F: __ B♭: __

Answer	Ref.	Frame
False.	(377-379)	5-5. The term *change of mode* refers to modulation from a major key to its relative minor or the reverse. (True/False) ______________
True.	(380)	5-6. Borrowed chords have the same harmonic function as their unaltered counterparts. (True/False)______________

Supplementary Assignments

ASSIGNMENT 5-1 Name________________________

1. Write the chords indicated by the chord symbols.

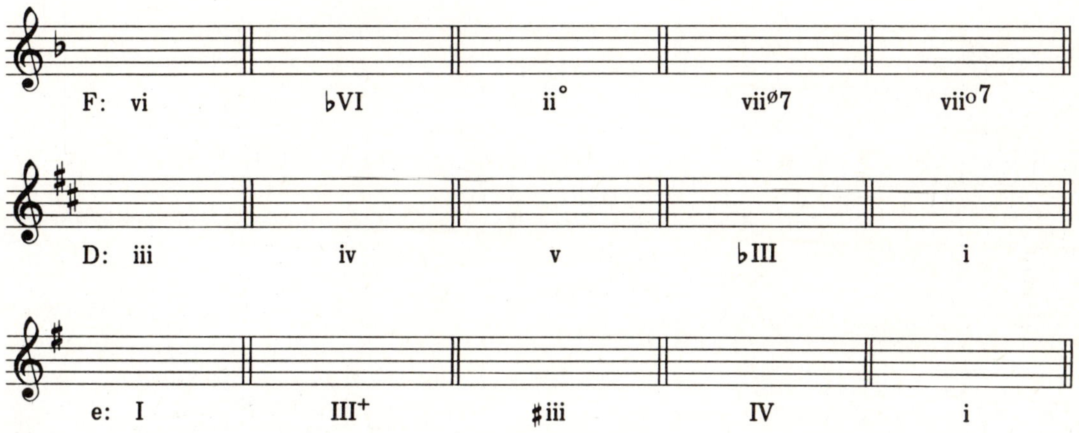

2. Which chords in question 1 are borrowed chords? ____________

3. Provide chord symbols for the chords below.

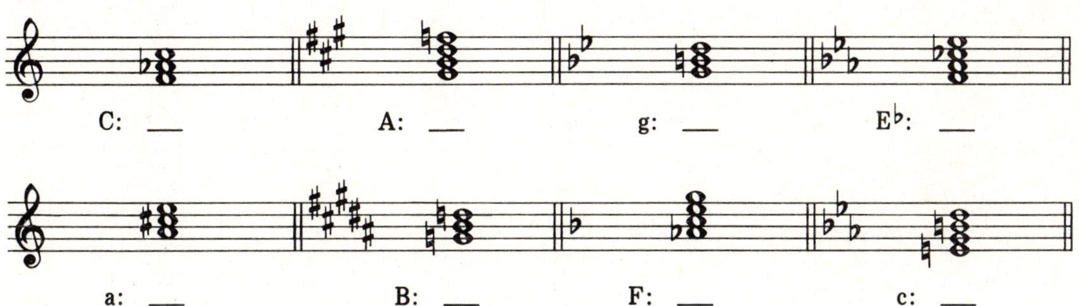

4. List (by chord symbol) the more common borrowed chords in major and minor keys.

Major: ________________________

Minor: ________________________

5. Which are borrowed chords? ____________

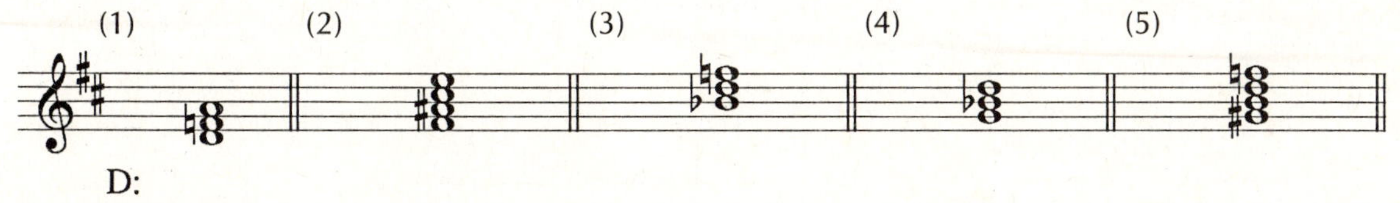

6. Which chord agrees with the chord symbol? __________

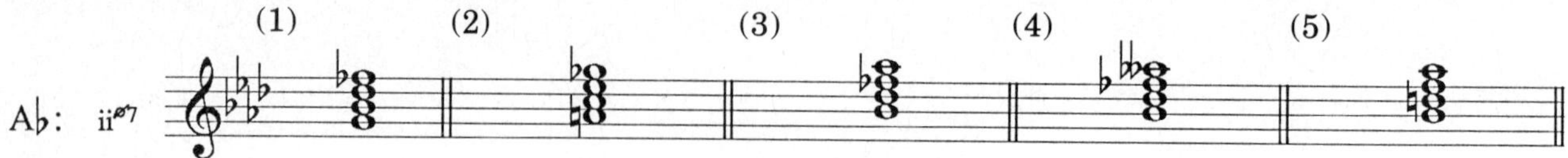

7. Which chord symbol is correct? __________

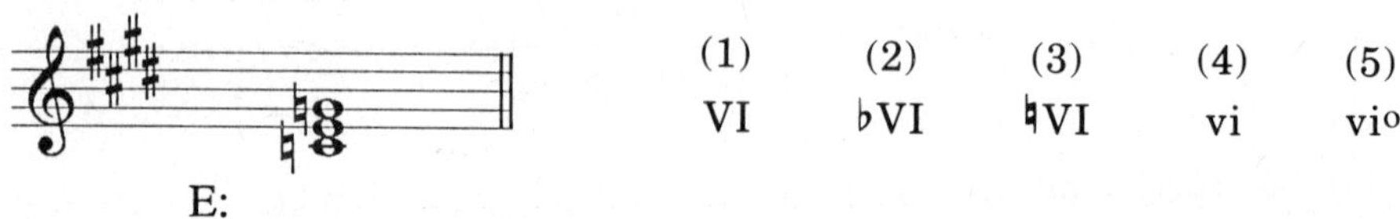

8. Which chord symbol is correct? __________

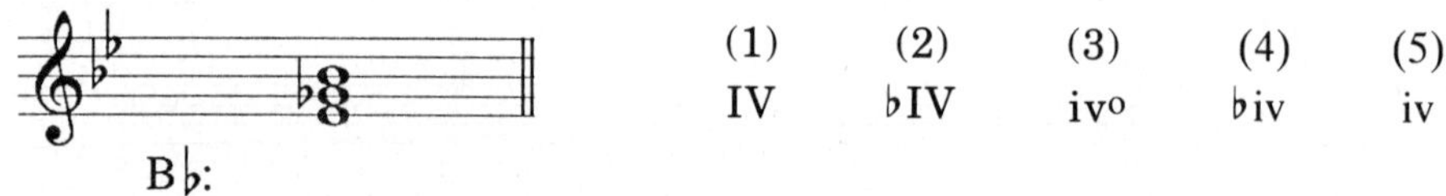

9. Provide chord symbols for the example below.

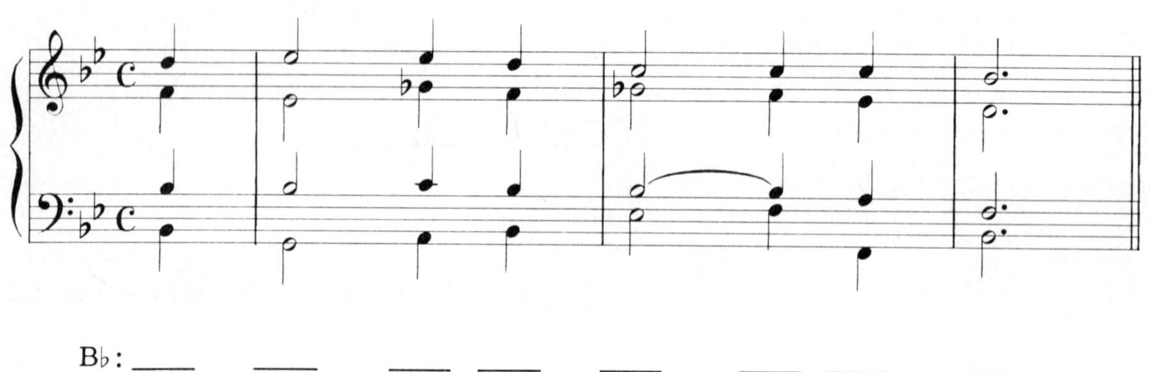

B♭: ____ ____ ____ ____ ____ ____ ____ ____

10. Provide the harmonic analysis for the example below.

Beethoven: *Sonata*, Op. 31, No. 1

G: ____ ____ ____ ____ ____ ____ ____ ____ ____ ____

ASSIGNMENT 5-2 Name____________________

1. Provide the harmonic analysis for the example below. Indicate, also, the nonharmonic tones.

Chopin: *Mazurka*, Op. 7, No. 4

2. Chords appear over a pedal in the example below. Provide the harmonic analysis. Take into account the nonharmonic tones.

Brahms: *Vier Ernste Gesänge*, No. 2 (voice omitted)

3. Harmonize the two melodies below in four-voice chorale style, using borrowed chords at the asterisks.

4. Supply the chord symbols for the examples below:

5. Complete other analyses or create short compositions involving borrowed chords, as directed by your instructor or tutor.

chapter six

Augmented Sixth Chords

The term "augmented sixth chord" derives from the interval of an augmented sixth which occurs between the bass and an upper voice when these chords are in their most common position. Although, like triads and seventh chords, the notes of augmented sixth chords can be arranged in thirds, chromatic alteration is so extensive that the written root surrenders its influence to another tone which functions as the actual or sounding root. For this reason augmented sixth chords are approached as unique sonorities containing a variety of intervals.

387. Each of the chords below contains the interval of an augmented sixth. Show with a bracket ([ ) the tones which produce this interval.

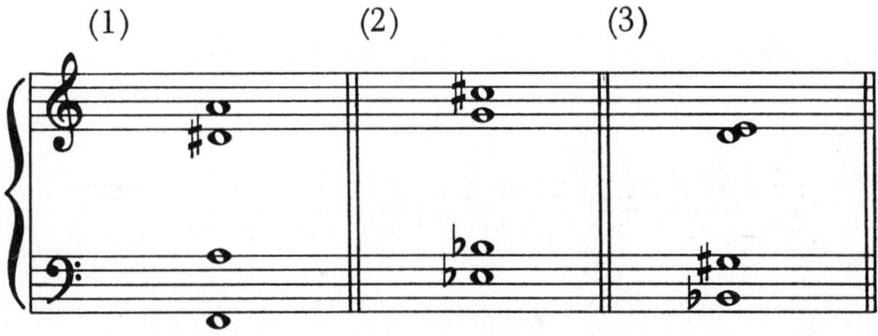

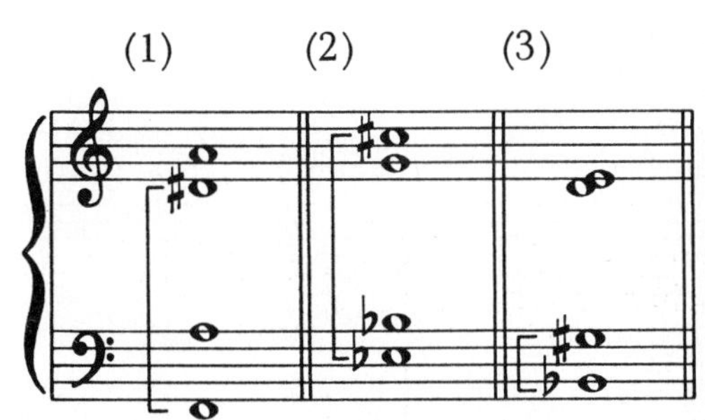

388. There are three commonly used types of augmented sixth chords, and the terms ITALIAN SIXTH, GERMAN SIXTH, and FRENCH SIXTH are used to identify them. Although the origin of these terms is unknown and their relevance is questionable, their use is so widespread that it is pointless not to avail ourselves of them.

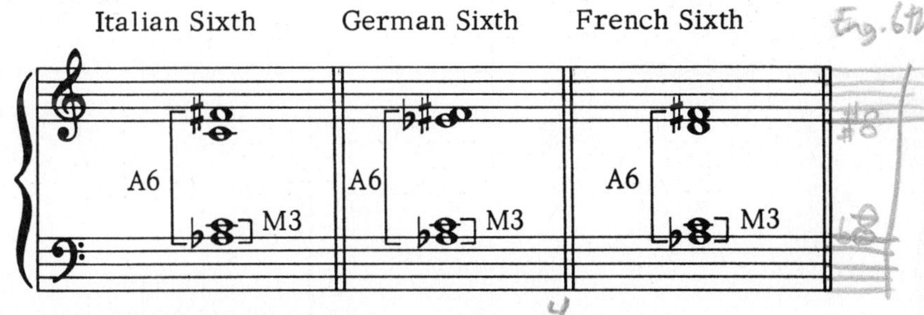

The example above shows that all three types of augmented sixth chords have two intervals in common: an augmented sixth, and a ____________________.

major third

(1) (2) (3) (4)

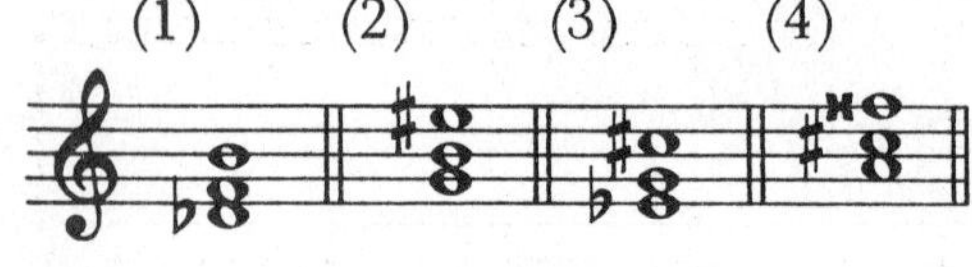

389. Each of the three types of augmented sixth chords contains the intervals of an augmented sixth and a major third above the lowest note.

Write these two intervals above each note.

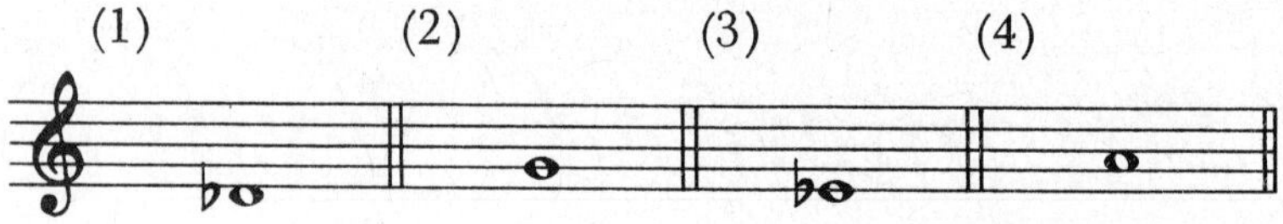

(1) (2) (3) (4)

(1) (2) (3) (4)

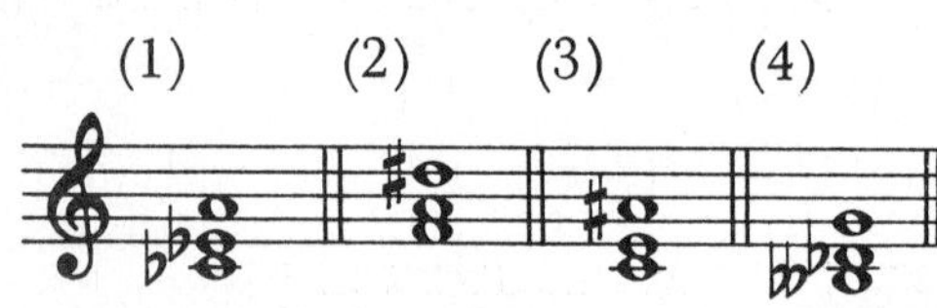

390. Write the intervals of an augmented sixth and a major third above each note.

(1) (2) (3) (4)

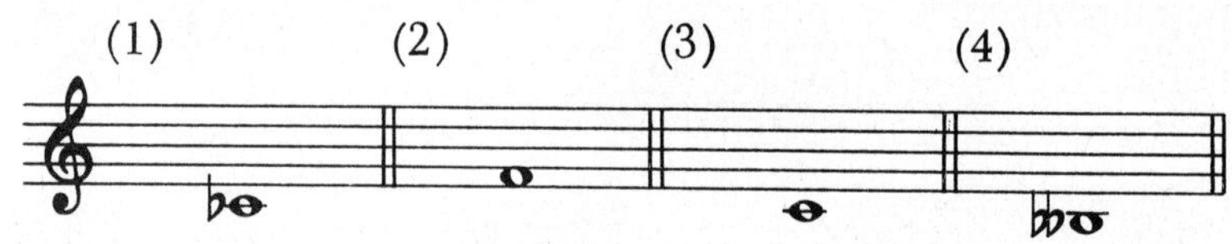

(1) (2) (3) (4)

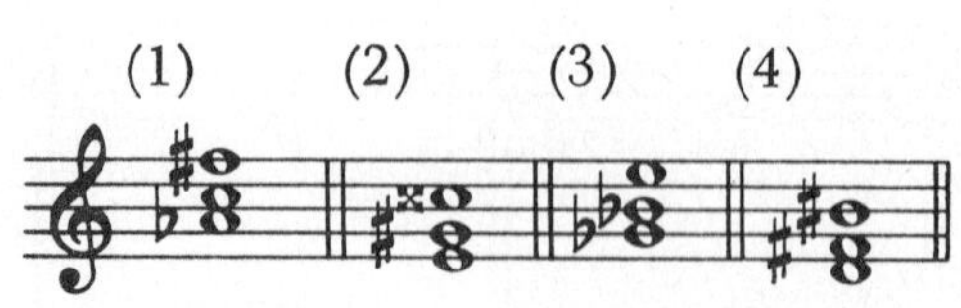

391. Continue as in the preceding frame.

(1) (2) (3) (4)

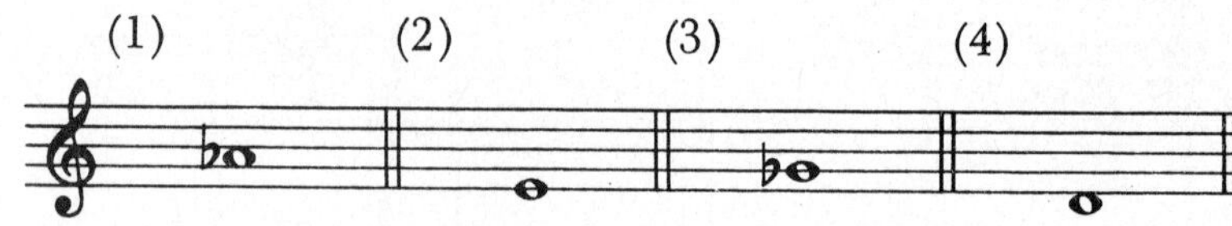

392. In the ITALIAN SIXTH chord, the major third above the bass is doubled by the fourth voice.

three

The Italian sixth is actually a chord of only ________ separate tones, one of which is doubled by the fourth voice. (Note that the altered tones are not doubled.)

(1) (2) (3)

393. Write the fourth voice in each of the *Italian sixth* chords below:

(1) (2) (3)

---

(1) (2)

or

394. Write the alto and tenor voices in accordance with the figured bass symbols.

(1) (2)

6 3 3   6 3 3

Yes.

395. Are both of the chords in the preceding frame Italian sixth chords? ______

---

(1) (2)

or   or

396. Write the alto and tenor voices in accordance with the figured bass symbols.

(1) (2)

6 3 3   6 3 3

The third above the bass.

397. Italian sixth chords consist of the following intervals above the bass: an augmented sixth and a major third. In four-part writing which tone is doubled? ____________

(a).

398. Since the interval of an augmented sixth is enharmonic with a minor seventh, the Italian sixth chord may sometimes have the same aural effect as a major-minor seventh chord *with the fifth omitted,* depending upon the particular context of a musical passage.

(a) (b)

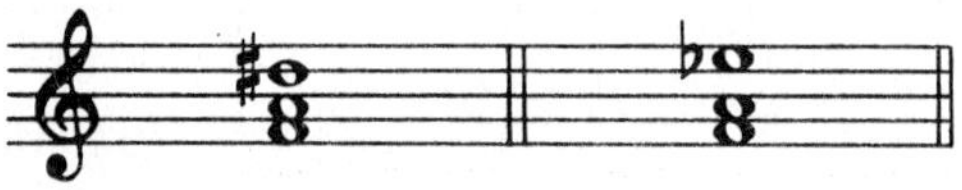

The two chords above sound the same. Which is notated as an Italian sixth chord? ______

(1) (2)

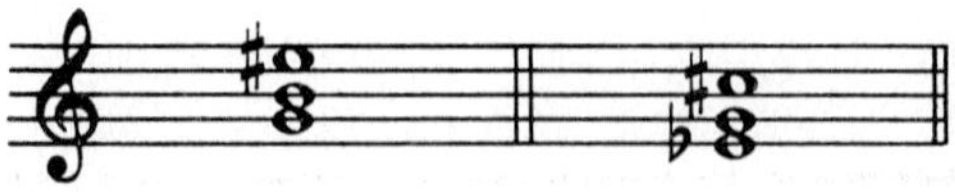

399. So, you may wish to avail yourself of the similarity between the major-minor seventh chord and the Italian sixth chord to assist in spelling the latter. To spell an Italian sixth chord, think first of a major-minor seventh chord; then omit the fifth and spell the seventh enharmonically as an augmented sixth.

Use this method to convert the major-minor seventh chords below into *Italian sixth* chords.

(1) (2)

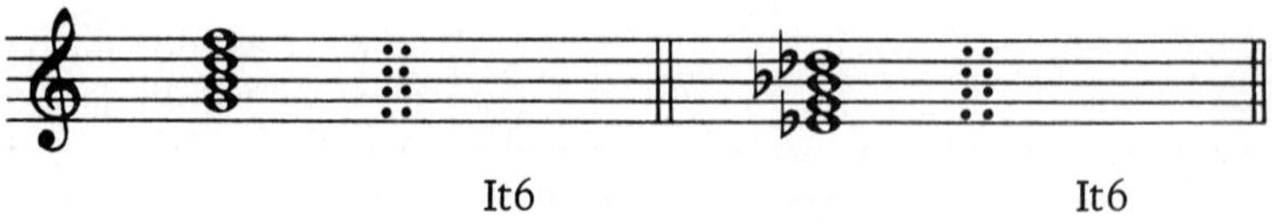

It6 It6

(1) (2)

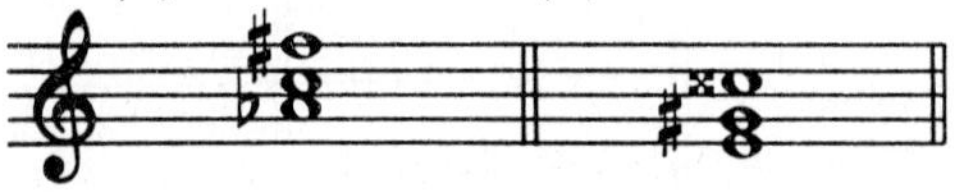

400. Continue as in the preceding frame.

(1) (2)

It6 It6

False.
(Chord (c) is not.)

401. All of the chords on the following page are Italian sixth chords. (True/False) __________

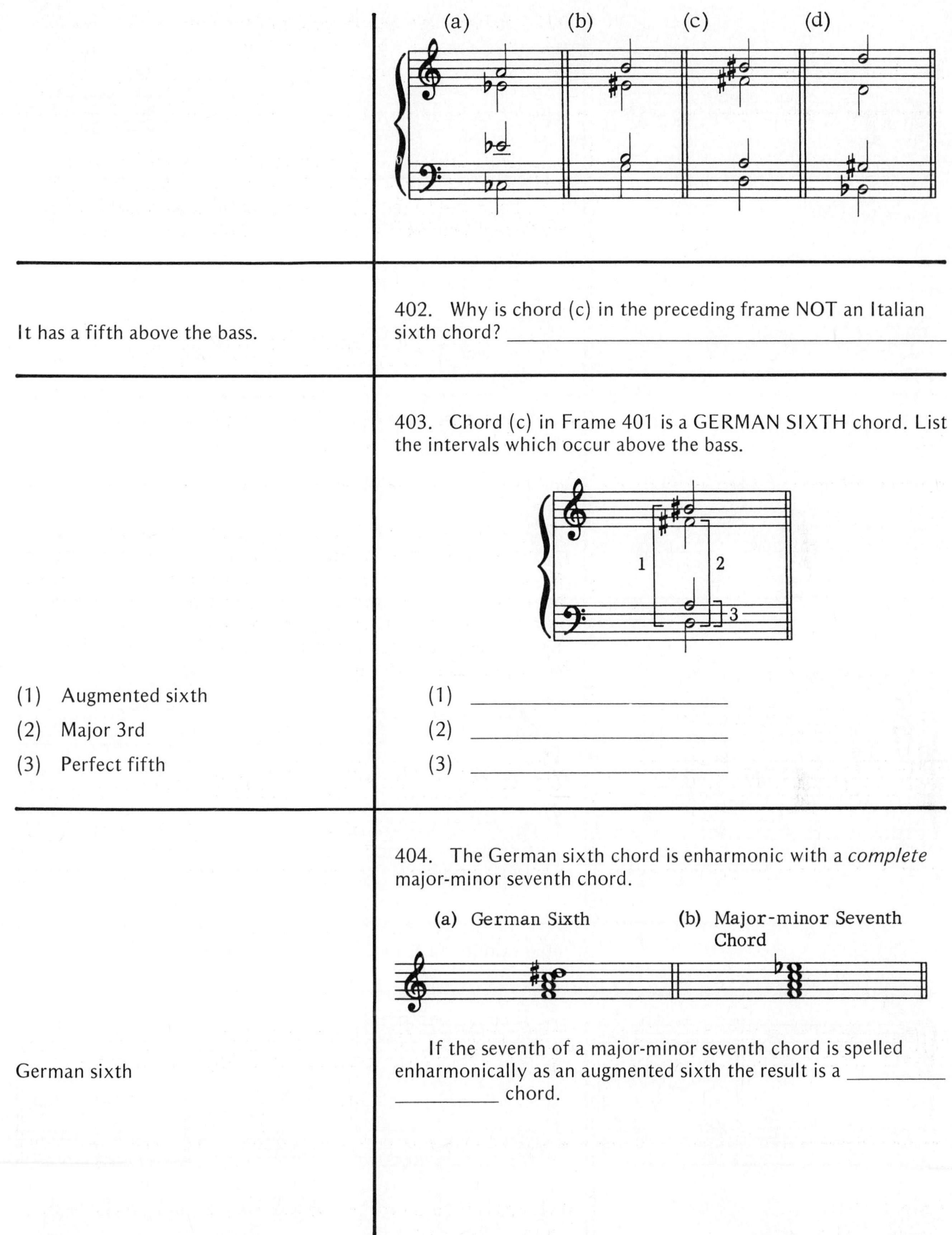

It has a fifth above the bass.

402. Why is chord (c) in the preceding frame NOT an Italian sixth chord? ______________________

403. Chord (c) in Frame 401 is a GERMAN SIXTH chord. List the intervals which occur above the bass.

(1) Augmented sixth
(2) Major 3rd
(3) Perfect fifth

(1) ______________
(2) ______________
(3) ______________

404. The German sixth chord is enharmonic with a *complete* major-minor seventh chord.

German sixth

If the seventh of a major-minor seventh chord is spelled enharmonically as an augmented sixth the result is a __________ __________ chord.

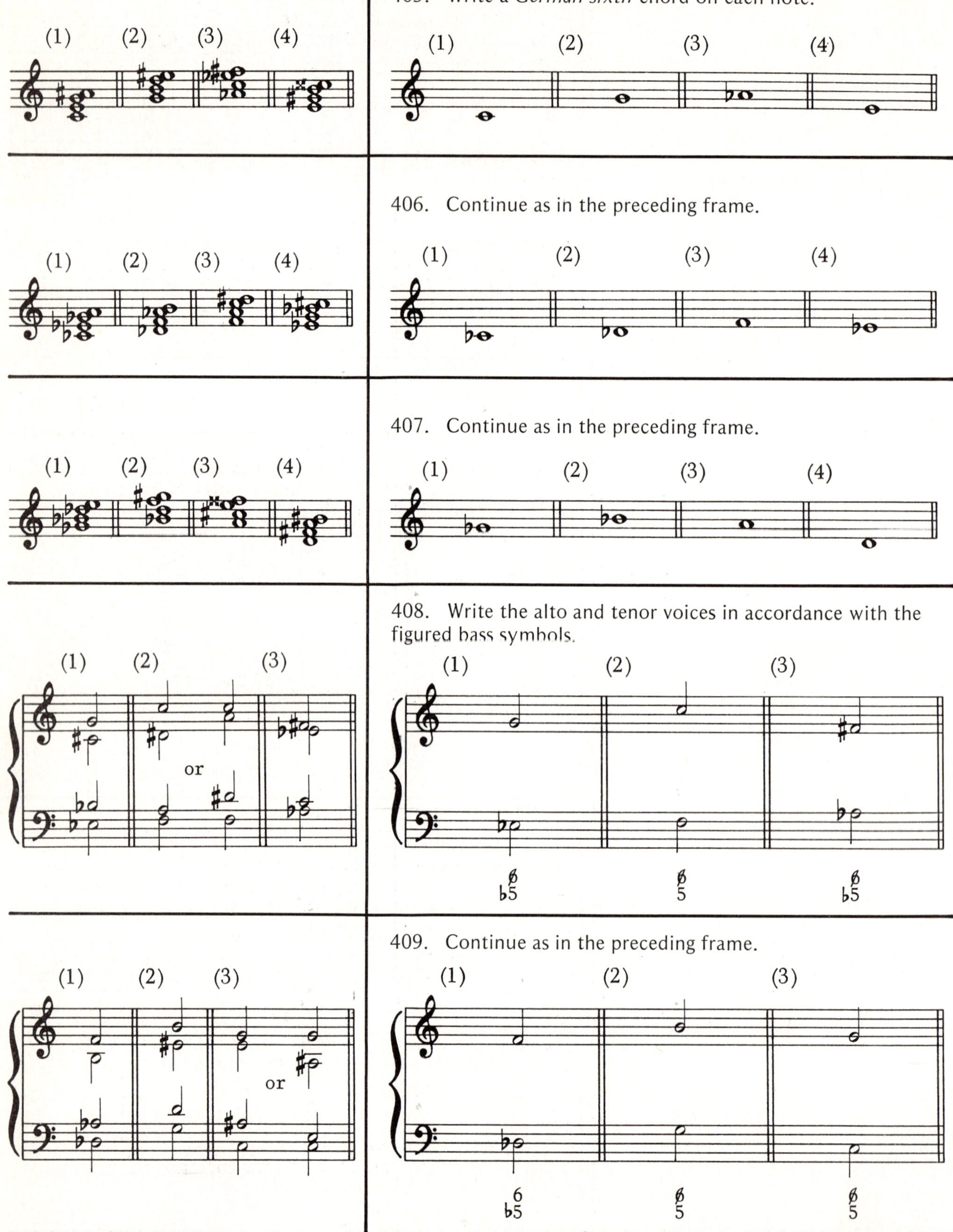
(1) (2) (3) (4)
405. Write a *German sixth* chord on each note.
(1) (2) (3) (4)
(1) (2) (3) (4)
406. Continue as in the preceding frame.
(1) (2) (3) (4)
(1) (2) (3) (4)
407. Continue as in the preceding frame.
(1) (2) (3) (4)
(1) (2) (3)
or
408. Write the alto and tenor voices in accordance with the figured bass symbols.
(1) (2) (3)
6̸ ♭5
6̸ 5
6̸ ♭5
(1) (2) (3)
or
409. Continue as in the preceding frame.
(1) (2) (3)
6 ♭5
6̸ 5
6̸ 5

6 (and) 5

410. The figured bass symbol which represents the Italian sixth chord includes the numbers 6 and 3; the symbol which represents the German sixth chord includes the numbers ______ and ______.

---

(1) (b), (d)
(2) (a), (c), (f)
(3) (e)

411. List each chord according to the categories provided below:

(a) (b) (c) (d) (e) (f)

(1) Italian sixth __________
(2) German sixth __________
(3) Neither of these __________

---

(1) Augmented 6th
(2) Major 3rd
(3) Augmented 4th

412. Chord (e) in the preceding frame is a FRENCH SIXTH chord. List the intervals which occur above the bass. *(Be specific.)*

1 2 3

(1) ____________________
(2) ____________________
(3) ____________________

False.
(See next frame.)

413. The FRENCH SIXTH CHORD contains an augmented sixth, a major third, and an augmented fourth above the bass.
The chords below are all French sixth chords. *(Check each interval before responding.)* (True/False) __________

(a) (b) (c) (d) (e)

(d) Italian sixth
(e) German sixth

414. Chords (d) and (e) in the preceding frame are not French sixth chords. Chord (d) is a(n) ________________ chord and chord (e) is a(n) ________________ chord.

415. Write a *French sixth* chord on each note.

416. Continue as in the preceding frame.

417. Continue as in the preceding frame.

418. Write the alto and tenor voices in accordance with the figured bass symbols.

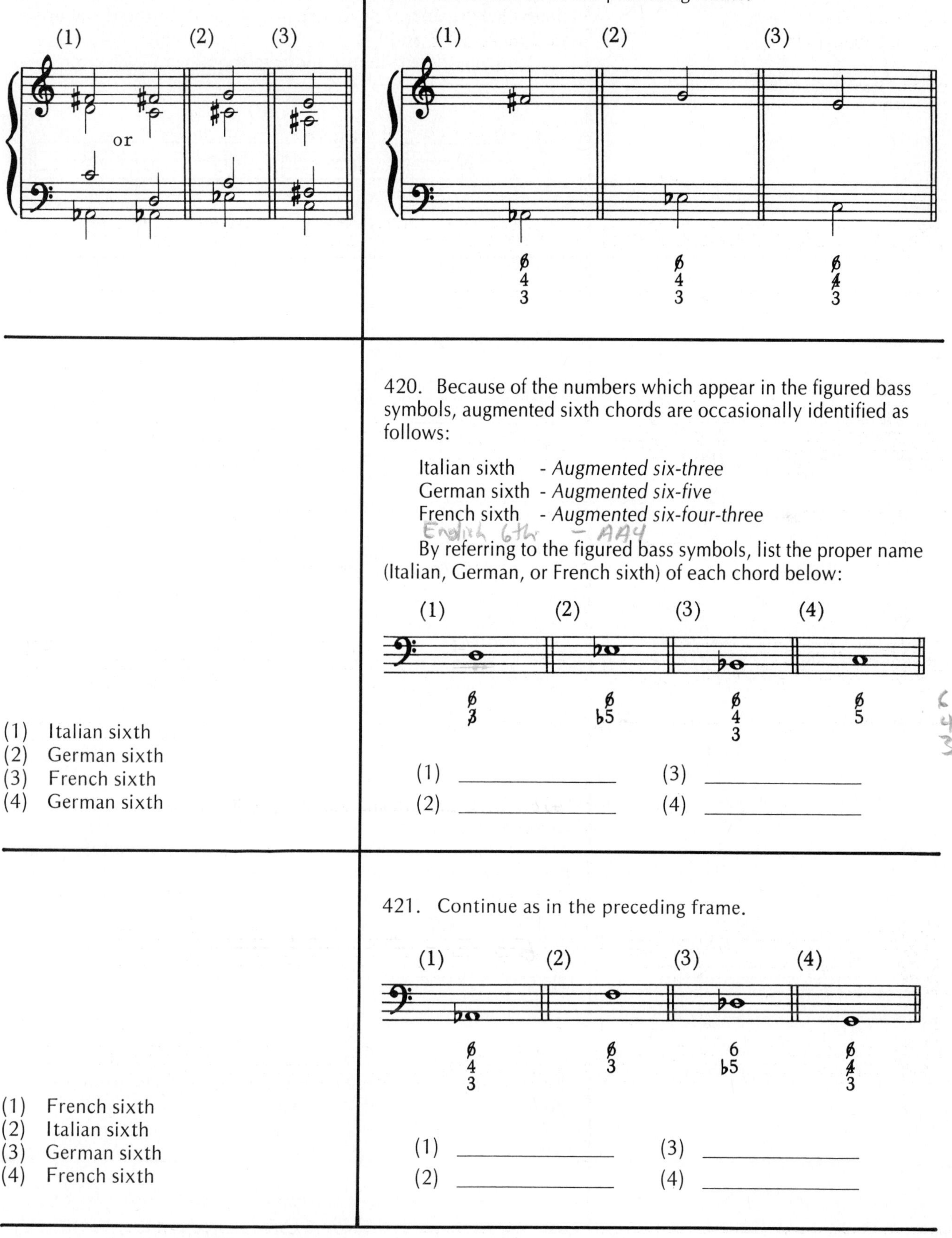

(1) (2) (3)

or

419. Continue as in the preceding frame.

(1) (2) (3)

---

(1) Italian sixth
(2) German sixth
(3) French sixth
(4) German sixth

420. Because of the numbers which appear in the figured bass symbols, augmented sixth chords are occasionally identified as follows:

Italian sixth - *Augmented six-three*
German sixth - *Augmented six-five*
French sixth - *Augmented six-four-three*

By referring to the figured bass symbols, list the proper name (Italian, German, or French sixth) of each chord below:

(1) (2) (3) (4)

(1) ______________ (3) ______________
(2) ______________ (4) ______________

---

(1) French sixth
(2) Italian sixth
(3) German sixth
(4) French sixth

421. Continue as in the preceding frame.

(1) (2) (3) (4)

(1) ______________ (3) ______________
(2) ______________ (4) ______________

422. We shall continue to identify augmented sixth chords by their proper names. For the purpose of analysis use the abbreviations It^6, G^6, and F^6.

Utilizing these symbols, indicate the type of each chord.

(1) ___ (2) ___ (3) ___ (4) ___

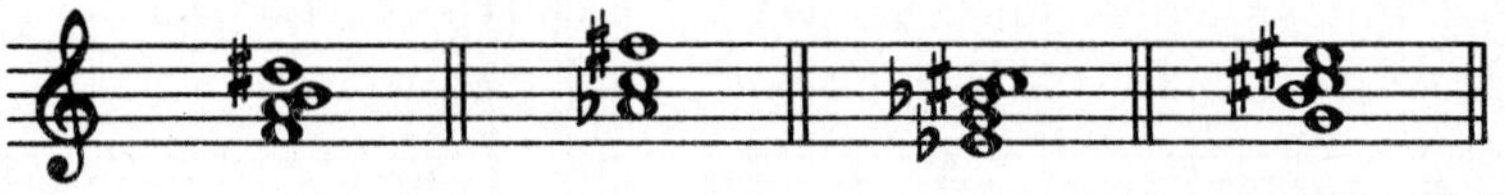

(1) F^6
(2) It^6
(3) G^6
(4) F^6

---

423. Continue as in the preceding frame.

(1) ___ (2) ___ (3) ___ (4) ___

(1) It^6
(2) G^6
(3) F^6
(4) G^6

---

424. The name augmented sixth chord derives from the interval of an augmented sixth which usually appears between the bass and an upper voice. These chords occur in other positions which cause the augmented sixth through inversion to become a diminished third.

The three types of augmented sixth chords are called Italian sixth, German sixth, and French sixth. The Italian sixth contains the intervals of an augmented sixth and a major third above the bass, and is enharmonic with a major-minor seventh chord with the fifth omitted. The German sixth contains the intervals of an augmented sixth, a major third, and a perfect fifth above the bass, and is enharmonic with a complete major-minor seventh chord. The French sixth has no counterpart in the diatonic chord vocabulary. Its tones could be derived from the whole-tone scale, and its aural effect is extremely colorful. The intervals which produce the French sixth are an augmented sixth, a major third, and an augmented fourth.

(No response.)

■ 425. You should now be able to spell and identify the various types of augmented sixth chords. Our task from this point will be to examine their use.

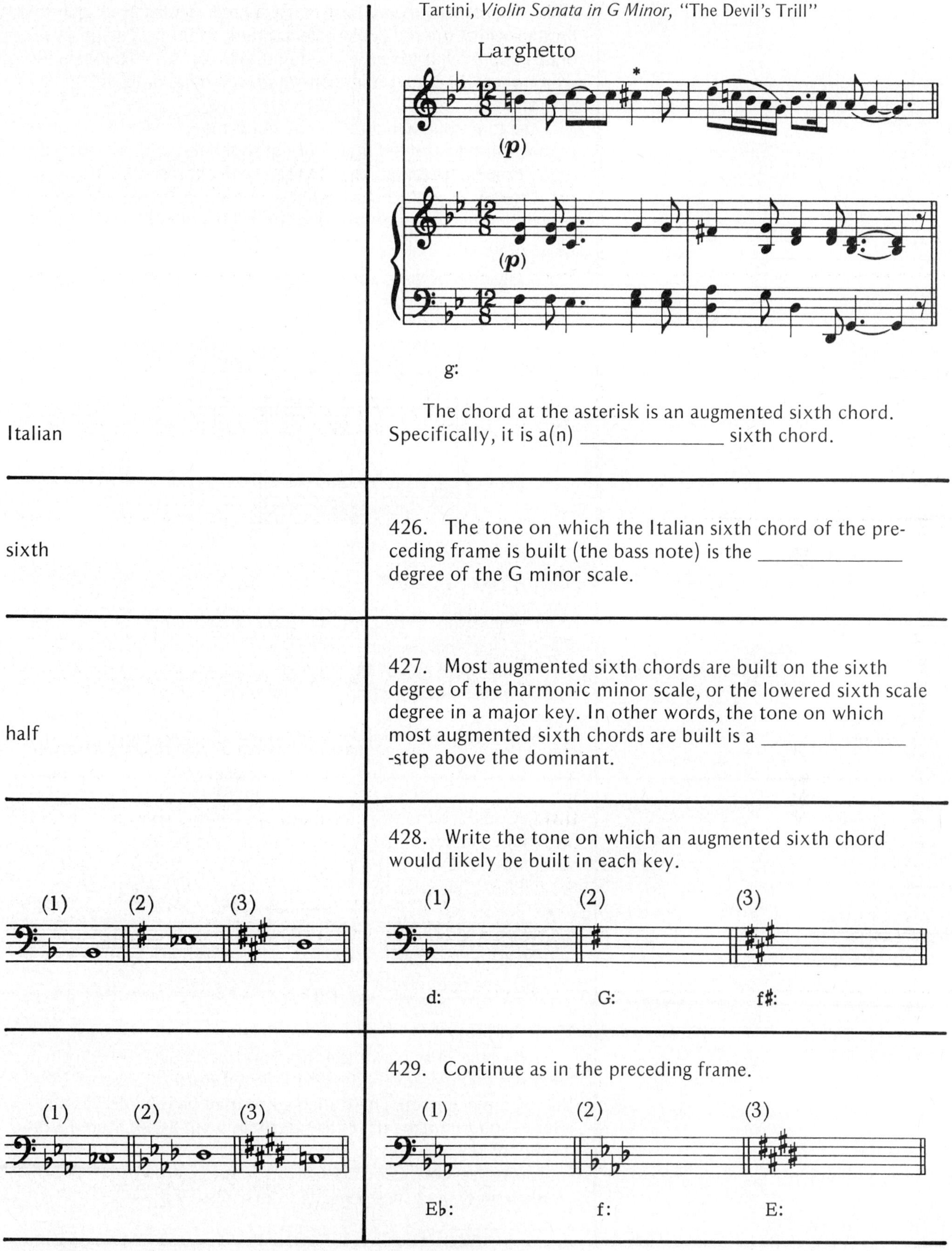

Tartini, *Violin Sonata in G Minor,* "The Devil's Trill"

Italian

The chord at the asterisk is an augmented sixth chord. Specifically, it is a(n) ____________ sixth chord.

---

sixth

426. The tone on which the Italian sixth chord of the preceding frame is built (the bass note) is the ____________ degree of the G minor scale.

---

half

427. Most augmented sixth chords are built on the sixth degree of the harmonic minor scale, or the lowered sixth scale degree in a major key. In other words, the tone on which most augmented sixth chords are built is a ____________ -step above the dominant.

---

428. Write the tone on which an augmented sixth chord would likely be built in each key.

---

429. Continue as in the preceding frame.

430. Augmented sixth chords have been presented as unique sonorities which are not constructed entirely of thirds. The purpose of this approach is to cause you to build these chords on the note which usually appears in the bass *and which has the aural effect of the root.*

The tones of augmented sixth chords may, in fact, be arranged in thirds; but the lowest note will not sound as the root, especially in the case of the Italian and German sixth chords.

The Italian sixth chord from the example in Frame 425 is shown with the notes arranged in thirds (a) and as it actually appears in the music (b).

(Play each of these chords at the piano.)

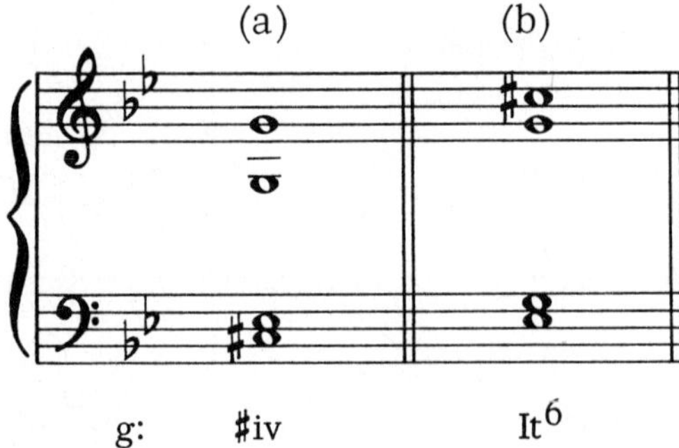

Comparison of the aural effect of the two chords above should make it clear that the note C-sharp does not sound like the root. The sounding root is E-flat, the note on which we consider the chord to be built. The chord symbol in (a) shows that the chord is an altered subdominant triad. The designation It^6 in (b), however, is the symbol which shall be used to identify this chord.

(No response.)

---

431. Compare the three types of augmented sixth chords which are arranged in thirds in the example below:

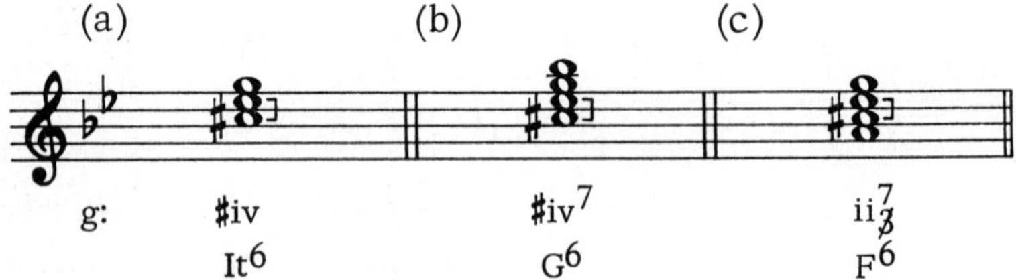

Arranged in this way the interval of the augmented sixth becomes through inversion a diminished third (bracketed in the example above). The Italian sixth may be regarded as an altered subdominant triad, the German sixth as an altered subdominant seventh chord, and the French sixth as an altered supertonic seventh chord. With this in mind, to what chord would you expect these chords to progress? To the ______________.

dominant *(or V)*

432. Augmented sixth chords (when built on the sixth degree of the harmonic minor scale, or the lowered sixth degree of the major scale) progress to the dominant triad or seventh chord or the tonic triad in a cadential six-four figure.

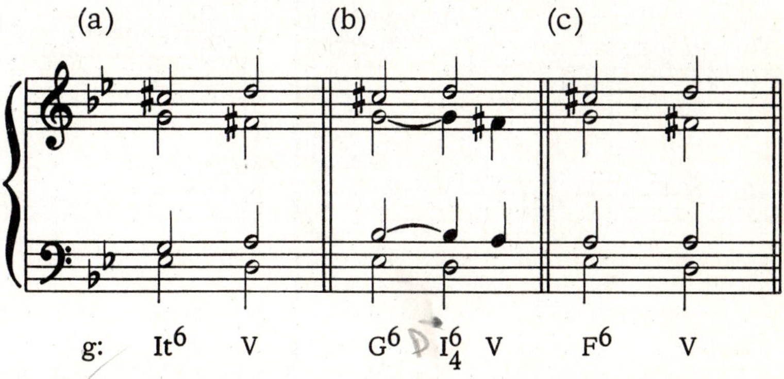

Because of their unusual color and highly active character, augmented sixth chords provide exceptional motivation to the dominant. They are used at points in musical form where this motivation is required. They often serve to focus attention on dominant harmony immediately prior to an important return of the tonic such as at the end of the development section in sonata form.

In each case above, the interval of an augmented sixth occurs between the ______________ and ______________ voices.

bass (and) soprano

---

433. Notice in the preceding frame that the interval of an augmented sixth expands outward to an octave.

This is the most characteristic feature in the resolution of augmented sixth chords. The remaining voices find their places in the following chord quite smoothly provided the augmented sixth resolves in this way.

The voices in the example above move by the interval of a ______________-step.

half

434. Complete the progression in each case. *(Be sure that the augmented sixth expands outward to an octave.)*

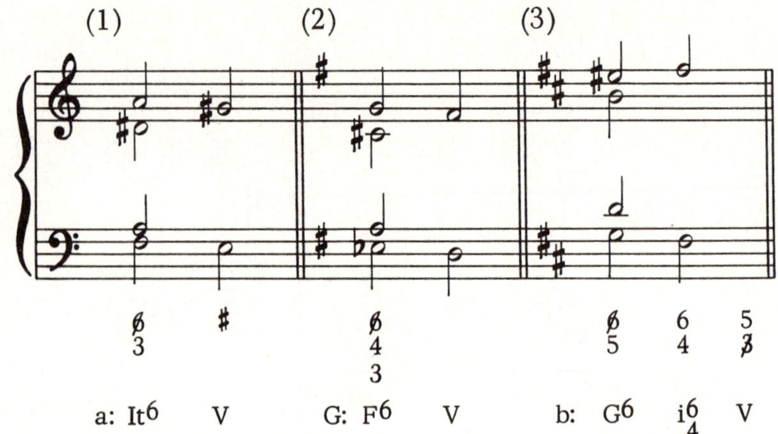

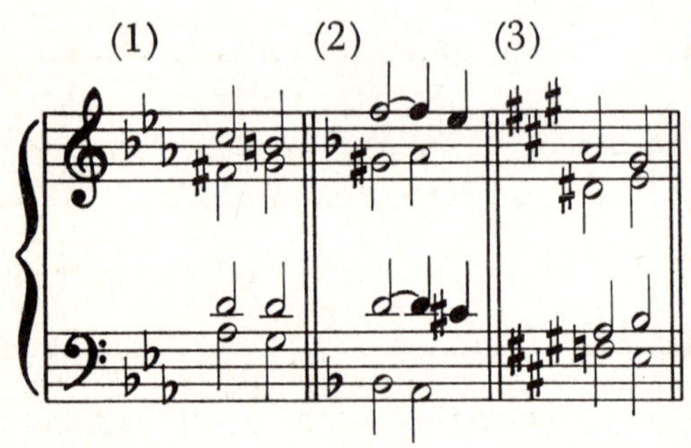

435. Continue as in the preceding frame.

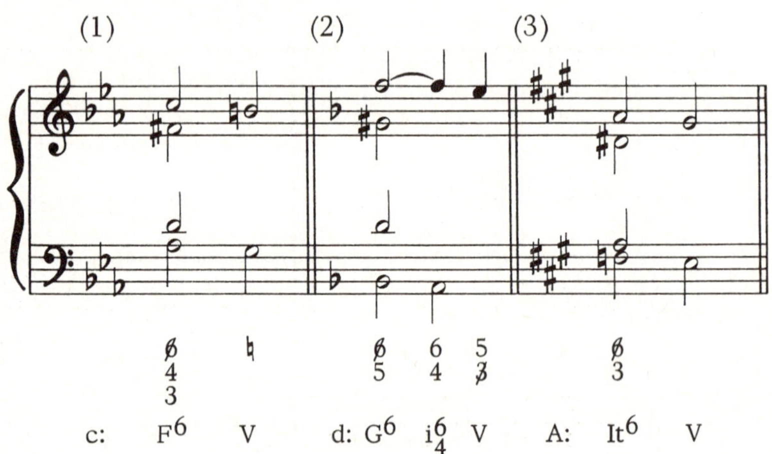

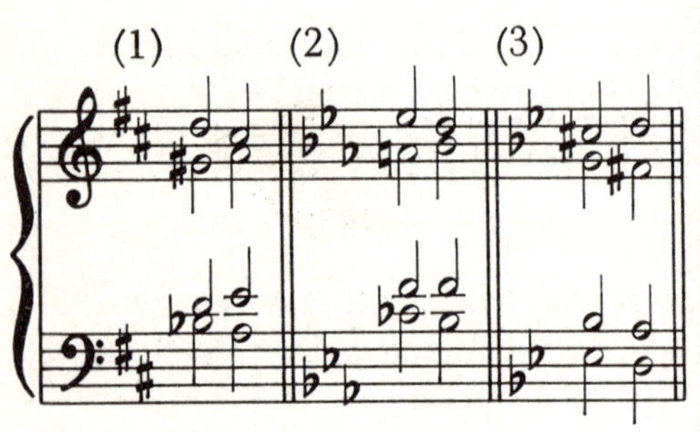

436. Continue as in the preceding frame.

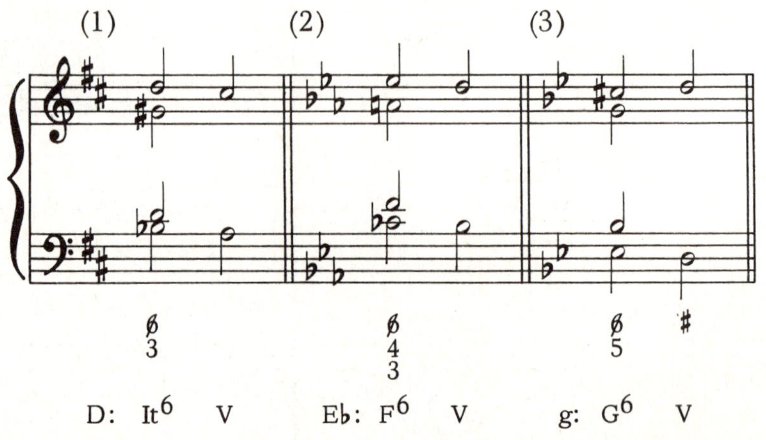

Parallel perfect fifths occur between the bass and the tenor.

437. What is the abnormality of part writing in the answer given for (3) of the preceding frame? ______________________

■

438. When the German sixth chord progresses directly to the dominant, parallel perfect fifths result. *These are not considered a mistake unless they occur between the bass and soprano voices.*

Draw lines between notes in the two chords at the asterisks to show the parallel fifths in the example below:

Chopin, *Nocturne*

■

439. Although parallel perfect fifths may occur when the German sixth chord progresses directly to the dominant, they are usually avoided or at least disguised by melodic movement.

Schubert, *Mass in G Major,* "Sanctus"

The chord at the asterisk is a German sixth chord. The melodic movement in the tenor from F-natural to D reduces the effect of parallel perfect fifths. Because of the melodic movement, the chord on the second beat (immediately following the asterisk) is an ______________ sixth chord.

Italian

440. For the sake of avoiding parallel perfect fifths, the German sixth chord often progresses first to the tonic triad in second inversion.

Mozart, *Sonata,* K. 284

Yes.

Does the interval of the augmented sixth resolve "normally" in the example above? ______

441. Complete the Roman numeral analysis for the following example:

Schubert, *Der Doppelgänger*

Sehr langsam

so man - che Nacht, in

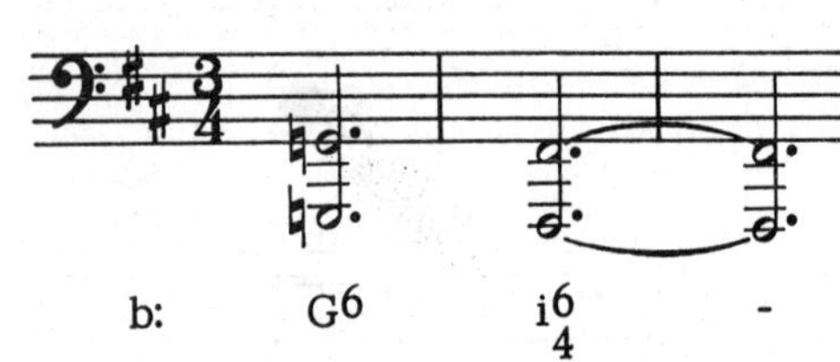

442. When the German sixth chord progresses to the tonic triad in second inversion in a major key, an alternate spelling is sometimes used.

Complete the Roman numeral analysis for the example below:

Schumann, *Dichterliebe*, Op. 48, No. 12

■ 443. The harmonic progression of the example in the preceding frame is shown in simplified form below:

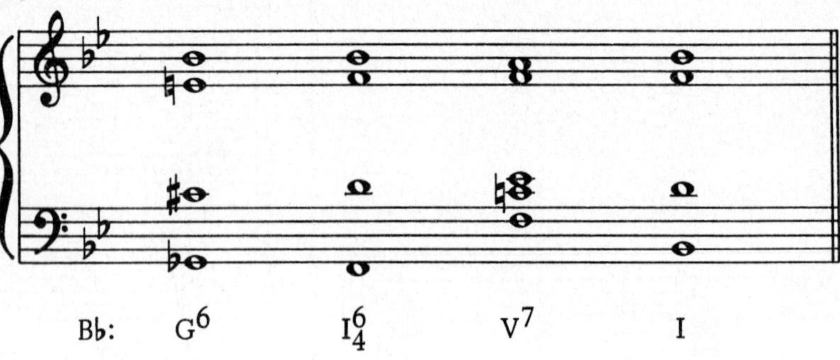

How does the German sixth chord above differ from the usual spelling? ______________________________

D-flat is spelled enharmonically as C-sharp.

---

444. The German sixth chord as spelled in the preceding frame is sometimes called the *doubly augmented six-four-three.** It contains these intervals: an augmented sixth, a major third, and a doubly-augmented fourth.

Bracket (]) the voices which produce the interval of the doubly augmented fourth.

*Note: Some writers may refer to this spelling of the German sixth chord as the *English sixth chord*.

---

445. The reason for the alternate spelling of the German sixth chord is to avoid the chromatic melodic movement which otherwise would occur when the following chord is a tonic six-four. Observe the tenor voice in the two examples below:

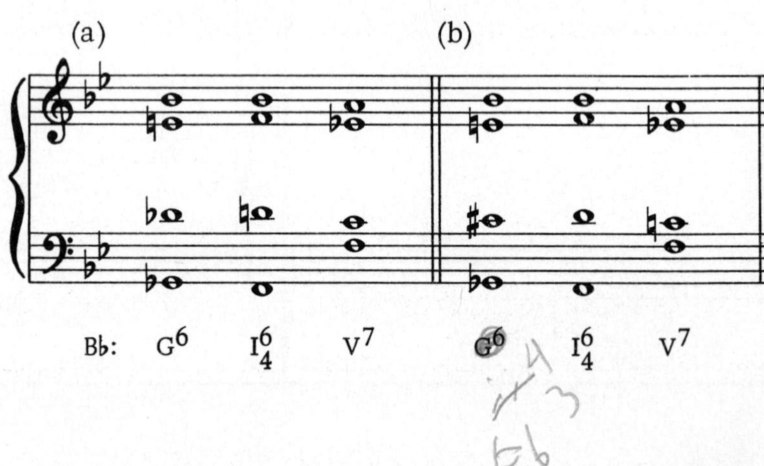

Disregard

In (a) the German sixth chord is spelled "normally." Its resolution to the tonic in second inversion results in chromatic movement in the tenor. This is avoided in (b) by spelling D-flat enharmonically as C-sharp. The German sixth chord in (b) is sometimes called a ______________________ ______________________ chord.

doubly augmented six-four-three

■ 446. The alternate spelling of the German sixth chord (doubly augmented six-four-three) is not always used.

Haydn, *Quartet,* Op. 64, No. 5

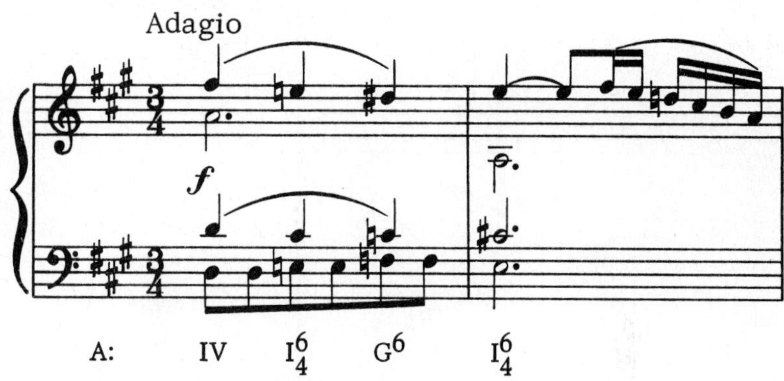

Composers show a lack of consistency in notating German sixth chords. When spelled as a doubly augmented six-four-three it is for the purpose of avoiding a chromatic melodic progression when resolving to the tonic six-four chord in a __________ key.

major

---

447. If the German sixth chord in the preceding frame were to be spelled as a doubly augmented six-four-three, what change would be required? ______________________

Change C-natural to B-sharp.

No.

448. Would you expect to encounter the doubly augmented six-four-three chord in a minor key? ______

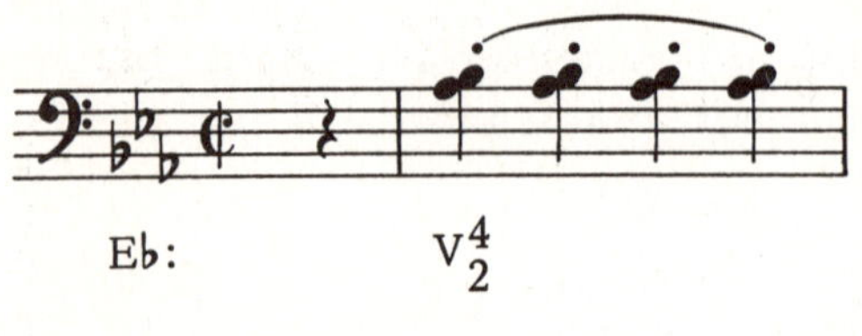

449. Supply the Roman numeral analysis for the example below:

Beethoven, *Sonata,* Op. 13

German

450. The example in the preceding frame illustrates the use of a French sixth chord. Sometimes the term augmented six-four-three is used to refer to the French sixth chord.

Do not confuse the augmented six-four-three with the doubly augmented six-four-three chord. The former is a French sixth, while the latter is a ______________ sixth chord with an enharmonic spelling.

451. Supply the Roman numeral analysis for the example below:

Mozart, *Symphony No. 40,* K. 550

■

452. Supply the Roman numeral analysis for the example below:

Schumann, *Papillons,* Op. 2

■

453. Augmented sixth chords occur frequently in the music of some late nineteenth-century composers. Used in combination with nonharmonic tones they often produce strikingly colorful effects.

Taking into account the nonharmonic tones which have been circled, supply the Roman numeral analysis for the example below:

Wagner, *Tristan und Isolde,* "Prelude"

454. Complete the alto and tenor voices and supply the Roman numeral analysis.

Bach, Chorale: *Ich hab' mein' Sach' Gott heimgestellt*

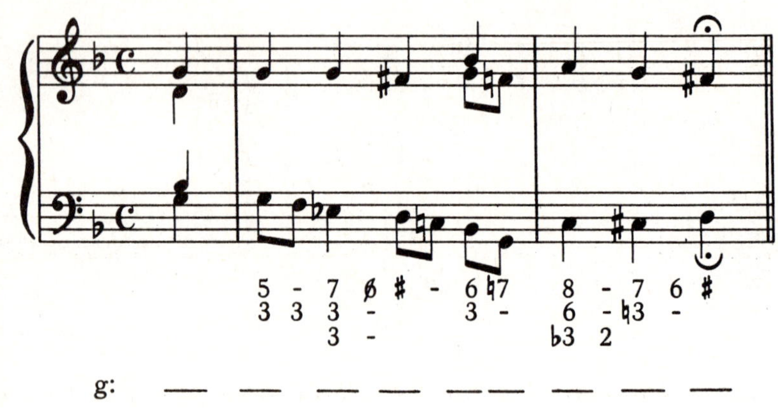

455. Complete the alto and tenor voices and supply the Roman numeral analysis.

Bach, Chorale: *Befiehl du deine Wege*

d: — — — — — — — — — — — — —

452. Supply the Roman numeral analysis for the example below:

Schumann, *Papillons,* Op. 2

453. Augmented sixth chords occur frequently in the music of some late nineteenth-century composers. Used in combination with nonharmonic tones they often produce strikingly colorful effects.

Taking into account the nonharmonic tones which have been circled, supply the Roman numeral analysis for the example below:

Wagner, *Tristan und Isolde,* "Prelude"

454. Complete the alto and tenor voices and supply the Roman numeral analysis.

Bach, Chorale: *Ich hab' mein' Sach' Gott heimgestellt*

455. Complete the alto and tenor voices and supply the Roman numeral analysis.

Bach, Chorale: *Befiehl du deine Wege*

456. A high degree of harmonic motivation is achieved through the use of various types of altered chords in the example below. There are two secondary dominants and one augmented sixth chord. Complete the Roman numeral analysis.

Bach, Chorale: *Wer nur den lieben Gott lässt*

457. All of the augmented sixth chords presented to this point have been in the "normal" position—*the interval of an augmented sixth has appeared between the bass and an upper part.* When the raised fourth scale degree is in the bass, the augmented sixth becomes by inversion a diminished third.

Tchaikovsky, *Eugene Onegin,* Act II, No. 17

Use a bracket ( ]) to identify the diminished third in the German sixth chord above.

A: V7 ♮VI G6

I6/4

458. Supply the Roman numeral analysis for the example below:

Chopin, *Valse Brillante,* Op. 34, No. 2

raised

459. In the preceding frame, the German sixth chord has the _____________ fourth scale degree in the bass.

460. The German sixth chord in the example below employs an enharmonic spelling.

Chopin, *Prelude,* Op. 28, No. 4

CEGA♯

The usual spelling of the German sixth chord in the example above is _____________.

461. Enharmonic spellings such as that in the preceding frame occur frequently in the chromatic harmonic style of the late nineteenth century. You must be alert to the function of a particular harmony as this is more important than the spelling which is often affected by mere convenience of notation.

3rd	The aural effect of the German sixth chord when the raised fourth degree is in the bass (Frames 457, 458, and 460) is the same as a major-minor seventh chord in (1st/2nd/3rd) _______ inversion.
diminished	462. Augmented sixth chords may be found in any position, but the two most common are shown below: 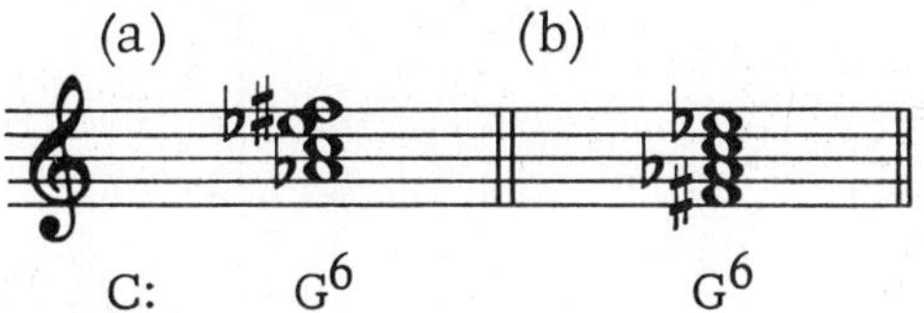 In (a), the lowered sixth scale degree is in the bass and the interval of an augmented sixth occurs between the bass and an upper part; in (b), the raised fourth scale degree is in the bass and the augmented sixth, through inversion, now appears as a _____________ third.
■ 5th	463. Since augmented sixth chords rarely occur in positions other than the two shown in the preceding frame, only a few examples will be cited. In the example below, the German sixth chord is spelled as a doubly augmented six-four-three. Franck, *Symphony in D Minor*  In the German sixth above, the note in the bass (G-sharp) is the sounding (root/3rd/5th/7th) ______ of the chord.
■	464. Augmented sixth chords are exploited by some composers for their novel color effects. The example on the following page makes effective use of a German sixth chord spelled enharmonically as a major-minor seventh chord.

Dvorak, *Symphony No. 9,* "From the New World," Op. 95

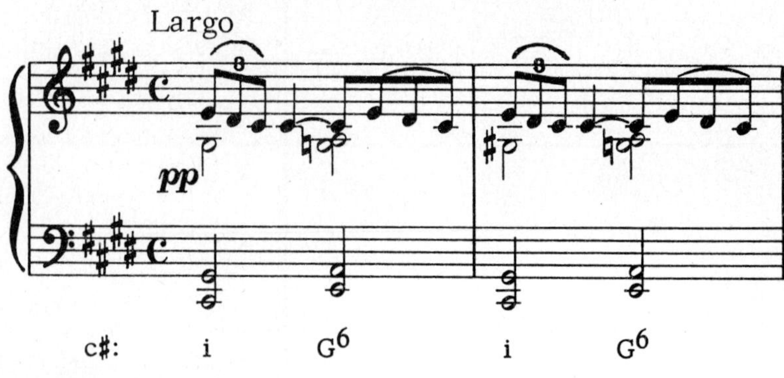

The colorful effect of this passage is due, in part, to the unusual resolution of the German sixth to the tonic triad in root position.

second

Augmented sixth chords (when built on the sixth scale degree) usually progress to the dominant triad or seventh chord, or to the tonic triad in ___________ inversion.

3rd

■ 465. The German sixth chord at the asterisk has the first scale degree in the bass. This note (D) is the sounding (root/3rd/5th/7th) ______ of the chord.

Franck, *Symphony in D Minor*

466. All of the augmented sixth chords presented to this point are built on the note which is a half-step above the dominant (the sixth scale degree in harmonic minor, or the lowered sixth-scale degree in major). But augmented sixth chords occur on other scale degrees as well.

We have learned that augmented sixth chords are highly active and that their usual resolution is to the dominant (a chord whose root is a half-step below the note on which the augmented sixth chord is built). This strong tendency to resolve in a particular way leads to a use of these chords which is analogous to secondary dominants. *Thus chords other than the dominant may be attended by augmented sixth chords.* Reference is occasionally made to the "augmented sixth of the supertonic," etc. Augmented sixth chords used in this manner are usually part of a highly chromatic style of writing as will be seen in examples which follow.

(No response.)

■ 467. The augmented sixth chord below precedes a secondary dominant.

Brahms, *Symphony No. 1,* Op. 68

The Italian sixth chord in this example relates to the chord which follows as if both were in the key of ____ major.

G

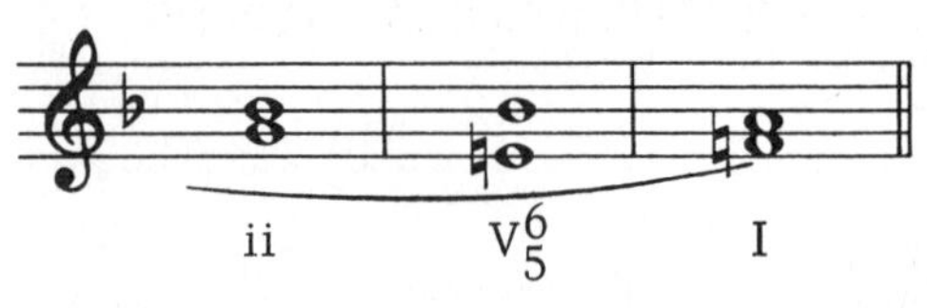

■ 468. Supply the Roman numeral analysis for the example below:

Beethoven, *Sonata,* for violin and piano, Op. 23

■ 469. The analogous function possessed by secondary dominants and augmented sixth chords is made especially clear in the example below. Here the supertonic triad is preceded by both a secondary dominant (V^4_3/ii) and a French sixth chord.

Wolf, *Wiegenlied*

Yes.

Does the interval of the diminished third resolve "normally" in the example above? ______

470. Check (√) the correct option:

1. Like secondary dominants, augmented sixth chords may relate to various triads in the key.
2. In augmented sixth chords the interval of an augmented sixth always occurs between the bass and an upper voice.

True statements:
(1) ______ (2) ______ Both ______ Neither ______

(1) √

---

471. The French sixth chord at the asterisk is built on E-flat, and thus would tend to resolve to the mediant (vi). It progresses instead to the subdominant in first inversion (IV⁶). Thus it becomes a "deceptive" resolution to a chord a third below the one expected.

Wolf, *Biterolf*

Does the interval of the augmented sixth resolve in the "normal" way? ______

Yes.

(1) iv (2) ii° (3) ii^ø7

472. In the preceding frame there are three borrowed chords. To review your knowledge of these chords, show them with chord symbols in the order of their occurrence.

(1) __________ (2) __________ (3) __________

Ab: G6 vi^{6}_{4}

■ 473. Complete the Roman numeral analysis for the example below:

Wagner, *Lohengrin*, Act I

Langsam

S

Herz - ens tief - stes Kla - gen er -

Ab: I vi7 vii°7/vi vi $\text{vii}^{\circ 6}_{5}$/iii ___

goss ich im Ge - bet,

___ vii^ø7/V I^{6}_{4} V I

False.
(Both are highly active.)

474. Augmented sixth chords are less active than secondary dominants. (True/False) __________

second

475. Most augmented sixth chords are built on the sixth degree of the harmonic minor scale or the lowered sixth degree of the major scale. They are also used in a manner similar to secondary dominants to embellish various diatonic triads. Two other uses remain to be examined: (1) built on the lowered second scale degree in major and minor, and (2) built on the fourth scale degree in major.

The chord at the asterisk is a French sixth built on the lowered ______________ degree of the E minor scale.

Brahms, *Symphony No. 4,* Op. 98

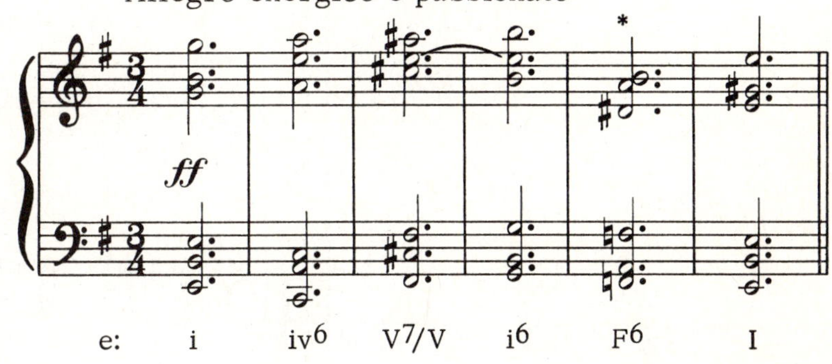

(c). The French sixth.

476. When built on the lowered second scale degree, augmented sixth chords usually resolve to the tonic in root position.

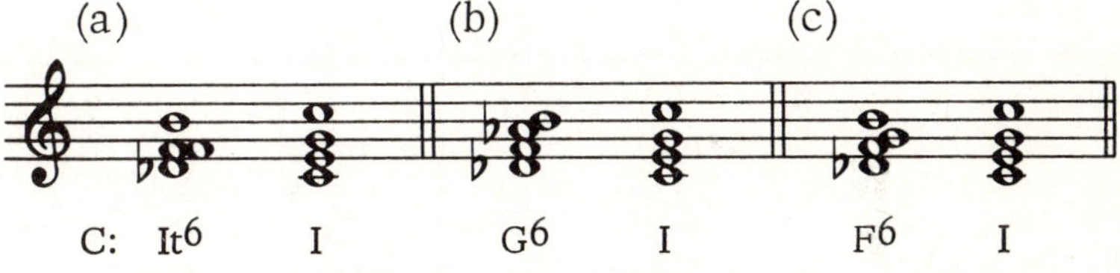

As usual, the interval of an augmented sixth expands outward to the octave. Progression to the tonic causes these chords to have dominant function. Which of the chords above could be regarded as an altered dominant seventh chord? ______________________________

---

477. When built on the lowered second scale degree, the French sixth may rightly be considered a dominant seventh chord with a lowered fifth. This is made clear by arranging the chord in (c) of the preceding frame in thirds.

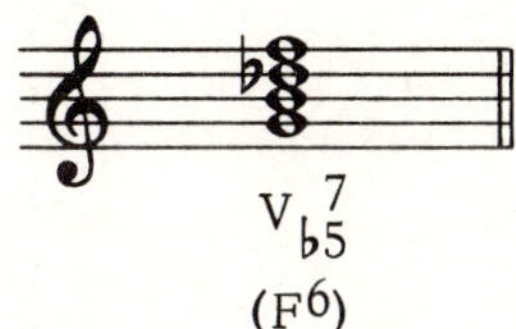

leading tone

Similarly, the Italian sixth in (a) of the preceding frame could be analyzed as an altered ______ ______ triad.

478. Augmented sixth chords built on the lowered second scale degree are often used at the cadence. Complete the Roman numeral analysis for the example below:

Fauré, *Au bord de l. Eau,* Op. 8, No. 1

479. Supply the Roman numeral analysis for the example below:

Sibelius, *Finlandia,* Op. 26

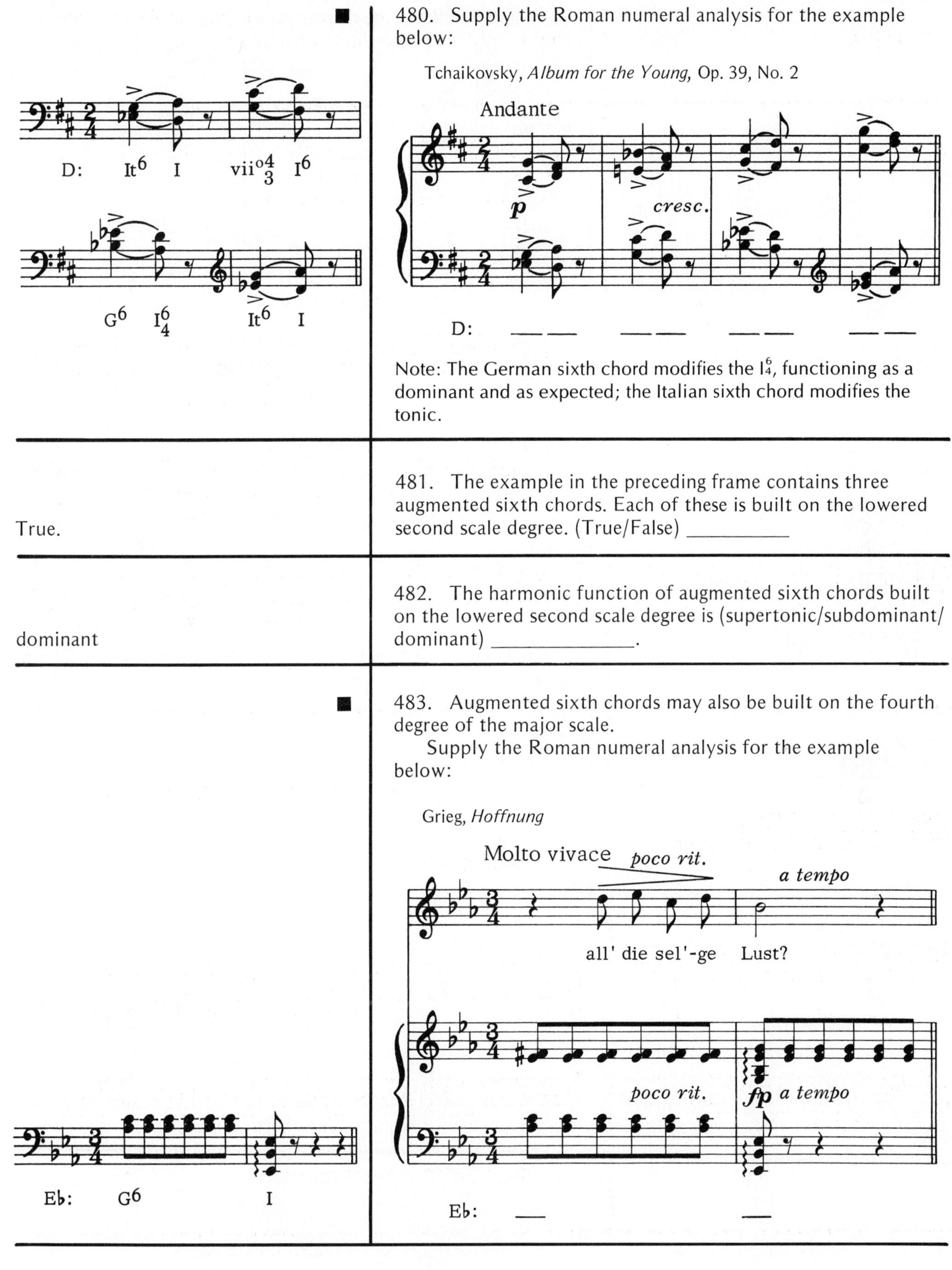

480. Supply the Roman numeral analysis for the example below:

Tchaikovsky, *Album for the Young*, Op. 39, No. 2

Note: The German sixth chord modifies the I^6_4, functioning as a dominant and as expected; the Italian sixth chord modifies the tonic.

True.

481. The example in the preceding frame contains three augmented sixth chords. Each of these is built on the lowered second scale degree. (True/False) __________

dominant

482. The harmonic function of augmented sixth chords built on the lowered second scale degree is (supertonic/subdominant/dominant) ______________.

483. Augmented sixth chords may also be built on the fourth degree of the major scale.

Supply the Roman numeral analysis for the example below:

Grieg, *Hoffnung*

484. When built on the fourth scale degree, augmented sixth chords may resolve to the tonic triad in either first inversion or root position. In the latter case, the effect is somewhat like a plagal cadence.

Complete the Roman numeral analysis for the example below:

Grieg, *First Meeting*

485. Complete the Roman numeral analysis for the example below:

Gounod, *Faust,* "Introduction"

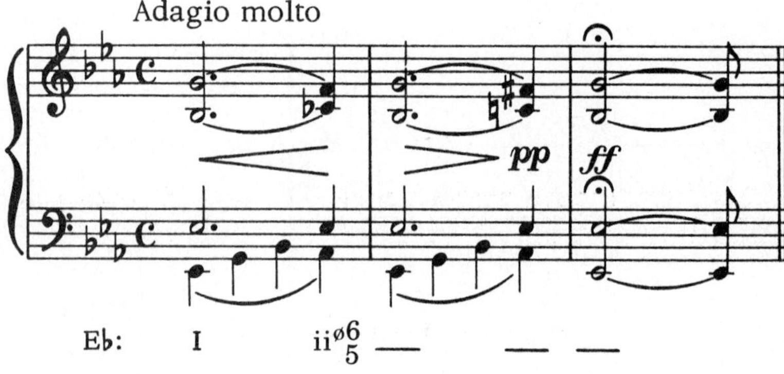

SUMMARY

The most common use of augmented sixth chords is to heighten the appearance of the dominant chord by providing a chromatic approach to it. Used in this manner, they are altered subdominant or supertonic chords. In the chromatic harmonic styles of some nineteenth-century composers these chords embellish diatonic chords other than the dominant, and even other altered chords such as secondary dominants.

Augmented sixth chords also appear on the lowered second scale degree as altered leading tone or dominant chords. They perform the same function as their diatonic counterparts, which is to progress to the tonic. When built on the fourth degree of the major scale, augmented sixth chords usually progress to the tonic triad in root position. The result is an effect similar to the plagal cadence.

Augmented sixth chords may be found which do not conform to any of the uses described in this chapter. In such cases their use may be termed "nonfunctional" (the result of chromatic nonharmonic tones), or merely the composer's desire to exploit the particular color which they possess.

Mastery Frames

6-1. Provide the proper name for each of the augmented sixth chords below.

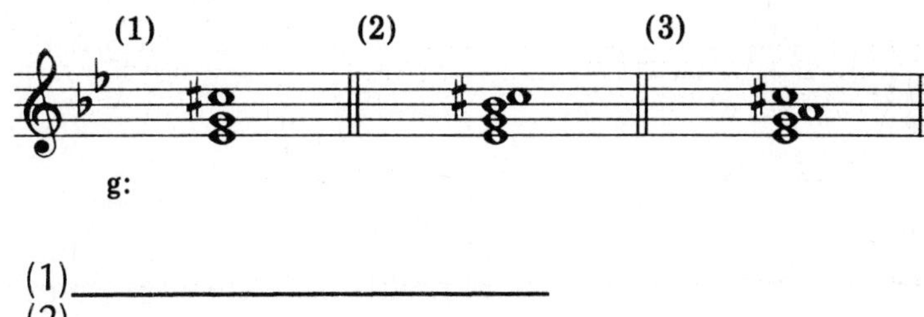

(1)________________________
(2)________________________
(3)________________________

(1) Italian sixth
(2) German sixth
(3) French sixth

(392, 403, 412)

6-2. Show the normal resolution of the interval of the augmented sixth in each case below.

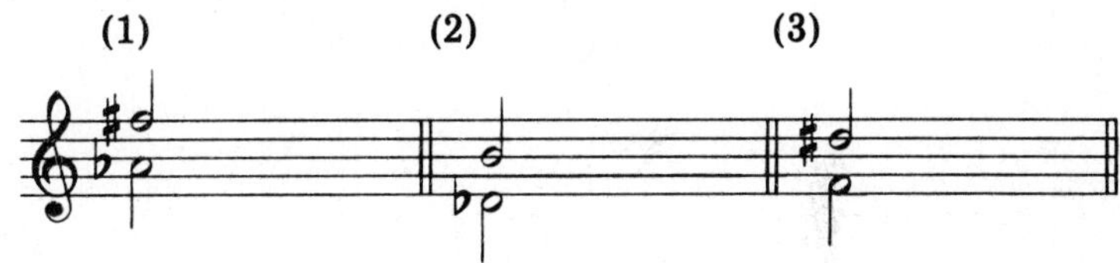

(433)

6-3. Resolve each augmented sixth chord and provide the appropriate chord symbols.

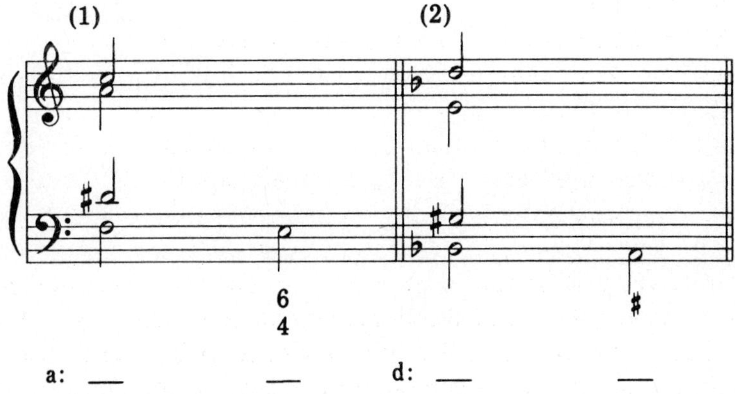

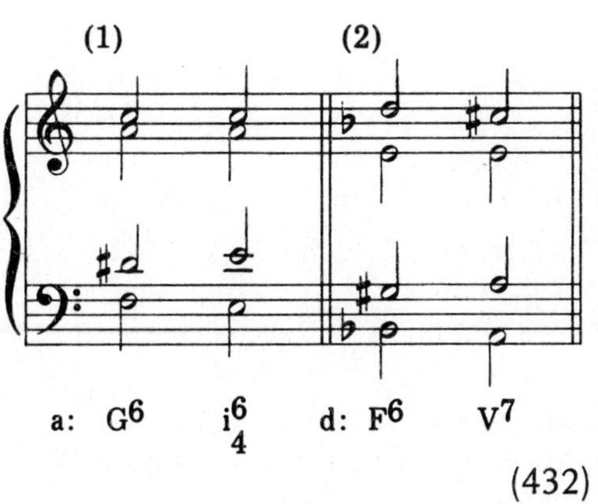

(432)

(477–485)

6-4. Continue as in the preceding frame.

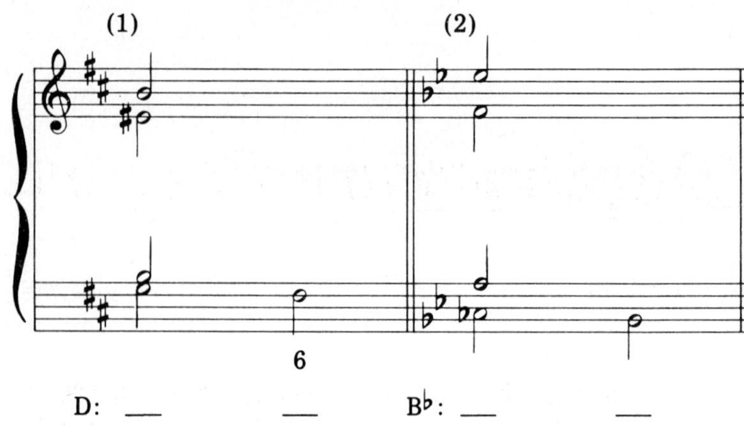

True. (442–448)

6-5. The "doubly augmented six-four-three" chord sounds the same as a German sixth chord. (True/False)____________

Supplementary Assignments

ASSIGNMENT 6-1 Name________________________

1. Write augmented sixth chords as directed. (The given notes are sounding roots.)

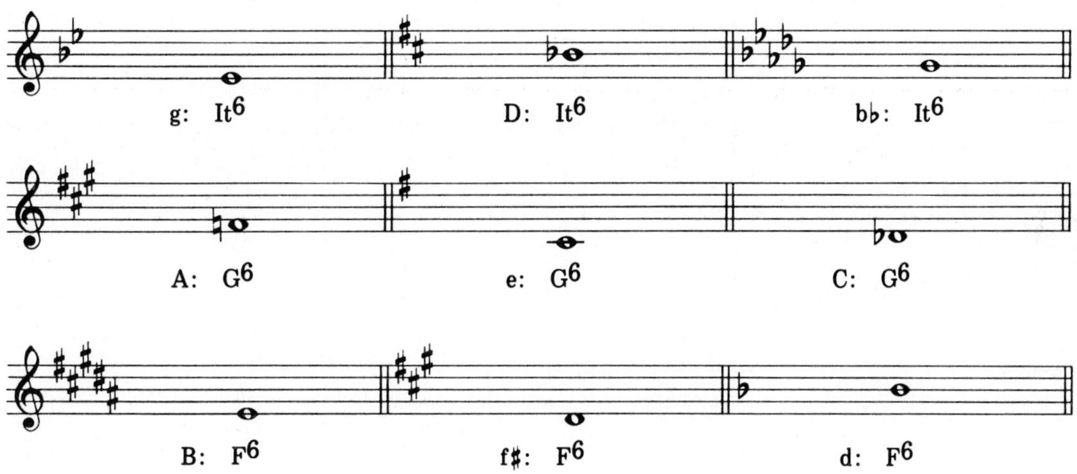

2. Which is the correct chord symbol? _______

1. iv^6_5
2. It^6
3. G^6
4. F^6

3. Which is the correct chord symbol? _______

1. It^6
2. G^6
3. F^6

4. Which chord agrees with the chord symbol? _______

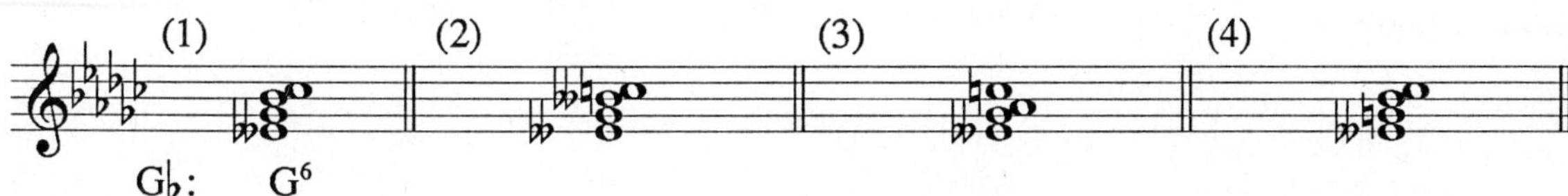

5. Which figured bass symbol represents a French sixth chord? ______

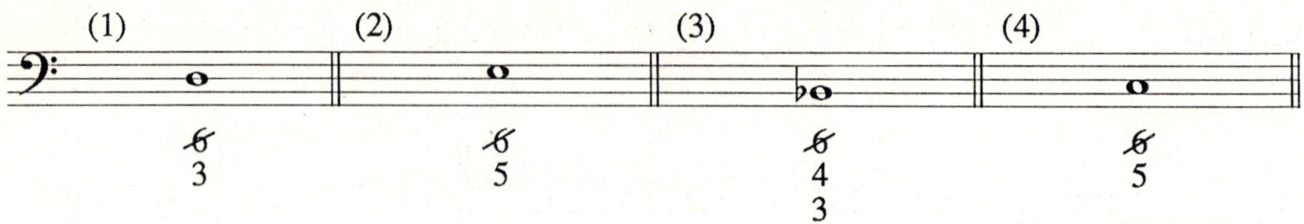

6. Is the augmented sixth chord used correctly? __________

7. Is the augmented sixth chord used correctly? __________

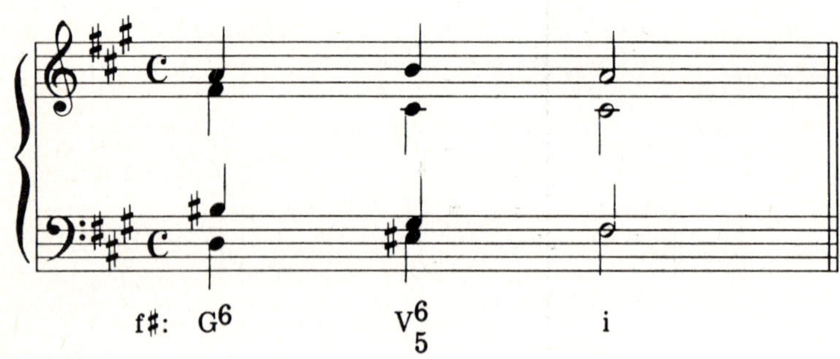

8. Is the augmented sixth chord used correctly? __________

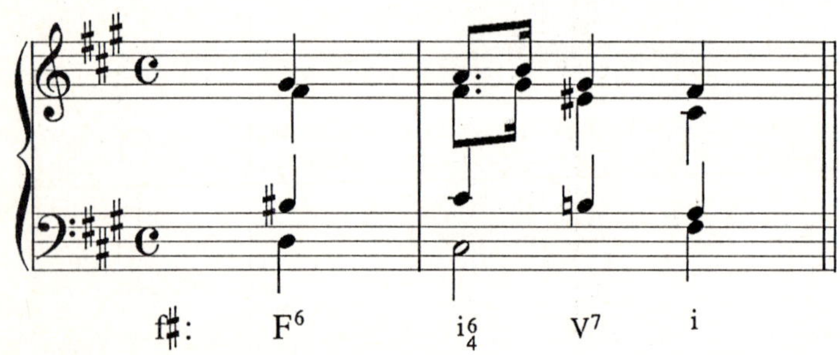

9. Add the soprano, alto, and tenor voices.

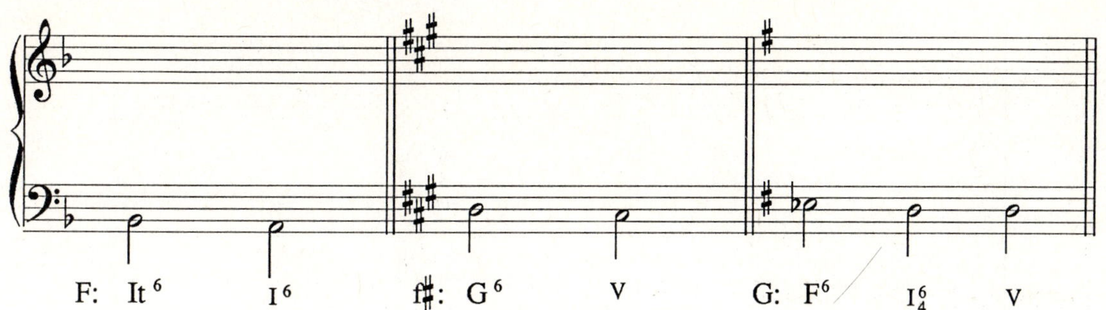

10. Identify the type of augmented sixth chord represented by each figured bass symbol.

(1)________________________

(2)________________________

(3)________________________

(4)________________________

ASSIGNMENT 6-2 Name____________________

1. Which chord is a "doubly augmented six-four-three" chord?__________

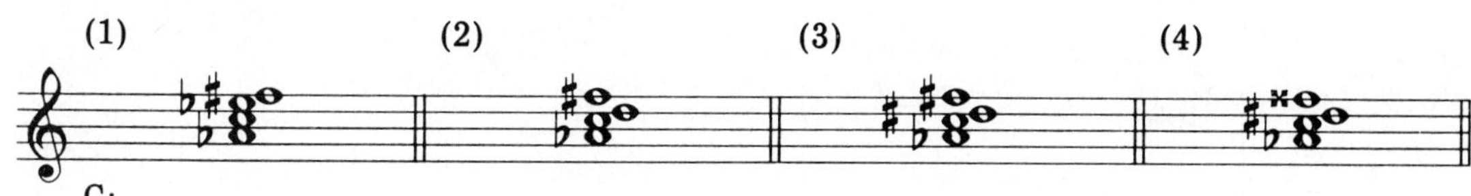

2. Add the alto and tenor voices in accordance with the figured bass symbols. Supply also the proper chord symbols.

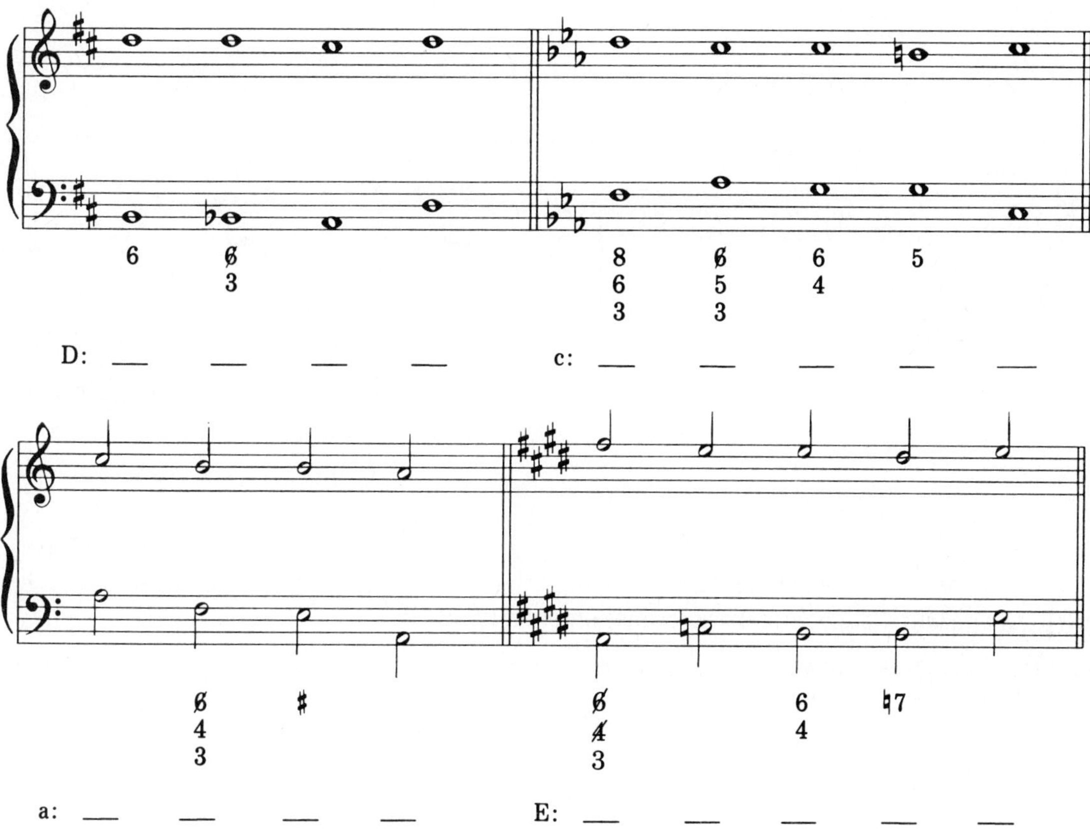

3. Supply the chord symbols.

Beethoven: *Sonata,* Op. 78

4. Provide the chord symbols and identify the nonharmonic tones in the examples below.

Chopin, *Mazurka*

Chopin, *Nocturne*, Op. 48, No. 2

5. Compose one or more phrases which contain augmented sixth chords. Choose your own key and time signature; take care to notate completely. Use piano or instrumental style.

6. Prepare additional analyses of examples, as selected by your instructor or tutor, in a format similar to that suggested in Supplementary Assignment 4-2, No. 8.

chapter seven

The Neapolitan Sixth, Altered Dominants, and Diminished Seventh Chords

Three types of altered chords are presented in this chapter: the Neapolitan sixth—an altered supertonic triad—dominants with increased activity due to alterations of the fifth, and two diminished seventh chords that do not have dominant function. All of these chords are used sparingly; they are saved for moments when their distinctive tonal qualities are most appropriate. Like all highly colored sonorities, overuse of these chords diminishes their effectiveness.

■

486. The chord at the asterisk is called a NEAPOLITAN SIXTH chord.

Chopin, *Valse Brillante,* Op. 34, No. 2

first

The Neapolitan sixth chord above is in ______________ inversion.

---

first

487. Although the origin of the term "Neapolitan sixth" is unknown, its use is universally accepted. The second part of this term (sixth) refers to the fact that the chord is usually in first inversion.

The word "sixth" in the term Neapolitan sixth chord refers to the interval of a sixth which occurs above the bass in any triad which is in ______________ inversion.

488. We shall use the symbol N^6 to represent the Neapolitan sixth chord. In the very few cases when it is in root position or second inversion the symbol will be N or N^6_4 and the reference can simply be Neapolitan or Neapolitan six-four, respectively.

(a) (b) (c)

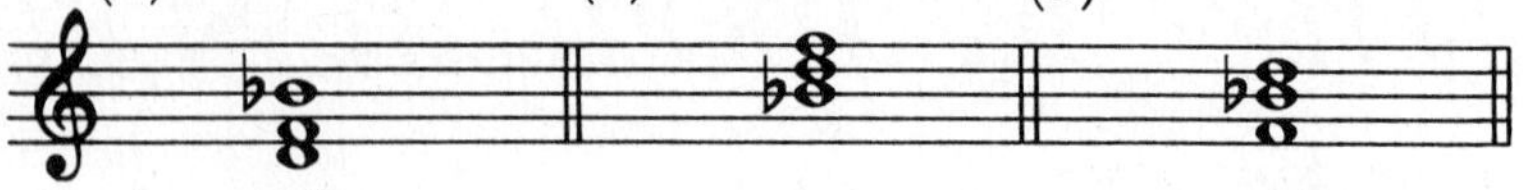

	(a)	(b)	(c)
a:	N^6	N	N^6_4
a:	$\flat II^6$	$\flat II$	$\flat II^6_4$

In (a) the chord is in first inversion (its usual position); (b) and (c) show the chord in root position and second inversion. The alternate analysis indicates that the Neapolitan sixth chord is a major triad built on the lowered second degree of the scale.

(No response.)

489. The earliest examples of the Neapolitan sixth chord are in minor keys, but they may occur in major keys as well. In either case, the chord is a major triad built on the lowered second degree of the scale. In the key of G minor, for example, the Neapolitan sixth chord is spelled A♭CE♭.

Spell the Neapolitan sixth chord in the key of C minor.

____

D♭FA♭.

490. Since the majority of Neapolitan sixth chords occur in first inversion, we shall write them on the staff with the third as the lowest note. In the key of A major, for example, the chord is spelled B♭DF. Written on the staff it appears as below:

A: N^6

Why is it necessary to place a natural sign before the note F in the example above? _______________

____

To produce a major triad.

491. Write the chord indicated. *(Remember that the third is the lowest note.)*

(1) (2) (3)

F: N^6 b: N^6 c: N^6

(1) (2) (3)

492. Continue as in the preceding frame.

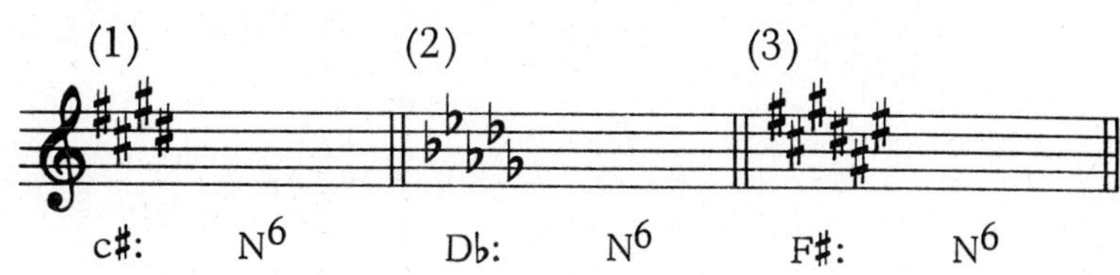

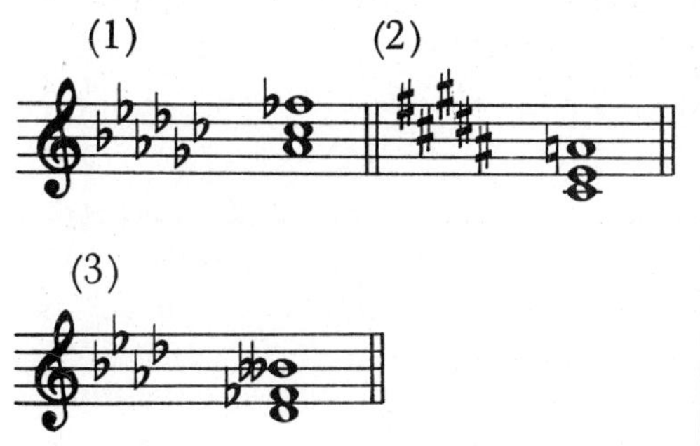

493. Continue as in the preceding frame.

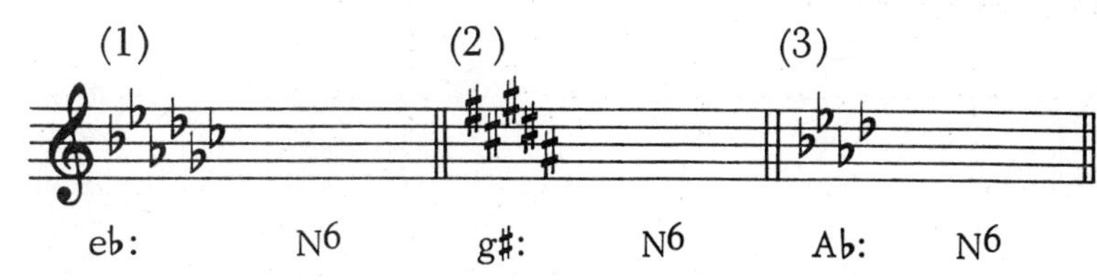

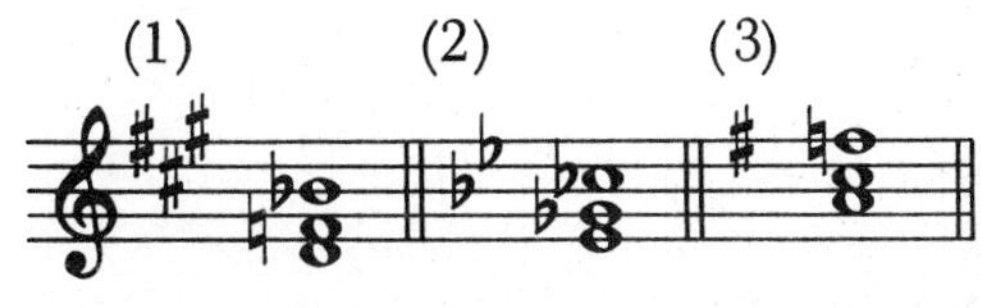

494. Continue as in the preceding frame.

■

495. Since the Neapolitan sixth chord is an altered supertonic triad, it normally progresses to a dominant chord.

Beethoven, *Sonata,* Op. 27, No. 2

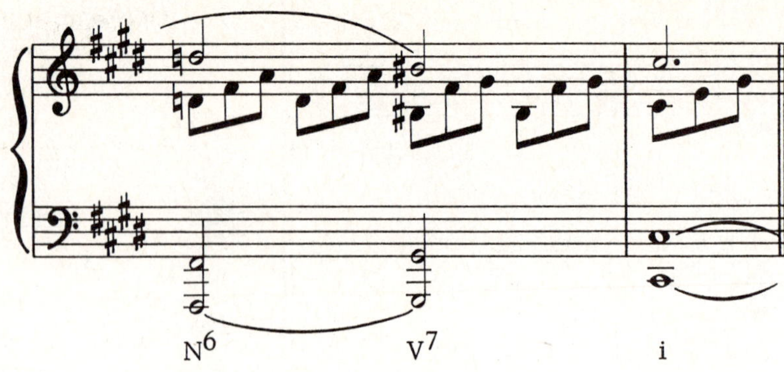

In the Neapolitan sixth chord above, the (root/3rd/5th) ______ is in the bass.

3rd

■ 496. The Neapolitan sixth chord produces a distinctive and colorful effect. The effect is most pronounced when the Neapolitan sixth chord is followed immediately by a dominant chord (as in the preceding frame). This is due to the tritone relationship which exists between the roots of the two chords.

Beethoven, *Sonata,* Op. 27, No. 2

(Adagio)

In addition to the tritone relationship between the roots of these chords, the melodic line contains an unusual interval (D-natural to B-sharp). Name this interval. ______________ ______________

Diminished third.

■ 497. The unusual features mentioned in the preceding frame are eliminated if a tonic six-four chord occurs between the Neapolitan sixth chord and the dominant.

Complete the Roman numeral analysis for the example on the following page.

Beethoven, *Sonata*, Op. 53

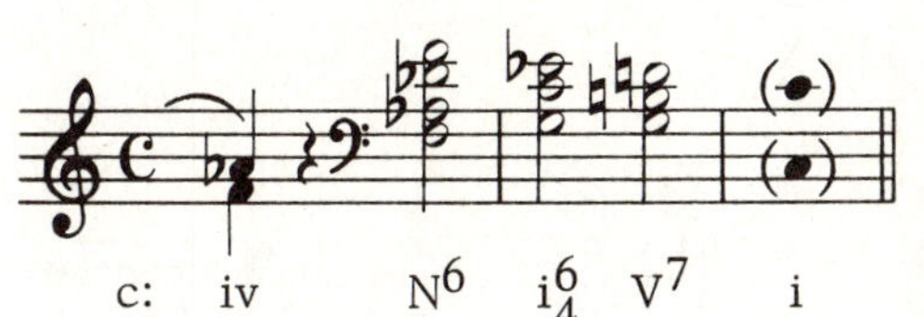

■

498. A secondary dominant sometimes appears between the Neapolitan sixth chord and the dominant.

Supply the Roman numeral analysis for the example below:

Schubert, *Erlkönig*, Op. 1

499. Supply the Roman numeral analysis for the example below:

Schubert, *Mass in G Major,* "Sanctus"

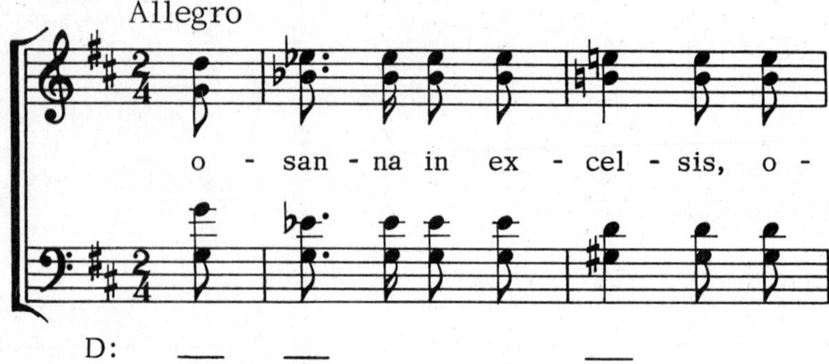

I I

---

500. Let us review some of the facts regarding the Neapolitan sixth chord. First of all, it is a major triad built on the lowered second scale degree of a major or minor scale, and it usually occurs in first inversion. The dominant triad or seventh chord is its ultimate harmonic goal. If it progresses directly to the dominant, however, a rather "exotic" relationship occurs due to the interval of a tritone between the roots of the two chords. This if often smoothed out by inserting a tonic in second inversion, a secondary dominant, or both, between the Neapolitan sixth and the dominant.

The examples in the next frame show that, in four-part writing the *third* of the Neapolitan sixth chord is often doubled. This doubling is used for the sake of smooth voice leading, and is quite prevalent.

(No response.)

---

501. Which example produces the *smoothest* harmonic effect? ______

(d).
(See the following frame for discussion of this choice.)

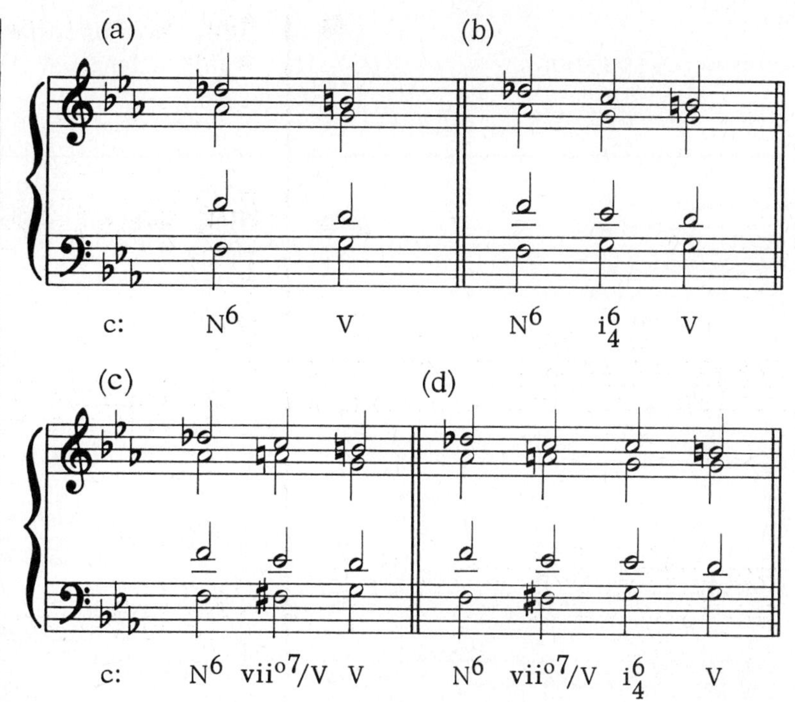

■

502. The progression in (d) of the preceding frame provides the smoothest effect, because the Neapolitan sixth and the dominant chords are separated by a greater number of chords than in either (b) or (c). Thus the dissonant effect caused by the tritone root relationship is considerably lessened.

Maximum smoothness, of course, is not always desired. The tritone relationship is often exploited for expressive purposes. Such a case is shown in the example below. Supply the Roman numeral analysis.

Chopin, *Prelude,* Op. 28, No. 20

It is in root position.

503. How does the Neapolitan sixth chord in the preceding frame differ from all those previously shown? ______________________________________

C: I N -

■ 504. Supply the Roman numeral analysis for the example below:

Brahms, *Intermezzo,* Op. 119, No. 3

Grazioso e giocoso

__ __ __ __

---

borrowed

505. The chords in the third and fourth measures of the preceding example are altered chords. Name the type of altered chord to which these chords belong. They are ____________ chords.

■ 506. Another example of the Neapolitan sixth chord in root position is shown below. Supply the Roman numeral analysis.

Wagner, *Die Walküre*, Act I, Scene 2

C: N^6_4 V^7 vi

■ 507. Although quite rare, the Neapolitan sixth chord may appear with the fifth in the bass. Supply the Roman numeral analysis.

Mozart, *Quintet,* K. 515

Allegro

(*p*)

PT

C: ___ ___ ___

Both √

508. Check (√) the correct option:

1. Neapolitan sixth chords are altered supertonic triads.
2. One or more chords may appear between the Neapolitan sixth chord and the dominant, which is its ultimate goal.

True statements:
(1) ______ (2) ______ Both ______ Neither ______

---

subdominant

509. The Neapolitan sixth chord may occur at any point in a phrase where its special color makes an appropriate effect. But because it is so distinctive, it should not be overused.

The harmonic function of the Neapolitan sixth chord is most like that of the (tonic/leading tone/subdominant/submediant) ____________ triad.

---

510. We shall now turn to a species of altered chords called *altered dominants.* Like the Neapolitan chords, altered dominants are highly colored and thus should be used with discretion.

Harmonic activity is heightened when a chord's urgency to resolve is increased. Dominant chords—active because of their position in the structure of tonality—are made more so by chromatic alterations of the fifth. The example on the following page shows the dominant triad and seventh chord with *raised* fifth.

(No response.)

In both (a) and (b) the fifth is inflected upward a half-step. The result is an augmented triad in (a), and an augmented minor seventh chord in (b). In each case the plus sign added to the Roman numeral refers to the augmented quality of the triad.

Three.
(The seventh, C; the leading tone, F♯; the raised fifth, A♯.)

511. The dominant triad (or seventh chord) is made more active by raising the fifth a half-step. Because altered tones tend to resolve in the direction of their inflection, the raised fifth resolves upward to the third of the tonic triad. Notice in (b) of the preceding frame that this causes irregular doubling to occur in the tonic chord as both the raised fifth and the seventh of the dominant seventh chord are compelled to resolve to the third of the tonic triad (B).

How many active tones does the first chord (V^{+7}) in (b) of the preceding frame contain? ______________

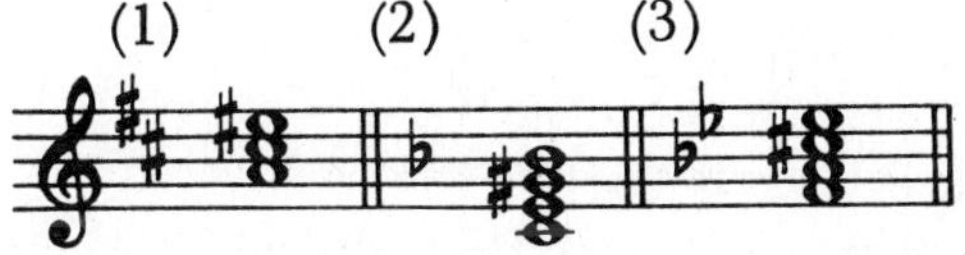

512. The dominant triad or seventh chord with raised fifth occurs only in major keys. Write the chords indicated by the chord symbols.

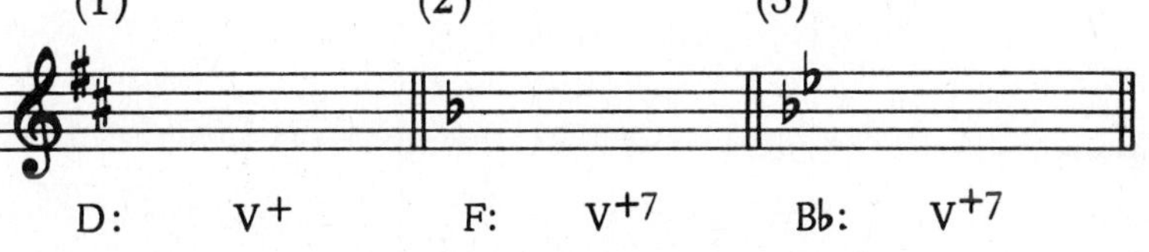

---

513. Altered dominants may be used in various inversions as well as root position. Write the chords as indicated by the chord symbols on the following page.

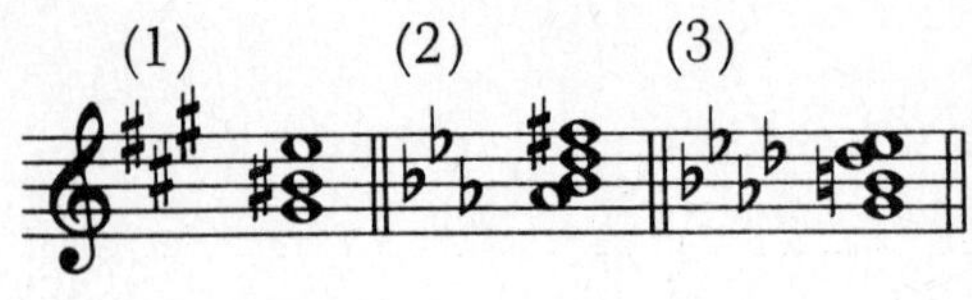

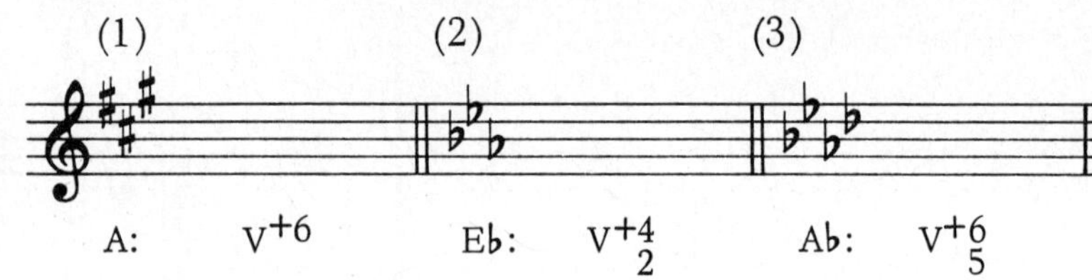

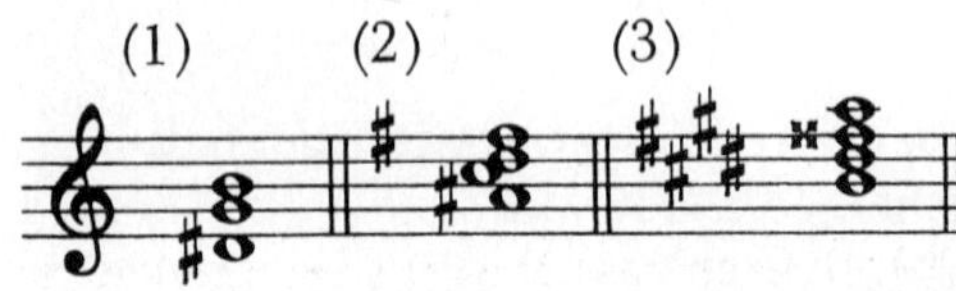

514. Continue as in the preceding frame.

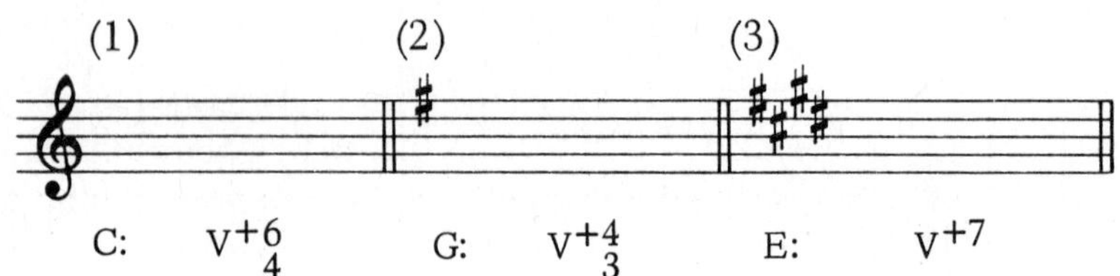

515. The activity of a dominant triad or seventh chord is increased by inflecting its fifth upward a half-step. It is important to remember that notes which are altered chromatically tend to resolve in the direction of their inflection.

Write the alto and tenor voices in accordance with the figured bass symbols. Supply, also, the Roman numeral analysis. *(Use close structure.)*

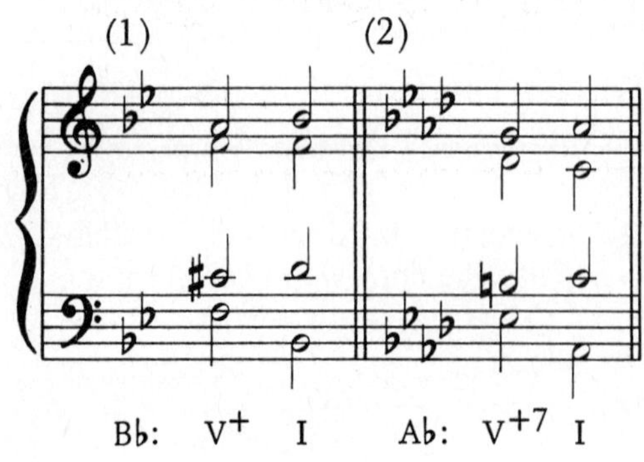

516. Write the alto and tenor voices in accordance with the figured bass symbols. Supply, also, the Roman numeral analysis. *(Use open structure.)*

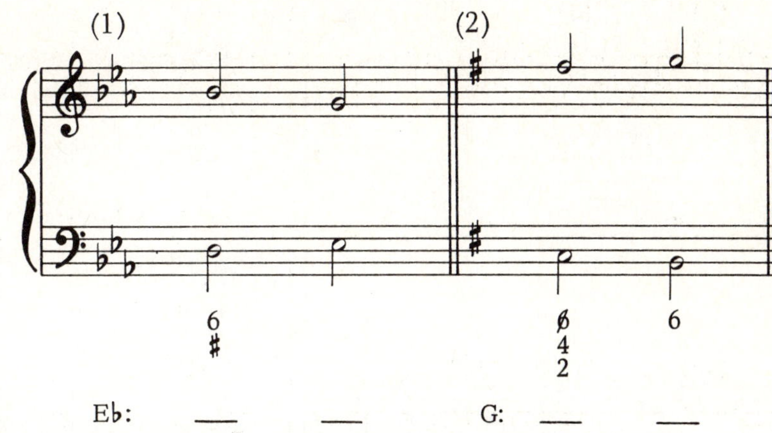

■

517. Supply the Roman numeral analysis for the example below:

Brahms, *Piano Concerto No. 2,* Op. 83

■

518. Supply the Roman numeral analysis for the final two chords in the example below:

Wolf, *Wo wird einst. . .*

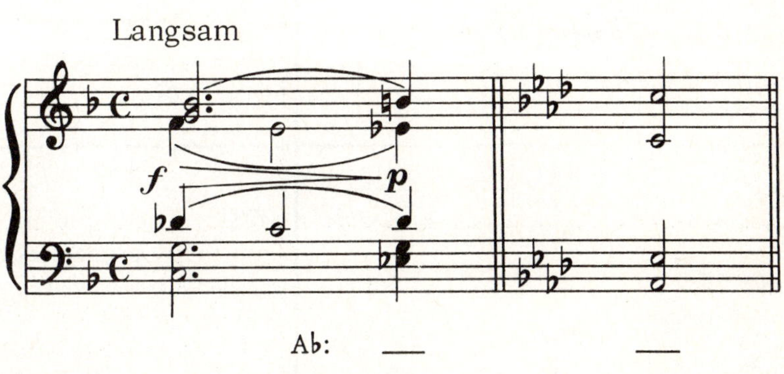

519. The raised fifth in the dominant triad or seventh chord often appears in a manner similar to a chromatic passing tone. Such a case is shown below. Supply the Roman numeral analysis.

Schubert, *Erlkönig,* Op. 1

520. Altered dominant chords such as those shown in the previous few frames may also be used as secondary dominants. In the example below, the subdominant is embellished by an altered dominant. Complete the Roman numeral analysis.

Strauss, *Till Eulenspiegels lustige Streiche,* Op. 28

3rd

521. The dominant triad or seventh chord with raised fifth normally progresses to a *major* tonic triad; the raised fifth resolves up a half-step to the (root/3rd/5th) ______ of the tonic chord.

522. The dominant triad or seventh chord sometimes contains a *lowered* fifth, and these chords may occur in either a major or minor key.

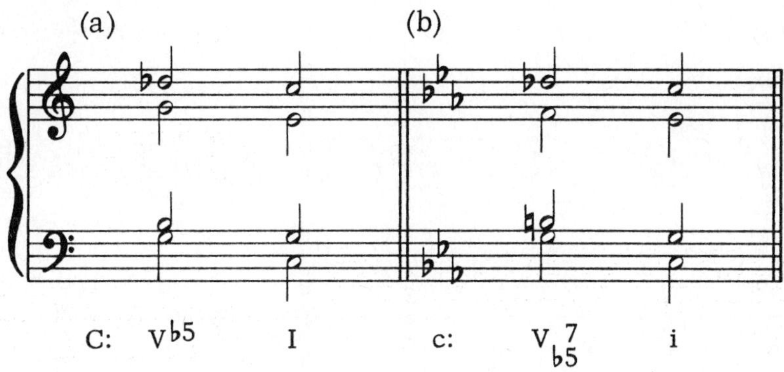

Is the altered dominant triad in (a) above (GBD♭) one of the four diatonic triad types (major, minor, diminished, or augmented)? ______

No.

523. Since the triad which results when the fifth of a dominant triad is lowered a half-step is not one of the four diatonic triad types, there is no symbol to express its quality. The altered tone is shown by an accidental applied to the chord symbol.

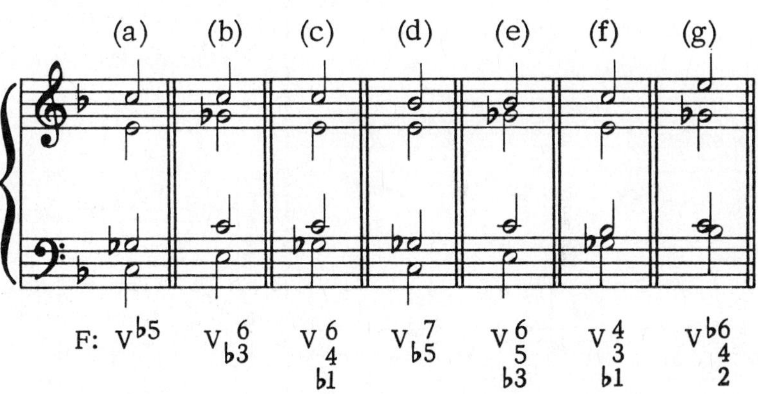

The altered note is represented variously as ♭5, ♭3, ♭1, or ♭6 according to the inversion, but in each case the altered note is the ______________ of the chord.

fifth

524. When in second inversion as in (f) of the preceding frame, the dominant seventh with lowered fifth consists of the same notes as one of the augmented sixth chords built on the lowered second scale degree. Name this chord. ___________ sixth.

French

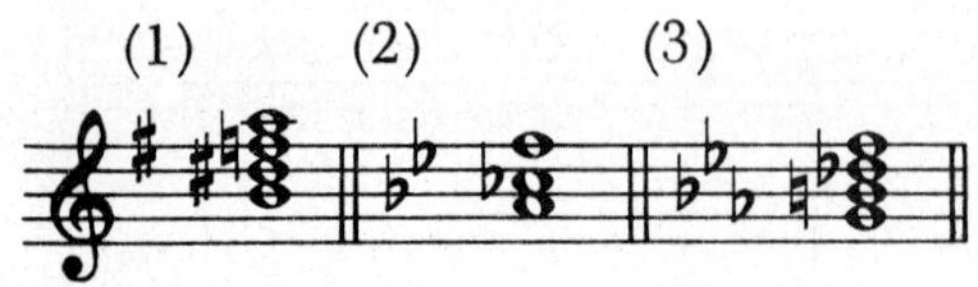

525. The chord in (f) of Frame 523 is the same as a French sixth built on the lowered second scale degree, and may be analyzed as such. In most cases this analysis is preferred.

Write the chords indicated by the chord symbols. *(Remember: raise the seventh scale degree in minor.)*

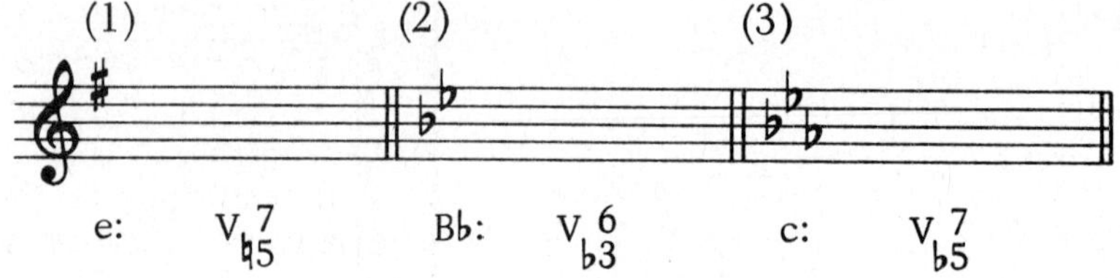

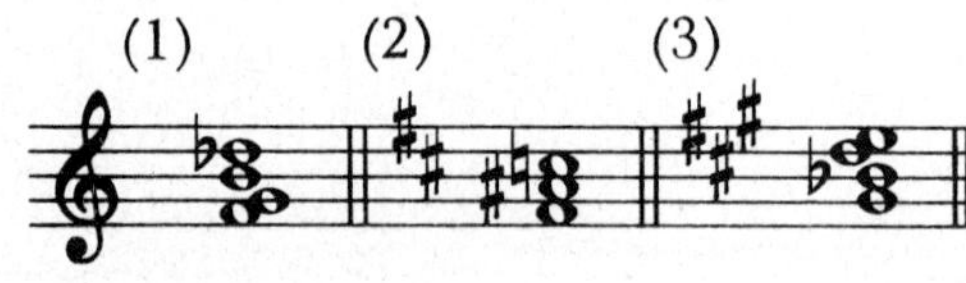

526. Continue as in the preceding frame.

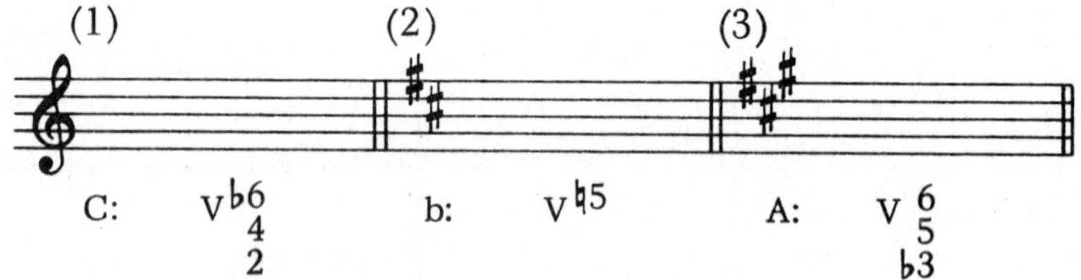

■

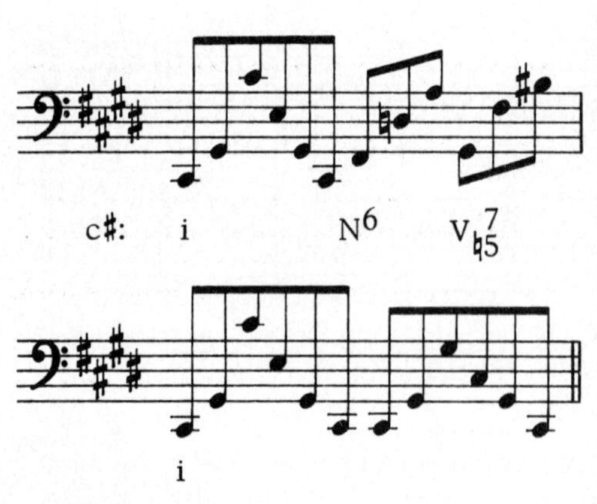

527. Supply the Roman numeral analysis.

Chopin, *Nocturne*, Op. 27, No. 1

528. As the harmonic vocabulary evolved during the nineteenth century, composers placed more and more stress upon chords of dominant function. The restless activity produced by increased numbers of dominant chords was appropriate to the subjective character of their music. This preoccupation with dominant harmonic activity caused an increase in the level of tension. Not only used more frequently, dominant chords were altered chromatically to increase their activity.

(No response.)

The dominant chord with raised fifth is one example of such alteration; the dominant chord with lowered fifth is another. All of these chords possess greater tension than do the same chords without alteration. The use of such chords adds to harmonic activity and provides additional color resources.

Extensive use of altered dominants is characteristic of late nineteenth-century music, and this style of writing is also encountered in music of a semi-popular vein in the twentieth century. By now, the sonorities—and harmonic function—of these chords are so familiar, that their usefulness in serious composition is limited. Like all highly-colored effects, they should be used sparingly and with discretion.

(b).
(See next frame.)

529. In which case is the dominant seventh chord with raised fifth resolved most satisfactorily? ______

(a) (b)

A♭: V^{+6}_{5} I V^{+6}_{5} I

The seventh does not resolve by step downward.

530. Why is the part writing weak in (a) of the preceding frame? ______________________________

(a).
(In (b), the seventh does not resolve properly.)

531. In which case is the dominant seventh chord with lowered fifth resolved most satisfactorily? ______

(a) (b)

b: $V^{7}_{\natural 5}$ i $V^{7}_{\natural 5}$ i

(2) √	532. Check (√) the correct option: 1. The dominant seventh chord with lowered fifth contains the same notes as a German sixth built on the lowered scale degree. 2. Altered tones tend to resolve in the direction of their inflection. True statements: (1) ______ (2) ______ Both ______ Neither ______
Neither √	533. Check (√) the correct option: 1. The chord GB♮DF is an altered dominant seventh in the key of C minor. 2. The chord C♯E♯G♯B is a dominant seventh with raised fifth in the key of F-sharp major. True statements: (1) ______ (2) ______ Both ______ Neither ______
first	534. We shall now turn from altered dominants to examine two diminished seventh chords which function in a unique manner. The diminished seventh chord, as either a leading tone seventh or secondary dominant, has dominant function. Its root is a half-step below the root of the following chord to which it relates. The two chords below do not function in this way and may be thought of as resolving "deceptively." (a) (b) C: ♯ii°7 I6 ♯vi°7 V^6_5 In (a), the SUPERTONIC SEVENTH CHORD WITH RAISED ROOT AND THIRD progresses to the tonic triad in first inversion; in (b), the SUBMEDIANT SEVENTH CHORD WITH RAISED ROOT AND THIRD progresses to the dominant seventh chord in ____________ inversion.
(c).	535. Which of the chords below is a *supertonic seventh chord with raised root and third*? ______ KEY OF A-FLAT MAJOR (a) (b) (c) (d)

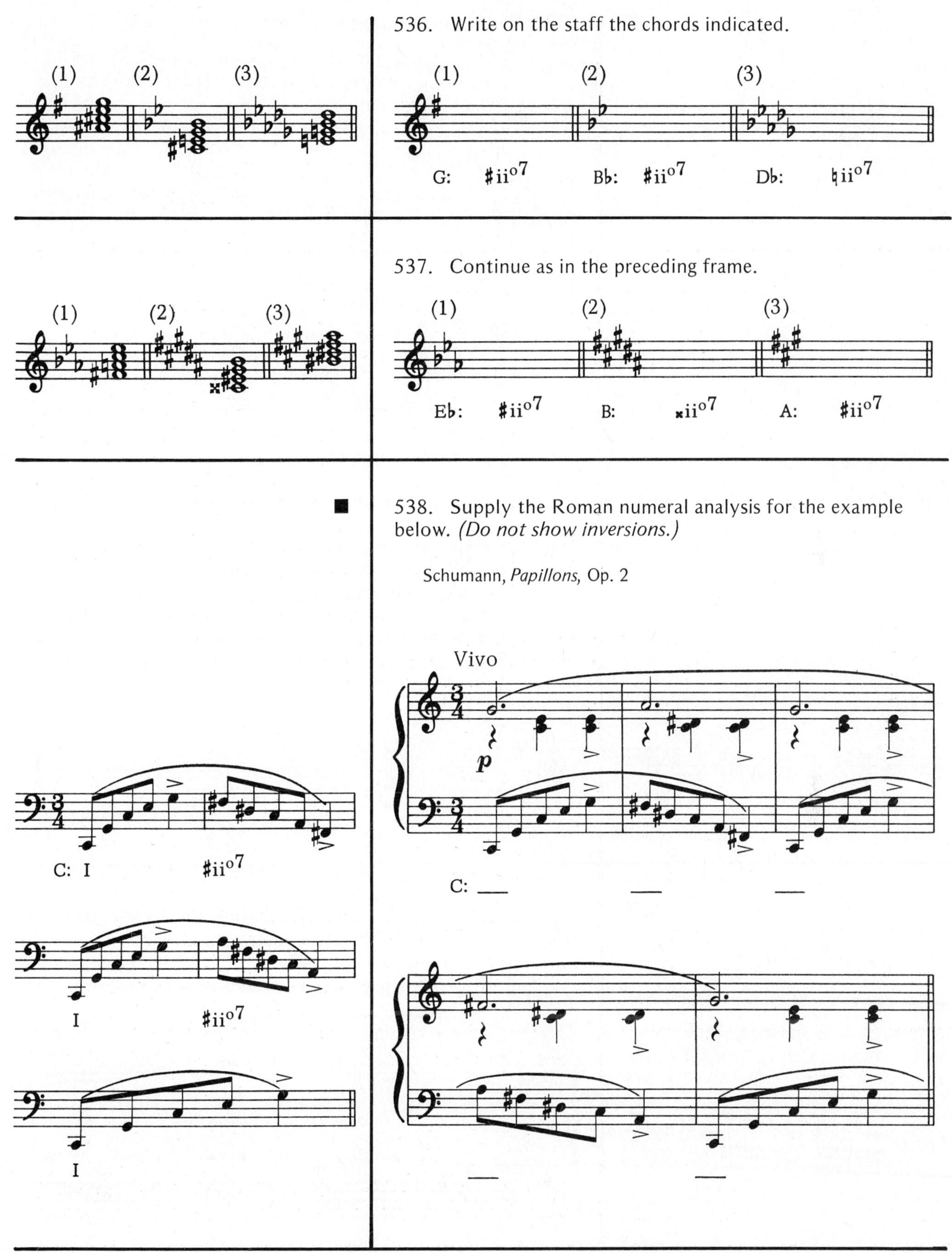
(1)
(2)
(3)
536. Write on the staff the chords indicated.
(1)
(2)
(3)
G: ♯ii°7
B♭: ♯ii°7
D♭: ♮ii°7
(1)
(2)
(3)
537. Continue as in the preceding frame.
(1)
(2)
(3)
E♭: ♯ii°7
B: 𝄪ii°7
A: ♯ii°7
538. Supply the Roman numeral analysis for the example below. *(Do not show inversions.)*
Schumann, *Papillons,* Op. 2
Vivo
p
C: I
♯ii°7
C: ___ ___ ___
I
♯ii°7
I
___ ___

third

539. The supertonic seventh chord with raised root and third may appear in various inversions. In the example below, this chord (at the asterisk) is in ______________ inversion.

Rossini, *William Tell,* "Overture"

(1) (2) (3)

540. Chord symbols may show inversions if desired.

Write the chords as indicated.

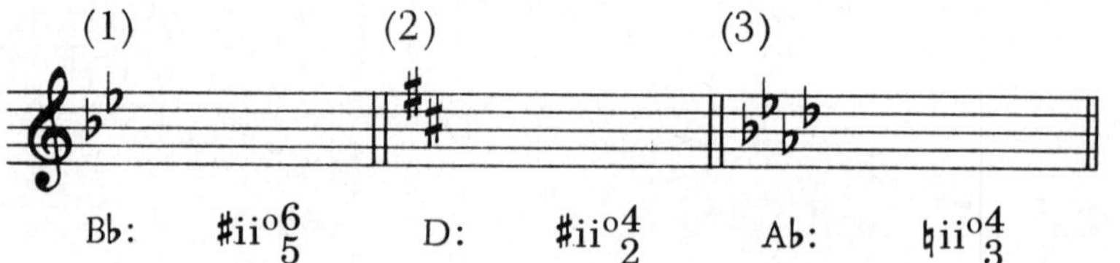

541. Supply the Roman numeral analysis for the example below. *(Indicate inversions.)*

Mozart, *Sonata,* K. 545

542. Supply the Roman numeral analysis for the example below. *(Indicate inversions.)*

Chopin, *Grande Valse Brillante,* Op. 18

B-flat

■ 543. As is often the case with diminished seventh chords, enharmonic spellings are used to simplify notation. In the example below, the altered supertonic seventh chord contains an enharmonic spelling of one note. The root, which normally would be spelled A-sharp, is notated as ______________.

Brahms, *String Quintet*, Op. 111

544. The chord symbol used in the preceding frame for the altered supertonic seventh chord needs to be explained. The sharp placed to the left of the Roman numeral refers to the root (A♯) which is spelled enharmonically as a B-flat. It follows, then, that a symbol is used which expresses the chord as *normally spelled.*

Each chord on the following page is a supertonic seventh chord with raised root and third but contains an enharmonic spelling. Supply the correct Roman numeral analysis in each case. *(Do not indicate inversions.)*

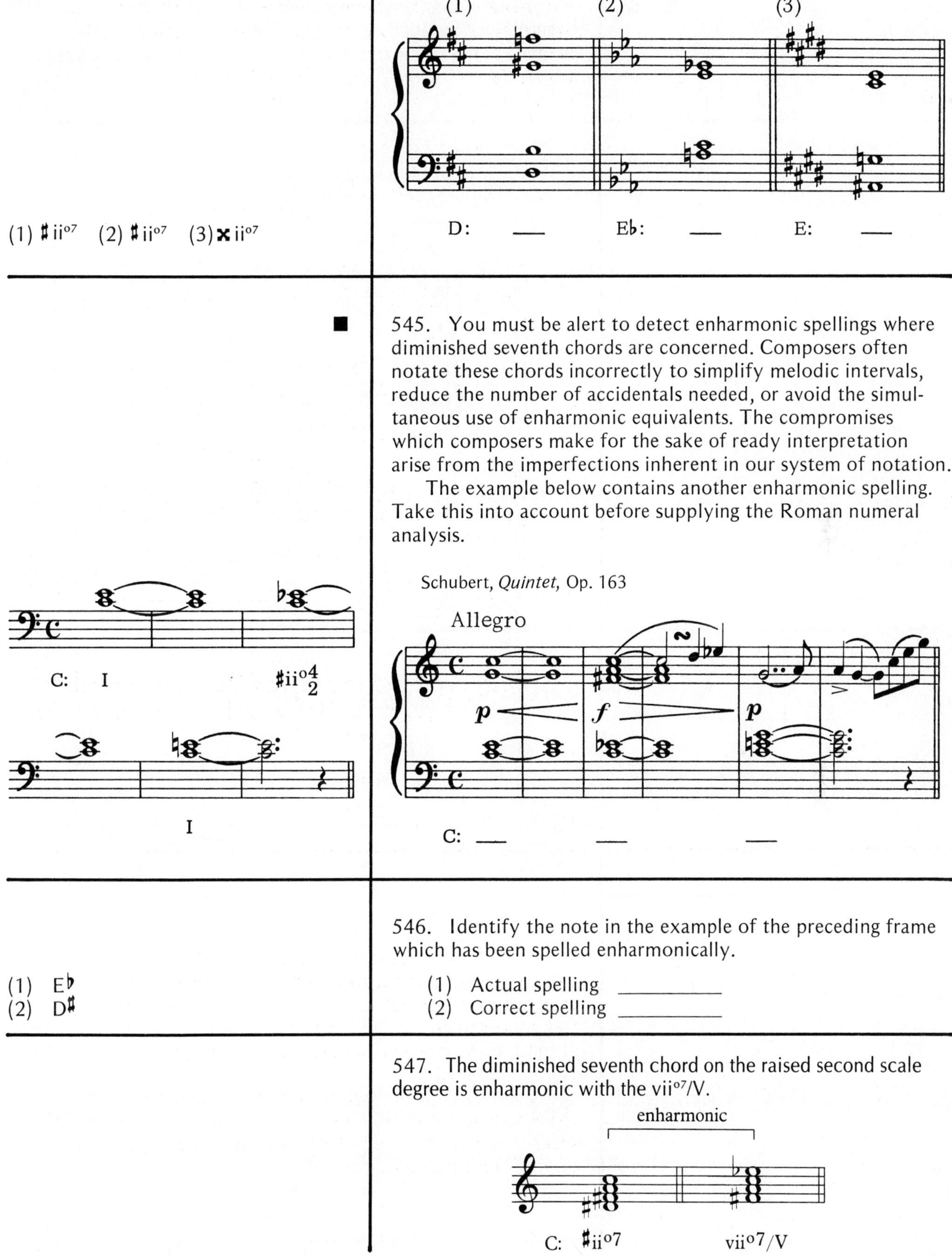

(1) ♯ii°7 (2) ♯ii°7 (3) ×ii°7

---

545. You must be alert to detect enharmonic spellings where diminished seventh chords are concerned. Composers often notate these chords incorrectly to simplify melodic intervals, reduce the number of accidentals needed, or avoid the simultaneous use of enharmonic equivalents. The compromises which composers make for the sake of ready interpretation arise from the imperfections inherent in our system of notation.

The example below contains another enharmonic spelling. Take this into account before supplying the Roman numeral analysis.

---

(1) E♭
(2) D♯

546. Identify the note in the example of the preceding frame which has been spelled enharmonically.

(1) Actual spelling ________
(2) Correct spelling ________

---

547. The diminished seventh chord on the raised second scale degree is enharmonic with the vii°7/V.

(No response.)	The resolution determines the analysis of enharmonic chords. Regardless of the spelling, the chord above is analyzed as vii°7/V if resolved to the dominant; if resolved to the tonic, it is analyzed as ♯ii°7.
dominant	548. In addition to being built on the raised second scale degree, the diminished seventh chord also appears on the raised sixth degree. C: ♯vi°7 V^6_5 I Whereas the supertonic seventh chord with raised root and third progresses to the tonic triad, the submediant seventh chord with raised root and third progresses to the ____________ triad or seventh chord.
(d).	549. Which of the chords below is a *submediant seventh chord with raised root and third*? ______ KEY OF D MAJOR (a) (b) (c) (d)
(1) (2) (3)	550. Write on the staff the chords indicated. (1) (2) (3) F: ♯vi°7 D: ♯vi°7 B: 𝄪vi°7

551. Continue as in the preceding frame.

552. Supply the Roman numeral analysis for the example below.

Schumann, *Dichterliebe,* Op. 48, No. 7

553. Complete the Roman numeral analysis below:

Wagner, *Die Meistersinger* "Vorspiel"

(Note the omission of the 5th in the altered submediant seventh chord.)

554. Supply the Roman numeral analysis for the example below:

Beethoven, *Quartet,* Op. 131

7th

■ 555. Like the altered supertonic seventh, the submediant seventh chord with raised root and third may appear in various inversions. The bass note of the chord at the asterisk is the (root/3rd/5th/7th) _________ of the chord.

Tchaikovsky, *Nutcracker Suite, "Valse des Fleurs"*

---

(1) G♮
(2) F𝄪

■ 556. Enharmonic spellings frequently occur. Identify the note in the chord at the asterisk which is spelled enharmonically.

Beethoven, *Symphony No. 2*, Op. 36

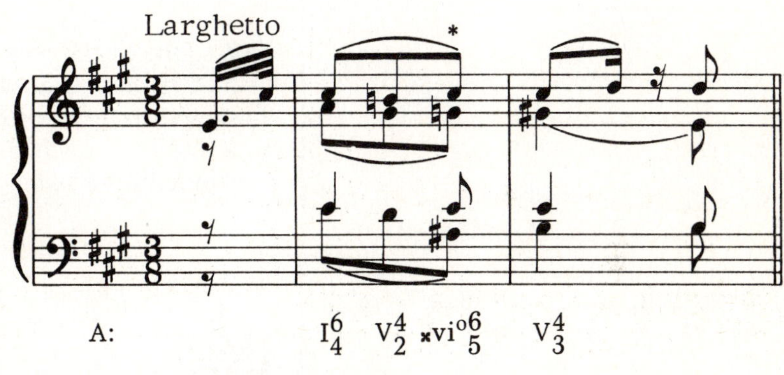

(1) Actual spelling _________
(2) Correct spelling _________

■ 557. Supply the Roman numeral analysis for the example on the following page.

Beethoven, *Quartet,* Op. 18, No. 3

B♭: __ __ __ __ __ __ __ __ __ __

__ __ __

Both are diminished, not perfect fifths.

558. One of the most important principles to observe when using altered chords is the proper resolution of altered tones. The supertonic and submediant seventh chords with raised root and third each contain two altered tones; these should continue in the same direction as their inflection (upwards).

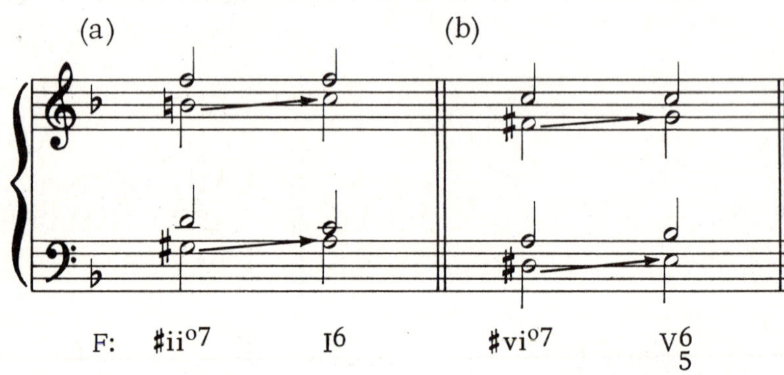

There are parallel fifths between the bass and tenor in (b). Why is this not an error? ________________________

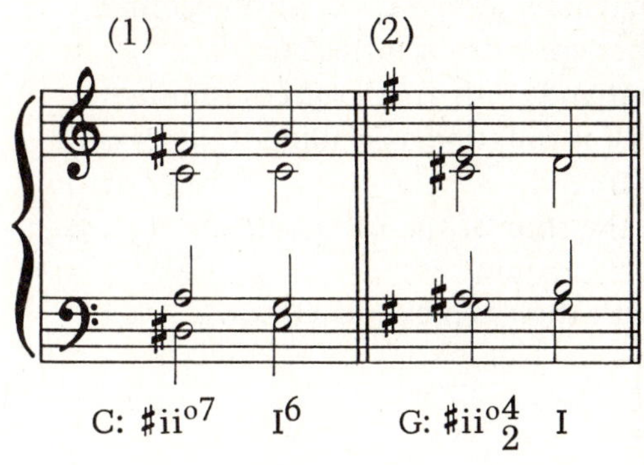

559. Write the alto and tenor voices in accordance with the figured bass symbols. Supply, also, the Roman numeral analysis. *(Indicate inversions.)*

560. Continue as in the preceding frame. *(Use open structure.)*

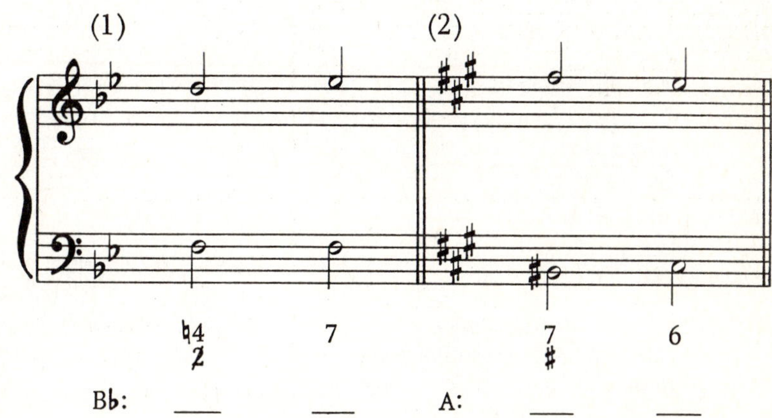

561. Continue as in the preceding frame.

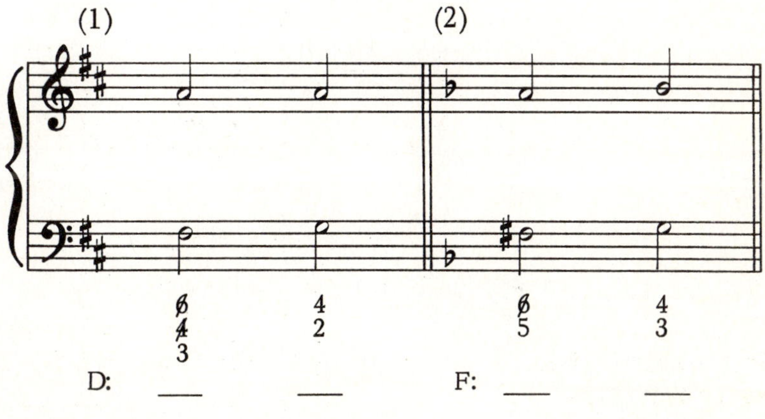

SUMMARY

The Neapolitan sixth is a colorful, but not especially active chord; it functions like any other supertonic triad—its normal resolution is to the dominant. Altered dominants, on the other hand, are highly active due to the raised or lowered fifth, which provides an additional active tone. Like most chromatically altered tones, the raised or lowered fifth tends to resolve in the direction of inflection.

The resolution of diminished seventh chords on the raised second and sixth scale degrees is unlike that of most other diminished seventh chords. These two chords do not function as leading tone seventh chords, but rather as colorful embellishments of the tonic or dominant. The root of the diminished seventh chord (as usually spelled) progresses down an augmented second to the root of the following chord, and it is this relationship which gives these progressions their distinctive character.

The altered chords presented in this chapter are shown below with their typical resolution.

Neapolitan Sixth

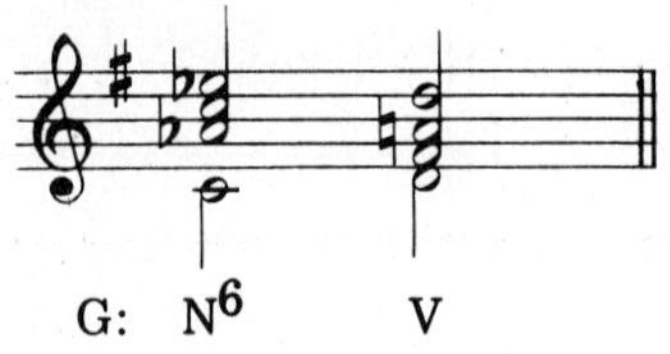

Altered Dominants

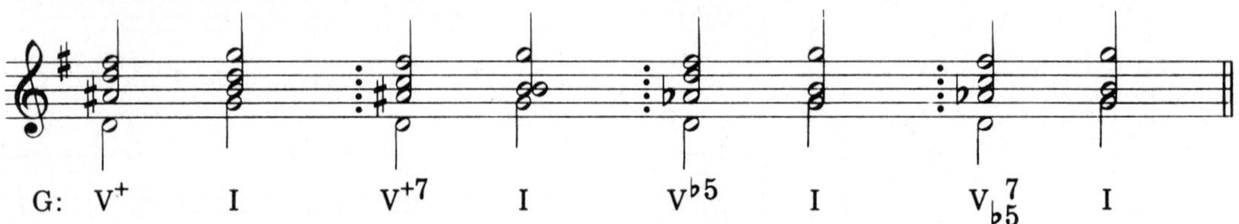

Diminished Seventh Chords on
Raised 2nd and 6th Scale Degrees

Mastery Frames

Neapolitan (486–488)	7–1. The major triad built on the lowered second scale degree is called the ____________________ sixth chord.
first third (500)	7–2. The Neapolitan sixth chord is usually used in __________ inversion with the __________ doubled.

(497)

7–3. Complete the upper voices and provide the appropriate chord symbols.

(1) (2) (3)

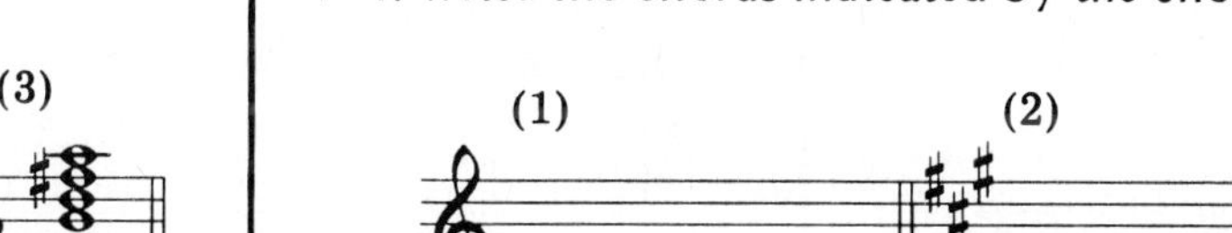

(510–514)

7–4. Write the chords indicated by the chord symbols.

(1) (2) (3)

C: V+ A: V+7 E♭: V+7

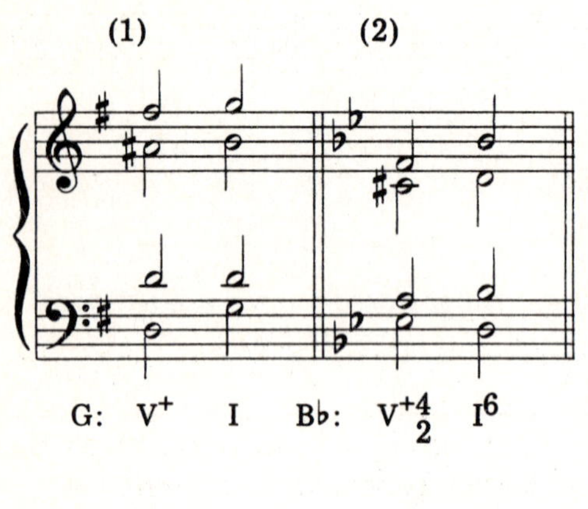

(515-516)

7-5. Complete the upper voices and provide the appropriate chord symbols.

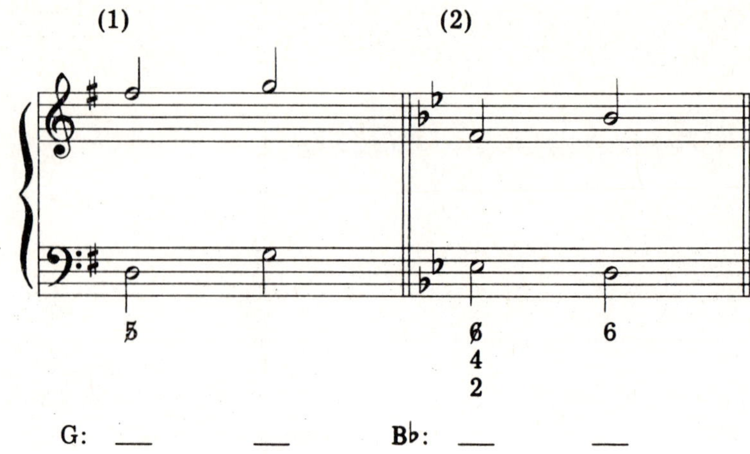

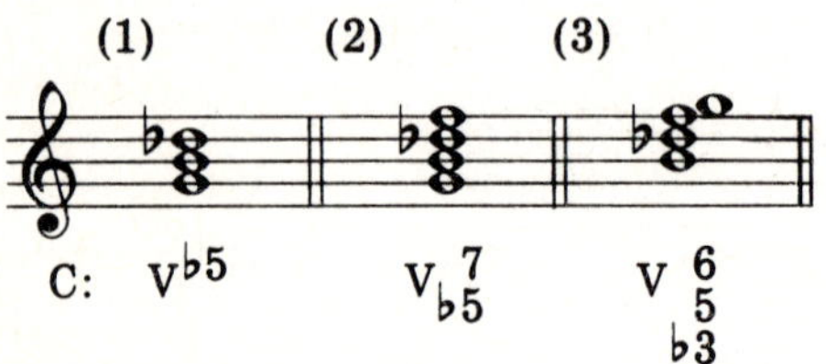

(522-526)

7-6. Write the chords indicated by the chord symbols.

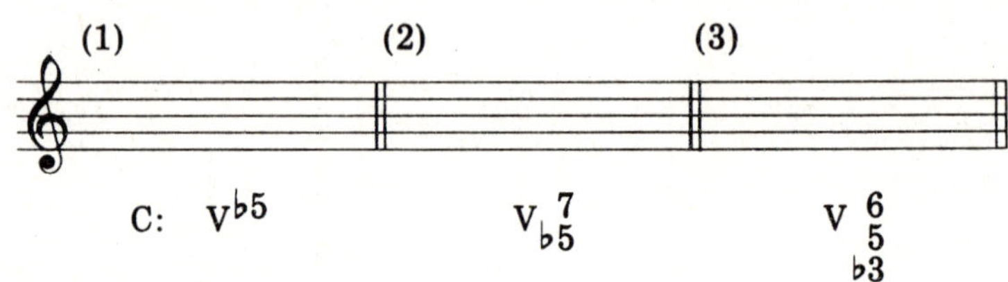

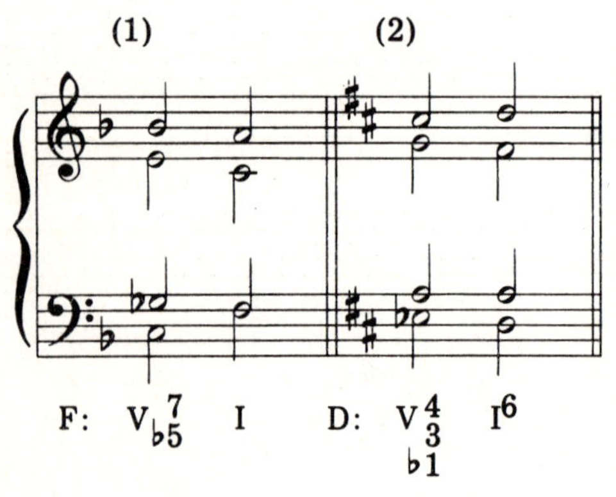

(523, 531)

7-7. Complete the upper voices and provide the appropriate chord symbols.

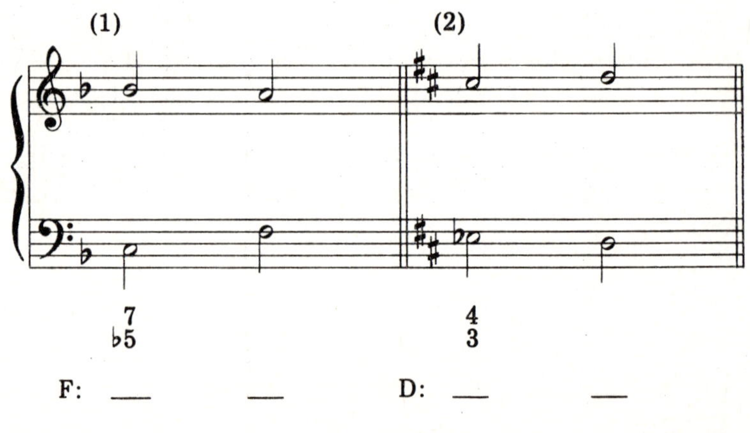

(534)

7-8. Write the chords indicated by the chord symbols.

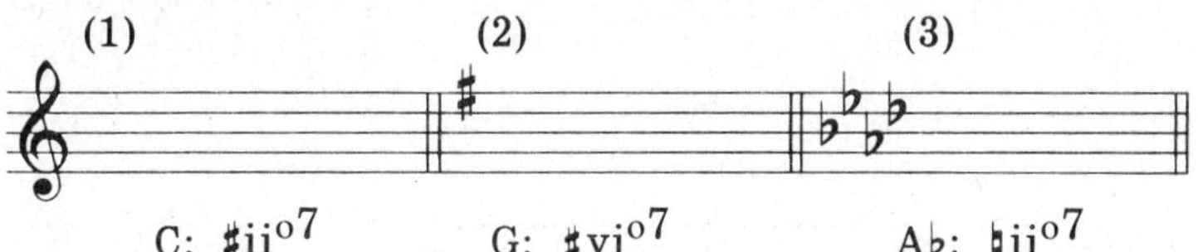

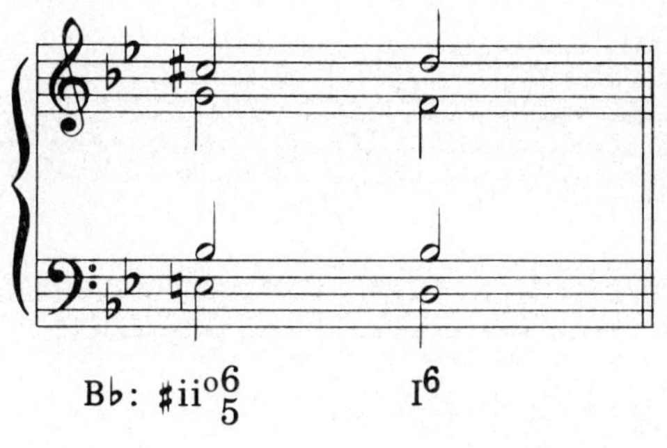

(534-547)

7-9. Complete the resolution of the altered supertonic seventh chord, and provide the appropriate chord symbols. *(Indicate inversions.)*

(548-556)

7-10. Complete the resolution of the altered submediant seventh chord, and provide the appropriate chord symbols. *(Indicate inversions.)*

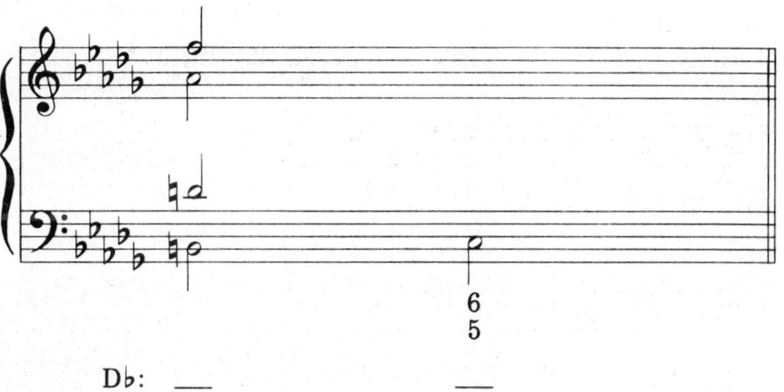

Supplementary Assignments

ASSIGNMENT 7-1 Name____________________________

1. Spell Neapolitan sixth chords in the indicated keys.

2. Write Neapolitan sixth chords on the grand staff for four-voice chorus. Place all chords in the normal position with preferred doubling. Also write resolutions for each.

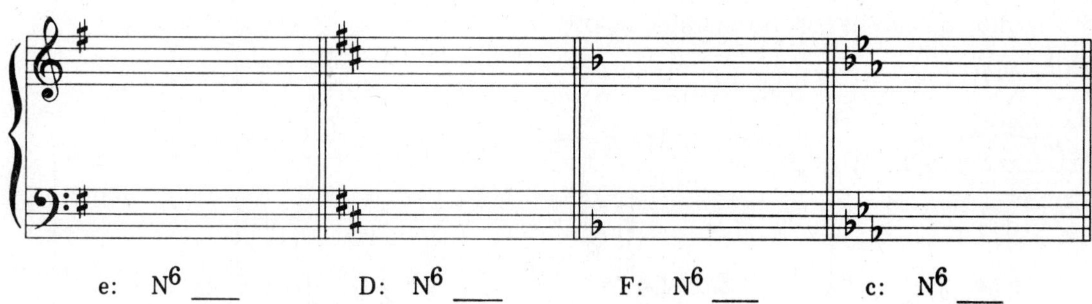

3. Which is the best resolution of the Neapolitan sixth chord?____________

4. Provide the harmonic analysis for the example below.

Beethoven: *Sonata*, Op. 90

5. Provide the harmonic analysis for the example below.

Schumann: *Waltz*

6. Show with chord symbols the expected resolution of each chord.

(a) N^6 ____________ (d) V^+ ____________

(b) $\sharp ii^{o7}$ ____________ (e) $\sharp vi^{o7}$ ____________

(c) $V\flat^7_5$ ____________ (f) V^{+7} ____________

ASSIGNMENT 7-2 Name______________________

1. Write the chords indicated by the chord symbols.

2. Resolve each chord so that all active tones move in the direction of their inflection. Provide also the proper chord symbols.

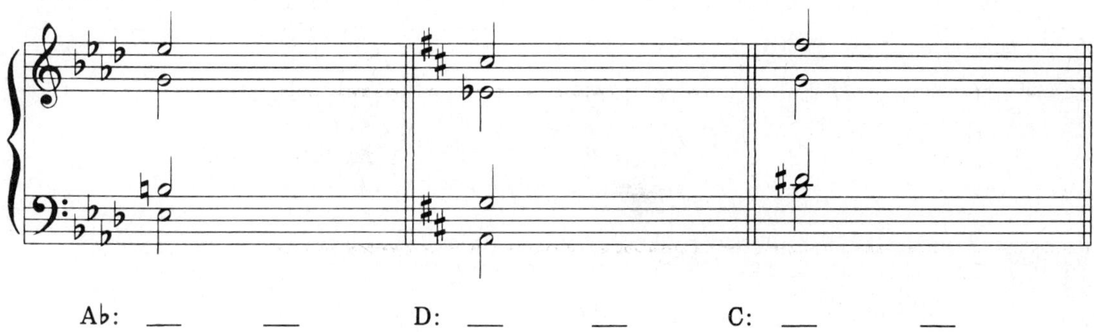

3. Write the alto and tenor voices, and provide the chord symbols.

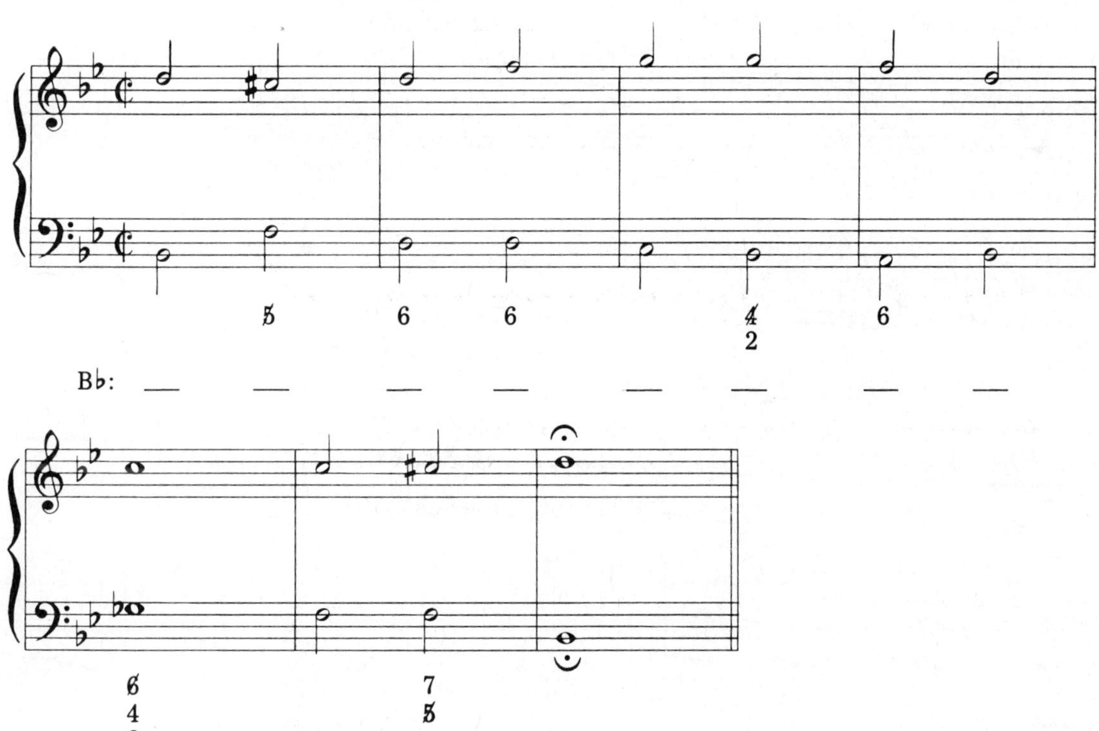

___ ___ ___ ___

4. Write the chords indicated by the chord symbols, and resolve appropriately. Provide the second chord symbol.

C: ♯ii°7 ____ A♭: ♮ii°7 ____ G: ♯vi°7 ____ D♭: ♮vi°7 ____

5. Provide the harmonic analysis for the example below.

Schubert: *Sechs Moments Musicaux,* Op. 94

6. Provide the harmonic analysis for the example below.

Chopin: *Nocturne,* Op. 32, No. 2

7. Compose one or more phrases which contain either a ♯ii°7 or a ♯vi°7 chord. Choose your own key and time signature; take care to notate completely. Use either piano or instrumental style.

chapter eight

Chromatic Third-Relation Harmony

During the nineteenth century, composers increasingly exploited root movement by thirds. Because the third is the basic constructive unit of chords in the tertian system, it follows that root relations by thirds should have a "fundamental" character. They generally produce an aurally pleasing effect for most listeners. Limited to diatonic chords, third-relation harmony is pleasing, but does not expand the tonal horizon. *Chromatic* third relations, however, lead to chords which are quite foreign to the tonality, yet may be used in such a way that the tonal center is not seriously undermined. The result is not necessarily tonal instability, but tonal expansion.

562. Mediant and submediant chords are called "mediants" because they are half-way between the tonic and either the dominant or subdominant.

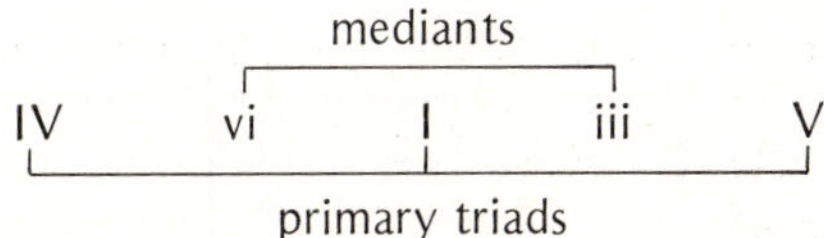

From this we can assert that any two chords whose roots are the interval of a third apart are in a "mediant" relationship with one another. The mediant and submediant triads relate to the tonic in this manner.

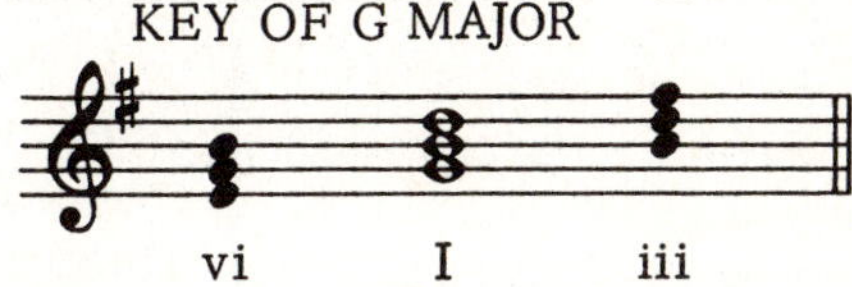

Extending this principle a step further, we can state that vii° and iii are in a "mediant" relation to the dominant.

Which two chords are in a "mediant" relationship with the subdominant?

(1) ________________
(2) ________________

Answer:
(1) Submediant
(2) Supertonic

---

563. Which chords have a mediant relationship to the D major triad on the following page? *(Don't be misled by inversions.)*

____

Answer: (a) and (c).

KEY OF D MAJOR

(a) (b) (c) (d)

(b) and (d).

564. Which chords have a mediant relationship to the F major triad below? _______________

KEY OF F MAJOR

(a) (b) (c) (d)

---

third

565. Within a tonality, mediant chords are built on the third and sixth scale degrees. (The mediant lies halfway between the tonic and dominant; the submediant lies halfway between the subdominant and the tonic.) The roots of mediant triads are related to the tonic by the interval of a ____________.

(No response.)

566. Whereas root relationships of fifths and seconds predominate in the music of earlier composers, mediant relationships (roots a third apart) are an important feature of many works by composers of the Romantic and post-Romantic eras. Of special importance is the use by these composers of *chromatic* mediant relationships. These, of course, involve the use of tones which are not part of the diatonic scale, and produce altered chords.

---

567. Limited to only major and minor triads, the mediants (both diatonic and altered) of the C major triad are shown in the diagram on the following page.

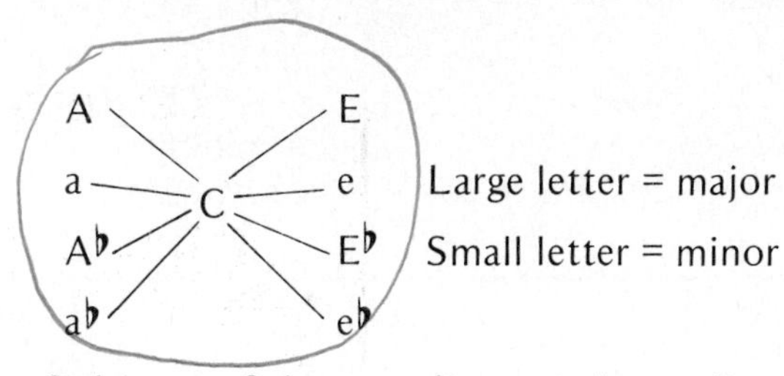

(1) ACE

(2) EGB
(Any order.)

Only two of these mediant triads are *diatonic* in the key of C major. Spell these chords.

(1) __________

(2) __________

---

chromatic

568. With the exception of the A minor and E minor triads, all of the mediant triads in the preceding frame bear a ______________ mediant relation to the C major triad.

569. Write the second chord in each case as directed. *(Observe the principles of correct voice leading and doubling.)*

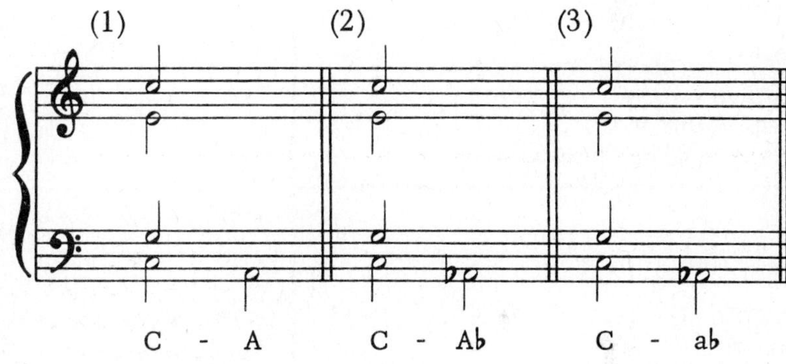

570. The chords you wrote in the preceding frame are the chromatic (sub)mediants of the C major triad.

Write the second chord in each case as directed. *(Continue to employ correct part writing procedures.)*

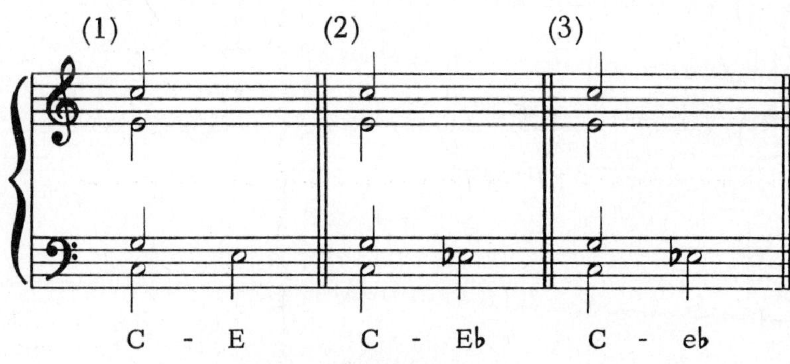

third

571. The root of a chromatic mediant may be either a major or minor ____________ from the root of the chord to which it relates.

---

572. It is chiefly major and minor triads which take part in chromatic mediant progressions. Diminished and augmented triads do not produce the novel tonal effect associated with this kind of writing and usually are best analyzed as some other type of altered chord. Seventh chords, on the other hand, sometimes are used in this manner, but we shall limit ourselves at this point to major and minor triads.

The mediant triads (both diatonic and altered) of the C minor triad are shown in the diagram below:

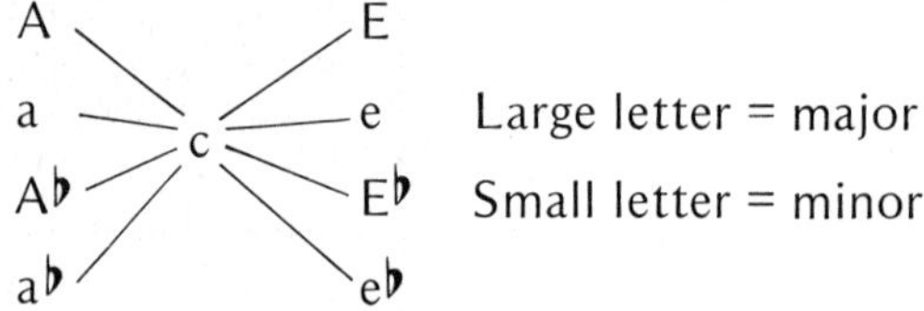

Spell the two mediant triads which are *diatonic* in the key of C minor.

(1) ____________

(2) ____________

(1) A♭CE♭

(2) E♭GB♭

(The note B♭ derives from natural minor.)

573. Write the second chord in each case as directed. *(Observe the principles of correct voice leading and doubling.*

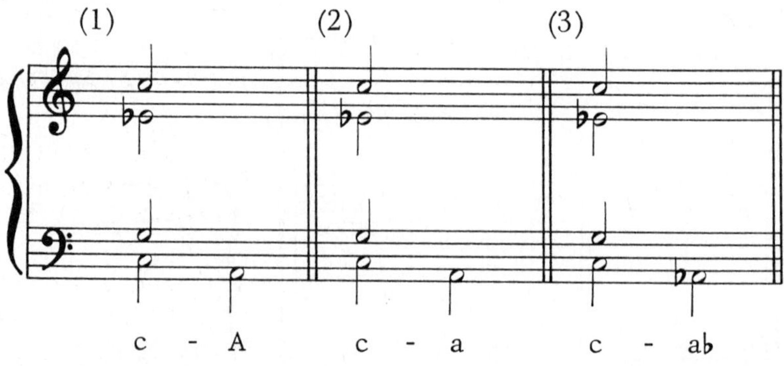

(1) (2) (3)

574. Continue as in the preceding frame.

(1) (2) (3)

c - E   c - e   e - eb

None.

575. Chromatic mediant relationships provide an important source of colorful harmonic effects. These effects were favored by composers of the late nineteenth century such as Wagner, Liszt, and Debussy. Progressions which feature a number of these relationships often have a nonfunctional harmonic character. The term "color harmony" sometimes is used to refer to this kind of writing. The ear apparently perceives as closely related two chords whose roots are a third apart, even though they may share few or no common tones. This is probably due to the long use in Western music of the third as the basic constructive interval for chords.

The D major and F minor triads bear a chromatic mediant relationship to one another. How many common tones do they share? ____________

---

(1) (2) (3) (4)

(Any order.)

576. Write the four *major* triads which are chromatic mediants of the A major triad.

(1) (2) (3) (4)

V/vi

577. Some of the chromatic mediants you wrote in the preceding frame are easily identified as possible borrowed chords or secondary dominants in the key of A major. The F major triad is a submediant chord borrowed from A minor, and the F-sharp major triad could be analyzed as V/ii. If analyzed as a secondary dominant, the C-sharp major triad would be represented by the chord symbol __________.

Keep in mind that the *root* relationships between chords will generally be the determining factor in how they are ultimately analyzed and classified.

578. Chromatic mediants may sometimes be identified as other types of altered chords. But when used as color sources rather than in accordance with functional harmonic principles, they open up new tonal relationships and effects. Progressions which contain a large number of such relationships take on a novel aspect. Chromatic mediants greatly enlarge the tonal vocabulary without necessarily undermining the stability of the tonality.

In Frame 576 one of the chromatic mediants given for the A major triad is the C major triad. Could this chord be analyzed as either a borrowed chord or a secondary dominant in the key of A major? __________

Yes.
(It is a diatonic triad in A (pure) minor. Thus it could be a borrowed chord.)

---

579. Write the two *minor* triads which are chromatic mediants of the A major triad. (Remember: *triads which are diatonic in the key of A major are excluded.)*

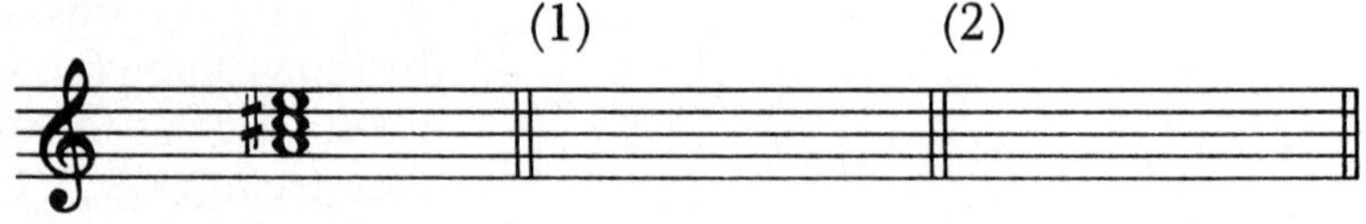

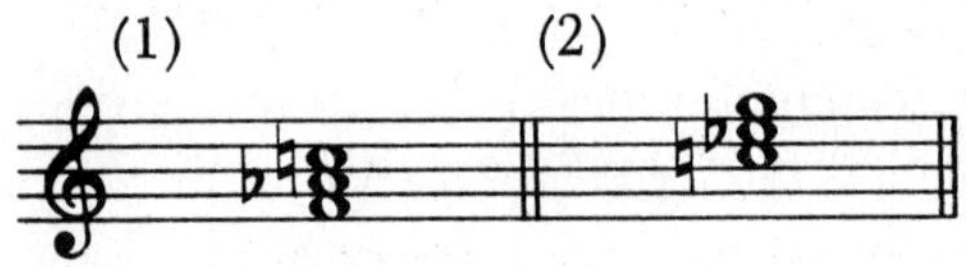

---

580. Write the four *minor* triads which are chromatic mediants of the G minor triad.

(1) (2) (3) (4)

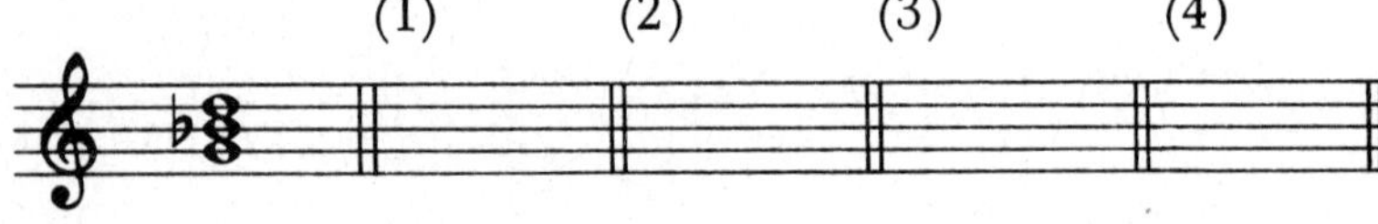

---

581. Write the two *major* triads which are chromatic mediants of the G minor triad. (Remember: *triads which are diatonic in the key of G minor are excluded.)*

(1) (2)

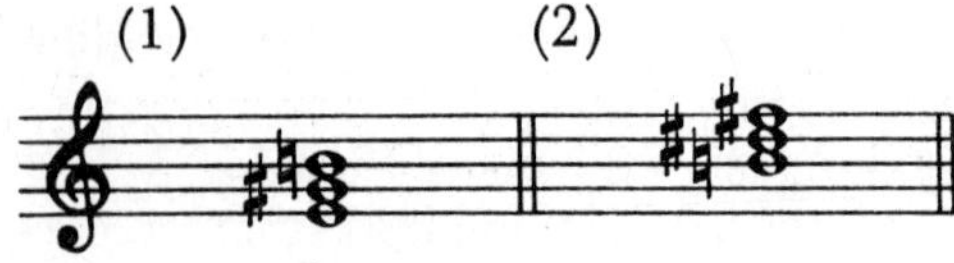

■

582. The chord symbol used to represent a chromatic mediant is determined by the quality of the chord and the scale degree on which it is built. The first chord in the example on the following page is a major triad on the third degree of the D-flat major scale. Thus a large Roman numeral (III) is used.

Liszt, *Sonetto 47 del Petrarca*

Con moto

Db: III V(13) V7 I

It does not function as a secondary dominant. As such, it would progress to vi.

Explain why the chord at the asterisk should not be analyzed as a secondary dominant (V/vi). ______________________

---

583. Observe the chord symbols used for each of the chords below:

(a) (b) (c) (d)

D: vi VI ♭VI ♭vi

Chord (a) is a diatonic (unaltered) submediant triad. A large Roman numeral is used in (b) to reflect the major quality of the chord. The flats placed at the lower left-hand corner of the Roman numerals in (c) and (d) indicate the lowered root in each case. What feature of the chord symbol in (d) indicates that the chord is a *minor* triad? ______________________

A small Roman numeral is used.

---

(1) (2) (3)

Eb: iii ♭III ♭vi

584. Write the proper chord symbol for each chord.

(1) (2) (3)

Eb: ___ ___ ___

False.
(Chord (1) is diatonic.)

585. All of the chords in the preceding frame are chromatic mediants. (True/False) __________

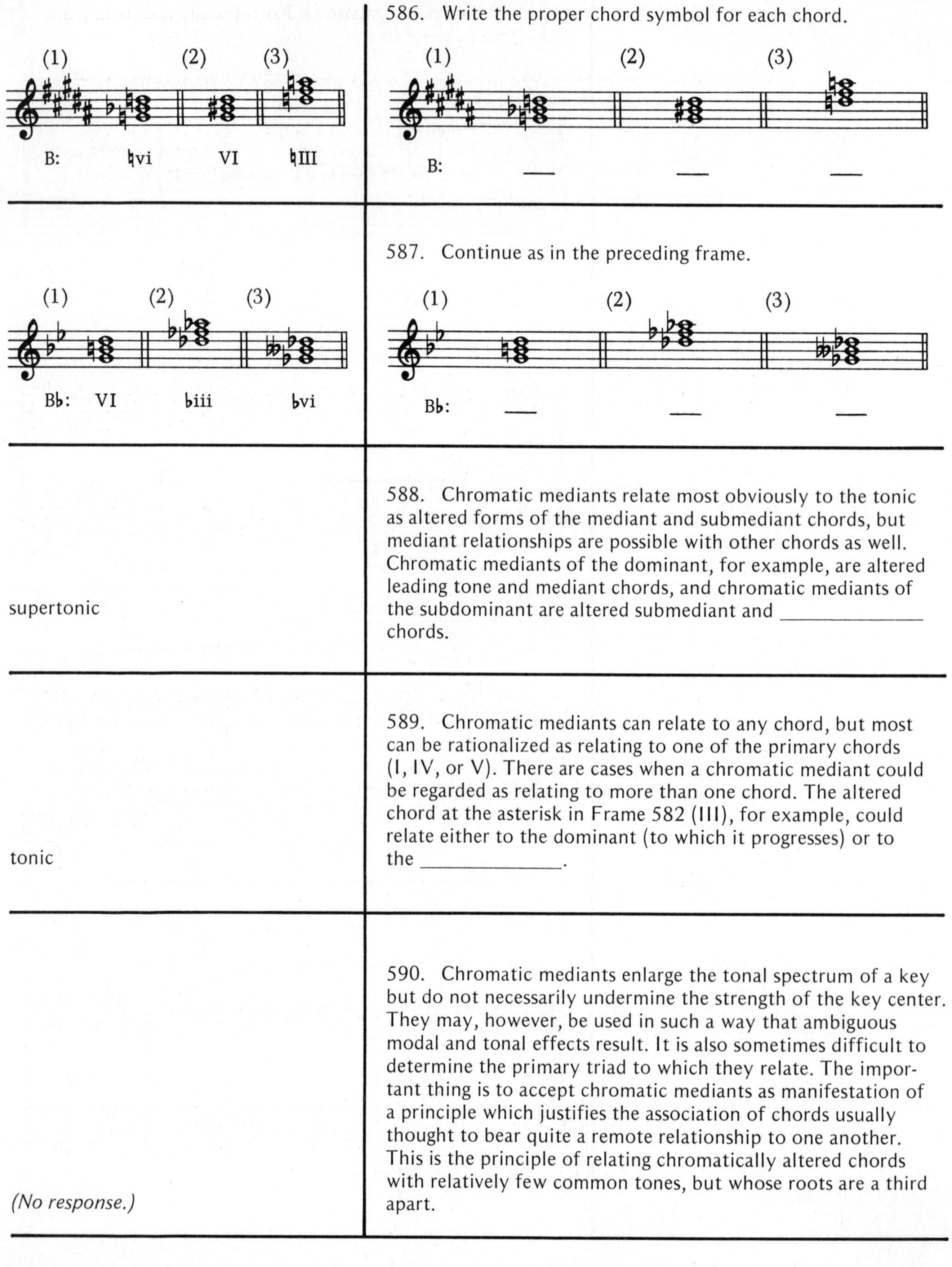

586. Write the proper chord symbol for each chord.

587. Continue as in the preceding frame.

supertonic

588. Chromatic mediants relate most obviously to the tonic as altered forms of the mediant and submediant chords, but mediant relationships are possible with other chords as well. Chromatic mediants of the dominant, for example, are altered leading tone and mediant chords, and chromatic mediants of the subdominant are altered submediant and _____________ chords.

tonic

589. Chromatic mediants can relate to any chord, but most can be rationalized as relating to one of the primary chords (I, IV, or V). There are cases when a chromatic mediant could be regarded as relating to more than one chord. The altered chord at the asterisk in Frame 582 (III), for example, could relate either to the dominant (to which it progresses) or to the _____________.

(No response.)

590. Chromatic mediants enlarge the tonal spectrum of a key but do not necessarily undermine the strength of the key center. They may, however, be used in such a way that ambiguous modal and tonal effects result. It is also sometimes difficult to determine the primary triad to which they relate. The important thing is to accept chromatic mediants as manifestation of a principle which justifies the association of chords usually thought to bear quite a remote relationship to one another. This is the principle of relating chromatically altered chords with relatively few common tones, but whose roots are a third apart.

nonfunctional

591. The use of chromatic mediants usually results in (functional/nonfunctional) ______________ harmony.

■

592. A passage which illustrates the vague or ambiguous tonal effect which may result from the use of chromatic mediant relationships is the "eternal sleep motive" from Wagner's opera, *Die Walkure.*

Wagner, *Die Walküre,* Act III, Scene 3

E

Harmony such as this is naturally open to a variety of interpretations. We shall discuss briefly one possibility in the next few frames.

One aspect of this passage is fairly obvious: the tonality established in measure nine is the key of ______ major.

(No response.)

593. In spite of the highly chromatic character of the passage in the preceding frame, it may be regarded as being entirely in the key of E major. Many of the chords can be explained as chromatic mediants, and these are the chords which concern us here. Melodically, this passage consists of a descending chromatic scale extending for more than an octave. It is organized rhythmically into a sequence which repeats every two measures.

---

third

594. Although the harmony varies, it is organized in accordance with the melodic sequence mentioned above. The units which comprise this sequence begin in measures 1, 3, 5, and 7. The last chord in the example (E major) closes the sequence. Obviously the chords which begin each unit of a sequence such as this have special significance. The example below shows the root progression of these chords. *(Numbers refer to measures.)*

① ③ ⑤ ⑦ ⑨

The notes are written in order to make clear their relation to one another. The root progression in each case is down a major ____________.

---

augmented

595. Chromatic mediants are often spelled enharmonically. The first chord of the example in Frame 592, for example, is an A-flat major triad. It is considered to have a chromatic mediant relation to the E major triad because the interval of a diminished fourth (A♭-E) is the aural equivalent of a major third (G♯-E).* You must not be misled by enharmonic spellings, for these occur frequently in highly chromatic music. Sound is more important than notation, which is often merely a matter of convenience.

The descending pattern of roots shown in Frame 594 outlines the ____________ triad.

*Chord 1 in Frame 592 can be viewed equally well as related to the dominant (B major triad) which follows.

596. The progression of chords which serves as the harmonic framework for the passage in Frame 592 is shown below:

All of these chords are easily related to the key of E major as either the tonic triad (I) or chromatic ______________.

mediants

---

597. The specific progressions in the example of Frame 592 which feature chromatic mediant relationships are shown below. *(Numbers refer to measures.)* Supply the proper chord symbols. *(Note the indication of C major in (b).)*

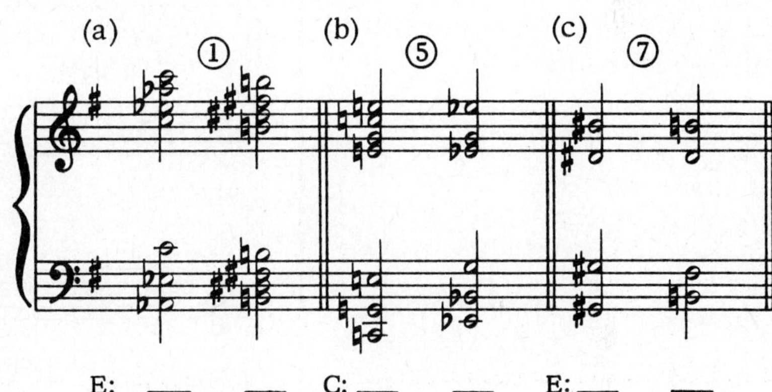

(a) E: III V

(b) C: I ♭III

(c) E: III V

---

598. You were asked to analyze the chords in (b) of the preceding frame in the key of C major as this makes them easier to comprehend. Even though the over-all tonal structure of Wagner's motive is in the key of E major, the momentary presence of other keys can be felt. This excerpt provides a good example of how the basic harmonic scheme can be endowed with extraordinarily colorful effects through chromatic mediants which suggest, but do not necessarily confirm, other keys.

Of course, the tonal fluidity produced in this manner can also result in actual changes of key. Whether or not keys are felt to be "established" is left to the discretion of the analyst. It is generally desirable to absorb as many chords as possible into a given tonality in order to obtain as large a view of the tonal organization as possible.

True.

All chromatic mediants are potentially in some key other than that in which they appear. (True/False) __________

■ 599. The harmony in the example below consists of major triads built on a series of roots which ascend in minor thirds.

Brahms, *Immer leiser wird mein Schlummer,* Op. 105, No. 2

Is the third chord (B♭D♮F♮) as closely related to the key of E major as the second (G♮BD♮)? ______

No.
(See next frame.)

600. Chord 3 in the preceding frame is a tritone removed from the tonal center of E major. This is the most remote tonal relationship possible. Note that B-flat divides the octave E-E into two equal parts.

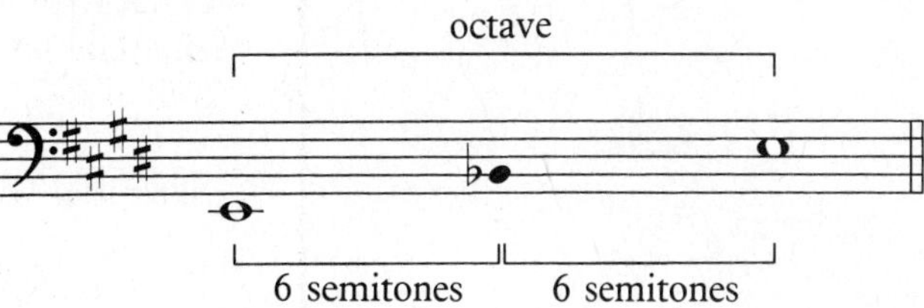

Such relations are called "symmetrical," and they tend to obliterate tonal distinctions.

(No response.)

---

601. The tonality of the progression in Frame 599 is ambiguous. Not only does the exclusive use of major triads provide the ear nothing to differentiate between, but furthermore, the sequence of roots quickly reaches a point which is so remote from the key of E major that it lies outside the orbit of this key.

Chromatic mediant relationships can be used to undermine the strength of a tonality. Do you think this is desirable?

____

It is not possible to give a simple yes or no answer. It depends upon circumstances and what a composer wishes to achieve at any given point in a composition.

---

602. The term FALSE RELATION* applies to chromaticism which occurs between two *different* voices. Compare the two examples below:

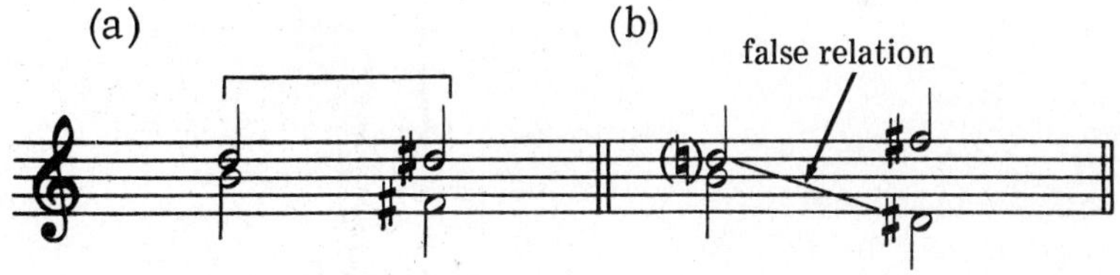

In (a), the chromaticism (D-D♯) occurs in the same voice. In (b), however, it not only occurs between the two voices but is displaced by the interval of an octave. *(Play these two examples at the piano.)*

Which example produces the "smoother" effect? ____________

*The term "cross relation" is also used.

(a).
(There should be no difference of opinion in this case.)

---

603. False relations may cause a kind of "chromatic stress." For this reason they are often avoided by means of careful part writing which limits chromatic movement to the same voice (as in (a) of the preceding frame). Sometimes false relations are exploited for their peculiar expressive value, particularly when a sudden, unexpected change of harmony is desired. Such a case is shown below:

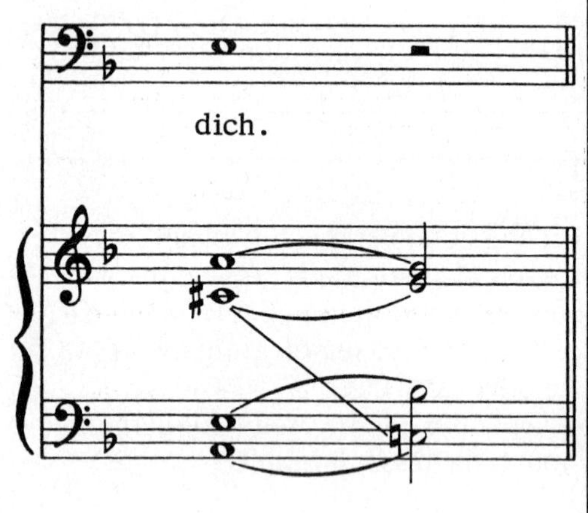

Find the false relation and draw a line connecting the notes which produce it.

(b) and (c).

604. Which example(s) contains a false relation? ___________

---

605. Chromatic mediants (or use of third relationships) bring about many false relations. These sometimes are exploited for their expressive value, but at other times are eliminated through careful part writing.

No.
(The chromaticism D♯-D♮ occurs in the same voice.)

A chromatic third relationship occurs in the example below between the second and third chords. Does this passage contain a cross relation? _______

Chopin, *Prelude,* Op. 28, No. 9

■

606. Supply the Roman numeral analysis for the example below. Analyze the chords at the asterisks as chromatic mediants.

Franck, *Chorale No. 1*

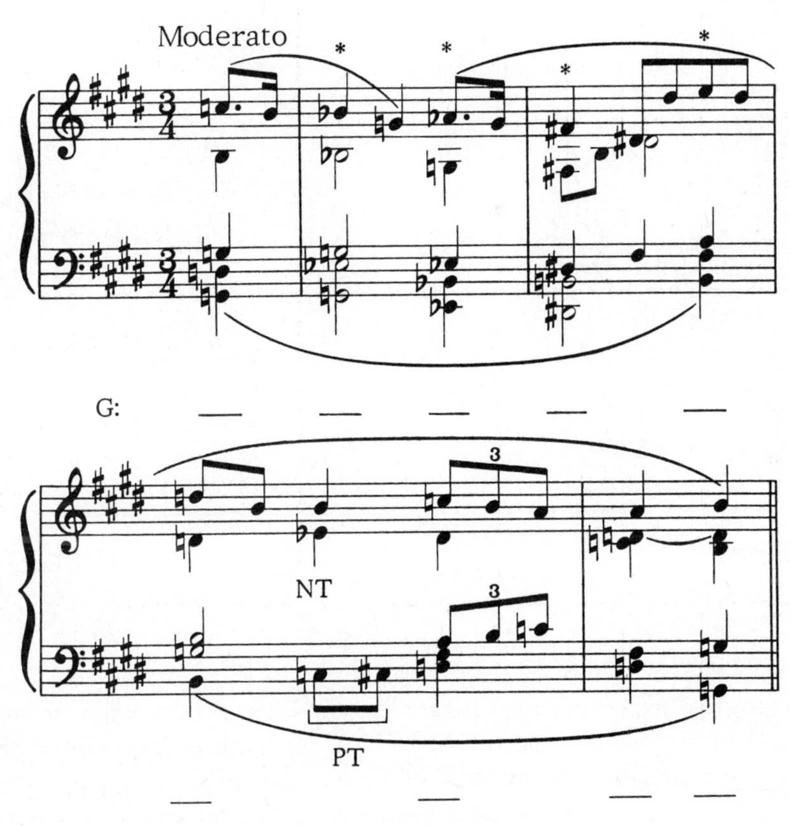

■ 607. In each of the two examples below, the B major triad is used as a different type of altered chord. Taking into account its function, indicate to what type each belongs.

KEY OF D MAJOR

(a) (b)

(a) ____________________

(b) ____________________

(a) Secondary dominant

(b) Chromatic mediant

---

608. Check (√) below the type of altered chord shown in the example.

D♭:

(a) Altered dominant ______

(b) Chromatic mediant ______

(c) Borrowed chord ______

(d) None of these ______

(b) √

---

609. The chord in the preceding frame could also be a secondary dominant (depending upon its use). Write the chord symbol which would be appropriate in such a case.

____

V/vi.

SUMMARY

Chords whose roots are separated by the interval of a major or minor third are said to be in a mediant relationship to one another. Chromatic mediants employ tones which are foreign to the key, and greatly enlarge the harmonic material of a particular tonality. Used with discretion (clearly related to primary triads), they do not undermine the strength of the key center. They may, however, depending upon the frequency of occurrence and the root relationships involved, cause ambiguity of modality and obscure the tonal center. Some chords can be analyzed either as chromatic mediants or other types of altered chords. The way a particular chord is used determines its classification.

Although chromatic mediants generally are not used as frequently as some of the other types of altered chords, they are capable of producing striking effects which cannot be achieved by other means. They are especially prevalent in music of late nineteenth-century composers who frequently exploited the third relation of roots to achieve novel tonal effects.

The examples below show how greatly the tonality of C major may be expanded by the use of chromatic mediants. The chromatic mediants are limited to major and minor triads that bear a mediant relationship to the tonic, subdominant, and dominant triads. (White notes denote diatonic triads; black notes denote altered chords.)

Examples (A), (B), and (C) show the generation of mediant triads (both diatonic and chromatic). Example (D) shows that, altogether, thirteen altered chords are produced as chromatic mediants.

KEY OF C

(Accidentals affect only the note that follows.)

Mastery Frames

vi, iii
ii, vi
iii, vii°

(562–565)

8-1. Use chord symbols to indicate the triads that have a *diatonic* mediant or third relationship with the tonic, subdominant, and dominant chords in a major key.

I __________
IV __________
V __________

(Any order.)

(566–571)

8-2. Write all of the major and minor triads that have a *chromatic* mediant or third relationship with the C major triad below.

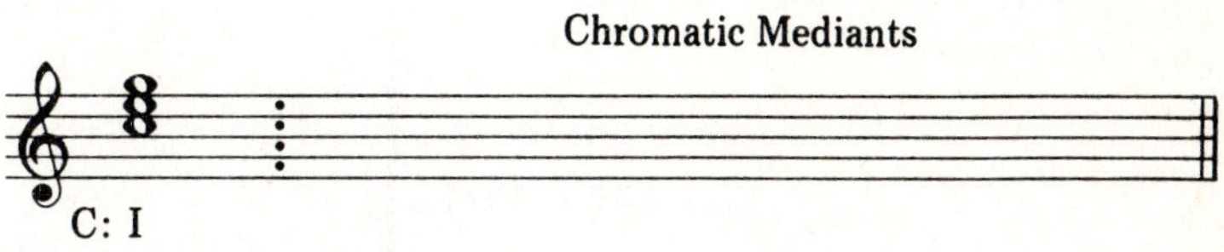

Chromatic Mediants

C: I

(1) (2) (3)

G: ♭VI ♭vi VI

(4) (5) (6)

III ♭iii ♭III

(583–587)

8-3. Write the appropriate chord symbol for each black note-head chord.

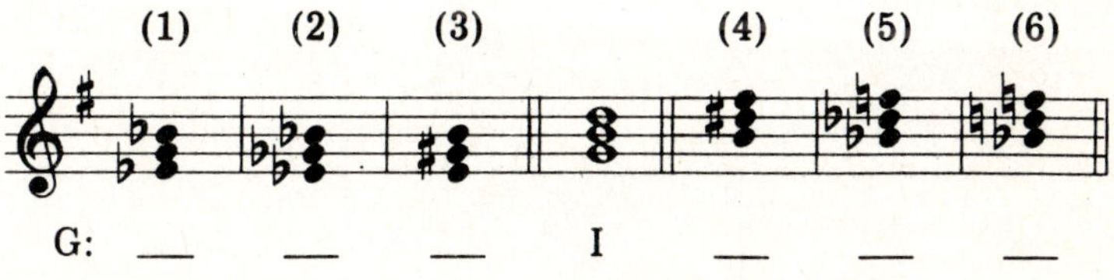

(1) (2) (3) (4) (5) (6)

G: ___ ___ ___ I ___ ___ ___

True. (566-568)	8-4. All of the black note-head chords in the preceding frame are chromatic mediants. (True/False)____________

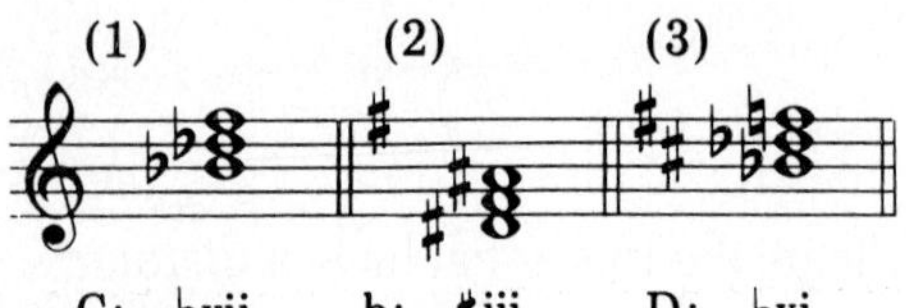

(583-587)

8-5. Write the chords indicated by the chord symbols.

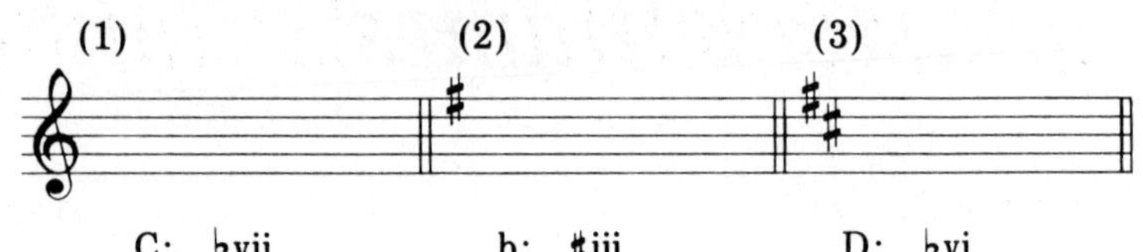

(583-587)

8-6. Write the chords indicated by the chord symbols.

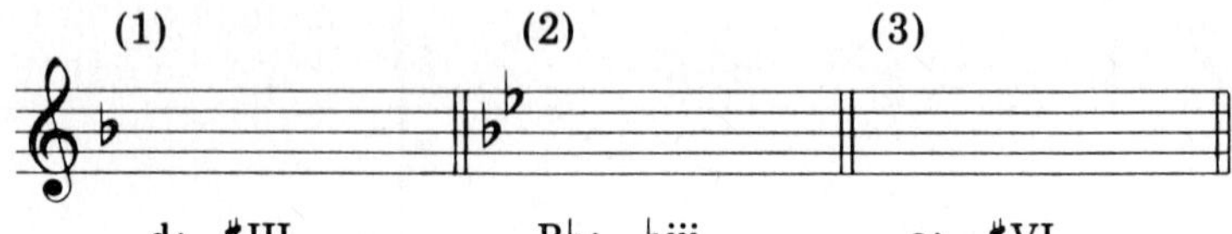

Supplementary Assignments

ASSIGNMENT 8-1 Name_______________________________

1. Which chords have a mediant relation to the B-flat major triad?__________

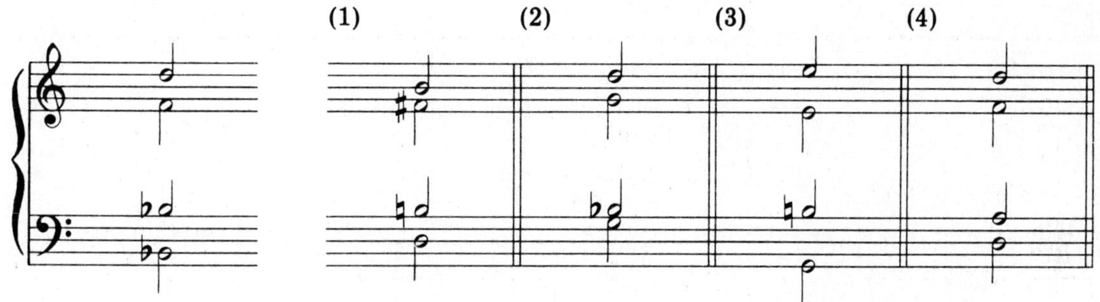

2. Which chords have a chromatic mediant relation to the C major triad?__________

3. Provide the missing chord symbols.

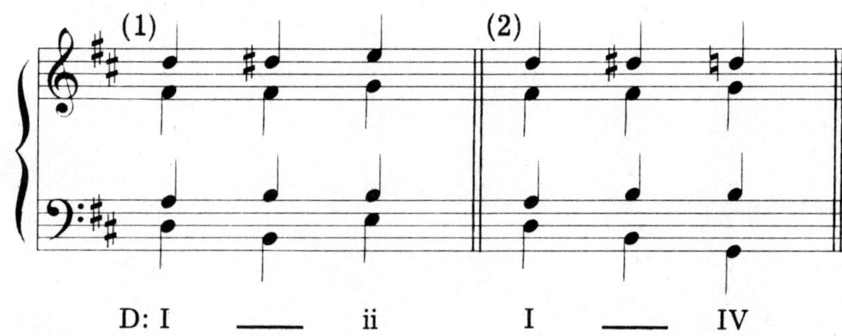

4. Identify each chord as one of the following types of altered chords. *(List by letter.)*

A. Augmented sixth
B. Borrowed chord
C. Chromatic mediant
D. Neapolitan sixth

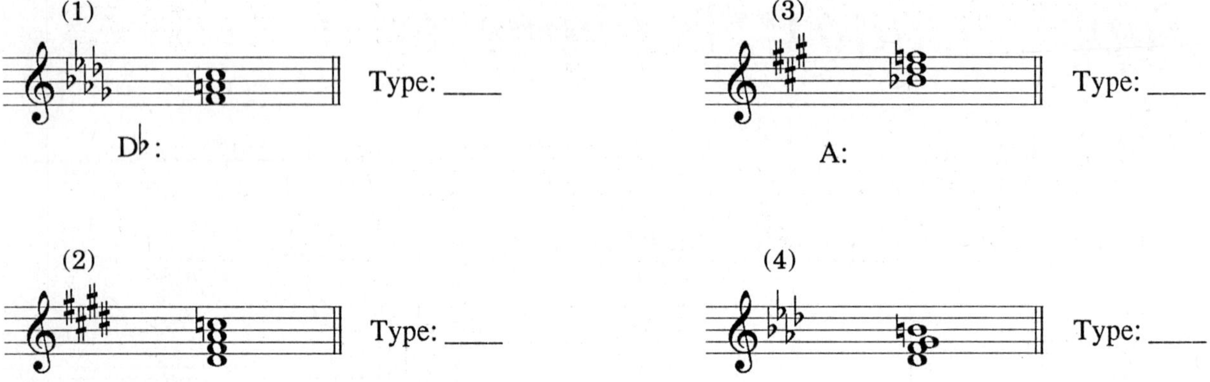

5. In the preceding question, the altered chord in (1) is a _____________; the altered chord in (2) is a _____________.

6. Provide the missing chord symbols.

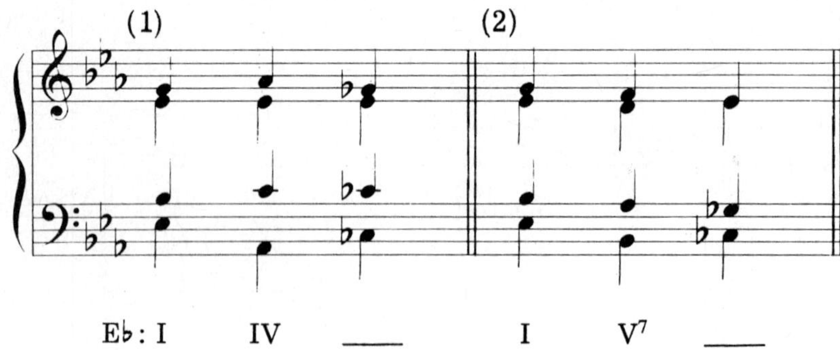

7. In the preceding question, the altered chord in (1) is a _____________; the altered chord in (2) is a _____________.

8. Reduce the notes over each bracket to a single chord by eliminating the nonharmonic tones. Write the chords on the lower staff, then supply the proper chord symbols.

Liszt: *Sonnetto 47 del Petrarca*

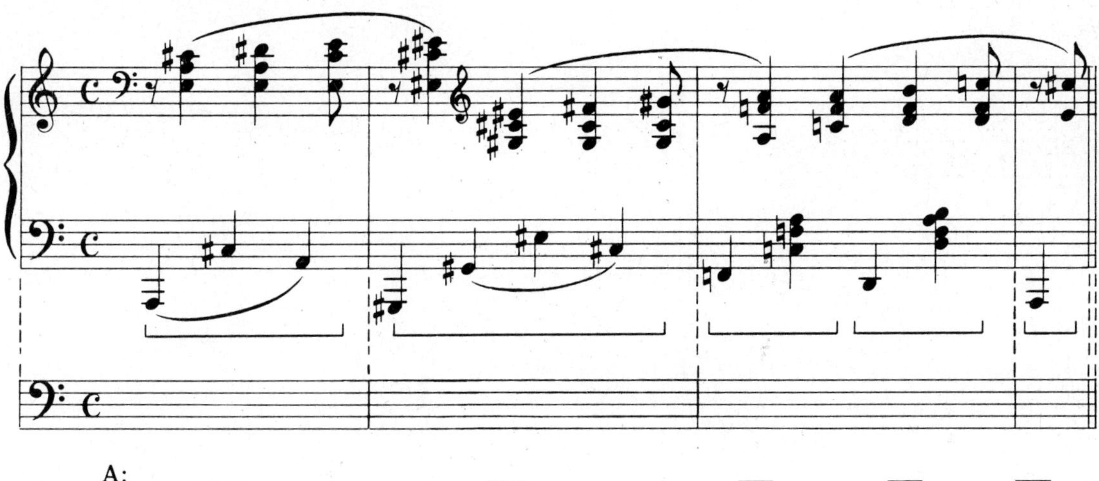

A: ___ ___ ___ ___ ___

9. Compose one or more phrases which contain several chromatic mediants. Choose your own key and time signature; take care to notate completely; use either piano or instrumental style.

chapter nine

Modulation to Foreign Keys Part 1

Extensive use of altered chords is generally accompanied by expansion of tonality beyond the limitations of closely related keys. The various techniques of modulation presented in this and the following chapter make available all of the tonal relationships contained in the chromatic scale; any key—no matter how remote—may be reached with ease. Due to the many ways diminished seventh chords can be resolved, they are especially mobile. In this chapter, we shall examine the use of these chords as springboards into distant tonal realms.

F minor.	610. Two keys whose signatures differ by more than one sharp or flat are called FOREIGN KEYS.* Although the techniques of modulation presented in this chapter may be used to modulate to closely related keys, they are associated chiefly with modulations to foreign keys. Which of the keys listed below is *not* closely related to B-flat major? __________ C minor E-flat major F minor G minor *The terms *remote* keys and *distant* keys are also used, as well as *semi-related*. Note that different writers may choose to define *foreign keys* differently than is done above.
foreign	611. Since the signature of B-flat major contains two flats and that of F minor four flats, these two keys are not closely related; they are called ____________ keys.
D minor (and) B major	612. Identify the two keys listed below which are foreign to the key of E minor. ____________ and ____________. D minor A minor G major B major
two	613. Modulations to foreign keys produce greater tonal variety than do modulations to closely related keys. This is because fewer tones are shared by foreign keys than by closely related keys. The signatures of foreign keys differ by at least ________ sharps or flats.

closely

614. The example below shows there are six common tones between the keys of D major and F-sharp minor (pure form).

D:

f♯:

D major and F-sharp minor are _____________ related keys.

Three.

615. How many common tones are there between the foreign keys of D major and F-sharp major? _____________

D:

F♯:

No.
(G major and G minor are foreign keys.)

616. Are all of the keys listed below closely related to G major? __________

D major
E minor
B minor
G minor

No.

617. Parallel major and minor keys are not closely related because of the difference of three sharps or flats between their signatures. Their identify is very close, however, due to the fact that they share the same tonic, subdominant, and dominant notes. The difference between them is of mode (quality) rather than key. Is it logical to speak of "modulating" from the key of G major to G minor? __________

Yes.

618. Modulation involves a shift of the tonal center from one pitch to another. Thus a change from a major key to its parallel minor (or the reverse) is not a modulation. This is called a *change of mode.*

Does change of mode result in tonal variety? __________

(*No response.*)

619. Change of mode is a useful device for introducing tonal variety into music. Because parallel major and minor keys share the same structural tones, the ear readily accepts a change from one to the other. While this in itself is not modulation, it leads to an expansion in the area of closely related keys, and interchangeability of mode makes available the closely related keys of both the major and minor in a given tonality.

ten

620. Interchange of mode expands tonality to include most of the tones of the chromatic scale. The composite modal structure thus created also possesses a greatly enlarged set of closely related keys. The diagram below shows the keys which are available to C major or minor as closely related keys through change of mode.

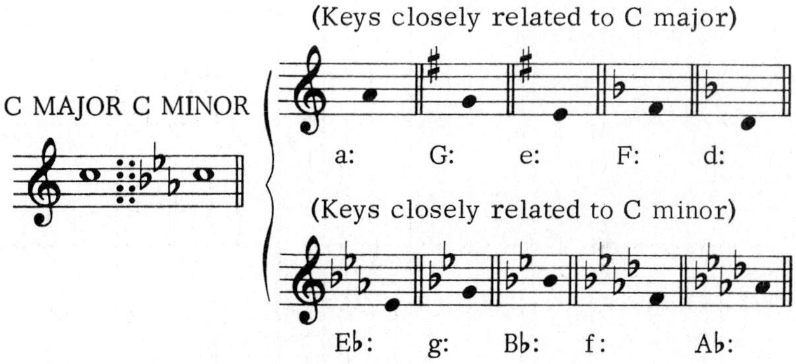

C MAJOR C MINOR

(Keys closely related to C major)

a: G: e: F: d:

(Keys closely related to C minor)

E♭: g: B♭: f: A♭:

Interchange of mode leads to a total of __________ keys which can easily be brought within the orbit of a single tonality.

■

621. The example on the following page demonstrates how change of mode can be used to lead to a foreign key. The first phrase shown is in F major. The second phrase begins with a change of mode to F minor, and quickly modulates to D-flat major, followed by B-flat minor.

F minor

Mozart, *Sonata,* K. 533

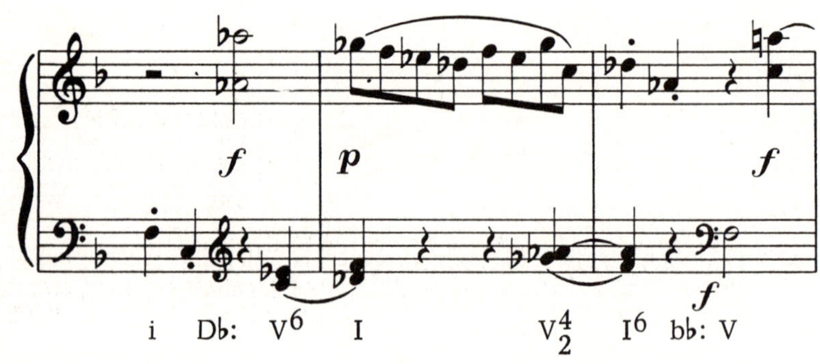

The keys of D-flat major and B-flat minor are both foreign to F major, but they are closely related to the key of ________ __________.

C minor

■ 622. Change of mode accounts for the ease with which the ear accepts the key of G minor in the second half of the example below.

Beethoven, *Sonata,* Op. 2, No. 3

The key of G minor is closely related to (C major/C minor) ___________.

(No response.)

623. Change of mode is not a modulation, but introduces tonal variety through contrast of major and minor modes. Further, change of mode has an important bearing upon modulation since it may serve as a steppingstone to more remote keys. In effect, change of mode increases the number of closely related keys from five to ten.

---

(1) √

624. Check (√) the correct option:

1. Modulations to foreign keys introduce greater tonal variety than modulations to closely related keys.
2. F-sharp minor and A major are foreign keys.

True statements:
(1) ______ (2) ______ Both ______ Neither ______

True.

625. Change of mode makes the key of C-sharp minor readily available to the key of A minor. (True/False) __________

No.

626. The process of "diatonic" common chord modulation is presented in Chapter Four. In this type of modulation the common chord is a diatonic (unaltered) chord in each of the two keys involved. Now we shall extend this principle to include the use of chords which are altered in one (or both) of the keys.*

Can altered chords be used as common chords in *diatonic* modulations? ______

*Some writers classify such modulations as *chromatic.* We shall refer to them simply as common chord modulations.

---

(2).
(diatonic = altered)

■

627. The chart below shows all of the possible relationships which the common chord may bear to the old and new keys.

	OLD KEY		NEW KEY
(1)	diatonic	=	diatonic
(2)	diatonic	=	altered
(3)	altered	=	diatonic
(4)	altered	=	altered

Which of these possibilities is used in the modulation on the following page? _________

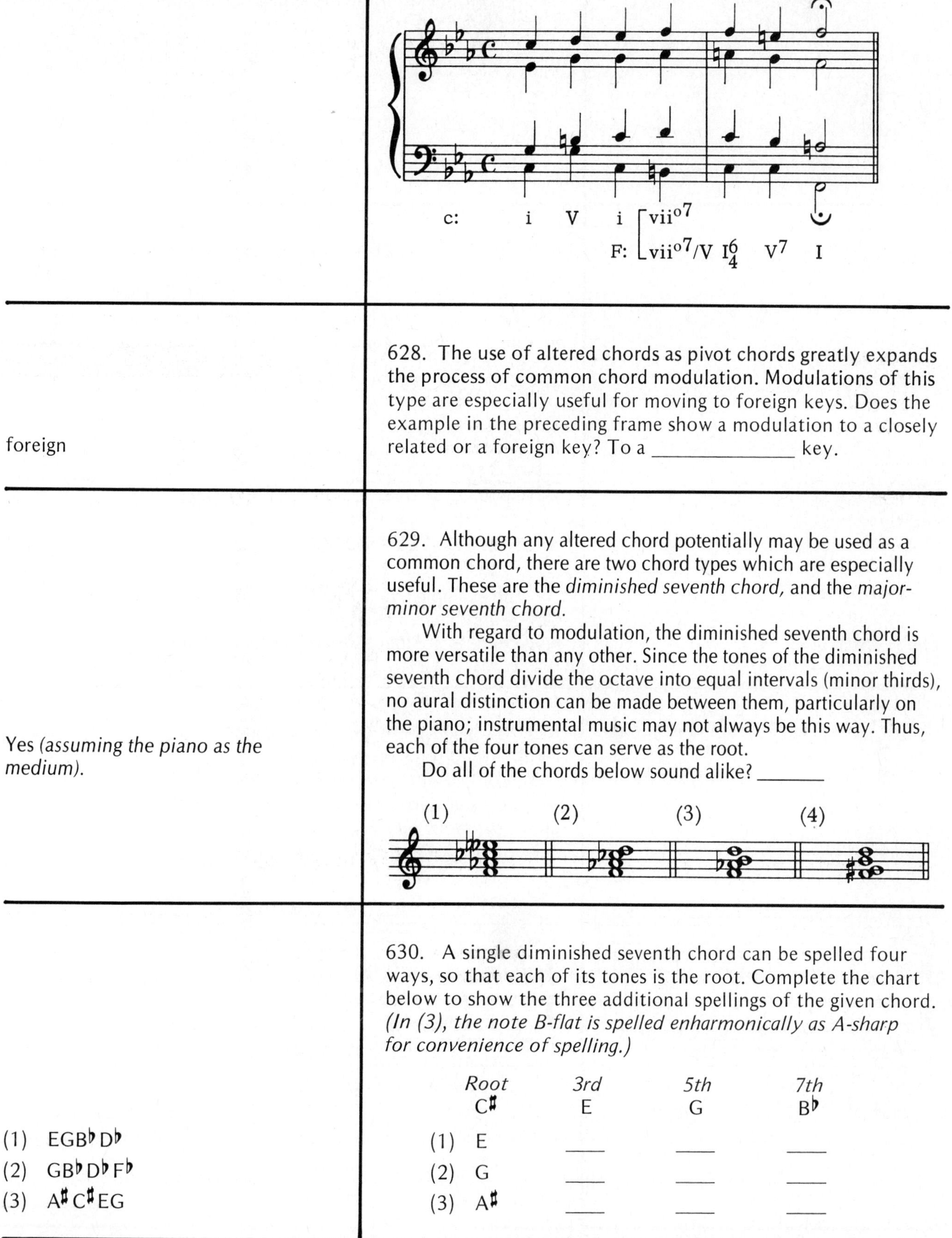

foreign

628. The use of altered chords as pivot chords greatly expands the process of common chord modulation. Modulations of this type are especially useful for moving to foreign keys. Does the example in the preceding frame show a modulation to a closely related or a foreign key? To a _____________ key.

Yes *(assuming the piano as the medium).*

629. Although any altered chord potentially may be used as a common chord, there are two chord types which are especially useful. These are the *diminished seventh chord,* and the *major-minor seventh chord.*

With regard to modulation, the diminished seventh chord is more versatile than any other. Since the tones of the diminished seventh chord divide the octave into equal intervals (minor thirds), no aural distinction can be made between them, particularly on the piano; instrumental music may not always be this way. Thus, each of the four tones can serve as the root.

Do all of the chords below sound alike? _______

(1) EGB♭D♭
(2) GB♭D♭F♭
(3) A♯C♯EG

630. A single diminished seventh chord can be spelled four ways, so that each of its tones is the root. Complete the chart below to show the three additional spellings of the given chord. *(In (3), the note B-flat is spelled enharmonically as A-sharp for convenience of spelling.)*

	Root	*3rd*	*5th*	*7th*
	C♯	E	G	B♭
(1)	E	___	___	___
(2)	G	___	___	___
(3)	A♯	___	___	___

(1) F♯ACE♭
(2) ACE♭G♭
(3) CE♭G♭B♭♭

631. Continue as in the preceding frame.

	Root	*3rd*	*5th*	*7th*
	D♯	F♮	A	C
(1)	F♯	____	____	____
(2)	A	____	____	____
(3)	C	____	____	____

(No response.)

632. Because any of the four tones of a diminished seventh chord can be the root, a high degree of mobility results. Consider, for example, the fact that the chord F♯ACE♭ is the vii°⁷/V in the key of C major, but is capable of performing the same harmonic function in three other major keys as well. *(Remember, too, that this chord could lead to the parallel minor in each case.)*

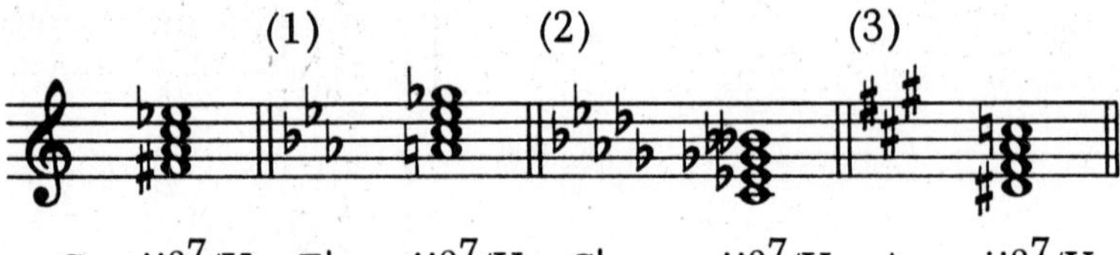

The example above shows that a diminished seventh chord can be approached as a vii°⁷/V in one key and left as the same type chord in another by merely respelling the chord.

■

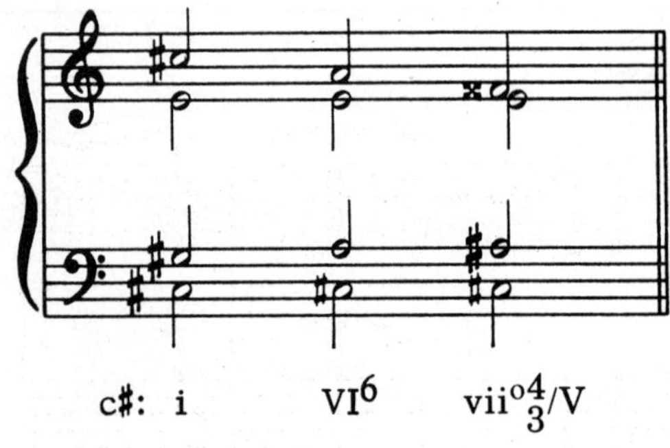

633. In order to pursue the possibility presented in the preceding frame a bit further, we shall construct a modulation from the key of C-sharp minor to G major. First write the notes on the staff which produce the chords indicated by the chord symbols. *(No key signature is given, so you must write the proper accidentals.)*

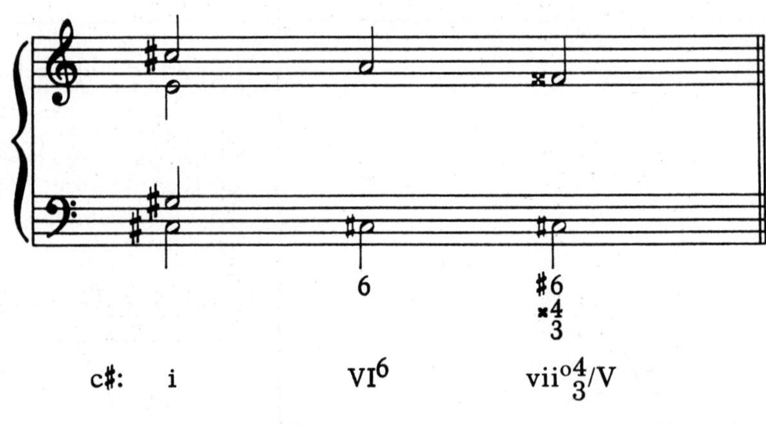

C♯EGB♭

634. Now respell the last chord in the preceding frame as a vii°⁷/V in the key of G major.

c : vii°⁷/V is spelled F𝄪A♯C♯E

G: vii°⁷/V is spelled __________

■

635. Complete the alto and tenor voices in accordance with the chord symbols. *(Since no key signature is given, be sure to ascertain the exact pitches required, and write the appropriate accidentals.)*

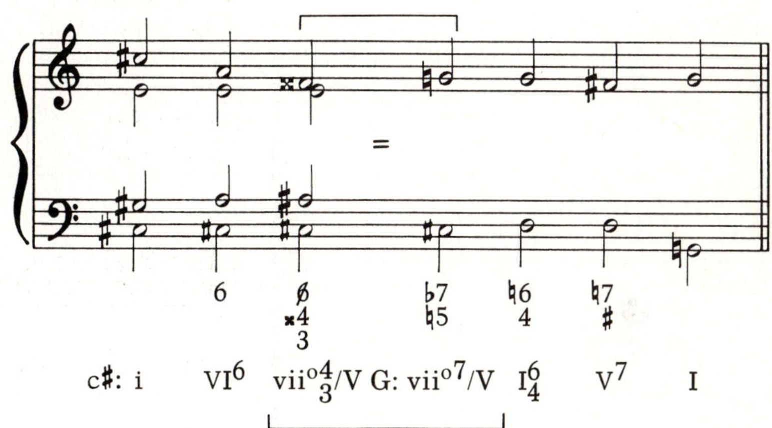

■

636. In actual music the pivot chord is usually not respelled.* In most cases, a single spelling is correct in only one of the two keys involved. Thus, a choice must be made between the possible spellings. That which is used should result in the simplest notation possible and cause the voices to lead smoothly into and out of the pivot chord.

Examine carefully the example below. It served as the basis for the chord progression presented in Frames 633-635.

Haydn, *Quartet,* Op. 74, No. 1

Is the pivot chord as notated spelled correctly in the key of C-sharp minor or G major? _______________

G major.

*Enharmonic spellings will be encountered frequently throughout this chapter. The term "enharmonic" modulation is sometimes used to refer to any type of modulation in which there is an enharmonic change of one or more notes.

---

637. The multiplicity of roots inherent in the diminished seventh chord results in a wide choice of possible resolutions. The mobility of this chord is extended by its numerous uses in both major and minor keys. The example below shows that a diminished seventh chord occurs on every degree of the major scale as an altered chord of one kind or another.

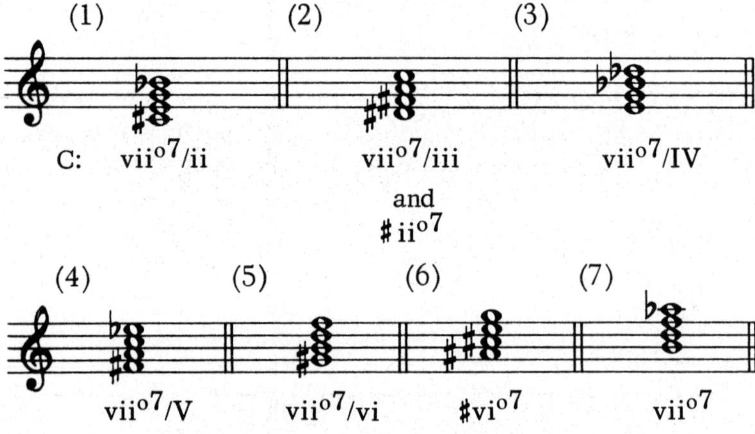

Note that the scale produced here by the "root" of each chord is actually very close to C-sharp minor.

(No response.)

---

638. The fact that a diminished seventh chord can appear on virtually every scale degree in both major and minor keys means that it may be both approached and left with ease. This, plus the possibility of regarding any one of the four tones as the root, results in a large number of possible uses.

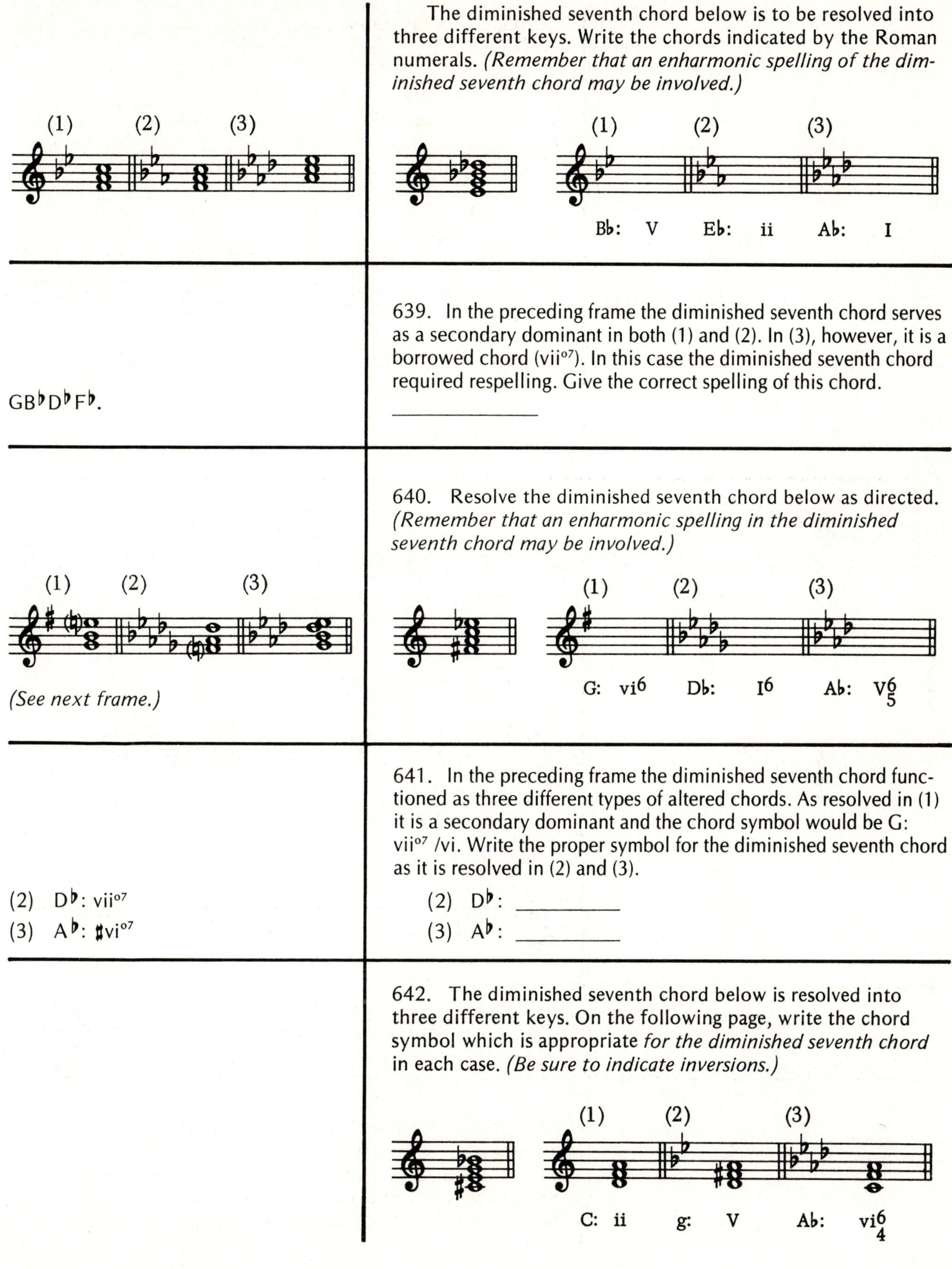

(1) (2) (3)

The diminished seventh chord below is to be resolved into three different keys. Write the chords indicated by the Roman numerals. *(Remember that an enharmonic spelling of the diminished seventh chord may be involved.)*

GB♭D♭F♭.

639. In the preceding frame the diminished seventh chord serves as a secondary dominant in both (1) and (2). In (3), however, it is a borrowed chord (vii°7). In this case the diminished seventh chord required respelling. Give the correct spelling of this chord.

____

(1) (2) (3)

(See next frame.)

640. Resolve the diminished seventh chord below as directed. *(Remember that an enharmonic spelling in the diminished seventh chord may be involved.)*

(2) D♭: vii°7

(3) A♭: ♯vi°7

641. In the preceding frame the diminished seventh chord functioned as three different types of altered chords. As resolved in (1) it is a secondary dominant and the chord symbol would be G: vii°7 /vi. Write the proper symbol for the diminished seventh chord as it is resolved in (2) and (3).

(2) D♭: __________

(3) A♭: __________

642. The diminished seventh chord below is resolved into three different keys. On the following page, write the chord symbol which is appropriate *for the diminished seventh chord* in each case. *(Be sure to indicate inversions.)*

(1) C: vii°7/ii (2) g: vii°7/V (3) A♭: vii°$^{4}_{2}$/vi	(1) C: ________ (2) g: ________ (3) A♭: ________
(1) f: vii°$^{4}_{2}$/V (2) A: vii°$^{6}_{5}$/vi (3) c: vii°$^{4}_{2}$	643. Continue as in the preceding frame. (1) (2) (3) f: V$^{6}_{4}$ A: vi6 c: i$^{6}_{4}$ (1) f: ________ (2) A: ________ (3) c: ________
(1) FA♭C♭E♭♭ (2) G♯BDF (3) BDFA♭	644. In each case below, the diminished seventh chord must be respelled in order for it to relate correctly to the chord to which it resolves. Supply the correct spelling in each case. (1) (2) (3) b♭: VI$^{6}_{4}$ D: V6 C: I6 (1) ________ (2) ________ (3) ________
(1) A♯C♯EG (2) GB♭D♭F♭ (3) EGB♭D♭	645. Continue as in the preceding frame. (1) (2) (3) b: i6 D♭: V$^{6}_{4}$ A♭: vi$^{6}_{4}$ (1) ________ (2) ________ (3) ________

646. The example below shows a modulation from the key of C major to E-flat major.

Haydn, *Quartet,* Op. 54, No. 1

The diminished seventh chord which serves as a common chord is spelled correctly in the key of C major. Its correct spelling in the key of E-flat major would be __________.

ACE♭G♭

647. In the example below, there is a modulation from the key of A major to B minor. The chord at the asterisk is the common chord. Supply the Roman numeral analysis.

Bach, Chorale: *Was mein Gott will, das g'scheh' allzeit*

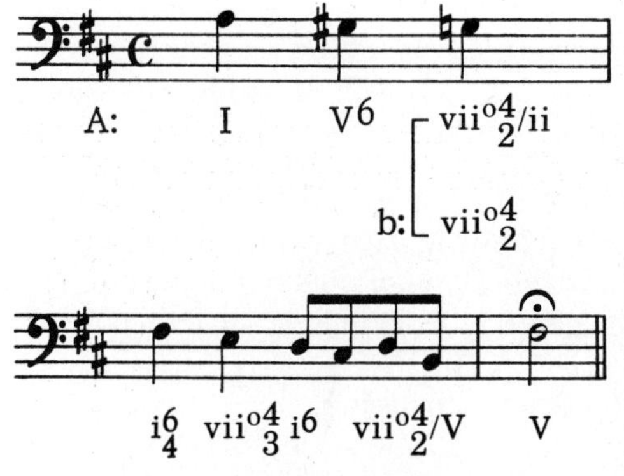

both

648. Although the use of altered chords as common chords is usually associated with modulations to foreign keys, the example in the preceding frame shows that modulations to closely related keys may be accomplished in this way too. The common chord in this example is spelled correctly in (the first/the second/both/neither) __________ key(s).

3.

■ 649. A modulation from the key of E-flat major to D major is shown below. In this example diminished seventh chords occur four times. Each of these chords is numbered. Write the number of the chord which is used to modulate. ______

Beethoven, *Sonata,* Op. 13

■ 650. Chord number three in the preceding frame is used to modulate from the key of E-flat major to D major. This chord is shown again in the example on the following page. Notice that it is spelled correctly in the new key (D major), but not in the old. The correct spelling of the chord (vii^{o7}/ii) in E-flat major would be EGB♭D♭.

Complete the Roman numeral analysis.

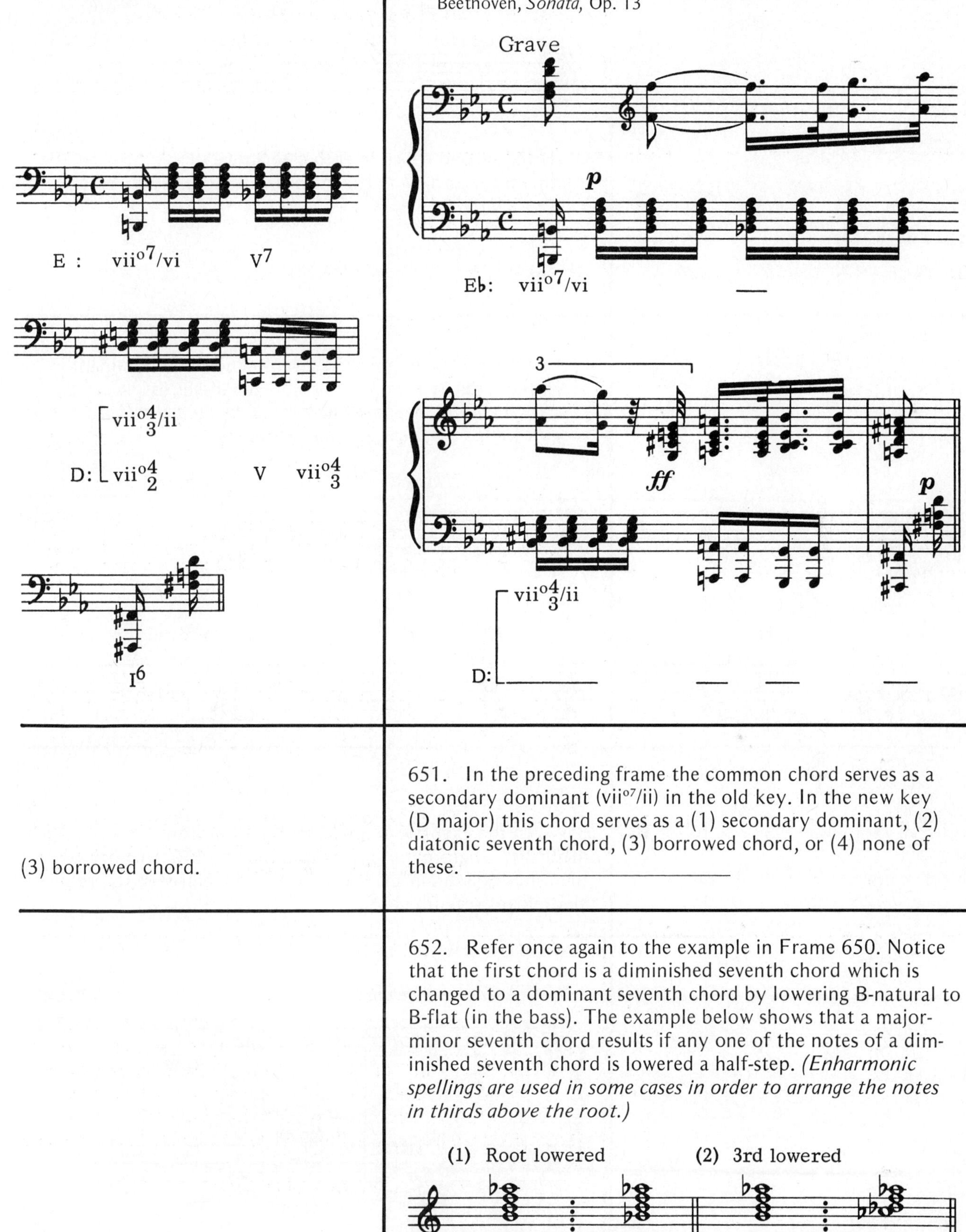

(3) borrowed chord.

651. In the preceding frame the common chord serves as a secondary dominant (vii°7/ii) in the old key. In the new key (D major) this chord serves as a (1) secondary dominant, (2) diatonic seventh chord, (3) borrowed chord, or (4) none of these. ______________________

652. Refer once again to the example in Frame 650. Notice that the first chord is a diminished seventh chord which is changed to a dominant seventh chord by lowering B-natural to B-flat (in the bass). The example below shows that a major-minor seventh chord results if any one of the notes of a diminished seventh chord is lowered a half-step. *(Enharmonic spellings are used in some cases in order to arrange the notes in thirds above the root.)*

(1) Root lowered (2) 3rd lowered

(1) E♭ (2) G♭
(3) A (4) C

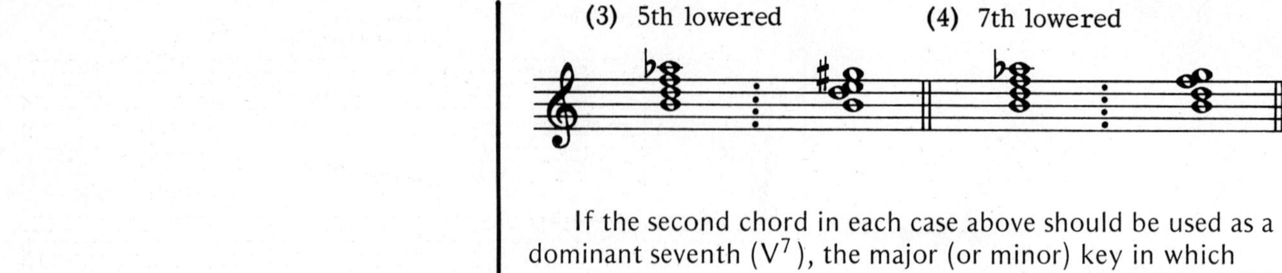

If the second chord in each case above should be used as a dominant seventh (V^7), the major (or minor) key in which each functions is:

(1) ______ (2) ______
(3) ______ (4) ______

---

653. Convert the diminished seventh chords to dominant seventh chords by lowering one note a half-step as directed. *(Use enharmonic spellings when necessary in order that each chord consists of thirds above the root.)*

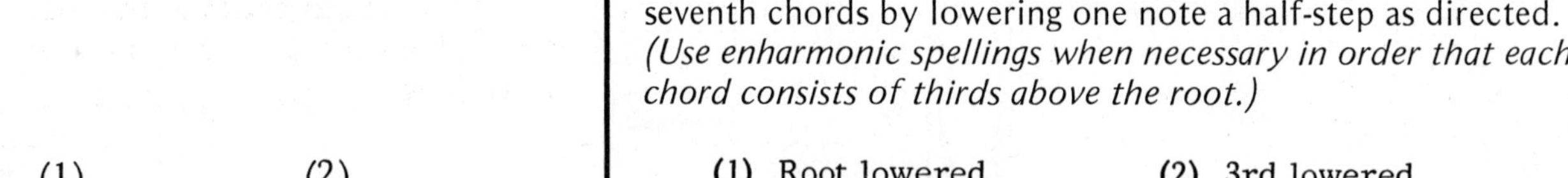

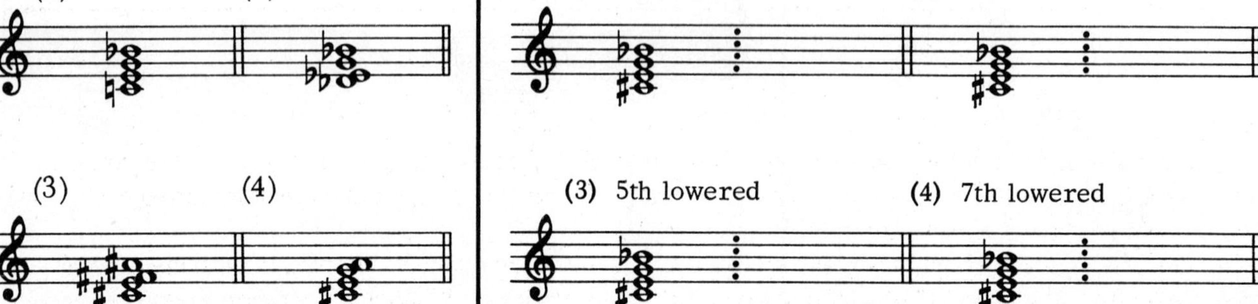

■

654. In the example below, a modulation from the key of G major to C-sharp minor is accomplished by lowering one of the tones of a diminished seventh chord a half-step to produce a dominant seventh chord.

Haydn, *Quartet,* Op. 74, No. 1

The note C is respelled B♯ (in the bass).

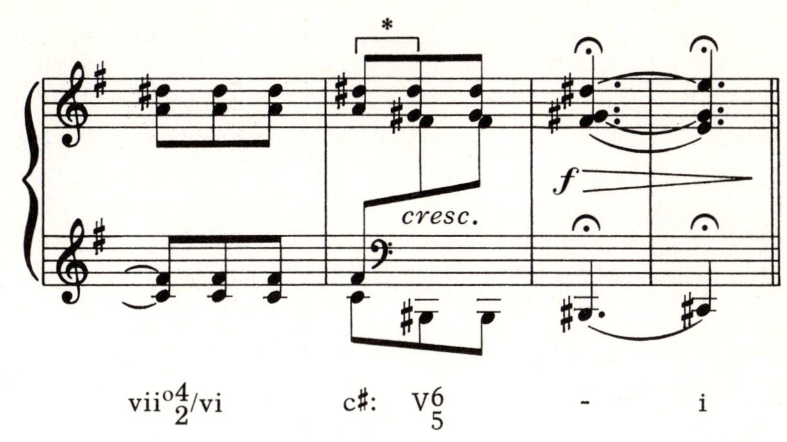

At the asterisk the fifth of the diminished seventh chord (A) is lowered a half-step to G-sharp, which becomes the root of the dominant seventh chord. What other change is made at this point to produce correct spelling? ____________________
____

SUMMARY

Keys whose signatures differ by more than one sharp or flat are called *foreign keys*. The degree of remoteness that two keys bear to one another is determined, in part, by the number of tones that are common to each. The fewer the common tones, the greater the remoteness.

Parallel keys (C major/C minor, for example) are foreign keys, even though they share the same tonic. A change from one to the other is not a modulation, but a change of mode. Change of mode provides easy access to five additional closely related keys—keys that are foreign to the original key.

Altered chords frequently can serve as common chords when modulating to foreign keys. There are four possible relationships that a common chord may bear to the old and new keys:

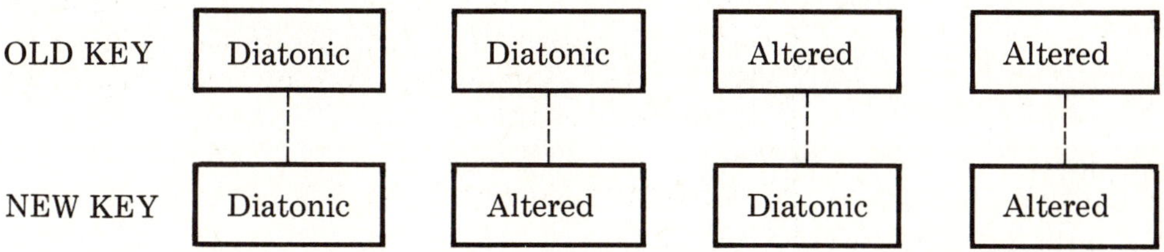

Diminished seventh chords are especially useful for modulating to foreign keys. The inherent ambiguity of root, plus many possible resolutions, cause them to be remarkably mobile. Like other symmetrical chords, such as the augmented triad, diminished seventh chords possess a neutral quality that facilitates both the approach to and departure from them. Movement from one diminished seventh chord to another, or several in succession, may produce the effect of suspended tonality.

Mastery Frames

(1) √

(3) √

(5) √
(6) √
(7) √

(610–612)

9–1. Check (√) the keys below that are foreign to the key of D major.

(1) C-sharp minor ________
(2) A major ________
(3) E major ________
(4) E minor ________
(5) D minor ________
(6) G minor ________
(7) A minor ________
(8) F-sharp minor ________

False. (617–618)

9–2. Change from major to minor (or the reverse) with the same tonic is rightly called a modulation because each key has a different signature. (True/False)____________

---

(2) (3) (4) (5)

D: b: C: a:

(7) (8) (9) (10)

d: F: c: E♭:

(Any order.) (620)

9–3. Complete the identification of the ten keys that are available as closely related keys, through the process of change of mode, with G major/G minor as the original tonality.

Keys closely related to G major.

(1) (2) (3) (4) (5)

e:

Keys closely related to G minor.

(6) (7) (8) (9) (10)

B♭:

chromatic (626-627)

9-4. A modulation in which the common chord is altered in either the old key or new key (or both) is called a _______________ modulation.

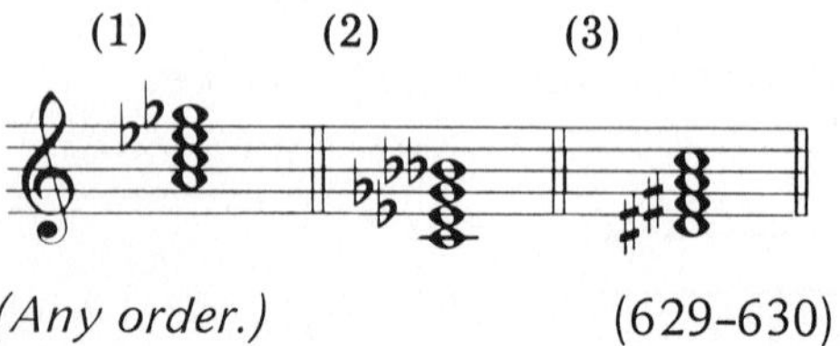

(Any order.) (629-630)

9-5. Write three additional spellings of the diminished seventh chord below. *(Each chord should be in root position; enharmonic spellings may be used.)*

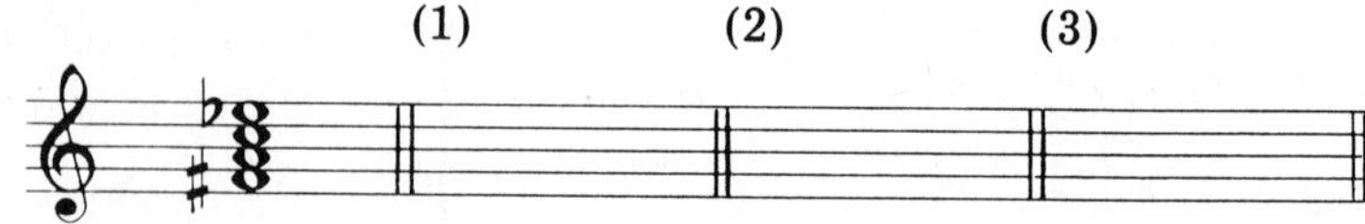

---

(1) G
(2) B♭
(3) D♭
(4) E
(Any order.) (630-632)

9-6. Indicate the four keys in which the diminished seventh chord below could appear as indicated by the chord symbol. *(Enharmonic spellings are necessary in some cases.)*

KEY

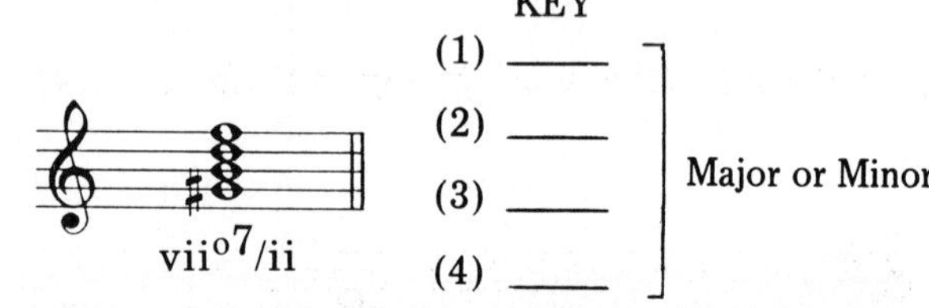

---

(1) E♭
(2) G♭
(3) A
(4) C
(Any order.) (637-641)

9-7. Indicate the four major keys in which the diminished seventh chord below could appear as indicated by the chord symbol. *(Enharmonic spellings are necessary in some cases.)*

KEY

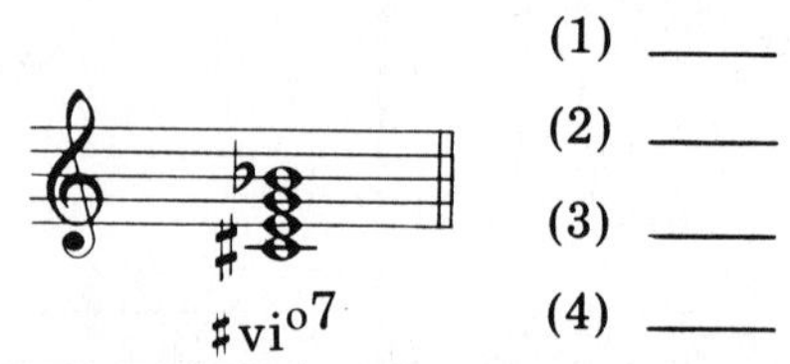

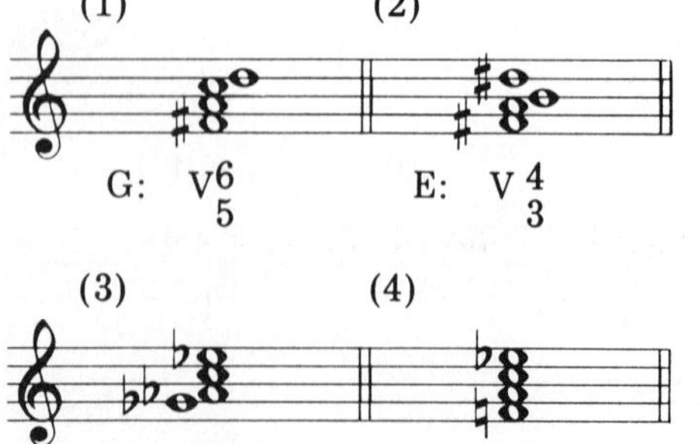

(652-654)

9-8. Transform the diminished seventh chord below into four different major-minor seventh chords by successively altering one of the chord tones. Indicate also the key into which each would resolve as a dominant seventh chord. *(Enharmonic spellings are necessary; write chord symbols to include inversions.)*

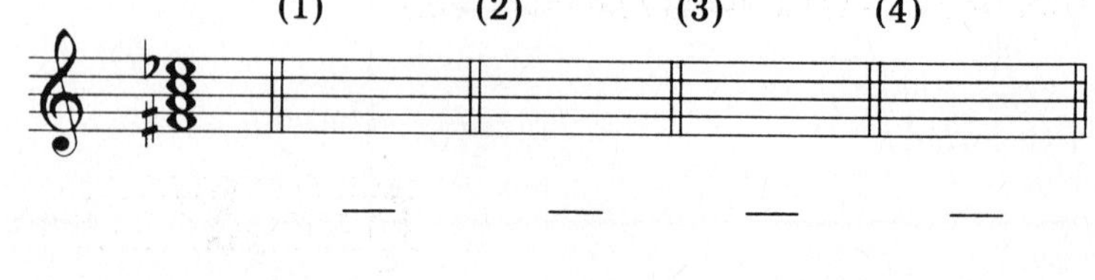

Supplementary Assignments

ASSIGNMENT 9-1 Name________________________________

1. Which of the keys below are foreign to the key of C major?____________

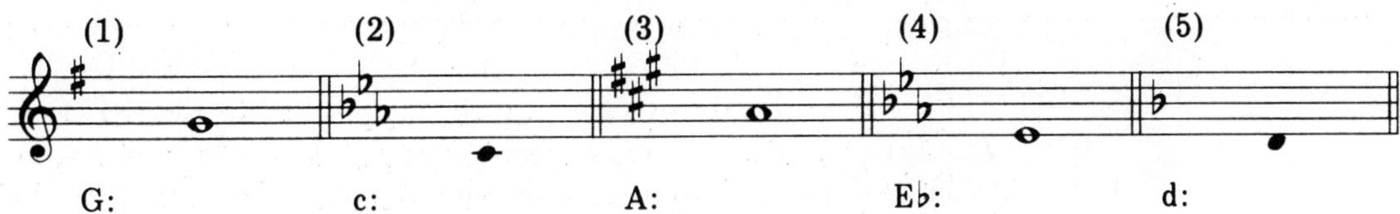

2. Which of the keys below are foreign to the key of C minor?____________

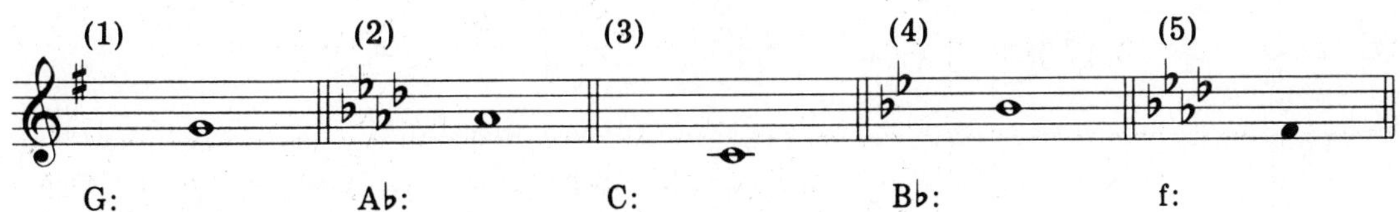

3. The single diminished seventh chord below may appear in any of the keys indicated. Supply the correct chord symbol for each key.

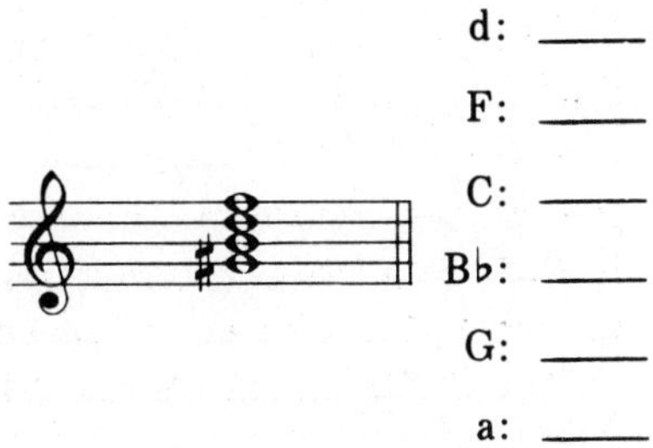

d: ____

F: ____

C: ____

B♭: ____

G: ____

a: ____

4. The diminished seventh chord below could function as a ♯ii°7 in four major keys. Identify the four keys. *(Enharmonic spellings may be involved.)*

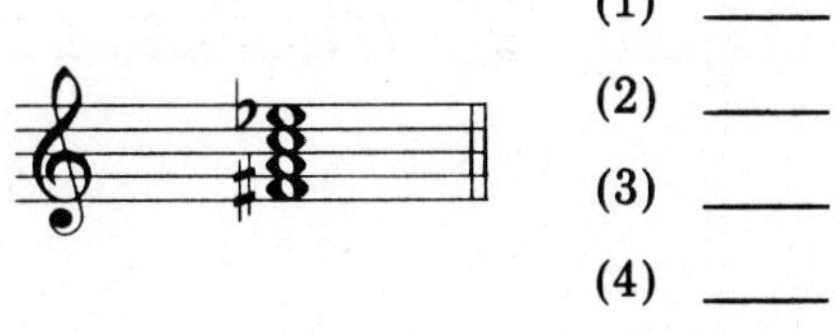

(1) ____

(2) ____

(3) ____

(4) ____

5. The diminished seventh chord below could function as a ♯vi°7 in four major keys. Identify the four keys. *(Enharmonic spellings may be involved.)*

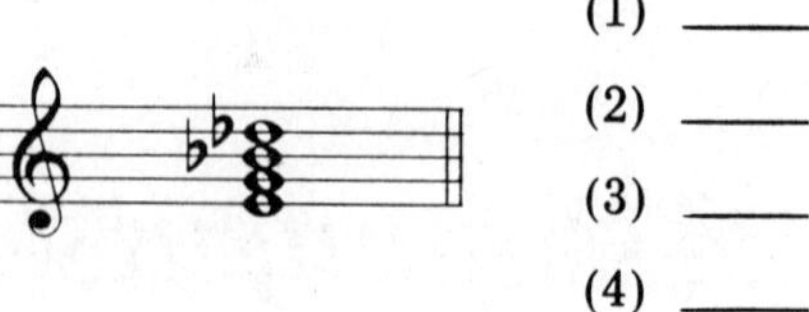

6. Supply the missing chord symbol.

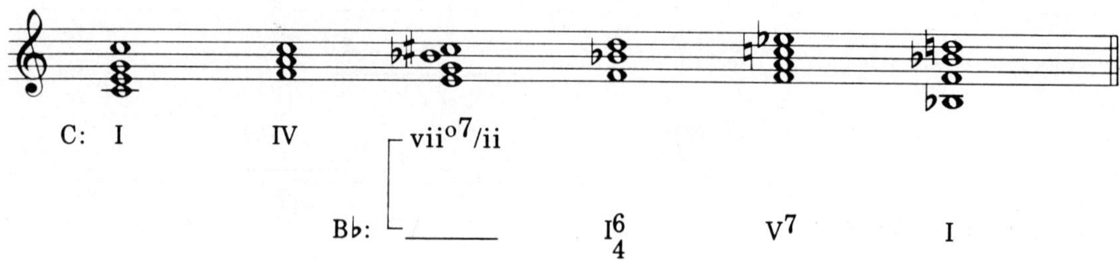

7. Supply the missing chord symbol.

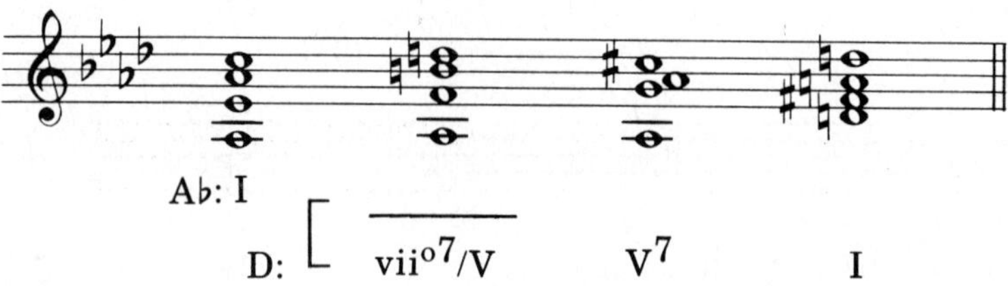

8. Explain the reasons why the diminished seventh chord is capable of so many different resolutions.

____

____

____

____

____

____

____

____

ASSIGNMENT 9-2 Name______________________

1. Complete the harmonic analysis.

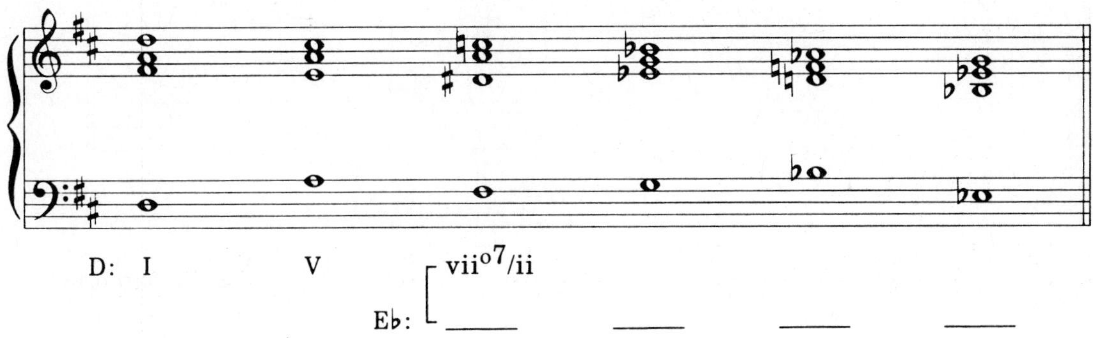

2. Complete the harmonic analysis.

3. The example below modulates from the key of E major to the key of B-flat major. Provide the harmonic analysis.

4. The example below modulates from the key of C minor to the key of B major. Provide the harmonic analysis.

5. The example below contains a modulation from F-sharp minor to E major. Provide the harmonic analysis.

6. Compose three single-phrase examples which modulate by means of the devices below. Analyze each phrase.

A. The common chord is vii°7/V in the new key.
B. The common chord is vii°7/ii in the new key.
C. The common chord is vii°7/vi in the new key.

chapter ten

Modulation to Foreign Keys Part 2

Chords which may be resolved several ways serve especially well as common chords in modulations to foreign keys. Like the diminished seventh chord, the major-minor seventh chord not only possesses strong activity, but is capable of performing many harmonic functions. This chapter focuses on modulations by means of the major-minor seventh chord; it also deals with the Neapolitan sixth chord, sequence modulation, and pivot tone modulation.

655. The major-minor seventh chord may function in three ways: (1) as a diatonic seventh chord (V^7); (2) a secondary dominant; and (3) enharmonically as a German sixth chord. To demonstrate these possibilities the major-minor seventh chord on G is resolved three different ways in the example below:

Indicate the function of the major-minor seventh chord in each case.

(1) ____________________

(2) ____________________

(3) ____________________

(1) German sixth

(2) Secondary dominant (V^7/ii)

(3) Diatonic seventh (V^7)

---

656. Resolve the major-minor seventh chord on D as directed, and supply the proper chord symbols.

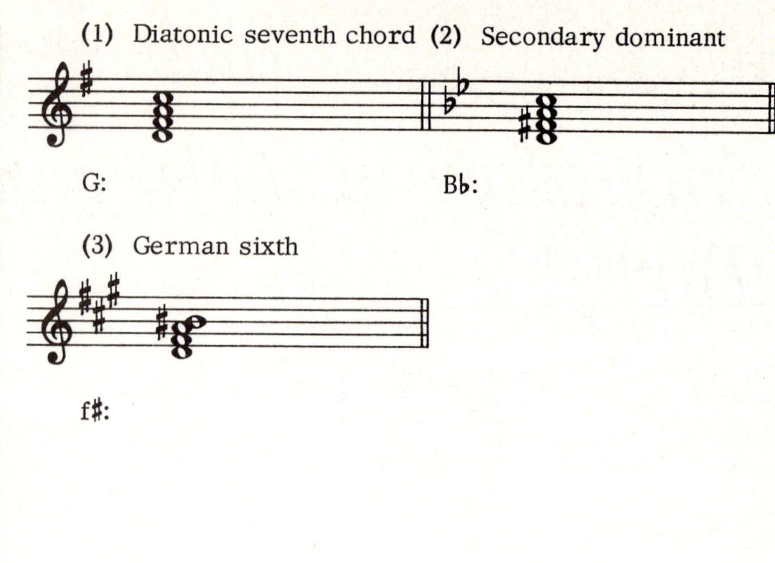

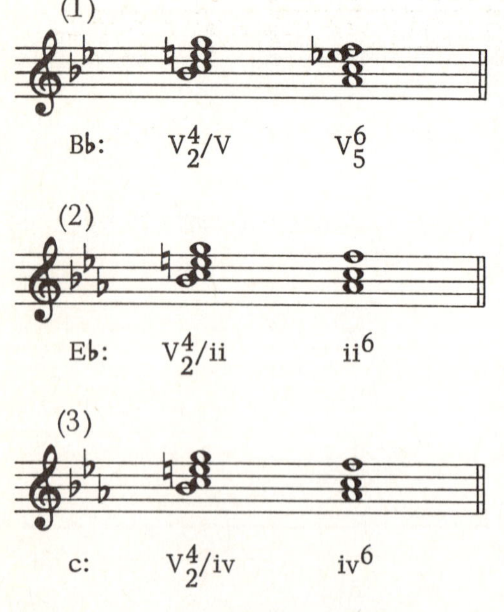

657. The next few frames demonstrate the versatility of the major-minor seventh chord. Supply the Roman numeral analysis. *(Indicate inversions.)*

(1) (2) (3)

Bb: ___ ___ Eb: ___ ___ c: ___ ___

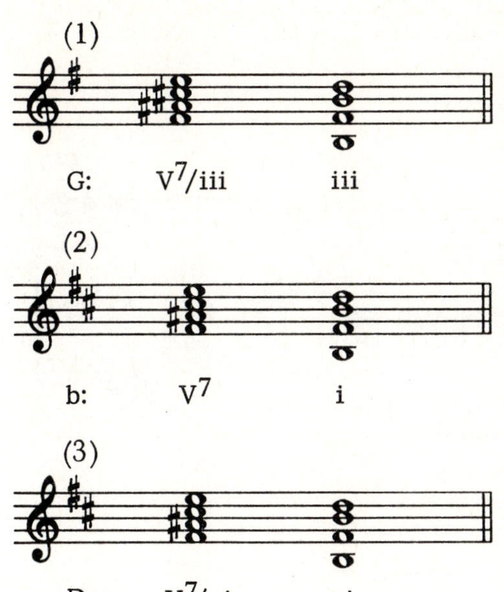

658. Continue as in the preceding frame.

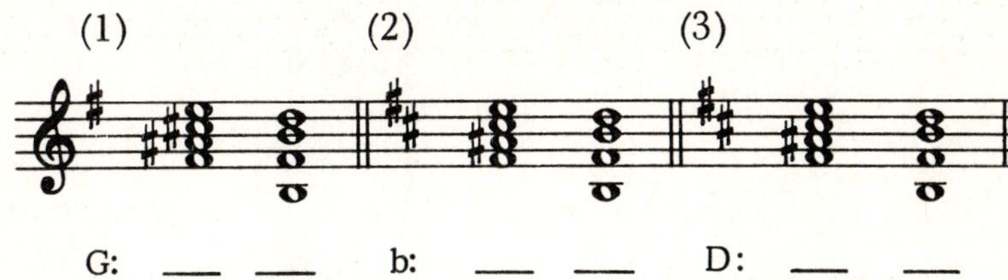

659. Continue as in the preceding frame.

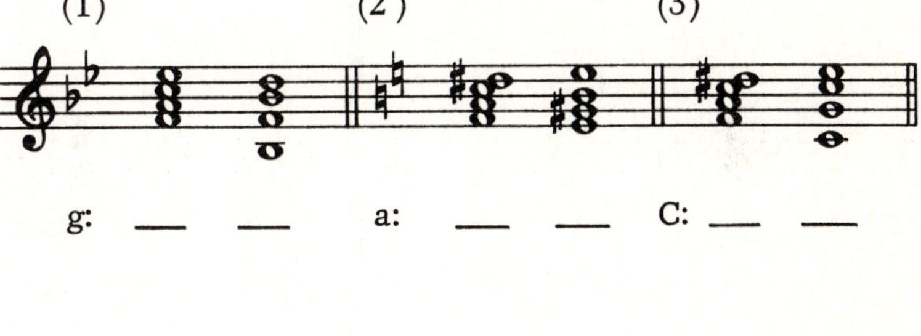

V^7/IV

■ 660. The chord at the asterisk is spelled and resolved as a German sixth in the key of C major. Supply the chord symbol for this chord in the key of A-flat major. *(Watch for enharmonic spelling.)*

Beethoven, *Symphony No. 5*, Op. 67

Andante con moto

(*p*) *pp*

A♭: I - - V^7 I - -

ff

vii^{o7}/ii -

C: G6

■ 661. In the example on the following page, the pivot chord (at the asterisk) is respelled by the use of enharmonic equivalents (D♯=E♭, B=C♭). This results in correct spelling in both of the keys involved. Supply the chord symbol for this chord in the new key (E-flat major).

G^6	Chopin, *Mazurka,* Op. 56, No. 1 Andante non tanto — Poco più mosso (*f*) rit. **p** *leggiero* B: V^7 - - I [V^7/IV E♭: [____ I^6_4
enharmonic	662. Modulations which involve enharmonic spellings (such as in the preceding frame) are sometimes called ____________ modulations.
Yes.	663. Is it correct to say that the keys of B major and E-flat major bear a chromatic mediant relation to one another? __________
■	664. The example below shows a modulation from the key of C minor to C-sharp minor. The chord at the asterisk is a pivot chord and is spelled correctly in the *new* key. Supply the chord symbols for this chord in both keys.

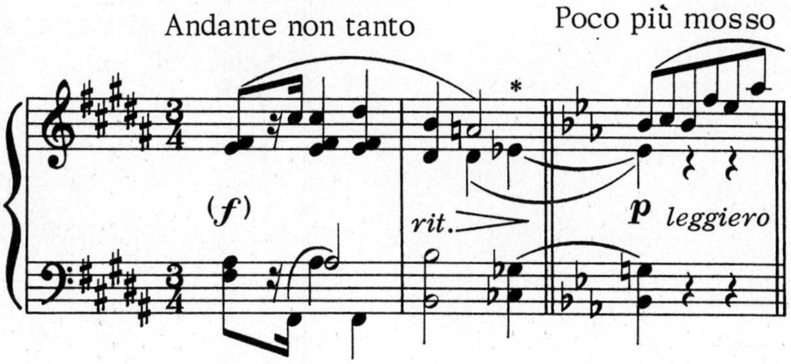

Beethoven, *Sonata,* Op. 90

665. In the preceding frame the chord at the asterisk is spelled correctly in the new key but not the old. Give the correct spelling of this chord in the key of C minor. __________

A♭CE♭F♯.

■ 666. We have seen that diminished seventh chords and major-minor seventh chords often serve as pivot chords. Actually, any altered chord may be used in this way. In the example below, the French sixth is used to modulate from the key of A-flat minor to D-flat major.

Wagner, *Die Walküre,* Act II, Scene 4

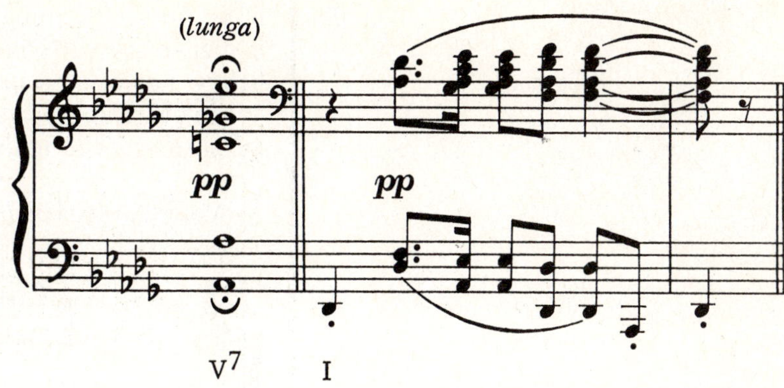

In the key of A-flat minor the French sixth is built on the lowered second scale degree. This chord is left as a French sixth built on the lowered ______________ degree in D-flat major.

sixth

■

667. The Neapolitan chord sometimes is used as a pivot chord. Complete the Roman numeral analysis.

668. In the example of the preceding frame, the pivot chord is spelled correctly in both keys. The chord at the asterisk below, however, is spelled correctly in the new key but not in the old. Supply the chord symbol for this chord in both keys. *(Be sure to take into account the enharmonic spelling.)*

Mozart, *Symphony No. 39,* K. 543

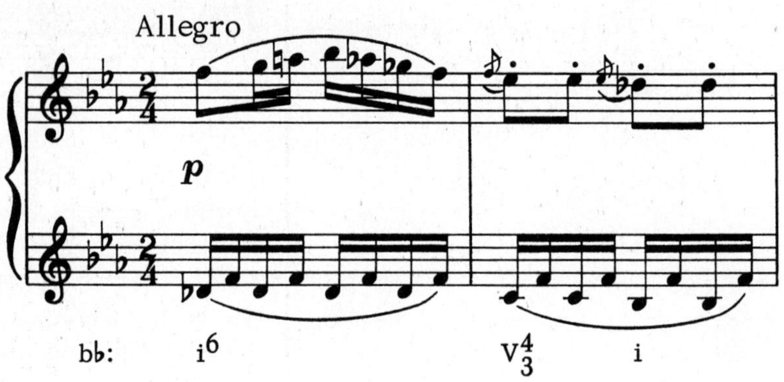

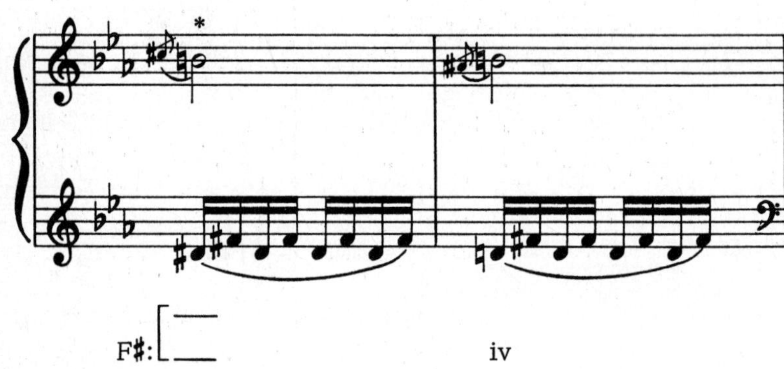

b♭: N6

F♯: IV6

---

669. Several enharmonic spellings are involved in the example on the following page. The modulation is from B-flat minor to B major, but not all of the voices move into sharps at the same time. Complete the Roman numeral analysis.

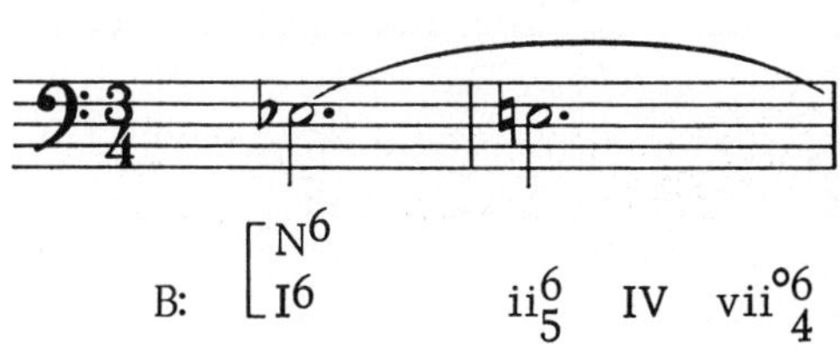

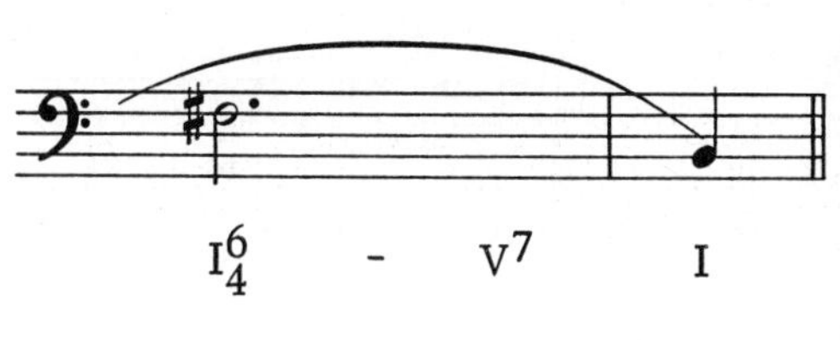

Haydn, *Quartet,* Op. 76, No. 6

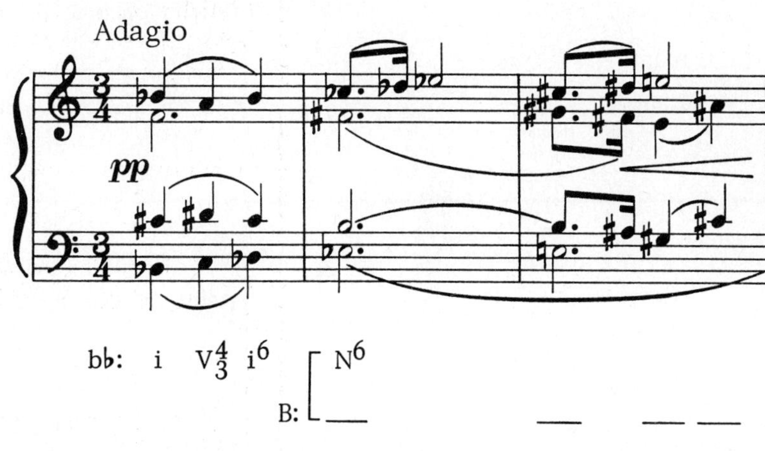

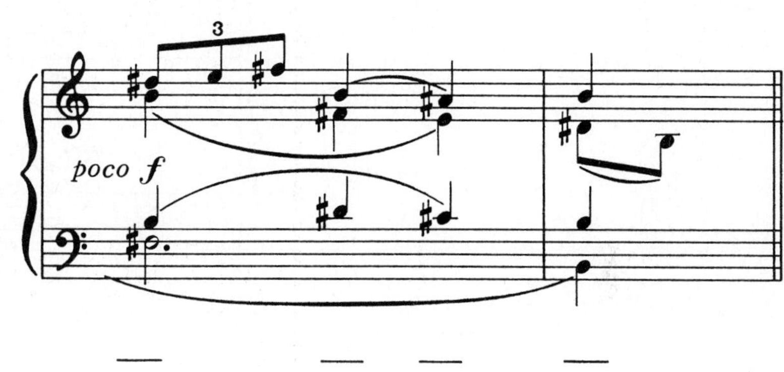

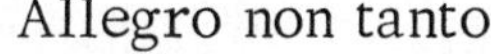

■ 670. Sequences may result in modulations to foreign keys.

Chopin, *Mazurka,* Op. 56, No. 1

Allegro non tanto

Play the example on the preceding page at the piano and identify each of the three keys involved in the sequence.

(1) ______________
(2) ______________
(3) ______________

(1) B major
(2) A major
(3) G major

■ 671. In the example below, modulations occur not only between the sequence units, but within them as well.

Franck, *Prelude, Aria et Final*

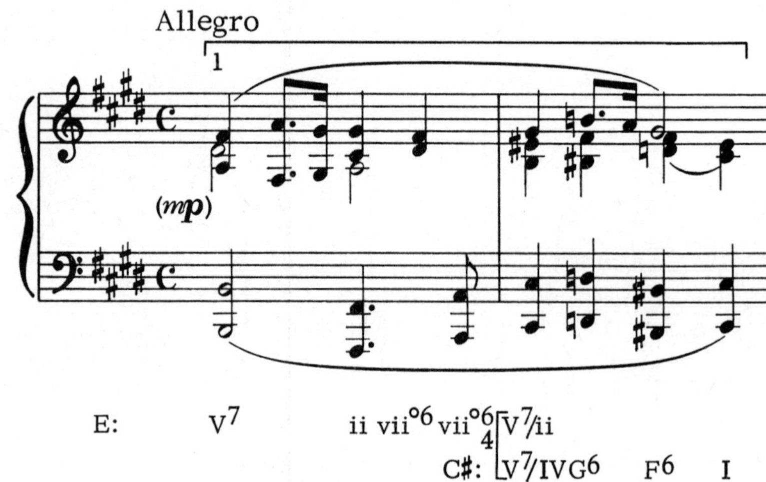

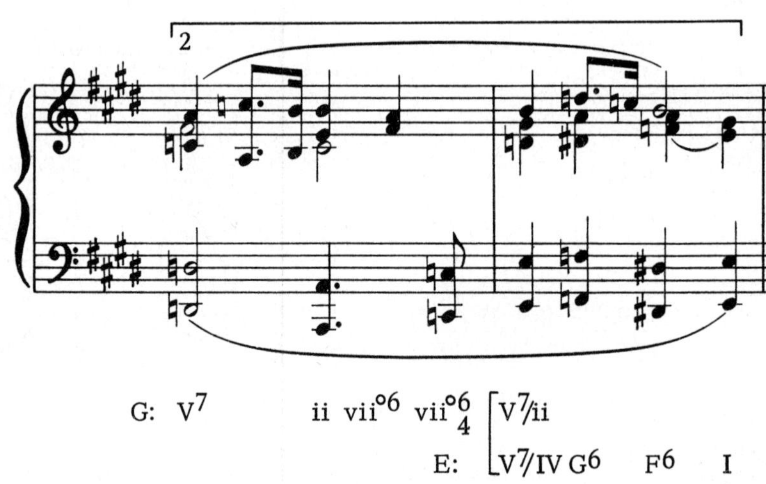

The sequence begins in the key of E major and modulates within the first unit to C-sharp major. The second unit begins in the key of G major and modulates to E major. If this pattern of key relationships were continued to complete a third sequence unit, the final key would be ______________.

G major

No.

672. Used excessively, sequences may result in "mechanical" effects. But they are useful in modulations involving foreign keys, for the repetition of a melodic, rhythmic, and harmonic pattern causes the ear to accept even the most remote tonal relationships.

Do all sequences result in modulation? ______

■

673. A single tone sometimes serves to link one key with another. Such a tone is called a "pivot" tone.

Chopin, *Mazurka,* Op. 33, No. 3

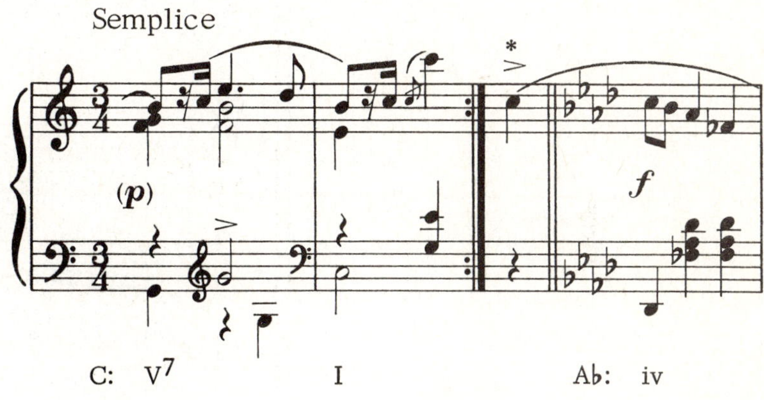

third

The note C is the first scale degree in the old key and the ____________ scale degree in the new key.

■ 674. The example below shows a pivot tone modulation from the key of B minor to D major.

Mozart, *Fantasia in C Minor,* K. 475

fifth
third

The note F-sharp is the ______________ scale degree in the old key and the ______________ scale degree in the new key.

■ 675. The pivot tone performs the same function as a common chord; it provides a link between two keys. In the example below, the pivot tone is G-sharp (at the asterisk). An enharmonic change is involved here.

Schumann, *Die Nonne,* Op. 49, No. 3

first	The note G-sharp is the third scale degree in the key of E major. It is the enharmonic equivalent of the ____________ scale degree in A-flat major.

SUMMARY

The major-minor seventh chord functions in three principal ways: as a dominant seventh chord; as a secondary dominant; and as an enharmonic equivalent of a German sixth chord. Thus, it is capable of many different resolutions. As a secondary dominant, for example, a particular major-minor seventh chord may resolve to a supertonic triad in one key, the mediant triad in another, the subdominant in another, and so forth. As the enharmonic equivalent of a German sixth chord, it has three possible resolutions: as if built on the lowered second scale degree; as if built on the fourth scale degree in a major key; and as if built on the note a half-step above the fifth scale degree in either major or minor.

The major-minor seventh chord often changes function as it resolves into the new key. It may, for example, be approached as a dominant seventh chord and resolved as a secondary dominant; or it may be approached as a secondary dominant and resolved as a German sixth chord.

The French sixth chord is also used as a common chord. It may, for example, be approached as if built on the lowered second scale degree, and resolved as if built on the lowered sixth scale degree in another key.

The Neapolitan chord is another altered chord that may perform as a common chord. Because it is a major triad (usually in first inversion), it is common with any diatonic triad of the same quality.

A single tone may perform the same function as a common chord; such a tone is called a *pivot tone.*

The stages of a modulating sequence may progress through several keys. The formal coherence provided by the repetition of melodic/harmonic patterns at different pitch levels causes the tonal shifts to be readily accepted by the ear.

Chapters Nine and Ten have shown that modulations to foreign keys may extend the range of keys related to a particular tonal center as far as the system of equal temperament permits. Frequent modulation (especially to foreign keys) tends to undermine the authority of the principal tonality. The degree of stability desired in a composition is not only a matter of style; it varies according to formal and expressive requirements. Fluctuations in tonal stability help elicit a variety of emotional responses. Insistence on the tonal resources of a single key provides the maximum degree of tonal stability, whereas liberal use of altered chords and frequent modulations to foreign keys produces tonal instability.

Mastery Frames

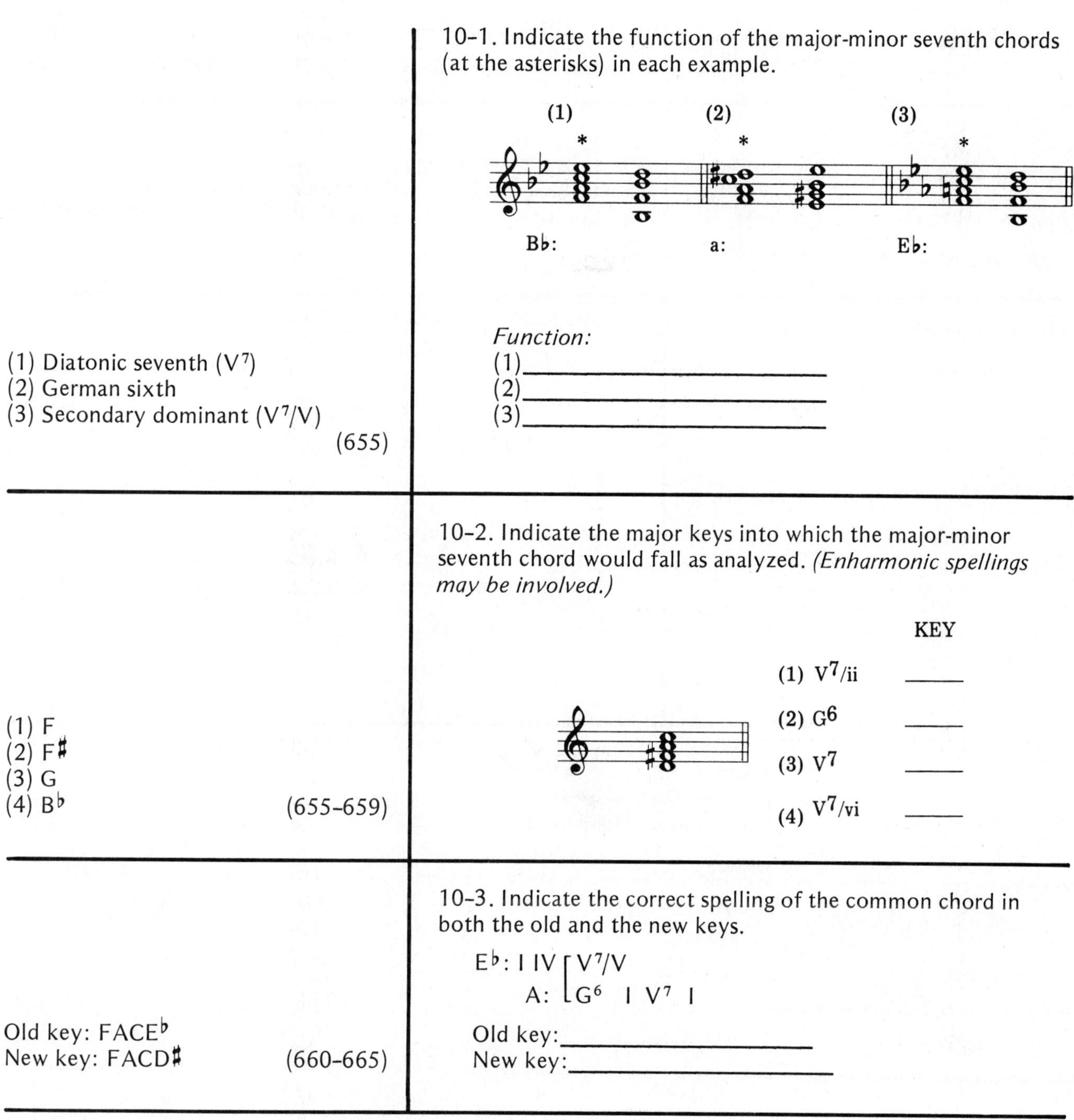

10–1. Indicate the function of the major-minor seventh chords (at the asterisks) in each example.

Function:
(1)____________________
(2)____________________
(3)____________________

(1) Diatonic seventh (V^7)
(2) German sixth
(3) Secondary dominant (V^7/V)
(655)

10–2. Indicate the major keys into which the major-minor seventh chord would fall as analyzed. *(Enharmonic spellings may be involved.)*

	KEY
(1) V^7/ii	_____
(2) G^6	_____
(3) V^7	_____
(4) V^7/vi	_____

(1) F
(2) F♯
(3) G
(4) B♭
(655–659)

10–3. Indicate the correct spelling of the common chord in both the old and the new keys.

E♭: I IV [V^7/V
A: [G^6 I V^7 I

Old key:____________________
New key:____________________

Old key: FACE♭
New key: FACD♯
(660–665)

Eb: [F⁶ / F⁶ I⁶] (666)

10-4. Complete the analysis of the modulation below.

C: I vi [—

Eb: [— — IV I IV⁶ V^6_5 I

---

fourth (666)

10-5. In the preceding frame the French sixth chord is built on the lowered sixth scale degree in the key of C major; it is built on the ____________ scale degree in the new key of E-flat major.

F: N⁶ vii°⁷/V I^6_4 V⁷ I (667-669)

10-6. Complete the analysis of the modulation below.

Db: I⁶ [IV⁶

F: [— — — — —

Supplementary Assignments

ASSIGNMENT 10-1 Name______________________________

1. Provide the missing chord symbol in each case.

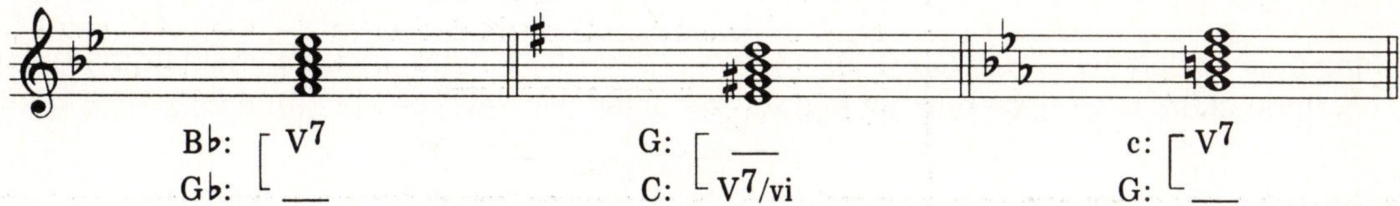

2. Provide the missing key indication. *(Enharmonic spellings may be involved.)*

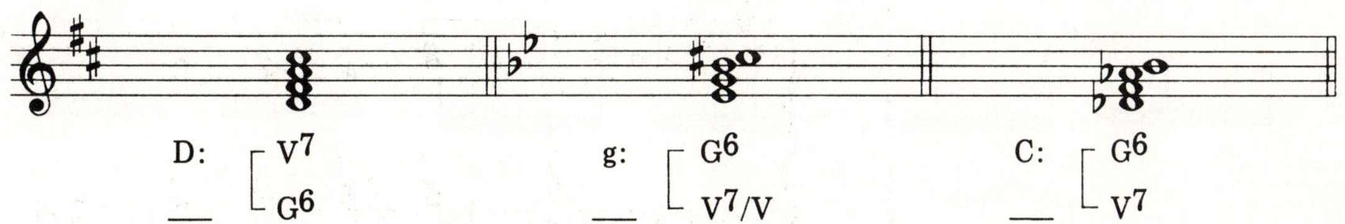

3. The chord AC♯EG is V^7 in D major; it is also V^7/vi in the key of ______________.

4. The chord B♭DFA♭ is V^7/ii in D-flat major; it is also ______________in the key of A-flat minor.

5. Which augmented sixth chord sounds the same as a major-minor seventh chord? ______________

6. The chord below is analyzed in the key of C major. Rewrite the chord (with enharmonic changes, if necessary) in the keys that are indicated.

7. Provide the proper chord symbols.

8. The example below modulates from the key of C major to the key of F minor. Provide the harmonic analysis.

9. The example below contains a modulation from C minor to C-sharp minor. Provide the harmonic analysis. Because the common chord is spelled correctly in only one of the two keys, be alert for enharmonic equivalents.

10. The modulation in the example below is from F major to E major. Provide the harmonic analysis. *(Analyze the chord at the asterisk as a common chord.)*

J. Strauss: *"Artist's Life Waltzes,"* Op. 316

ASSIGNMENT 10-2 Name________________________________

1. The example below contains a modulation from the key of D major to the key of D-flat major. Provide the harmonic analysis. *(The common chord is at the asterisk.)*

Schubert: *Waltz*, Op. 9, No. 14

2. Compose a single phrase example that contains a modulation as represented below.

C: ~~~~~~~~ ⌈ V^7
B: ⌊ G^6 ~~~~~~~~

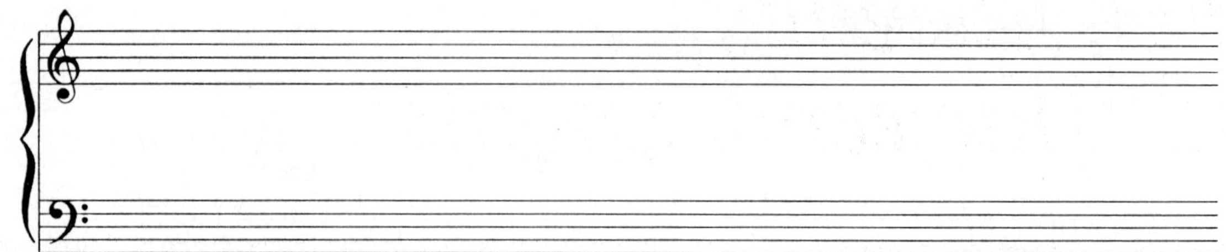

3. Compose a single phrase example that contains a modulation as represented below.

D: ~~~~~~~~ ⌈ I^6
c♯: ⌊ N^6 ~~~~~~~~

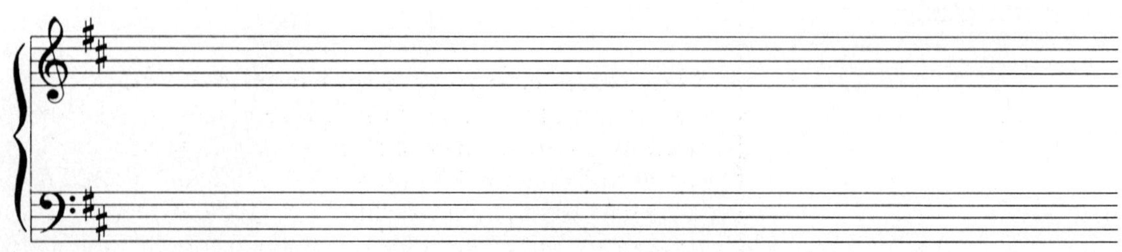

chapter eleven

Ninth, Eleventh, and Thirteenth Chords

The interval of a third is the basic unit for building chords in tonal music. Two superimposed thirds produce a triad, three a seventh chord. Continuing further, chords of four, five, and six thirds form harmonic structures called ninth, eleventh, and thirteenth chords after the interval which occurs between the root and the highest note. Consisting of as many as seven tones, these chords are fairly dissonant, and are used only when colorful effects are desired. Used sparingly by earlier composers, ninth, eleventh, and thirteenth chords occur more frequently toward the end of the nineteenth century. They are especially characteristic of impressionistic music.

676. Chords of more than four tones can be produced by superimposing additional thirds above the seventh of seventh chords. These are knows as NINTH, ELEVENTH, and THIRTEENTH CHORDS.

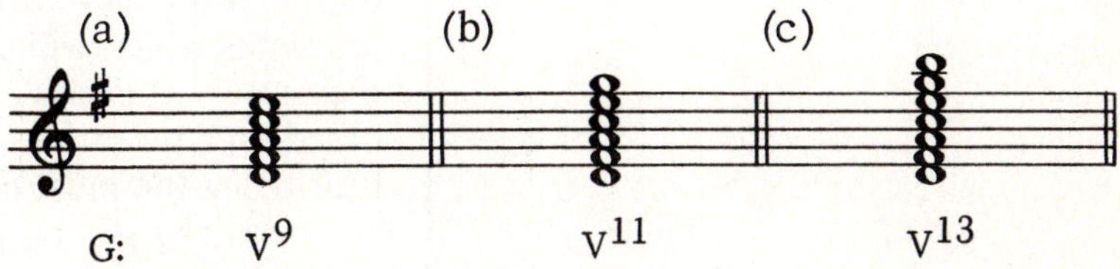

If an additional third were to be added above the thirteenth chord, a fifteenth would result. Since the fifteenth merely duplicates the root two octaves higher, the thirteenth chord is the limit of tertian extention possible unless chromatic notes are used.

The thirteenth chord consists of ____________ notes.

seven

---

677. Ninth, eleventh, and thirteenth chords may occur on any scale degree, but the majority are dominant chords. This results from the desire evidenced by many composers to increase the activity of dominant harmony. Extended and altered dominant sonorities were exploited chiefly by late nineteenth-century composers, but ninth, eleventh, and thirteenth chords are part of the harmonic vocabulary of earlier composers as the examples which follow will show.

(No response.)

The chord in example (a) of the preceding frame is called a dominant ninth chord; chord (b) is called a dominant eleventh chord.

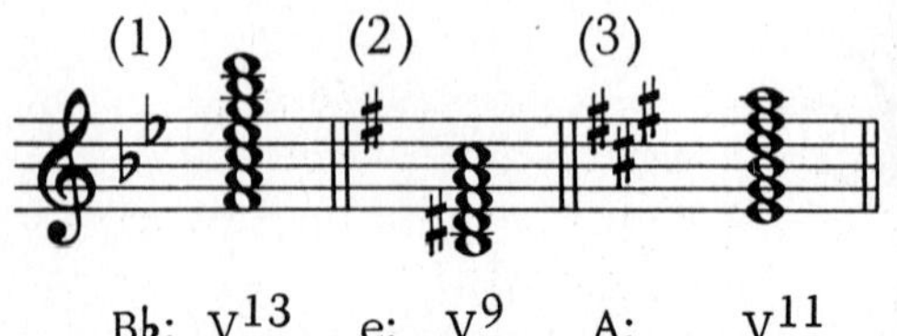

678. Write the chord symbol for each chord.

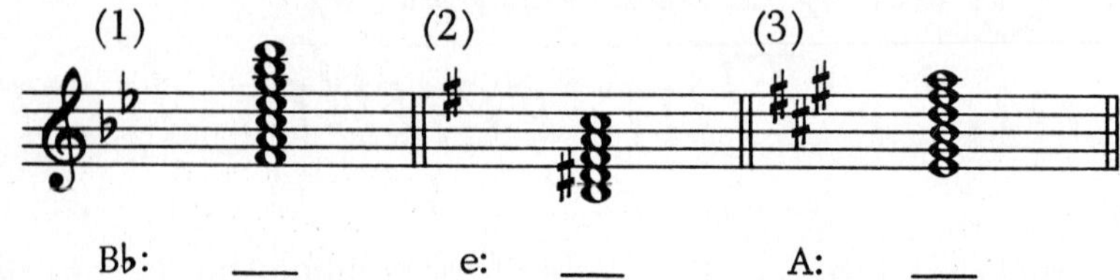

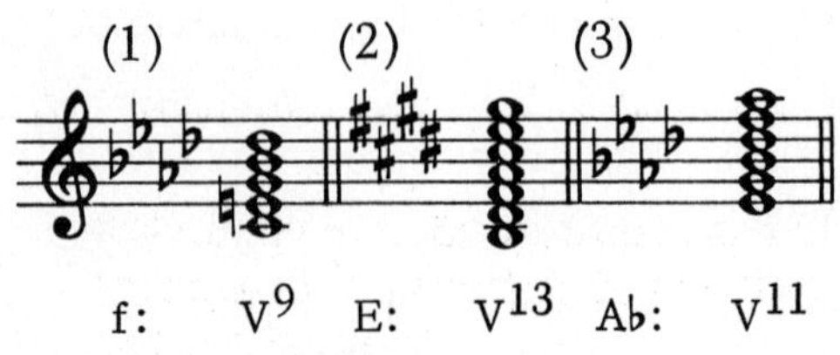

679. Continue as in the preceding frame.

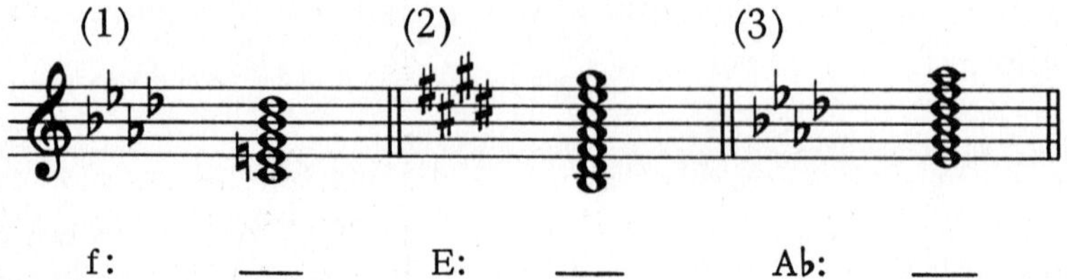

(No response.)

680. Ninth, eleventh, and thirteenth chords pose two special problems which will concern us throughout this chapter. First, they rarely appear as complete chords. Since most music is based on a texture of three, four, or five separate parts, with four being the most prevalent, one or more tones are usually omitted. The second problem results from the manner in which the higher chord members are introduced into the musical texture. Since these tones often appear as nonharmonic devices, it is sometimes difficult to decide whether they should be interpreted as members of the harmony or as incidental melodic occurrences.

---

681. Now we shall direct our attention to ninth chords. The most frequently used ninth chords are shown below:

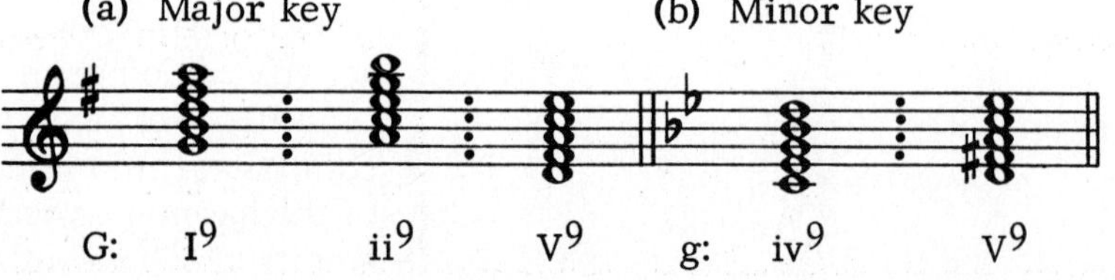

No. *(See next frame.)*	The dominant ninth chord is used more frequently than any other, so we shall start with this chord. In the preceding example, the dominant ninth chord (V^9) is shown in both a major and minor key. Do these chords sound the same in each case? ______
minor	682. The two forms of the dominant ninth are identified according to the type of interval between the root and ninth of the chord. The interval in (a) below is a major ninth whereas the interval in (b) is a ____________ ninth. (a) G: V^9 (b) g: V^9
major	683. The chord in (a) of the preceding frame is commonly referred to as the "major ninth chord." It consists of a major-minor seventh chord plus a ____________ ninth above the root.
major-minor	684. The chord in (b) of Frame 682 is called a "minor ninth chord." This term derives from the interval of a minor ninth which appears above the root. The sonority also includes a ____________-____________ seventh chord.
major-minor-minor	685. The terms "major ninth chord" and "minor ninth chord" refer to *dominant* ninths. Thus the seventh chord to which the ninth is added is assumed to be major-minor in quality. When it is necessary to refer accurately to the various qualities of ninth chords, one may extend the system used for seventh chords. The major ninth, for example, could be termed a "major-minor-major ninth chord." *(The quality of the ninth is added to the term which designates the quality of the seventh chord.)* The chord in example (b) of Frame 682 is commonly called a "minor ninth chord." Its more specific term is ____________-____________-____________ ninth.

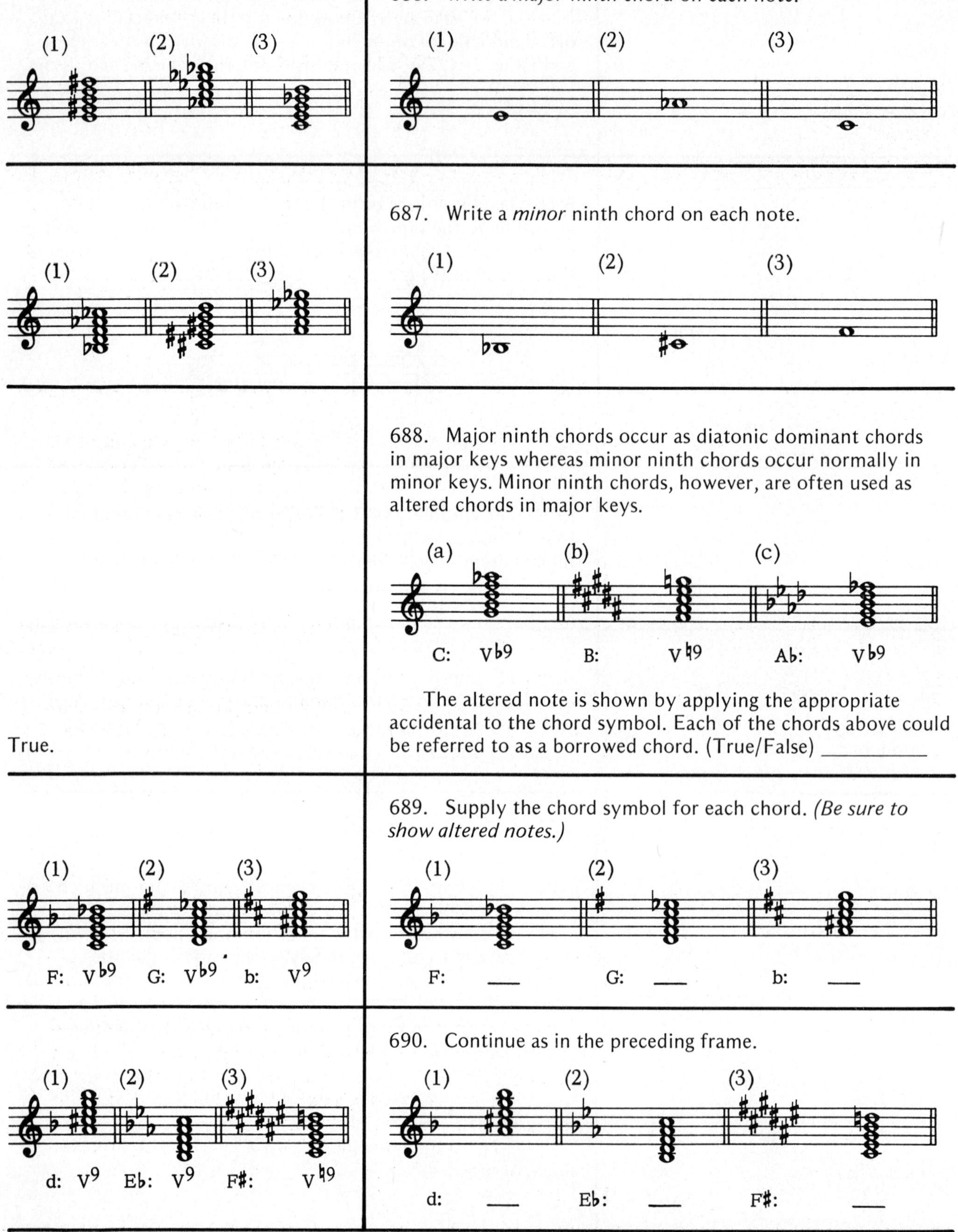

686. Write a *major* ninth chord on each note.
(1)
(2)
(3)
687. Write a *minor* ninth chord on each note.
(1)
(2)
(3)
688. Major ninth chords occur as diatonic dominant chords in major keys whereas minor ninth chords occur normally in minor keys. Minor ninth chords, however, are often used as altered chords in major keys.
(a)
(b)
(c)
C: V♭9
B: V♮9
A♭: V♭9
The altered note is shown by applying the appropriate accidental to the chord symbol. Each of the chords above could be referred to as a borrowed chord. (True/False) __________
True.
689. Supply the chord symbol for each chord. *(Be sure to show altered notes.)*
F: V♭9
G: V♭9
b: V9
F: ___
G: ___
b: ___
690. Continue as in the preceding frame.
d: V9
E♭: V9
F♯: V♮9
d: ___
E♭: ___
F♯: ___

No.
(In (c) the 7th is omitted; in (d) the third is omitted.)

691. A ninth chord contains five tones. Obviously one of these tones must be omitted in four-part writing. *Usually the fifth is omitted.*

Check the doubling in each chord below. Is the fifth omitted in each case? ______

(a) (b) (c) (d)

C: V^9 D: V^9 e: V^9 F: $V^{\flat 9}$

(c) and (d).

692. Although the fifth is the chord member which is usually omitted when a ninth chord is sounded by four voices, a satisfactory sonority can be produced by omitting either the third or seventh. The root and ninth, of course, must be present.

Which of the chords in the preceding frame are minor ninth chords? ____________

(No response.)

693. Ninth chords are usually in root position and the ninth is at least a ninth above the root (often in the highest voice). The effect of a chord built in thirds may be lost if the higher chord members are set too close to the root.

(a) (b)

The effect in (a) is of a dominant seventh chord with an added second. In (b) the tones of the ninth chord are placed as close together as possible with the seventh in the lowest voice. Rather than sounding like a chord built in thirds, this arrangement produces the effect of a "tone cluster."

The ninth of a ninth chord is usually more than an octave above the bass.

694. Write the alto and tenor voices and supply the chord symbol in each case. (Remember: *Omit the fifth unless the figured bass indicates otherwise.)*

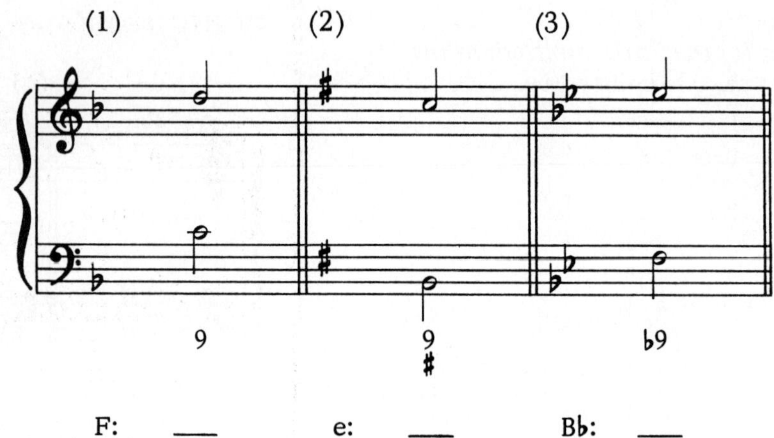

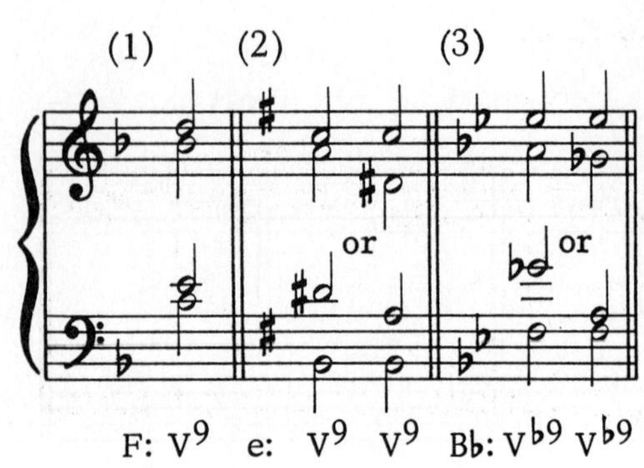

---

695. Continue as in the preceding frame.

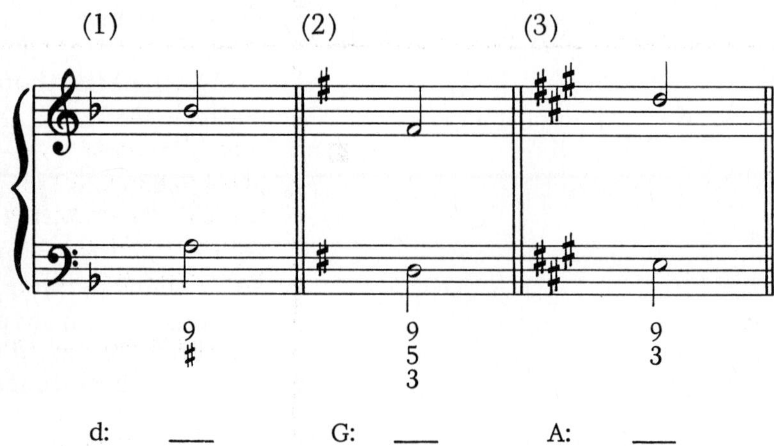

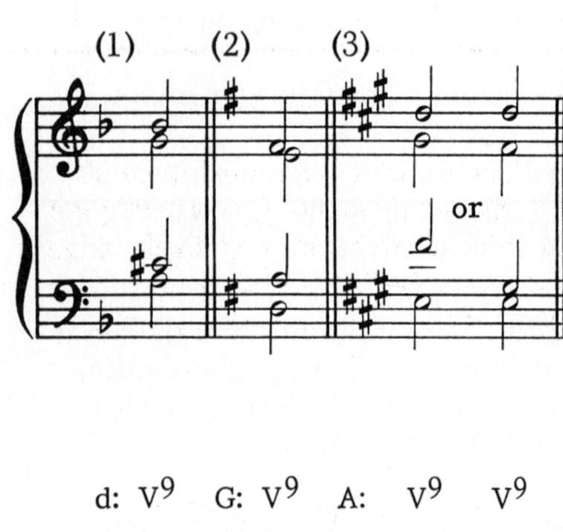

---

696. In (2) of the preceding frame the chord member which has been omitted is the ______________.

seventh

---

697. When ninth chords are sounded by four parts, the fifth of the chord is usually omitted. The ninth is often in the highest part, and usually at least a ninth above the root. Although ninth chords occasionally are in first, second, or third inversion, fourth inversion is practically never used.

Most ninth chords are built on the dominant. There are two types of dominant ninth chords, the *major ninth chord* which consists of a major-minor seventh chord plus a major ninth, and the *minor ninth chord,* which consists of a major-minor seventh chord plus a minor ninth.

(No response.)

Appoggiatura.

698. The ninth of a ninth chord is a dissonant element. It often appears as a nonharmonic tone as at the asterisk in the example below:

Beethoven, *Symphony No. 6,* Op. 68

The nonharmonic function of the ninth (D) is obvious. This passage shows that like the seventh, the ninth tends to resolve downward by step. What type of nonharmonic tone is the ninth in this example? _______________

major

699. The ninth at the asterisk below is perhaps more forcefully perceived than the one in the preceding frame. This is because it occurs on a stronger portion of the beat and is of relatively longer duration. Still, the note G is perhaps best analyzed as a appogiatura, rather than a chord member.

Chopin, *Mazurka,* Op. 7, No. 1

If analyzed as a ninth chord, the dominant ninth above is a (major/minor) ____________ ninth.

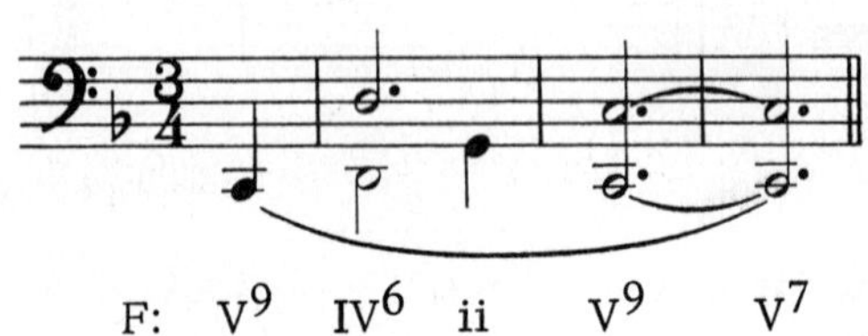

■ 700. Supply the Roman numeral analysis for the example below:

Wagner, *Die Walküre,* Act I, Scene 1

(Lento)

F: ___ ___ ___ ___ ___

f: vii°$^6_5$ V^9

■ 701. Supply the Roman numeral analysis for the example below. *(Analyze all of the notes in the second measure as constituting a single chord even though they do not sound simultaneously.)*

Beethoven, *Quartet,* Op. 135

Grave, ma non troppo tratto

(one chord)

f: ___ ___

minor

702. The dominant ninth chord in the preceding frame is a (major/minor) ____________ ninth.

■ 703. The ninth of a ninth chord is not always resolved. In the example below there is no doubt that the ninth (at the asterisk) is an integral part of the chord. Although brief, it appears in a strong metrical position. Supply the Roman numeral analysis.

Beethoven, *Piano Concerto No. 3,* Op. 37

■ 704. When the ninth is not resolved, it may appear as part of an arpeggio, as it does here:

Beethoven, *Quartet,* Op. 18, No. 1

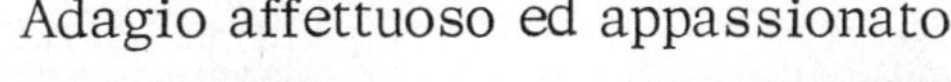

minor

The dominant ninth chord above is a (major/minor) ______________ ninth.

■ 705. Although the majority of ninth chords are dominant chords, they may be built on other scale degrees as well. They often appear in sequence patterns such as in the example below:

Mozart, *Sonata,* for violin and piano, K. 380

No.

Are all of the ninth chords in the preceding example the same quality? ______

■

706. Supply the Roman numeral analysis for the example below. *(Analyze the chord at the asterisk as a ninth chord.)*

Beethoven, *Sonata* for violin and piano, Op. 30, No. 2

suspensions

707. The chord at the asterisk in the preceding frame is analyzed as a subdominant ninth chord. This chord could be analyzed as a supertonic triad in first inversion by regarding the two upper notes as nonharmonic tones. Specifically, they would be ______________.

■

708. Supply the Roman numeral analysis for the example below:

Grieg, *Wedding Day at Troldhaugen,* Op. 65, No. 6

■ 709. The major ninth chord appears on the tonic as an altered chord in the example below:

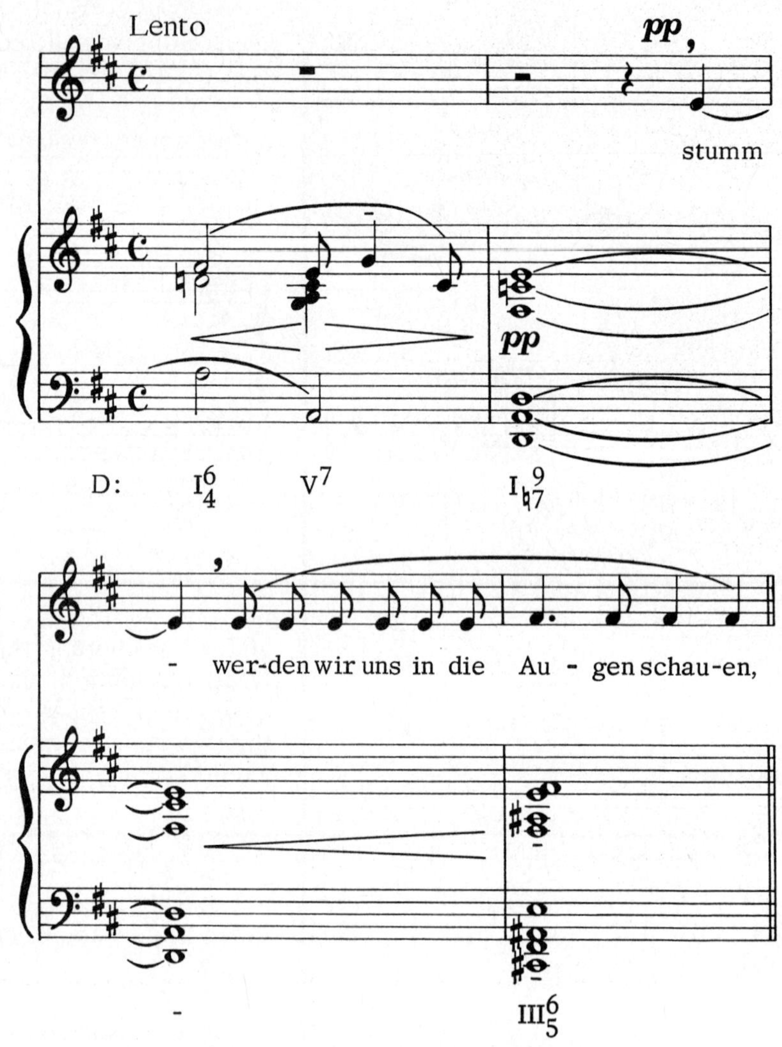

The ninth chord resolves to a chromatic mediant seventh chord (F♯A♯C♯E). This is an example of (functional/nonfunctional) ________________ harmony.

nonfunctional

■ 710. Although quite rare, ninth chords may be used in various inversions. To avoid undue complications chord symbols need not show inversions. If it is necessary to do so, the intervals which actually appear above the bass may be included as part of the chord symbol.

In the example on the following page, the chord at the asterisk is a ninth chord. Which chord member is in the lowest part? The ____________.

seventh

Haydn, *Piano Sonata,* in D major

■ 711. Supply the Roman numeral analysis for the example below. *(The chords at the asterisks need not be analyzed; they serve purely a nonharmonic function.)*

Schumann, *Scenes from Childhood,* Op. 15, No. 2

---

third

712. Since the ninth chord in the preceding frame has the seventh in the lowest part, it is in _____________ inversion.

---

third

■ 713. In the ninth chord on the following page, the chord member which is in the bass is the _____________.

Dvořák, *Quartet,* Op. 105

■ 714. Ninth chords may be used as secondary dominants. Complete the Roman numeral analysis for the example below:

Tchaikovsky, *Nutcracker Suite,* "Overture"

■ 715. The ninth chord in the example below appears in arpeggiated form. Take this into account in writing the Roman numeral analysis.

Bach, *Well-Tempered Clavier,* Vol. I, Prelude XII

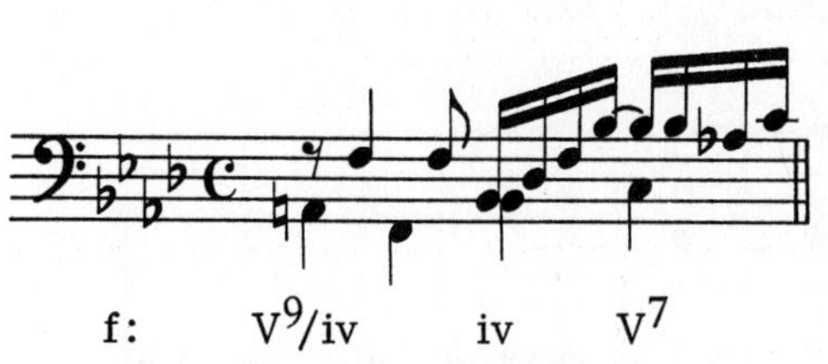

■ 716. The analyzed portion of the example below shows a secondary dominant (V/ii), which becomes a ninth chord by the gradual addition of tones.

Schumann, *Album for the Young,* Op. 68, No. 15

(No response.)

■ 717. Complete the Roman numeral analysis.

Fauré, *Après un Rêve,* Op. 7, No. 1

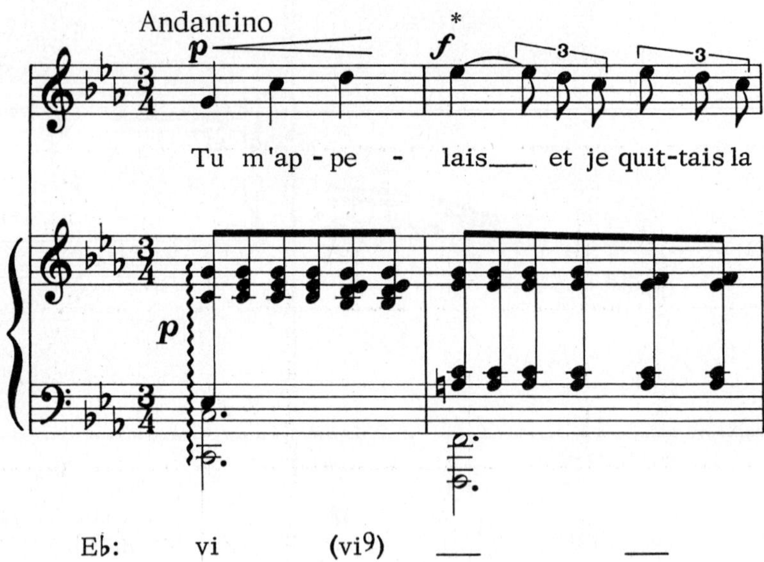

Eb: vi (vi9) ___ ___

___ ___

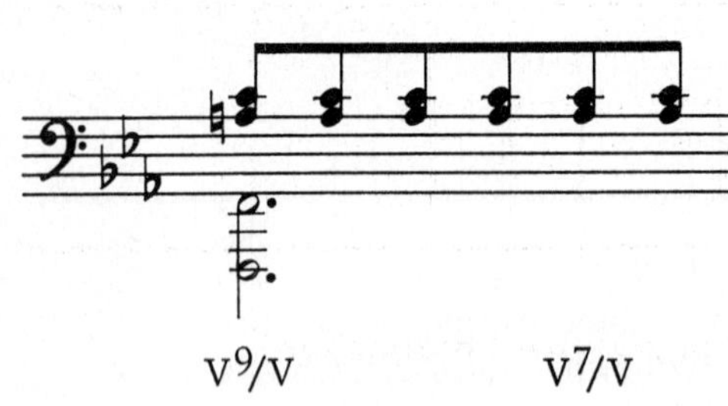

V9/V V7/V

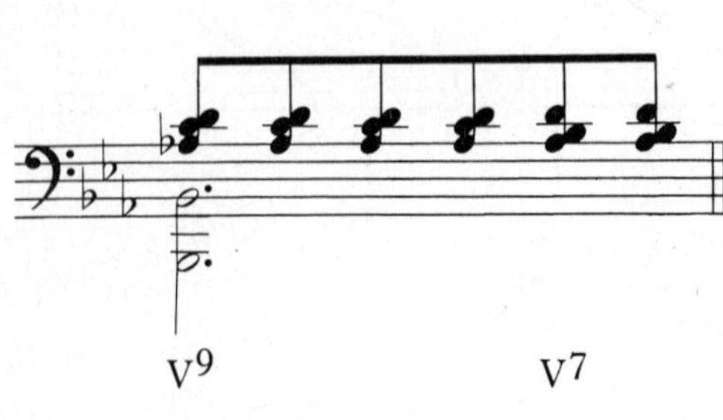

V9 V7

718. The ninth chords at the asterisks in the preceding frame could be eliminated from the analysis by regarding the ninths as nonharmonic tones. What type of nonharmonic tone is employed? Both are ______________.

suspensions

(You are entitled to your opinion.)

719. Ninth chords frequently are the result of nonharmonic tones; but if the ninth is sufficiently prolonged or made prominent through rhythmic accentuation, the effect of an actual ninth chord may be strong enough to warrant the acceptance of the tone as integral member of the chord.

Referring again to the example in Frame 717, do you think the ninths in this case are best analyzed as nonharmonic tones or as members of actual ninth chords? ______________

True.

720. The majority of ninth chords are dominant ninths. (True/False) __________

False.

721. There is only one type of dominant ninth chord. (True/False) __________

---

1. Major ninth chord
2. Minor ninth chord

722. Name the two types of dominant ninth chords.

1. ________________________
2. ________________________

False.
(The minor ninth chord may occur in major as a borrowed chord.)

723. Minor ninth chords may be used only in minor keys. (True/False) ___________

---

six

724. An ELEVENTH CHORD is written by superimposing another third on top of a ninth chord.

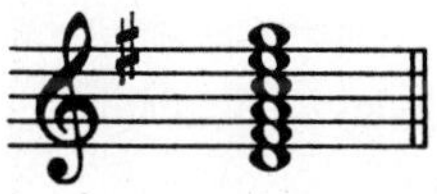

G: V^{11}

The chord above is called a *dominant eleventh chord.* Complete eleventh chords consist of __________ tones.

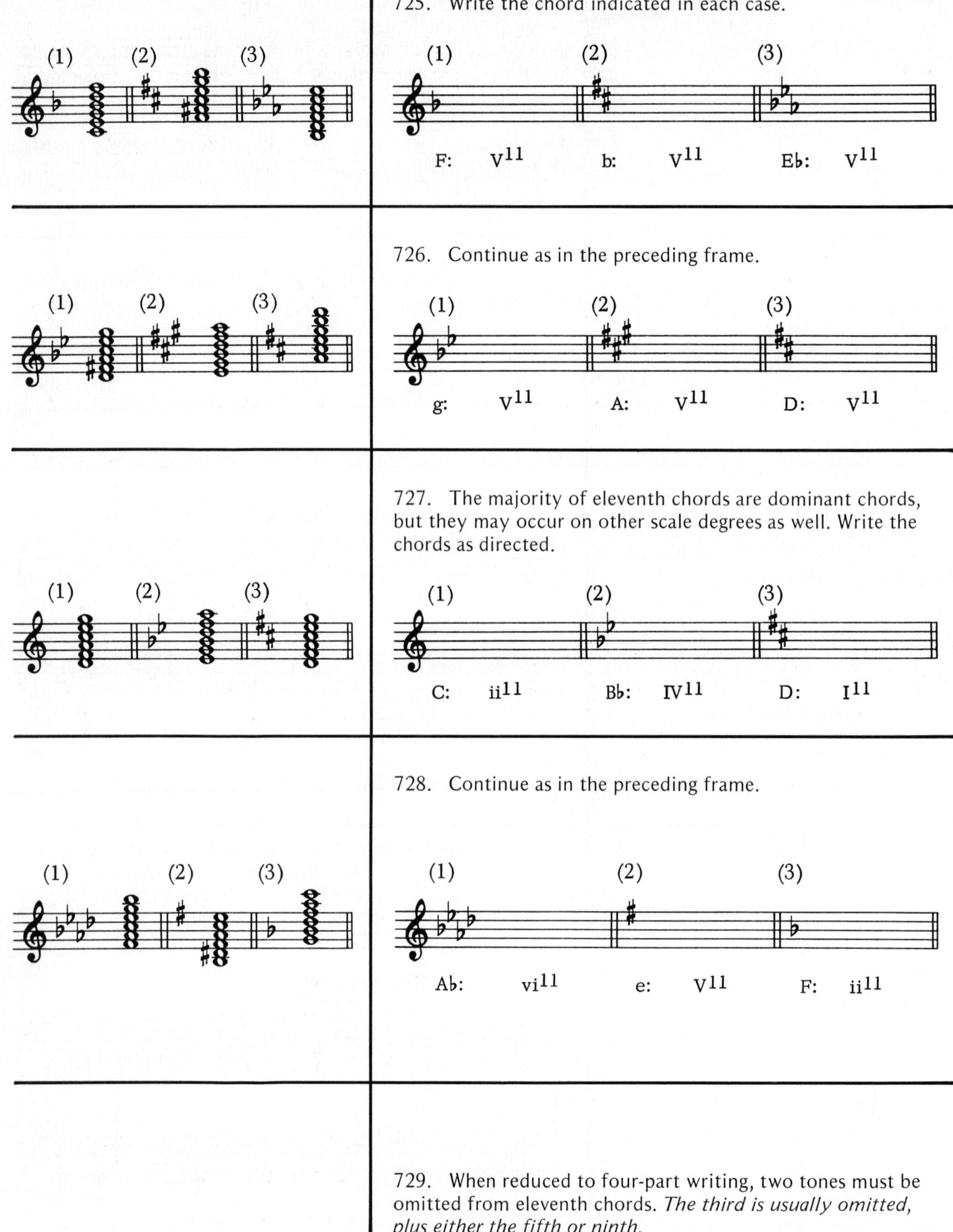

729. When reduced to four-part writing, two tones must be omitted from eleventh chords. *The third is usually omitted, plus either the fifth or ninth.*

Name the chord members which are omitted from each of the eleventh chords above.

(1) __________ and __________.

(2) __________ and __________.

(1) Third (and) fifth

(2) Third (and) ninth

730. Write each chord according to the figured bass symbols.

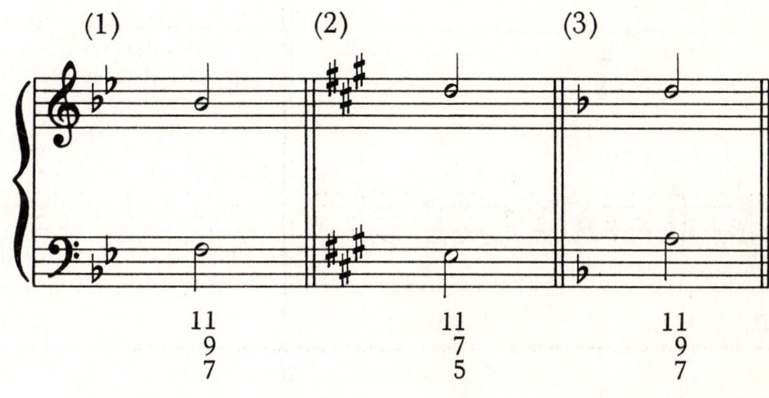

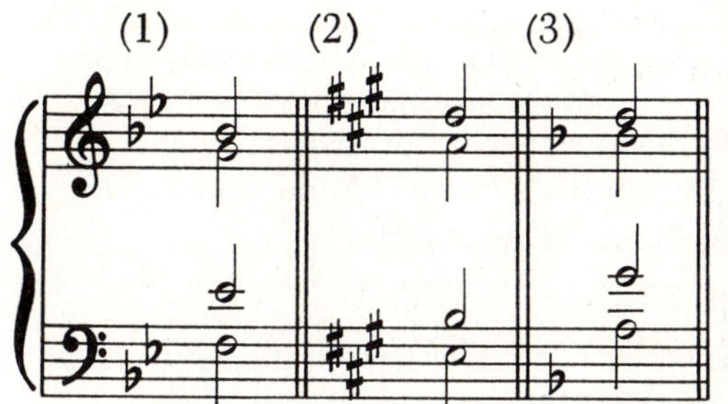

■ 731. Composers of the Classical and early Romantic eras used eleventh chords largely in a nonharmonic fashion.

Mendelssohn, *Songs Without Words*, Op. 53, No. 2

suspension	In the dominant eleventh chord (at the asterisk) the ninth ($F^{\flat}$) appears as a neighboring tone, and the eleventh ($A^{\flat}$) can be analyzed as a ____________.
third	732. What chord member has been omitted from the dominant eleventh in the preceding frame? The ____________.
Active. *(Activity is relative, of course, but in terms of traditional music, this is an active sonority.)*	733. Notice in the example below that the tonic eleventh chord contains not only the tones of the tonic triad, but also the dominant seventh chord. KEY OF A MAJOR dominant seventh chord tonic triad While all ninth, eleventh, and thirteenth chords may be approached as resulting from combinations of two or more triads or seventh chords, the effect of a "polychord"* is strongest in the case of the tonic eleventh. Would you expect a sonority such as this to be active or inactive? ____________ *A polychord consists of two or more triads or seventh chords sounded simultaneously.
True.	734. If you will play the tonic eleventh below at the piano, you will find that the tones which are the seventh, ninth, and eleventh tend to be attracted to the root and third of the tonic triad as indicated by the arrows. A: I^{11} I The upper three tones of a tonic eleventh chord may be regarded as nonharmonic tones. (True/False) __________

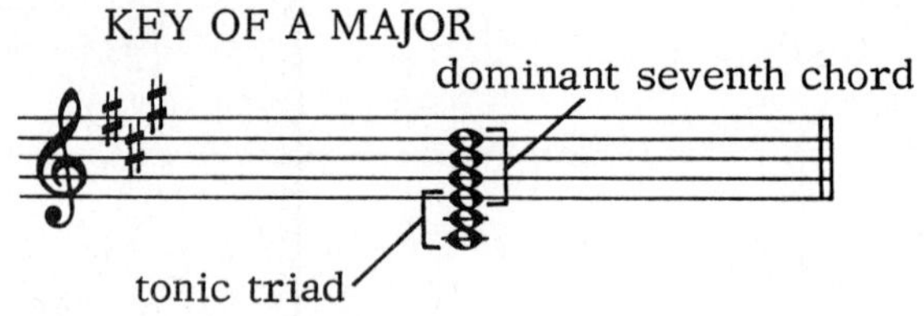

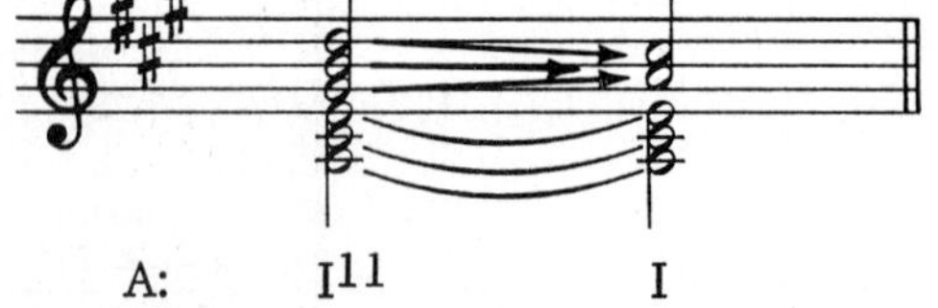

■ 735. The example below shows a chord which can be analyzed as a tonic eleventh chord, but which actually is the result of a combination of the tonic triad and the dominant seventh chord.

Beethoven, *Sonata,* Op. 2, No. 2

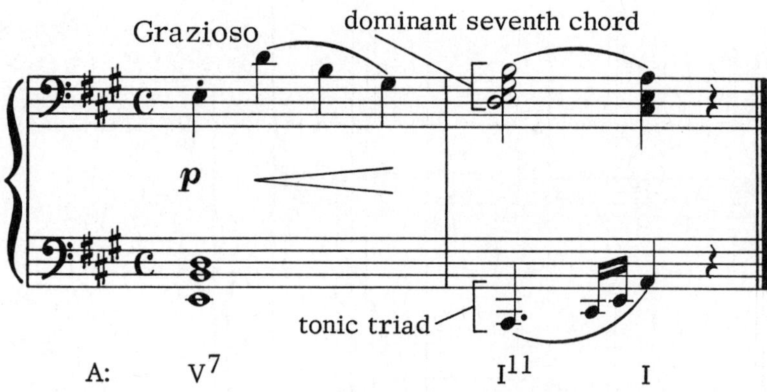

Cadence effects such as this occur fairly often in traditional music. While these sonorities are undoubtedly the result of nonharmonic factors (the dominant seventh chord can be called an appoggiatura chord), they can also be related to expanded tertian sonorities such as eleventh chords, and provide a logical steppingstone to the use of polychords by later composers.

The dominant seventh chord superimposed on a tonic triad contains the tones of a tonic eleventh. The term which refers to a sonority consisting of two different chords sounding simultaneously is ____________.

polychord

■ 736. The first chord in the example below is an eleventh chord with the third and ninth omitted. Since this is the beginning of the composition, there can be no question as to the harmonic status of the eleventh. No nonharmonic interpretation is valid here. Analyze with Roman numerals.

Schumann, *Noveleten,* Op. 21

■

Ab: I V11 I V11

I V11 I G6

737. In contrast to earlier practice, composers of the late nineteenth century tended to use eleventh chords more as integral harmonic units for the sake of their color. Supply the Roman numeral analysis for the example below:

Wolf, *Goethe Lieder,* No. 45

The 3rd and 5th.

738. Which chord members have been omitted from the dominant eleventh chords in the previous example? ____________________

■

739. Seventh, ninth, and eleventh chords are used in a non-functional manner in the example below:

Debussy, *Pelléas et Mélisande,* Act II, Scene 1

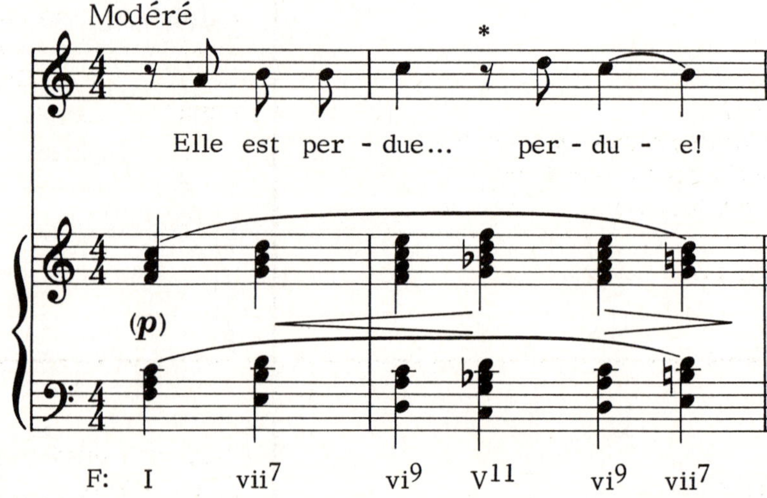

No. *(The 3rd is missing.)*	Is the chord at the asterisk a complete dominant eleventh chord? ______
True.	740. The style of writing shown in the preceding frame is characteristic of impressionist composers. Chords are often used for their color effect, and the concept of active and inactive tones is broadened so that ninth, eleventh, and thirteenth chords perform as relatively consonant sonorities. Further, roots progress more freely (with a higher incidence of seconds) than in music which is more strongly governed by traditional harmonic principles. All chords in the preceding frame are in root position. (True/False) __________
Yes. *(Roots progress entirely by seconds—from F down to C, then back up to E. This symmetrical pattern is an expressive factor.)*	741. Another feature of the example in Frame 739 warrants further comment. Notice that each chord from the first to the fourth is progressively more complex. The first is a triad, the second a seventh chord, the third a ninth chord, and the fourth (at the asterisk) an eleventh chord. From this point the sequence is reversed. Since this subtle gradation of tension coincides with the contour of the melody and is reinforced by the dynamic indications, it is obvious that the composer used the varying degrees of tension possessed by these chords to help accomplish his expressive purpose. Gradations of tension, produced not only by harmony, but through rhythm, dynamics, melody, and timbre as well, lie at the root of musical expression. Does the progression of roots in Frame 739 contribute to the tension pattern of the phrase? __________
True.	742. The third is usually omitted from eleventh chords. (True/False) __________

False.
(The dominant eleventh is the most common.)

743. Eleventh chords occur with approximately equal frequency on all scale degrees. (True/False) __________

---

(2) √
(The first statement is false because TWO tones must be omitted.)

744. Check (√) the correct option:

1. An eleventh chord may be set into four parts if one of the tones (usually the third) is omitted.
2. In music prior to the nineteenth century most eleventh chords are the result of nonharmonic tones.

True statements:
(1) ______ (2) ______ Both ______ Neither ______

---

seven

745. A chord consisting of six superimposed thirds is called a THIRTEENTH CHORD.

F: V^{13}

Limited to diatonic tones further extension in thirds beyond the thirteenth is impossible because additional tones merely duplicate lower members of the chord.

A complete thirteenth chord consists of ______________ tones.

5th, 9th, (and) 11th

746. We shall concentrate on the dominant thirteenth chord as all others are extremely rare. When set into four parts, three chord members must be omitted. There are several acceptable possibilities, but generally *the third and eleventh are not present at the same time.* In other words, the third is omitted if the eleventh is present, but is included if the eleventh is omitted.

The example on the following page shows a dominant thirteenth chord and its resolution to a tonic triad. Which chord members are omitted from the thirteenth chord? The __________, __________, and __________.

Note: Keep in mind the following examples are to offer some general illustrations. Many examples to be found in the literature are *not* limited to four parts.

3rd, 5th, (and) 9th

747. Which chord members are omitted from the thirteenth chord below? The __________, __________, and __________.

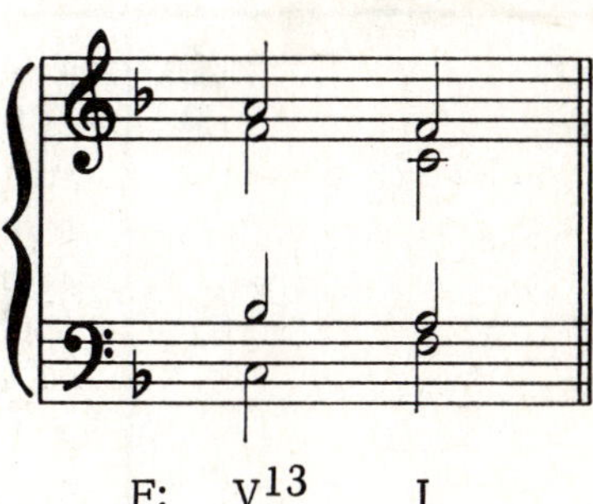

■

748. Write the alto and tenor voices in accordance with the figured bass symbols. Supply, also, the Roman numeral analysis.

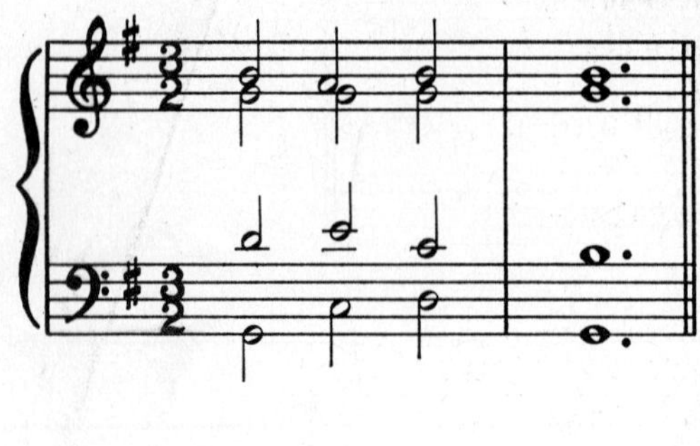

G: I ii^6_5 V^{13} I

■ 749. Continue as in the preceding frame.

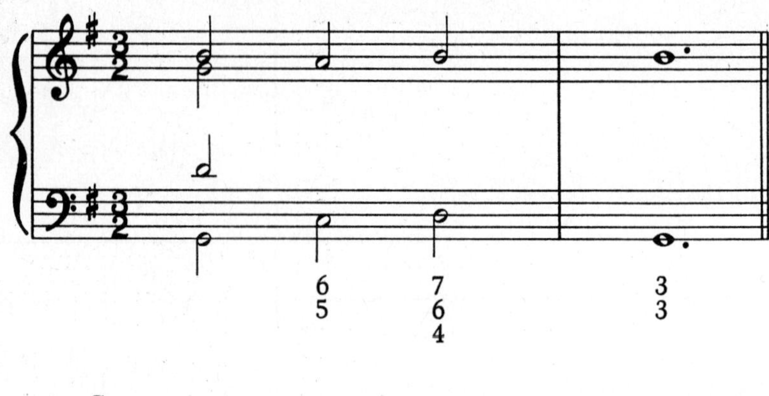

a: V V/V V V^7 i

■ 750. The thirteenth often is the result of a nonharmonic tone. A typical example is shown below. The escape tone (C) is the thirteenth over the dominant seventh chord. Supply the Roman numeral analysis.

Chopin, *Prelude,* Op. 28, No. 2

___ ___ ___

■ 751. In the preceding frame the thirteenth is merely suggested by the escape tone. While still nonharmonic, the thirteenth at the asterisk in the example below is a bit closer to achieving harmonic status. This is due to its longer duration, and being placed in a relatively strong rhythmic position.

Chopin, *Prelude,* Op. 28, No. 20

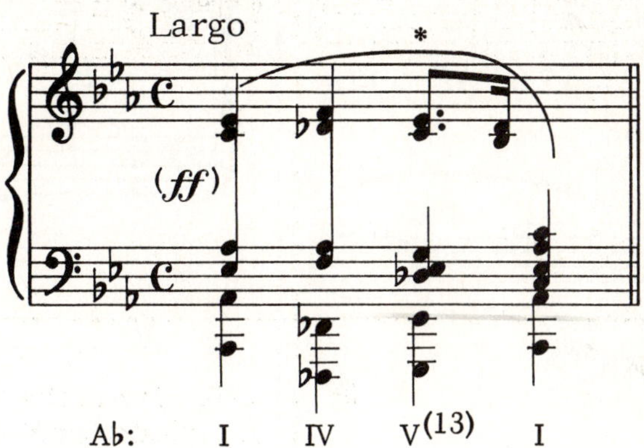

passing

The nonharmonic tone used to produce the effect of a dominant thirteenth above is called an accented _____________ tone.

---

escape tone

■ 752. The note which is circled in the example below could be analyzed as a free tone or as an eleventh. Likewise, the note C (at the asterisk) may be regarded as a thirteenth or as a(n) __________________.

Chopin, *Valse Brillante,* Op. 34, No. 2

Note: Some writers might consider this C a "free anticipation" of the C in the inner voice occuring on the next beat in the following measure.

■ 753. The thirteenth chord at the asterisk on the following page is not the result of a nonharmonic tone; it has complete harmonic status. Take into account the pedal tones (G and D) as indicated when writing the Roman numeral analysis.

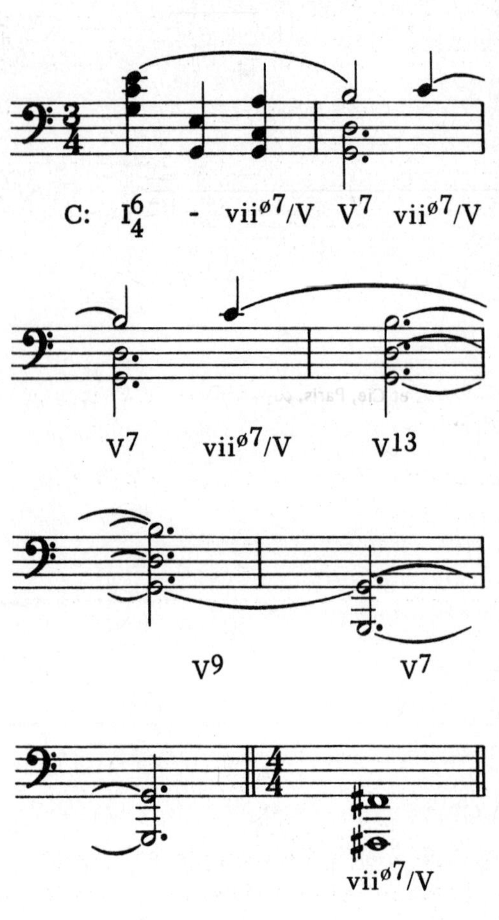

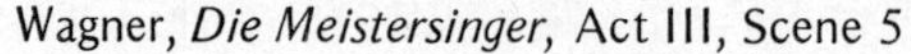
Wagner, *Die Meistersinger,* Act III, Scene 5

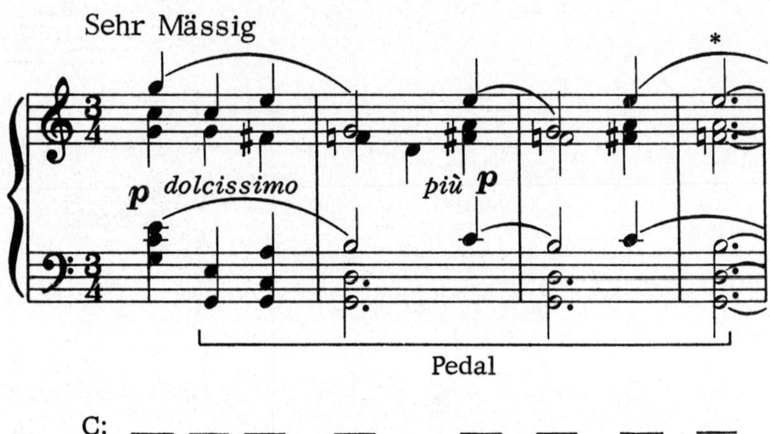

■

754. Dominant thirteenth chords are used prominently in the example below.

Ravel, *Valses noble et sentimentales,* No. 1

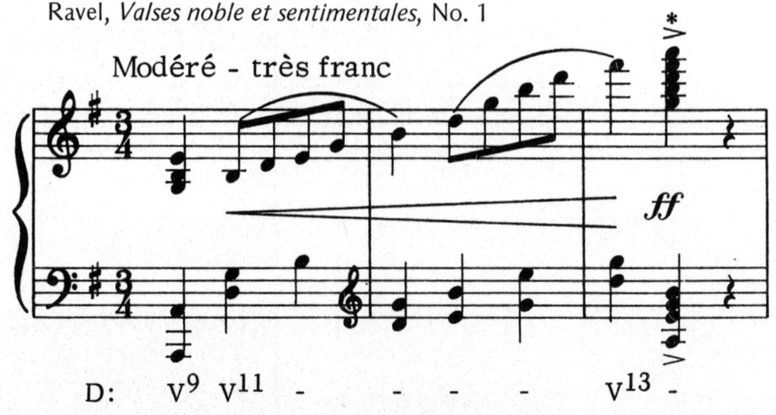

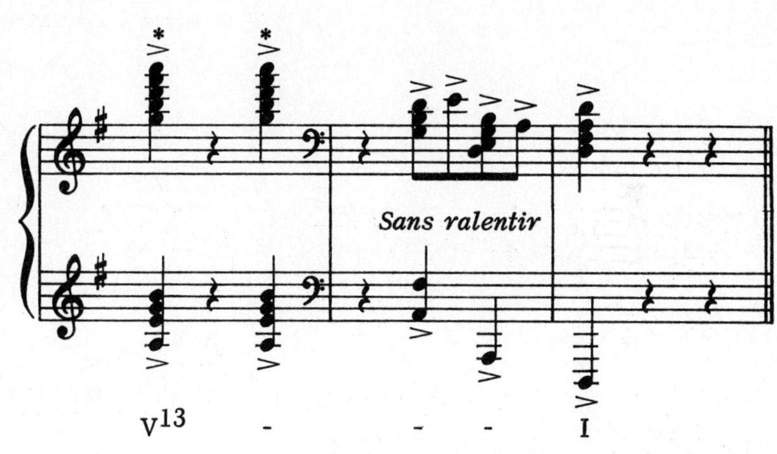

Are any triad tones omitted from the thirteenth chords at the asterisks? __________

Yes.
(The 3rd is not present.)

SUMMARY

Ninth, eleventh, and thirteenth chords are used sparingly except in late nineteenth-century music. Impressionist composers, in particular, made extensive use of these chords to achieve the shimmering harmonic effects which are characteristic of their music.

Extensive use of these chords tends to produce a "diffuse" harmonic idiom. The complete thirteenth chord, for example, contains all seven tones of a diatonic scale. Ambiguity of root and even tonal center often result when these chords are used extensively. Spacing and doubling is of crucial importance, and delicate decisions must be made as to which tones should be omitted in order to produce the desired effect. The judgment of the ear must be relied on, since principles and rules are not adequate to control all of the variable factors present in this kind of writing.

We are dealing here with material that stands at the boundary between functional harmonic practices and more modern techniques. It is but one short step to techniques such as pandiatonicism in which the tones of the diatonic scale lose their functional values, and atonality in which the stabilizing and referential influence of the key center is rejected entirely.

Mastery Frames

The fifth. (677)

11–1. Upon which scale degree do most ninth, eleventh, and thirteenth chords occur?________________________

---

(1) (2) (3)

D: V^{9} g: V^{11} F: V^{13}

(678–679)

11–2. Write the chord symbol for each chord.

(1) (2) (3)

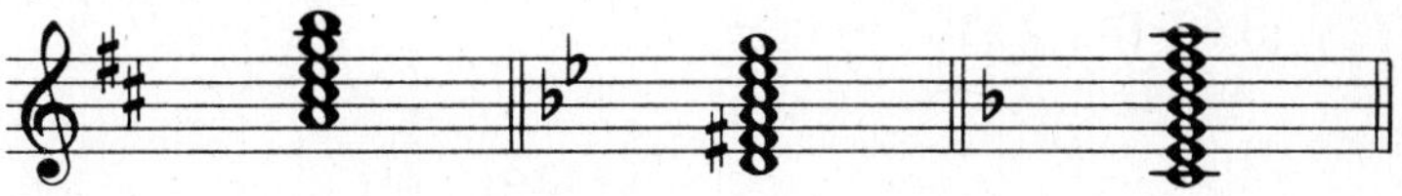

D: __ g: __ F: __

---

(1).

(682–688)

11–3. Which of the two chords below is called a "minor ninth chord"?________

(1) (2)

a: V^{9} A: V^{9}

True. (693)

11–4. Ninth chords are usually found in root position. (True/False)____________

---

(1) (2) (3)

G: V^{11} E♭: ii^{11} F: $vii^{ø11}$

(724–728)

11–5. Write the chords indicated by the Roman numerals.

(1) (2) (3)

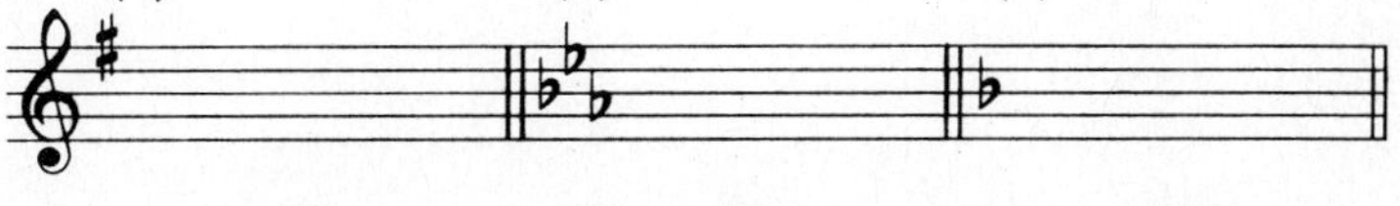

G: V^{11} E♭: ii^{11} F: $vii^{ø11}$

---

third (729–730)	11-6. When an eleventh chord appears in four-part writing, the ____________ of the chord is usually omitted, plus either the fifth or the ninth.
Seven. (745)	11-7. How many notes are needed to write a complete thirteenth chord?____________
(1) (2) (3) b: V13 A♭: IV13 F: I13 (745)	11-8. Write the chords indicated by the Roman numerals. (1) (2) (3) b: V13 A♭: IV13 F: I13
3rd, 5th, (and) 9th (746–747)	11-9. Which chord members are omitted from the dominant thirteenth chord below? The ______, ______, and ______. E: V13 I9

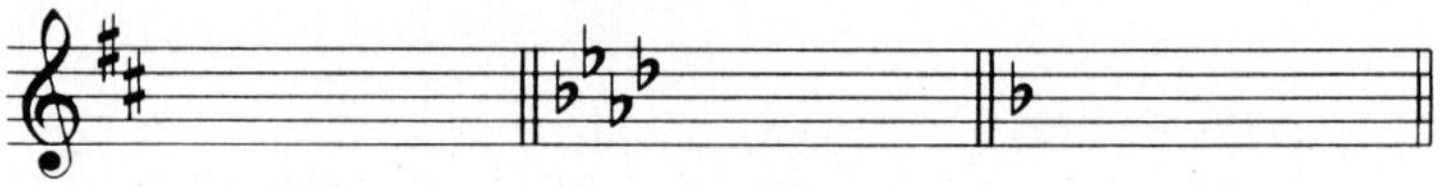

Supplementary Assignments

ASSIGNMENT 11-1 Name________________________________

1. Add a single note to each chord to produce a dominant major ninth chord.

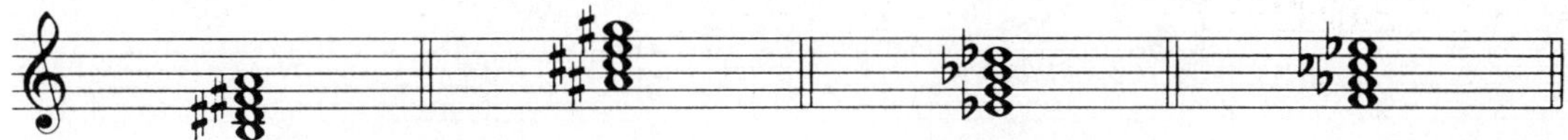

2. Add a single note to each chord to produce a dominant minor ninth chord.

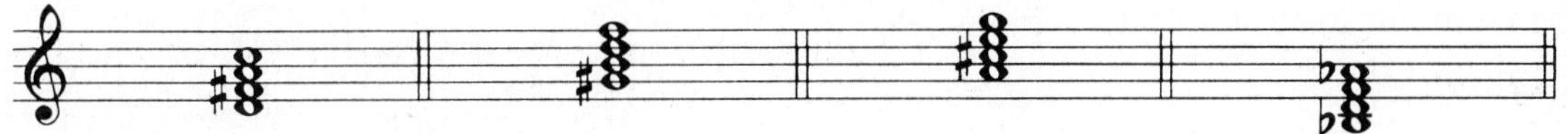

3. Write major ninth chords. The given note is the fifth in each case.

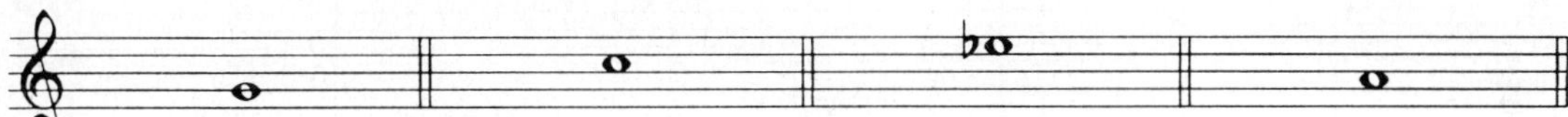

4. Write minor ninth chords. The given note is the seventh in each case.

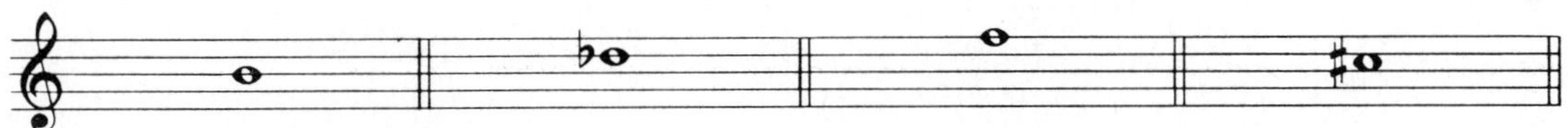

5. Write the chord symbol for each chord.

6. Write the chords indicated by the chord symbols. *(Take care to provide the needed accidentals.)*

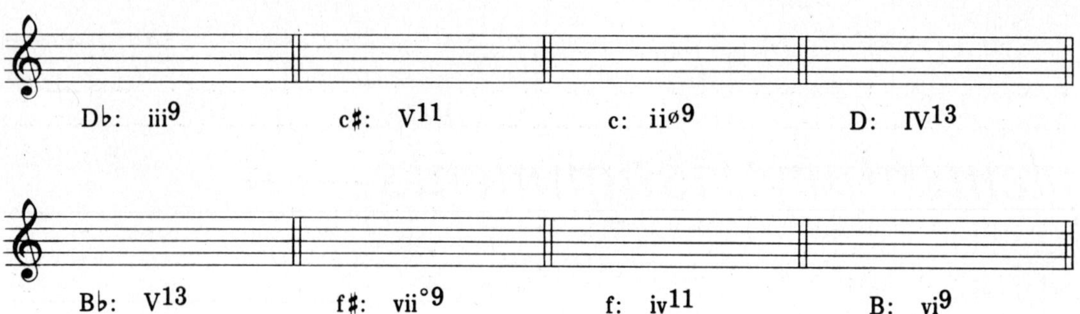

7. Provide the proper chord symbol for each chord.

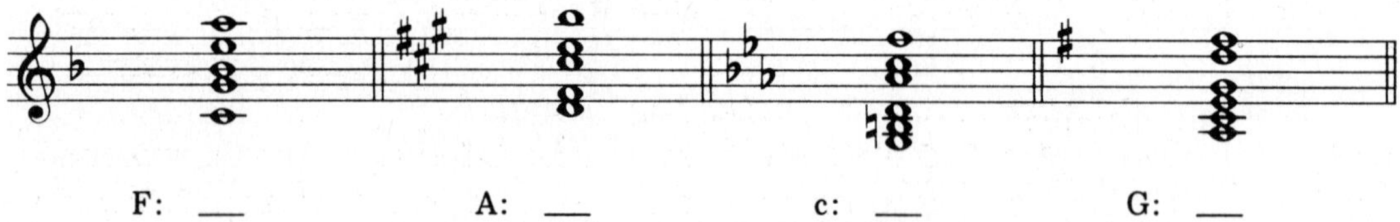

8. Provide the harmonic anaysis for the example below.

J. Strauss: "Artist's Life Waltzes," Op. 316

ASSIGNMENT 11-2 Name________________________________

1. Does the addition of a ninth, eleventh, or thirteenth alter a triad's harmonic function? *(Qualify your response.)*____

____

2. How many notes are needed to complete a ninth chord?________________

3. How many notes are needed to produce a complete thirteenth chord?________________

4. Provide the harmonic analysis for the example below.

Chopin: *Etude*, Op. 10, No. 3

5. Provide the harmonic analysis for the example below.

Chopin: *Fantasie*

6. Provide the harmonic analysis for the example below.

Chopin: *Polonaise-Fantasie,* Op. 61

7. On the staves below, compose one or more phrases that contain at least one ninth, eleventh, or thirteenth chord.

appendix a

Chord Glossary

CHORD SYMBOLS

Since early in the nineteenth century, symbols have been used to show the harmonic function of chords. These symbols consist of Roman and Arabic numerals as well as letters, accidentals, and figures such as the circle and plus sign. Chord symbols provide a vocabulary for verbal and written reference, and serve as a quick means of identifying not only a chord's relation to the tonal center, but also its quality and structure.

Musical analysis may take many forms, ranging from mere descriptive observation to complex interpretations made with reference to some explanatory system. Symbolism varies with the degree of exactness required by the analysis. The symbols used in this book are a compromise between simplicity and exactness; they may easily be adapted to serve the purpose of a particular type of analysis. Inversions, for example, generally are shown as part of the chord symbol; but, if the purpose of analysis is served merely by showing how chords function in a progression, symbols may be simplified by representing chords in root position only. Chord symbols are not precise enough to permit music to be reconstructed from them alone. They do, however, indicate the specific quality of diatonic triads and seventh chords (either directly or by inference), and usually show inversions. Thus the basic harmonic structure may readily be traced. In the case of certain altered chords, undue complexity is avoided at the expense of precision. To be completely consistent, logical, and devoid of ambiguity, chord symbols would be so complex that many no longer would serve as convenient references to harmonic entities.

As in many areas of music theory, there is a lack of standardization regarding chord symbols. Whenever possible, the most widely accepted practices have been observed. The following information summarizes the symbols used in this book.

DIATONIC TRIADS

Roman numerals are used to identify triads and are directly related to scale degrees. Further, the quality of triads is shown by the form of the symbols (capital letters = major, small letters = minor, small letters with circle = diminished, and capital letters with plus sign = augmented).

First and second inversions of triads are shown by adding the figured bass symbols 6 or ${}^{6}_{4}$ to the Roman numerals.

Notice that the figures are placed at the upper right-hand corner of the Roman numerals. When more than one number is involved, the largest appears at the top and the remainder are placed in descending order.

SYMBOLS FOR CHORDS NOT PRESENTED IN THIS BOOK

Some of the examples in this book include chords which are not treated fully until Part II. In no case does comprehension of the material depend upon an understanding of these chords.

DIATONIC SEVENTH CHORDS

The figure 7 added to the Roman numeral indicates a seventh chord in root position. In a major key the form of the Roman numeral is the same as for the corresponding triad.

The symbols used in harmonic minor are shown below:

Notice that in the diminished minor, or so-called "half-diminished" seventh chord ($ii^{ø7}$, $vii^{ø7}$), the circle which denotes the diminished triad is replaced by a circle with a slash. For the fully diminished, or so-called "diminished" seventh chord (vii^{o7}), the circle which denotes the diminished triad is an indicator that the seventh is diminished as well. All half or fully diminished seventh chords are shown in these ways regardless of their use. This attempts to keep the nomenclature in conformity with that used by many writers and instructors. As somewhat traditional symbols, the circle and circle with slash are appropriate in reflecting the theoretical practices currently in use.

Inversions of seventh chords are shown by figured bass symbols.

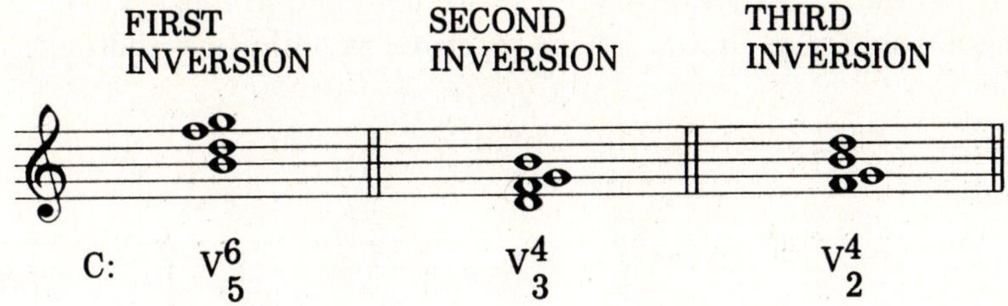

THE DOMINANT NINTH CHORD

The symbol V^9 is used to represent a dominant chord consisting of four superimposed thirds.

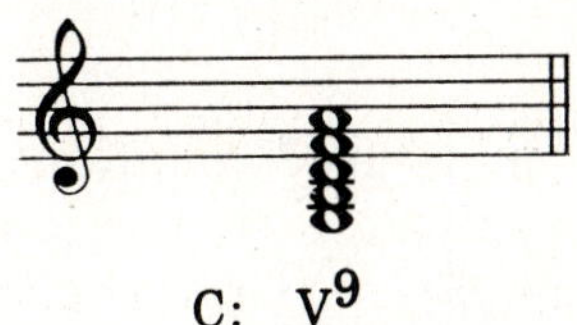

THE MEDIANT MAJOR TRIAD IN MINOR KEYS

The mediant triad generated by the descending form of the melodic minor scale is a major triad. The chord symbol is an upper-case Roman numeral. For example:

ALTERED CHORDS

Most of the altered chords which occur in traditional music are included in this list. The usual resolutions are given for each chord. These resolutions should not be regarded as definitive; there are many other possibilities which may occur.

Chord Types	*Symbols*	*Resolutions*
Secondary dominants	V/x V^7/x vii^{o} $vii^{ø7}$ vii^{o7}	Root down a P5 Root up a m2
Borrowed chords	ii^{o} $ii^{ø7}$ ♭III ♭III^{+} iv $IV^{♭7}$ (in major) ♭VI vii^{o7} I (in minor)	V ♭VI I V V IV iv ii^{o} I Various
Augmented sixth chords	It^6 G^6 F^6 (on 6) (on 2) (on 4)	V I I I^6
Neapolitan sixth chords	N^6 (N N^6_4)	V I^6_4
Altered dominants	V^{+} V^{+7} $V^{♭5}$ $V^{7}_{♭5}$	I I
Diminished seventh chords on raised 2nd and 6th scale degrees	♯ii^{o7} ♯vi^{o7}	I^6 V^6 V^6_5
Chromatic mediants	II ♭II ♭ii III ♭III ♭iii VI ♭VI ♭vi	IV I V I IV

appendix b

Piano Styles

Creative writing is possibly the best way to demonstrate command of the concepts and materials presented in this text. In original compositions students may apply the knowledge gained in terms of their own creativity. It is desirable that a variety of media (piano, voice, small ensembles, etc.) be used, but because of its availability, the piano is the most practical. The brief exposition of piano styles presented here provides a guide for those who have had little experience with keyboard techniques. Effective writing is possible—even by non-pianists—if typical styles are utilized. The material which follows—used in conjunction with the suggested supplementary assignments—facilitates the creative work which helps develop a heightened sensitivity to the rhetoric of harmonic music.

There are three textures into which all music falls: *monophonic* (a single melodic line), *homophonic* (a melody with accompaniment); and *polyphonic* (several voices approximately equal in melodic interest). Of these, homophonic texture is the most practical for music in which the harmonic element is stressed. Thus we shall concentrate on various homophonic piano styles.

I. FIGURATED BLOCK CHORDS. In the example below, the melody is provided a simple accompaniment in block chords.

Mozart: *Sonata,* K 545 (altered)

Block chords are easy to play because the left hand does not move over the keyboard. Care should be taken that principles of doubling and voice leading are applied. Active tones (the leading tone and chord sevenths) should not be doubled, and should be resolved properly. Notice in measure two, for example, that the leading tone (B) is omitted from the left hand, and also that the chord seventh (F) is resolved down by step to E.

Figuration patterns give rhythmic interest to block chords.

Mozart: *Sonata,* K 545

The way that the three notes of the block chords are transcribed into the figuration pattern is clear.

This technique of providing rhythmic animation for block chords is called "Alberti bass," after the Venetian composer Domenico Alberti (1710-1740?), who used such patterns extensively, perhaps even to excess.

Styles 3-12 show some of the many figurations which may be devised. The meter, as well as the degree of animation desired, affects the choice of pattern.

4

5

6

7

8

9

10

II. JUMP BASS (AFTER-BEAT PATTERNS). In these styles the left hand jumps from bass notes to block chords. The best sonority results when the block chords are set in the vicinity of middle C.

Schubert: *Waltz in A minor*

As in figurated block chords, care must be taken that principles of part writing are observed. In the above example there are four voices in the left hand. Notice how each of these traces a smooth line, and also the way active tones resolve properly.

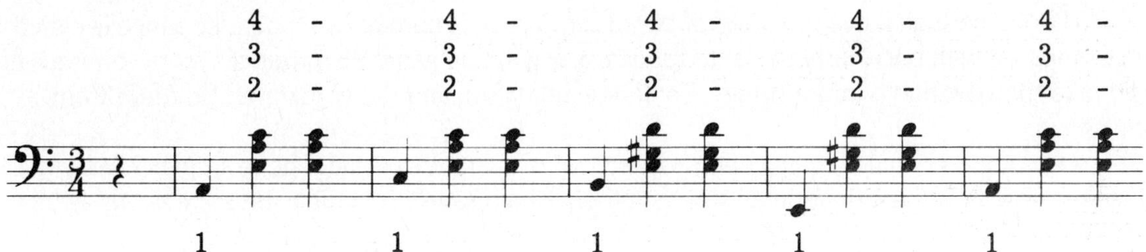

Of course the relation of the accompanying voices to the melody must also be considered. *Undesirable doubling and incorrect parallel motion must be avoided.*

Jump bass patterns are exploited mostly in waltzes and mazurkas, but are also useful in duple or quadruple meter for march-like effects. Some typical patterns are shown in styles 14-18.

(14)

(15)

(16)

(17)

(18)

III. ARPEGGIATION. The successive sounding of chord tones over a more or less extended range is called arpeggiation. Compared with previously presented styles, arpeggiation generally produces more sonorous effects. This is due to the vibration of more strings. Rhythmic animation and richer texture also result from arpeggiation.

There is scarcely any limit to the arpeggiation patterns which can be devised. The examples which follow demonstrate a few typical patterns; these may suggest others which satisfy specific expressive needs as they arise.

In style 19, arpeggiation is used exclusively throughout the entire composition. The effect is of figurated harmonies.

Schumann: *Album für die Jugend* ("Kleine Studie")

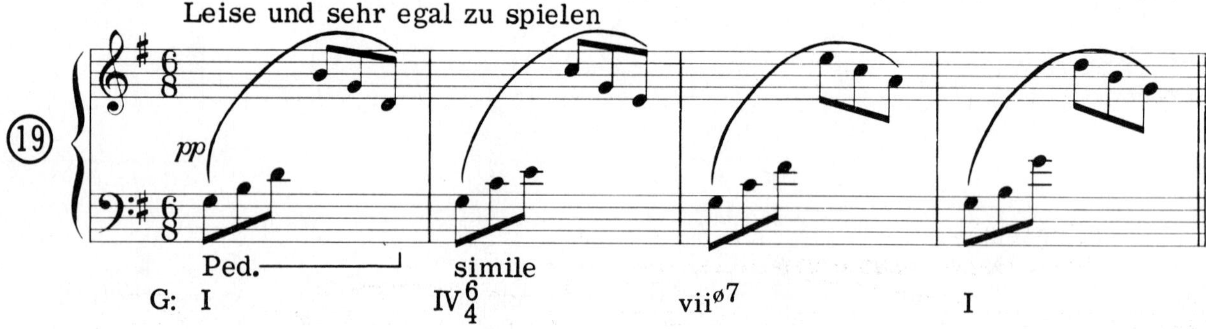

The example below shows fairly simple left hand arpeggiation, which supports a melody in the right hand.

Chopin: *Nocturne,* Posthumous

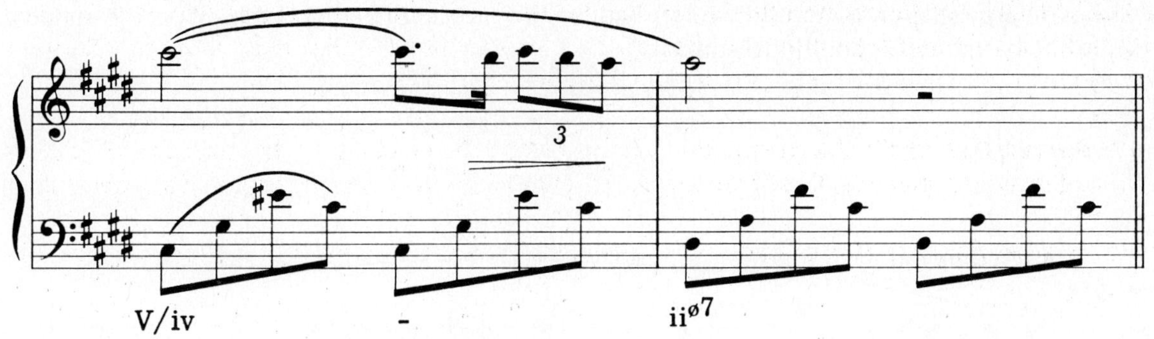

The arpeggiation in the next example is more extended in range.

Leybach: *Nocturne,* Op. 52

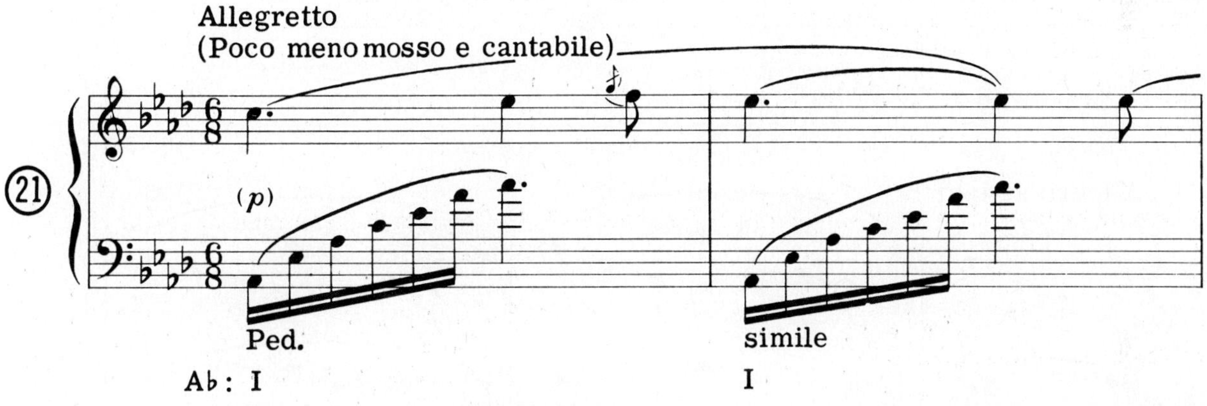

Style 22 has an arpeggiation pattern in the left hand while the right hand not only plays the melody, but also fills in the harmony for additional sonority.

Brahms: *Intermezzo,* Op. 119, No. 2

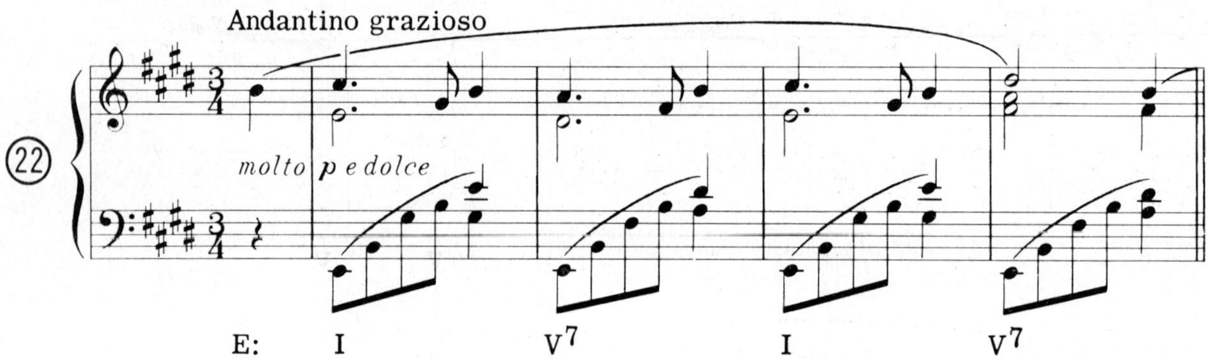

Arpeggiation takes a different form in the next example. The treble and bass move mostly in parallel tenths, while the middle voice completes the harmony, and fills in the eighth note rhythm.

Mendelssohn, *Lieder ohne Worte,* Op. 85, No. 2

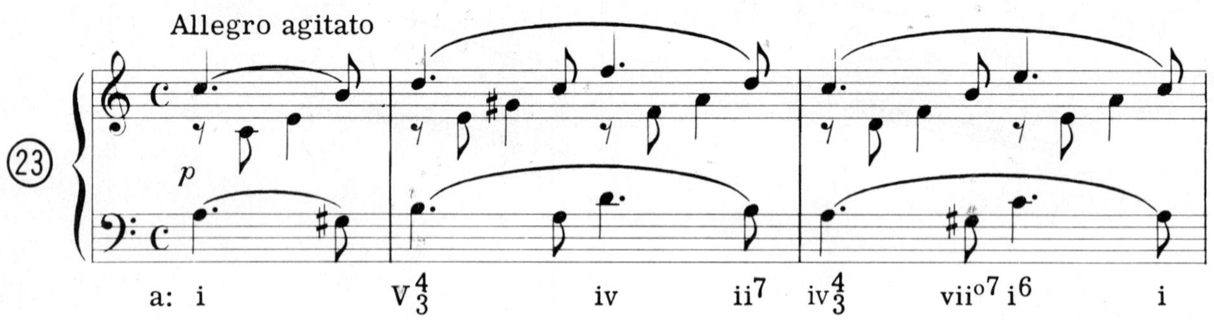

In style 24 the arpeggiation is in the tenor register, divided between the right and left hands.

Schumann: *Kinderscenen* ("Von Fremden Ländern und Menschen")

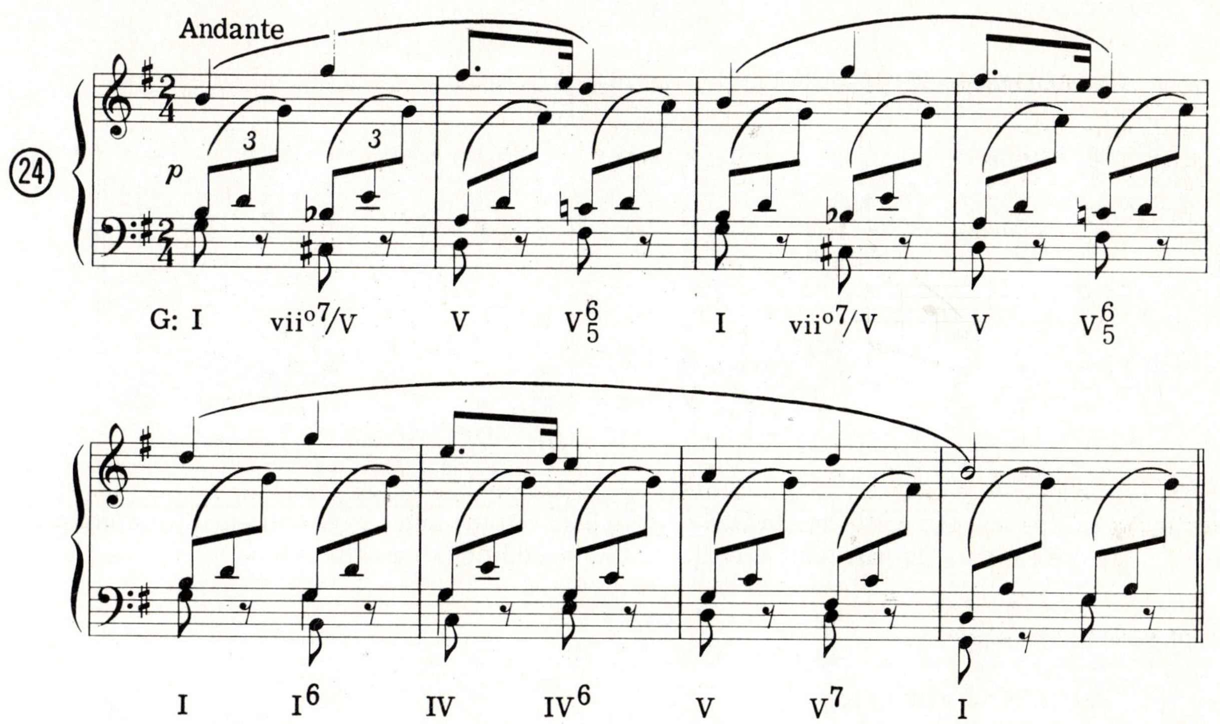

In the next example the arpeggiation is in descending motion, divided between the two hands.

Burgmüller: *Lullaby*

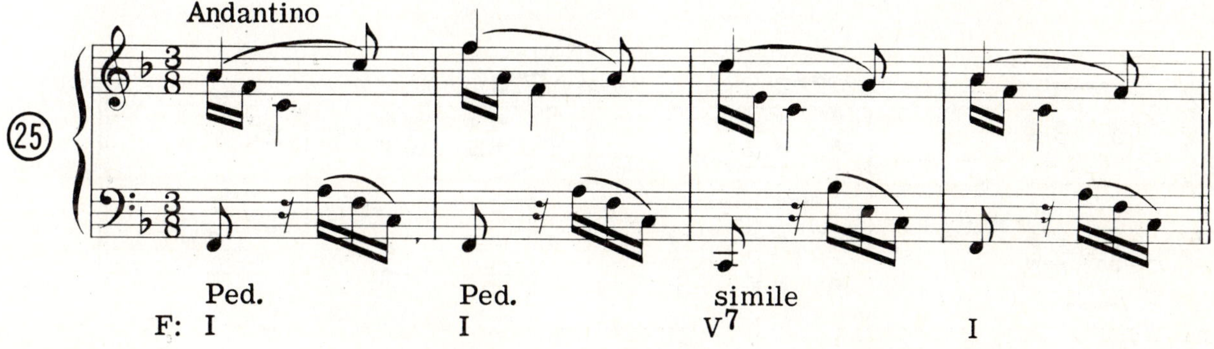

IV. HYMN STYLE. For serious, dignified, or stately effects, melodies may be accompanied in a fashion similar to vocal settings of hymns. In this style chords change for almost every melody note. The resulting rapid harmonic rhythm makes figuration impractical. The number of voices may be consistent, or fluctuate to produce the desired sonorities.

Close style: The example below shows octave doubling of the bass, with the remaining voices in the right hand.

Schumann: *Album für die Jugend* ("Nordisches Lied"), Op. 26

Open style: In this case the voices are divided equally between the two hands, and open structure predominates. Only once is the four-part texture enriched by the addition of a fifth tone.

Chopin: *Mazurka,* Op. 68, No. 3

V. RIGHT-HAND PATTERNS. Of the several typical ways to treat the right hand, the single line melody is the simplest. This style has been amply demonstrated in previous examples (see styles 2, 13, 20, and 21). A few others are shown in the remaining examples.

Added alto in thirds and sixths:

Mozart: *Sonata,* K 333

Filled in chords:

Schubert: *Waltz in B-flat Major*

Melody in octaves: Increased sonority and prominence for the melodic line can be supplied by octave doubling.

Beethoven: *Sonata,* Op. 10, No. 1

Melody with after beats: This technique is used when fuller sonorities are desired. Such patterns also produce a more intricate rhythmic texture.

Mendelssohn: *Lieder ohne Worte,* Op. 102, No. 1

Polyphonic texture has not been touched on here, but even casual use of imitation between melodic and accompaniment elements is effective. In addition, placement of the melody in the tenor or bass registers with the accompaniment above, provides variety. Above all, avoid using only a limited range. The compass of the piano is more than seven octaves, and effective writing requires that the hands range rather widely over the keyboard. In this way the color contrasts of the various registers are exploited.

appendix c

Glossary of Terms

Accessory tone *See* Nonharmonic tone.
Accidental A sign that affects the pitch of a note.
Acoustics The science that deals with sound.
Active tone A tone that has a strong tendency to resolve in a specific direction, e.g., the leading tone.
Altered chord A chord that contains one or more tones which are foreign to the prevailing tonality. Most altered chords fall into four classes: secondary dominants, borrowed chords, chromatic mediants, and augmented sixth chords.
Altered dominants Dominant triads or seventh chords with heightened activity due to chromatic alteration of the fifth.
Altered nonharmonic tone A nonharmonic tone that is inflected so as to be foreign to the prevailing tonality.
Altered tone A tone that is not included in the prevailing tonality.
Alto A low female voice. The next-to-the-highest voice of the four-part chorus.
Amen cadence *See* Plagal cadence.
Anticipation A nonharmonic tone that is approached by step and left by repetition.
Appoggiatura A nonharmonic tone that is approached by leap and left by step, usually with a change of direction.
Appoggiatura chord A chord that is used in a nonharmonic capacity similar to the appoggiatura.
Arpeggiation Sounding the tones of a chord in succession, rather than simultaneously.
Arpeggio six-four chord A second inversion chord formed by arpeggiated movement in the lowest voice.
Atonality The absence of a tonal center.
Augmented fourth An interval that is a half step larger than a perfect fourth.
Augmented major seventh chord A seventh chord consisting of an augmented triad plus a major seventh.
Augmented second An interval that is a half step larger than a major second.
Augmented six-five chord *See* German sixth chord.
Augmented six-four-three chord *See* French sixth chord.
Augmented six-three chord *See* Italian sixth chord.
Augmented sixth An interval that is a half step larger than a major sixth.
Augmented sixth chords A group of chords, all of which contain the interval of an augmented sixth (or diminished third). *See* French sixth chord, German sixth chord, and Italian sixth chord.
Augmented triad A chord consisting of two major thirds.
Authentic cadence A closing harmonic progression consisting of the dominant chord (sometimes the leading tone) followed by the tonic chord.
Auxilliary six-four chord *See* Pedal six-four chord.
Auxilliary tone *See* Neighboring tone.

Baroque era The musical period from 1600 to 1750 characterized by elaborate ornamentation, strict forms, and the establishment of functional harmonic tonality.
Bass A low male voice. The lowest voice of the four-part chorus.
Bass staff The staff modified by the bass clef sign, which designates F below middle C as occurring on the fourth line.
Borrowed chord A diatonic chord in one mode (major or minor), which appears as an altered chord in the opposite parallel mode. Most borrowed chords appear in major, borrowed from the parallel minor key.
Bytone *See* Nonharmonic tone.

Cadence A melodic-harmonic formula that brings a phrase to a more or less definite close.
Cadential six-four chord A second inversion chord that is part of a cadence formula—most frequently, the tonic chord in second inversion followed by the dominant.
Chain of suspensions Several suspensions in succession in which the resolution of one suspension becomes the preparation for the following.
Changing tone *See* Neighboring tone.
Changing tones The middle two notes of a four-note figure, of which the first and fourth are chord tones, and the second and third are nonharmonic tones.

Change of mode A change from major to minor (or the reverse) with the same tonal center retained.

Chord A combination of several tones sounded simultaneously.

Chord changes Changes of harmony.

Chord function Chords function differently depending upon the relation of their root to the tonal center. The tonic chord, for example, is relatively static, whereas the dominant chord is active.

Chord of repose The tonic triad.

Chord quality Chords differ in quality according to their intervallic structure. Diatonic triads, for example, may be major, minor, diminished, or augmented.

Chord seventh The chord member that is a seventh above the root.

Chord spacing The placement of the various chord members in part writing. *See* Close structure; Open structure.

Chord symbol A figure composed of a Roman numeral and sometimes various figured bass symbols. Chord symbols identify the root of the chord in relation to the key center, as well as the quality.

Chord tone One of the tones that constitute a chord.

Chromatic 1) Melodic movement by half steps. 2) Music that incorporates many tones and chords foreign to the prevailing tonality.

Chromatic harmony Harmony that features many altered chords and frequent modulations to foreign keys.

Chromatic mediants Chords whose roots are related by the interval of a third and that contain one or more tones foreign to a single diatonic scale.

Chromatic modulation 1) Modulation in which not all voices move diatonically. 2) Modulation to a foreign key. 3) Modulation in which the common chord is an altered chord in one or both of the keys involved.

Chromatic movement Half-step movement that involves only one basic note.

Chromatic scale A scale consisting entirely of half steps.

Chromatic third relation *See* Chromatic mediants.

Chromatic third-relation harmony *See* Chromatic mediants.

Classical era The musical period from about 1750 to 1800, characterized by simplicity and order.

Closely related keys Keys whose signatures differ by not more than one sharp or flat.

Close structure The spacing of voices so that no vacant chord members occur between the three upper voices.

Color harmony *See* Nonfunctional harmony.

Common chord A chord that functions in two or more keys.

Common chord modulation A modulation that involves a common chord.

Common tone A tone that occurs in two or more chords.

Consecutive perfect intervals Perfect unisons, fourths, fifths, or octaves that occur in succession between the same two voices.

Contrary motion Two voices that move in opposite directions.

Crossed voices The abnormal vertical distribution of voices in a chord, *e.g.*, the alto placed above the soprano.

Cross relation *See* False relation.

Damper pedal The right-hand pedal of the piano, which, when depressed, allows the strings to continue vibrating.

Deceptive cadence A nonfinal cadence consisting of the dominant chord followed by the submediant chord.

Deceptive resolution An unexpected resolution of a chord. Typically, the resolution of the dominant chord to the submediant, rather than to the expected tonic.

Development section In sonata form, the section following the exposition. Previously stated themes undergo various types of variation, and there is usually frequently modulation.

Diatonic Literally "by step"—having to do with scale tones; tonal material derived from a scale.

Diatonic modulation A modulation that involves diatonic melodic movement, and in which the common chord is a diatonic chord in both keys.

Diatonic scale A scale limited to the half and whole steps.

Diatonic seventh chords Seventh chords that are limited to tones of a diatonic scale.

Diatonic triad A triad consisting of tones included in a scale.

Diminished fifth An interval that is a half step smaller than a perfect fifth.

Diminished-minor seventh chord A seventh chord consisting of a diminished triad plus a minor seventh.

Diminished seventh chord A seventh chord consisting of a diminished triad plus a diminished seventh.

Diminished third An interval that is a half step smaller than a minor third.

Diminished triad A chord consisting of two diminished thirds.

Dissonance Auditory tension produced by two or more tones when sounding intervals of the major or minor second, major or minor seventh, or tritone.

Dissonant elements A chord member or nonharmonic tone that creates a dissonance, e.g., the chord seventh.

Distant keys *See* Foreign keys.

Dominant The fifth degree of the scale, or the chord built thereupon.

Dominant eleventh chord A chord of six tones built in thirds on the fifth scale degree.

Dominant function A chord that relates to the following chord as a dominant or leading tone triad, seventh, ninth, etc.

Dominant ninth chord A chord of five tones built in thirds on the fifth scale degree.

Dominant relation The relation between a dominant chord and its tonic.

Dominant seventh chord A chord of four tones built in thirds on the fifth scale degree, a major-minor seventh chord.

Dominant seventh chord with lowered fifth Equivalent to the French sixth chord built on the lowered second scale degree.

Dominant thirteenth chord A chord of seven tones built in thirds on the fifth scale degree.

Double flat A sign that causes a basic note to be raised in pitch a whole step.

Double pedal Two tones (usually tonic and dominant) used simultaneously as a pedal.

Double sharp A sign that causes a basic note to be raised in pitch a whole step.

Doubled tones The same chord member sung by two or more voices.

Doubling The assignment of the same chord member to two or more voices. This is necessary when a triad is set for four or more voices

Doubly augmented six-four-three chord A German sixth chord with the perfect fifth above the sounding root spelled enharmonically as a doubly augmented fourth.

Downward stem A stem that extends downward from a notehead. When the grand staff is used for the four-voice chorus, alto and bass stems go downward.

Dyad A two-note chord.

Dynamics The aspect of music concerning varying degrees of loudness and softness.

Dynamic indications Signs that indicate varying degrees of loudness (amplitude).

Echappée *See* Escape tone.

Elements of Music The basic properties of music, which include rhythm, melody, timbre, texture, and harmony.

Eleventh chord A chord of six tones built in thirds.

Embellishing harmony The chords that are not vital to the stability of the phrase, in contrast to structural harmony.

Embellishing six-four chord *See* Pedal six-four chord.

Enharmonic change Alternate notation of the same pitch, e.g., C-sharp changed to D-flat.

Enharmonic modulation Modulation in which there is an enharmonic change of one or more notes.

Enharmonic spelling A single pitch spelled differently, e.g., G-sharp/A-flat

Equal temperament Tuning of the tones contained within an octave so that all half steps are of equal size.

Escape tone A nonharmonic tone that is approached by step and left by leap, usually with a change of direction.

Essential chord A chord that serves a structural function; often one of the three primary triads (tonic, subdominant, or dominant).

Essential dissonance Dissonance that is part of the harmony.

Expanded tertian sonorities Chords constructed by adding thirds above the triad (seventh, ninth, eleventh, and thirteenth chords).

False relation Chromaticism that occurs between two different voices.

Fifteenth The interval of a double octave.

Figured bass A shorthand notation widely used during the baroque era. *See* Figured bass symbols.

Figured bass symbols Various signs, including numerals and accidentals, placed beneath the bass to indicate chords and melodic motion in the upper voices. Figured bass symbols basically show the intervals that occur above the lowest voice.

Final cadences The cadences that produce a sufficient sense of closure to conclude principal sections of the music. The two final cadences are the authentic and plagal.

First inversion A chord that employs the third in the lowest voice.

Flat A sign that causes a basic note to be lowered in pitch a half step.

Foreign keys Keys whose signatures differ by more than one sharp or flat.

Foreign tone *See* Nonharmonic tone.

Four-part texture Music set in four parts. *See* Four-voice chorus.
Four-part writing Music set in four parts.
Four-voice chorus A chorus consisting of soprano, alto, tenor, and bass.
Free tone A nonharmonic tone that is approached and left by leap.
French sixth chord An augmented sixth chord consisting of a major third, augmented fourth, and augmented sixth above a given note. The French sixth chord is sometimes called an augmented six-four-three chord.
Functional harmony The employment of chords and root progressions that serve to establish a tonality.

German sixth chord An augmented sixth chord consisting of a major third, perfect fifth, and augmented sixth above a given note. The German sixth chord is sometimes called an augmented six-five chord.
Grand staff Two staves joined together, usually with the treble clef sign on the upper and the bass clef sign on the lower.
Gregorian chant The monodic liturgical music of the Roman Catholic Church.

Half cadence A nonfinal cadence, usually terminating with the dominant chord.
Half step The smallest interval of the tempered scale, equivalent to a minor second.
Harmonic action The effect of chords moving from one to another.
Harmonic analysis The process of examining critically the harmonic element of music. The identification of tonalities and the labeling of chords are basic types of harmonic analysis.
Harmonic cadence Closure produced by harmonic action. The strong dominant-tonic progression, for example, contributes to the positive effect of the authentic cadence irrespective of the rhythmic and melodic elements.
Harmonic function The movement of chords to one another defines tonal space and delineates form. Harmonic function basically is either "structural" or "embellishing."
Harmonic interval The interval produced by two tones sounding simultaneously.
Harmonic minor scale A scale that consists of the following half- and whole-step pattern: W H W W H W+ H H.
Harmonic phrase A succession of chords that constitutes a phrase.
Harmonic progression The movement from one chord to another.
Harmonic rhythm The rhythm defined by chord changes
Harmonic sequence The sucessive repetition of a harmonic pattern at a different pitch.
Harmonic tension Tension created by the use of relatively dissonant chords.
Harmonic tonality The definition of a tonal center by means of chords relating in various ways to the tonic.
Harmonic tone A tone that is included as part of a chord.
Harmonization The technique of selecting chords to accompany a melody.
Harmony The element of music concerning chords and their relation to one another.
Horizontal aspect of harmony Successions of chords.

Imperfect cadence An authentic or plagal cadence that lacks a complete sense of finality. *See* perfect cadence.
Impressionist music Music that utilizes techniques developed by impressionist composers, particularly Debussy and Ravel. Features of this music include liberal use of expanded tertian sonorities, unresolved dissonance, parallelism, the whole tone and pentatonic scales, and flexible rhythms.
Inactive tones Tones of the tonic triad are relatively inactive unless part of a dissonant sonority.
Inner pedal An alternate term for a pedal that occurs in an inner voice. *See* Pedal.
Interval The difference in pitch between two tones.
Inversion 1) Altering an interval so that the higher note becomes the lower. This is usually done by moving the upper note an octave lower, or vice versa. 2) Placing a chord member other than the root in the bass.
Inverted pedal An alternate term for a pedal that occurs in an upper voice. *See* Pedal.
Irregular doubling The exigencies of part writing sometimes make it necessary to employ an alternate doubling to avoid a more serious weakness.
Italian sixth chord An augmented sixth chord consisting of a major third and augmented sixth above a given note. The Italian sixth chord is sometimes called an augmented six-three chord.
Iteration Emphasis by repetition, immediate or delayed.

Key The tonality of a composition or segment thereof.
Key center The tonal center; the first degree of the scale upon which the music is based.

Key signature A group of sharps or flats that produce the desired half- and whole-step pattern of a given scale.

Keynote *See* tonal center.

Leading tone The seventh scale degree (a half step below the tonic), or the chord built thereupon.

Leading tone relation A chord that relates to the following chord as a leading tone triad, seventh chord, etc.

Leading tone seventh chord A chord of four tones built in thirds on the seventh scale degree (a half step below the tonic).

Major key The tonality formed by a major scale.

Major-minor-major ninth chord A ninth chord consisting of a major triad, a minor seventh, and major ninth; a dominant ninth chord in a major key.

Major-minor seventh chord A seventh chord consisting of a major triad plus a minor seventh; the dominant seventh chord.

Major ninth chord Equivalent to a dominant ninth chord in a major key.

Major scale A scale that consists of the following half- and whole-step pattern: W W H W W W H.

Major seventh chord A seventh chord consisting of a major triad plus a major seventh.

Major triad A chord consisting of a major third and a superimposed minor third.

Mediant The third scale degree, or the chord built thereupon.

Mediant relationship Chords whose roots are the interval of a third apart are in a mediant relationship with one another.

Mediant seventh chord A seventh chord built on the third scale degree.

Melodic activity Interest created by the melodic element of music.

Melodic contour The shape defined by the rising and falling pitches of a melody.

Melodic function Performance of a linear, rather than a harmonic role.

Melodic line *See* Melodic contour.

Melodic minor scale A scale that consists of two forms:
Ascending: W H W W W W H
Descending: W W H W W H W

Melodic phrase A phrase etched by the melodic contour.

Melodic sequence The successive repetition of a melodic unit at a different pitch.

Melody A musical line produced by a series of single tones.

Minor-major seventh chord A seventh chord consisting of a minor triad plus a major seventh.

Minor ninth chord Equivalent to a dominant ninth chord in a minor key.

Minor seventh chord A seventh chord consisting of a minor triad plus a minor seventh.

Minor triad A chord consisting of a minor triad and a superimposed major third.

Modal mixture The exchange of diatonic chords between parallel major and minor keys.

Modulating sequence A melodic and/or harmonic pattern stated successively at different pitch levels and in different keys.

Modulation The act of establishing a new tonal center.

Natural minor scale A minor scale that uses the same tones as its relative major scale. It consists of the following half- and whole-step pattern: W H W W H W W.

Neapolitan sixth chord A major triad built on the lowered second scale degree, usually in the first inversion.

Neighboring tone A nonharmonic tone that is approached and left by step with a change of direction. Neighboring tones usually occur on an unaccented portion of the beat and may be either a step above or below the harmonic tone.

New key The tonal destination of a modulation.

Ninth chord A chord of five tones built in thirds.

Nonchord tone *See* Nonharmonic tone.

Nondominant seventh chord Any seventh chord other than the dominant seventh.

Nonfinal cadences Cadences that are incapable of bringing a composition to a close. The two nonfinal cadences are the half and the deceptive.

Nonfunctional Harmony that performs an embellishing, rather than a tonality-defining role.

Nonharmonic tone A tone that is extraneous to the harmony.

Normal resolution The usual, predictable movement of an active tone or chord.

Notehead The part of a note that indicates the pitch.

Oblique motion Movement of two voices, one of which remains stationery while the other moves either upward or downward.

Octave An interval in which the frequency of the higher note is double that of the lower.

Old key The original tonality of a modulation.

Open structure The spacing of voices so that there is a vacant chord member between the tenor and alto, and between the alto and soprano.

Opening progression Harmonic movement away from the tonic at the beginning of the phrase.
Organ point *See* Pedal.
Ornamentation One or more notes appearing between a suspension and its resolution.

Pandiatonicism The use of the tone of a diatonic scale without observing its usual functional idiosyncrasies.
Parallel keys Two keys (major and minor) that employ the same tonic.
Parallel fifths Movement in fifths between the same two voices. If both fifths are perfect, the individuality of the voices is diminished. Such movement is generally avoided.
Parallel motion Two or more voices moving by the same intervals in the same direction.
Parallel perfect fifths Movement in perfect fifths between the same two voices; generally avoided.
Part writing The technique of writing chords and leading voices from one to another.
Passing chord A chord that performs a nonharmonic function similar to a passing tone.
Passing six-four chord A second-inversion chord that usually occurs between a triad in first inversion and the same triad in root position. Typical is the following: tonic in first inversion—dominant in second inversion—tonic in root position.
Passing tone A nonharmonic tone that is approached and left by step in the same direction. It may occur either ascending or descending, and may be either accented or unaccented.
Passive resolution The retention of an active tone, e.g., the chord seventh, in the same voice in the following chord.
Pedal A nonharmonic tone that is sustained (usually in the bass), against which other voices produce harmonies that are foreign to it.
Pedal point *See* Pedal.
Pedal six-four chord A second-inversion chord that occurs over the same (or repeated) bass note, e.g., the subdominant six-four preceded and followed by the tonic in root position.
Perfect cadence An authentic or plagal cadence that meets the following conditions:

1. Both the final and penultimate chords must be in root position.
2. The final (tonic) chord must have the keynote in the highest voice.

Phrase A basic unit in the formal organization of music, usually four measures in length, used especially during the classical period.
Phrase modulation A modulation that occurs at the beginning of a new phrase.
Phrase structure The underlying harmonies stripped of embellishing chords. Most phrases fall into one of three types:

1. A single chord followed by a cadence.
2. Harmonic embellishment by a single chord followed by a cadence.
3. A cadence formula (or basic harmonic progression) spread over the entire phrase.

Phrygian cadence In traditional harmony, a type of half cadence. The subdominant in first inversion moving to the dominant (in a minor key) is a typical example.
Picardy third The raised third in the tonic chord of a minor key. This effect is usually reserved for the final chord, to provide a more emphatic conclusion.
Pitch The "highness" or "lowness" of sound.
Pivot chord *See* Common chord.
Pivot tone A single tone that is common to two keys and serves as a link from one to the other.
Pivot tone modulation Modulation by means of a tone that is common to two keys.
Plagal cadence A closing harmonic progression consisting of the subdominant chord followed by the tonic chord.
Polychord Two or more chords sounding simultaneously.
Polyharmony Two or more chords that occur simultaneously.
Polytonality The simultaneous occurrence of two or more tonalities.
Preparation The initial note of the suspension figure. *See* Suspension.
Primary triads The tonic, subdominant, and dominant triads.
Progression 1) The movement from one chord to another. 2) More specifically, harmonic movement that creates a sense of forward motion. Root movements down in fifths, up in seconds, and down in thirds generally produce strong effects. *See also* Retrogression.
Pure minor scale *See* Natural minor scale.

Range The normal compass of a given voice or instrument.
Relative keys Major and minor keys that have the same signature, but different tonics.
Remote keys *See* Foreign keys.
Resolution 1) The movement from one chord to another; the term often denotes movement from an active chord to a less active one. 2) The final note of the suspension figure. *See also* Suspension.
Retardation A suspension that resolves upward. *See also* Suspension.

Retrogression A relatively weak harmonic movement. *See also* Progression.
Returning note *See* Neighboring tone.
Rhythm The temporal aspect of music. Involved is the division of time into beats, accent patterns of meter, and rhythmic figures.
Roman numerals Symbols used to identify chords built on the various degrees of the scale.
Roman numeral analysis The use of Roman numerals and other figures associated with chord symbols to indicate the quality of chords and their position in relation to the key center.
Romantic era The musical period from about 1800 to 1900 characterized by emphasis on emotional qualities, freedom of form, increased use of chromaticism, and expanded tonality.
Root The note on which a chord is built.
Root movement The intervallic relationship of the root of a chord to the root of an adjoining chord.
Root position The arrangement of a chord so that the root is in the lowest voice.

Scale A stepwise arrangement (ascending or descending) of the tones contained in an octave.
Scale degrees The tones contained in a scale.
Secondary dominant An altered chord that functions as dominant (a leading tone) to a diatonic triad other than the tonic.
Secondary seventh chord *See* Nondominant seventh chords.
Secondary triads Triads that are built on the second, third, sixth, and seventh scale degrees.
Second inversion The arrangement of a triad so that the fifth is in the lowest voice.
Sequence The successive statement or repetition of a melodic and/or harmonic unit at a different pitch level.
Sequence modulation Modulation caused by sequence units that move successively through different keys.
Sequential pattern A melodic and/or harmonic unit that is repeated successively at a different pitch.
Seventh 1) An interval encompassing seven basic notes. 2) The highest note of a seventh chord when in root position.
Seventh chord A chord consisting of four tones built in thirds.
Sharp A sign that causes a basic note to be raised a half step.
Signature *See* Key signature.
Similar motion Two voices that move in the same direction, but not by the same interval.
Six-four chord *See* Second inversion.
Slash (/) A sign that is used in conection with figured bass symbols. When drawn through a number, the note represented by the number is raised a half step.
Sonata form A form consisting of three principal sections: exposition, development, and recapitulation. Sometimes called "first movement" form because of its use in most opening movements of the classical symphony, sonata, and concerto.
Sonority The aural effect of a tone or group of tones.
Soprano A high female voice. The highest voice of the four-voice chorus.
Sounding root The chord member of the Italian and German sixth chords that has the aural effect of the root, as opposed to the "written" root. *See* Written root.
Spacing The placement of the various chord members in part writing. *See also* chord spacing.
Staff The five parallel horizontal lines and intervening spaces upon which musical symbols are placed.
Stationary six-four chord *See* Pedal six-four chord.
Stem The vertical line attached to a notehead.
Stepwise motion Melodic movement to adjacent scale degrees.
Strong beat A beat that has relatively strong metric stress, e.g., the first beat of the measure.
Structural harmony Harmony that appears at strategic formal points and serves to establish the tonal organization.
Structural points Locations that have special formal significance, e.g., the beginning and end of the phrase.
Structural tones The first, fourth, and fifth tones of the scale are the roots of the three primary triads: tonic, subdominant, and dominant.
Structure of tonality The tonal pattern created by the three principal triads: the tonic, the dominant (a perfect fifth above), and the subdominant (a perfect fifth below).
Subdominant The fourth scale degree, or the chord built thereupon.
Subdominant seventh chord A seventh chord built on the fourth scale degree.
Submediant The sixth scale degree, or the chord built thereupon.
Submediant seventh chord A seventh chord built on the sixth scale degree.
Submediant seventh chord with raised root and third A diminished seventh chord built on the raised sixth scale degree in major. Resolution is

usually to the dominant triad or seventh chord in first inversion.

Subtonic The tone a whole step below the tonic, or the chord built thereupon.

Supertonic The second scale degree, or the chord built thereupon.

Supertonic seventh chord A seventh chord built on the second scale degree.

Supertonic seventh chord with raised root and third A diminished seventh chord built on the raised second scale degree in major. Resolution is usually to the tonic chord in first inversion.

Suspended tonality The effect produced by a series of nonfunctional chords or rapid modulations.

Suspension A nonharmonic tone that is approached by the same note (usually tied) and left by step (usually downward).

Symmetrical chords Chords that incorporate some form of symmetry, e.g., the augmented triad and the diminished seventh chords that divide the octave into equal intervals.

Symmetrical relationship Tones, chords, or rhythms that bear some kind of equal relationship to one another, e.g., a passage of chords in which roots are related consistently by the interval of the third.

Tenor A high male voice. The next-to-the-lowest voice of the four-voice chorus.

Tension *See* Harmonic tension.

Texture The structure of sound created by tones sounding together.

Third inversion A chord that employs the seventh in the lowest voice.

Third relation Tones or chords related by the interval of the third.

Thirteenth chord A chord of seven tones built in thirds.

Timbre The quality of sound determined by the number and relative intensity of its overtones.

Tonal center The first degree of the scale: the tonic.

Tonal harmony Harmony based on diatonic scales that demonstrates loyalty toward the tonic.

Tonal music Music that adheres to a central tone, the tonic.

Tonal spectrum The array of tones utilized in a given passage or composition.

Tonal system *See* Tonality.

Tonal vocabulary The tonal resources available within a particular style.

Tonality The organization of the tones and chords of a key with reference to the tonic.

Tone cluster A relatively dissonant chord produced by sounding several tones close together.

Tonic The first degree of the scale, or the chord built thereupon.

Tonic-dominant axis The tonality-defining relationship governed by the tonic and dominant chords, whose roots are a perfect fifth apart.

Tonic eleventh chord A chord of six tones built in thirds on the first scale degree.

Tonic seventh chord A chord of four tones built in thirds on the first scale degree.

Tonicization The emphasis of a particular diatonic chord by embellishing it with an altered chord that bears a dominant relationship to it.

Traditional music Music that is based on tonal, harmonic, rhythmic, and formal practices of the so-called "common practice" period—the baroque, classical, and romantic eras.

Transient modulation Modulation to a key that is passed through quickly on the way to another key.

Treble staff The staff modified by the treble clef sign, which designates G above middle C as occurring on the second line.

Triad A chord of three tones. Most triads are built in thirds.

Triad tone A tone that is part of a triad.

Triple pedal *See* Pedal.

Tritone Three whole steps. The interval of the augmented fourth (or diminished fifth). The tritone divides the octave into two equal parts.

Unessential chord A chord that is not vital to the stability of the phrase. *See also* Embellishing harmony.

Unessential dissonance Dissonance that appears incidentally, as a nonharmonic tone.

Upper voices All voices other than the lowest.

Upward stem A stem that is attached to the right-hand side of the notehead and extends upward. When the grand staff is used for the four-voice chorus, soprano and tenor stems go upward.

Vertical aspect of harmony Chords, as opposed to chord progressions.

Voice leading The technique of moving the various voices from one chord to another.

Weak beat A beat that has relatively light metric stress.

Western music Music of Western Europe and music that has been derived therefrom.

Whole step The major second; two half steps.

Written root The lowest tone of a chord when arranged in thirds, as opposed to the sounding root in the case of the Italian and German sixth chords. *See* Sounding root.

appendix d

Orchestration Chart

Note that conservative, practical ranges have been given here: In compositional assignments the extreme ranges of the instruments would probably be best avoided to facilitate classroom performances. See orchestration books in the Bibliography for information on instruments not listed here. The sounding range of the instrument is given first in wholenotes, followed by the written range in quarternotes. The transposition interval, if needed, is given just to the right of the range staff.

WOODWINDS

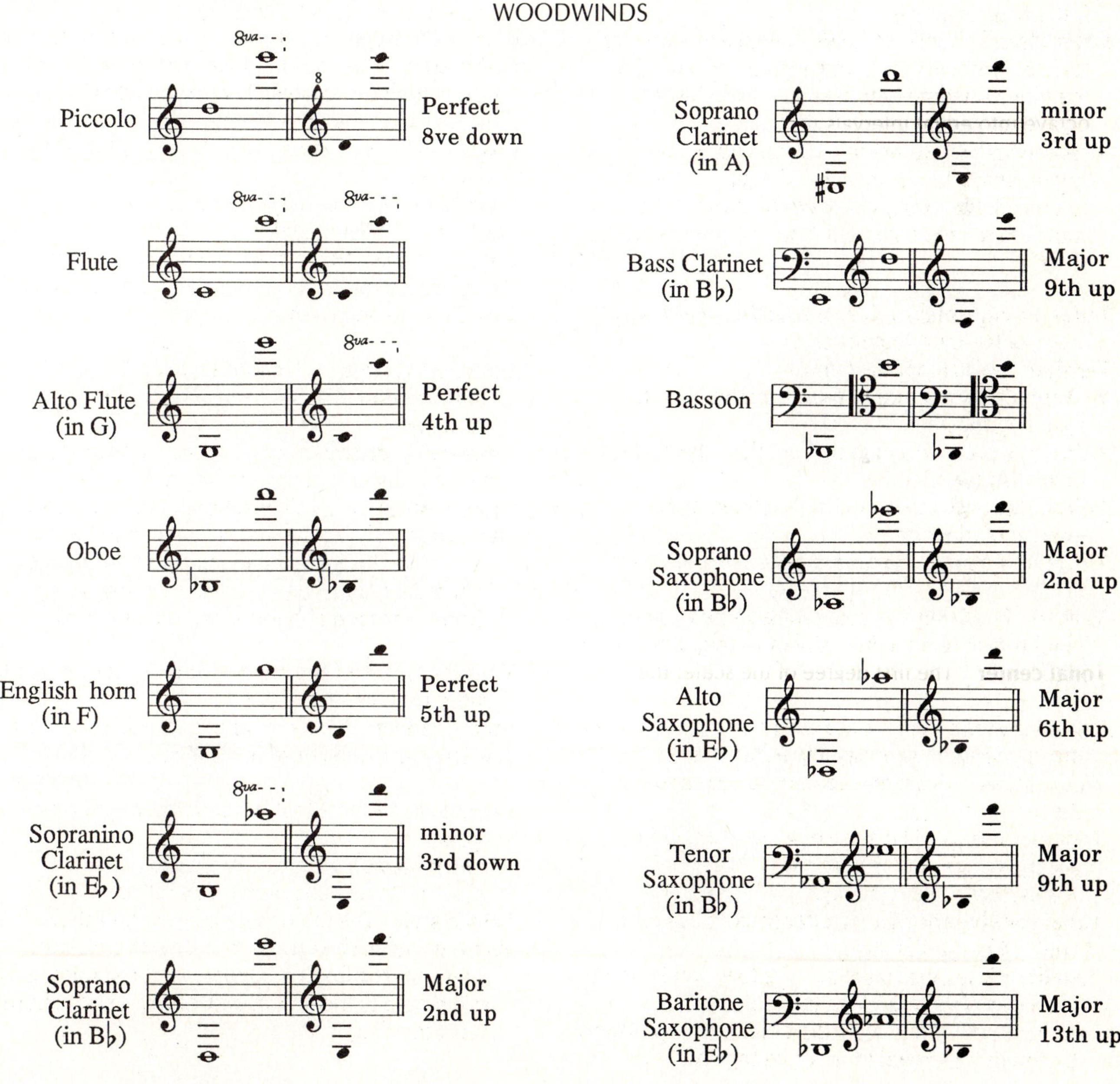

BRASS

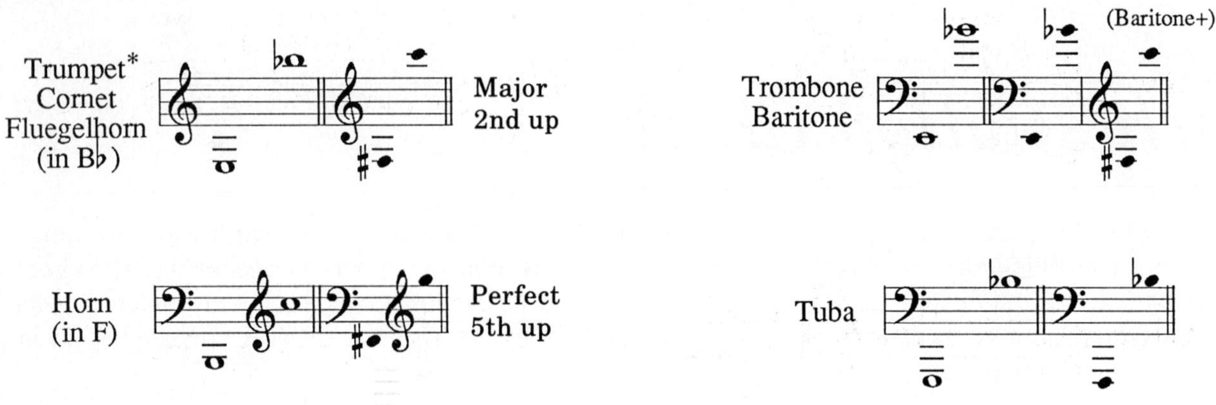

*C trumpet's sounding and written range is same as B♭ trumpet's written range.

+If baritone is written in treble clef, then it is written as a B♭ transposition; always check with your player to see which clef should be used for your part.

STRINGS

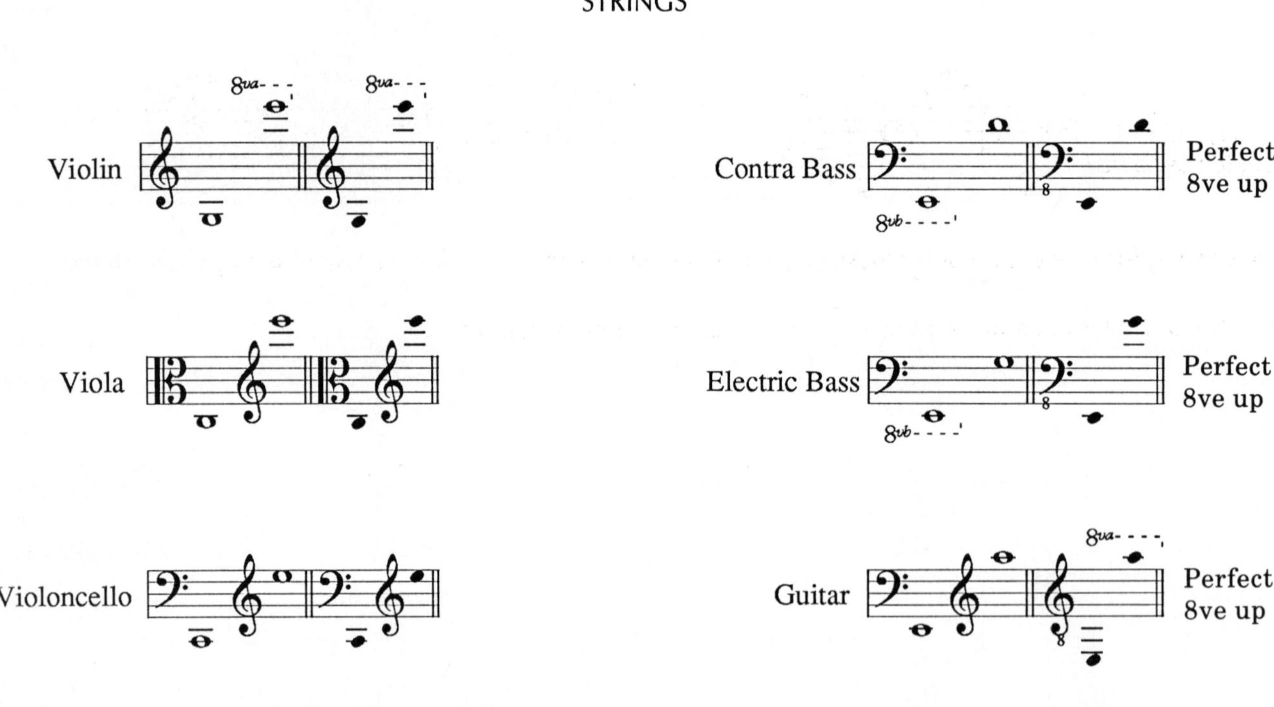

KEYBOARD RELATED*

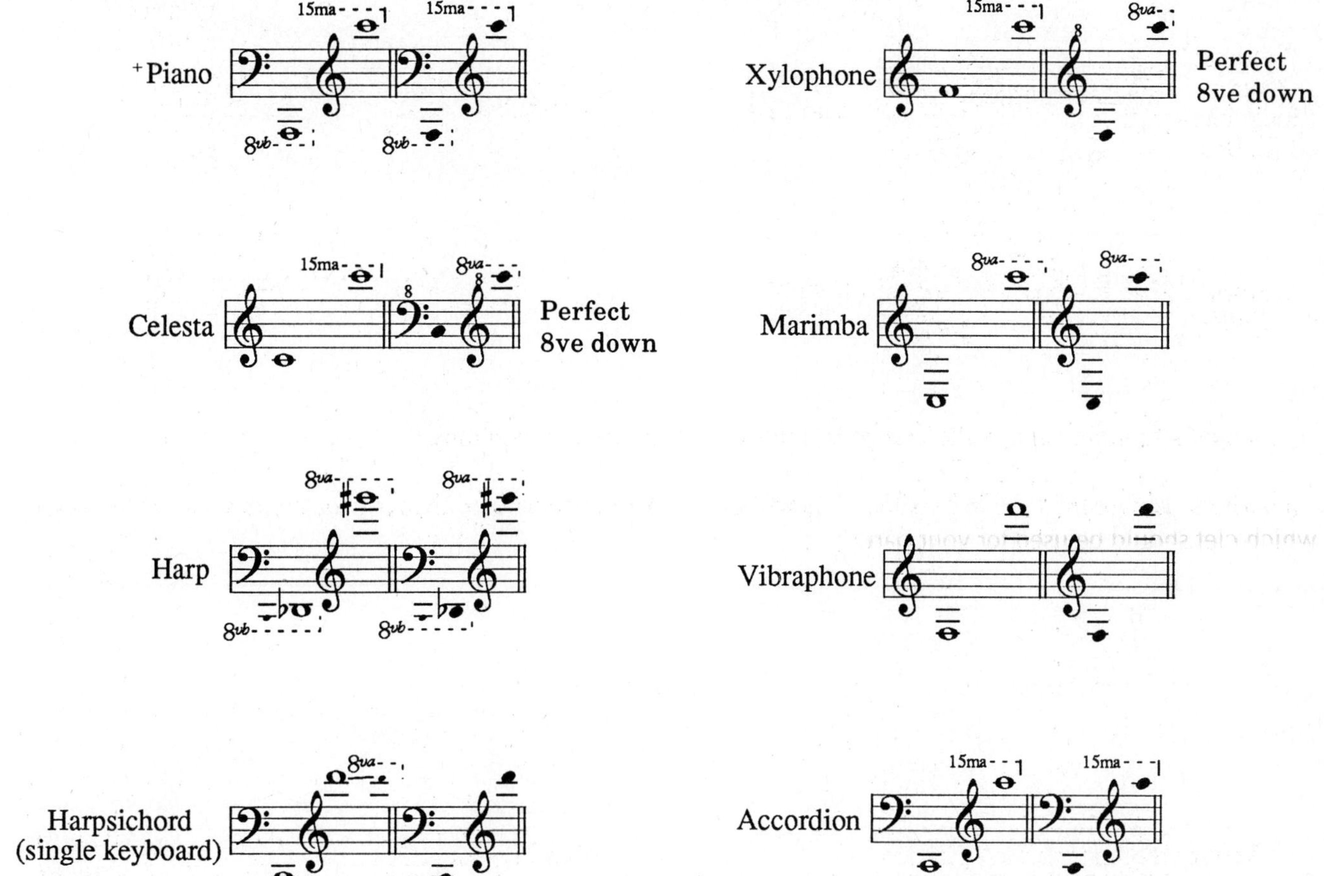

*For organ (pipe or electric) or synthesizers, check with instrument or performer available to you for ranges.

+Electric or synthesized piano ranges may vary from this normal piano range.

Bibliography for Further Study

ACOUSTICS

Backus, John. *Acoustical Foundations of Music,* 2nd ed. 1977. (ISBN 0-393-09029-9). New York: W. W. Norton.

Benade, A. H. *Fundamentals of Musical Acoustics.* 1976. (ISBN 0-19-502030-8). Fairlawn, N.J.: Oxford University Press.

______. *Horns, Strings, & Harmony.* 1979. Reprint of 1960 ed. (ISBN 0-313-20771-2, BEHO). Westport, Conn.: Greenwood Press.

Campbell, D. W., & Greated, Clive A. *The Musicians Guide to Acoustics.* 1987. (ISBN 0-02-870161-5). New York: Schirmer Books.

Erickson, Robert. *Sound Structure in Music.* 1975. (ISBN 0-520-02376-5). Berkeley, Calif.: University of California Press.

Moravcsik, Michael J. *Musical Sound: An Introduction to the Physics of Music.* 1987. (ISBN 0-913729-39-6). New York: Paragon House.

Pierce, John R. *The Science of Musical Sound.* 1983. (ISBN 0-7167-1508-2). New York: W. H. Freeman.

Stawson, Wayne. *Sound Color.* 1985. (ISBN 0-520-05185-8). Berkeley, Calif.: University of California Press.

COMPOSITION

Austin, Larry, & Clark, Thomas. *Learning to Compose—Modes, Materials, and Models of Musical Invention.* 1989. (ISBN 3495). Dubuque, Iowa: William C. Brown.

Cope, David. *New Music Composition.* 1977. (ISBN 0-02-870630-7). New York: Schirmer Books.

Dallin, Leon. *Techniques of Twentieth-Century Composition: A Guide to the Materials of Modern Music,* 3rd ed. 1974. (ISBN 0-697-03614-6). Dubuque, Iowa: William C. Brown.

Marquis, G. Welton. *Twentieth-Century Music Idioms.* Reprint of 1964 ed. 1981. (ISBN 0-313-22624-5, MATC). Westport, Conn.: Greenwood Press.

Russo, William, & Ainis, Jeffrey. *Composing Music: A New Approach.* 1983. (ISBN 0-13-164756-3). Englewood Cliffs, N.J.: Prentice-Hall.

Wourinen, Charles. *Simple Composition.* 1979. (ISBN 0-582-28059-1). New York: Longman.

COUNTERPOINT

Benjamin, Thomas. *Counterpoint in the Style of J. S. Bach.* 1986. (ISBN 0-02-870280-8). New York: Schirmer Books.

______. *The Craft of Modal Counterpoint: A Practice Approach.* 1979. (ISBN 0-02-870480-0). New York: Schirmer Books.

Gauldin, Robert. *A Practical Approach to Sixteenth-Century Counterpoint.* 1985. (ISBN 0-13-689258-2). Englewood Cliffs, N.J.: Prentice-Hall.

Kennan, Kent. *Counterpoint,* 2nd ed. 1972. (ISBN 0-13-184291-9). Englewood Cliffs, N.J.: Prentice-Hall.

Mason, Neale B. *Essentials of Eighteenth-Century Counterpoint.* 1968. (ISBN 0-697-03605-7). Dubuque, Iowa: William C. Brown.

Merriman, Margarita. *A New Look at Sixteenth-Century Counterpoint.* 1982. (ISBN 0-8191-2392-7). Lanham, Md.: University Press of America.

Parks, Richard S. *Eighteenth-Century Counterpoint & Tonal Structure,* 2nd ed. 1984. (ISBN 0-13-246744-5). Englewood Cliffs, N.J.: Prentice-Hall.

Piston, Walter. *Counterpoint.* 1947. (ISBN 0-393-09728-5). New York: W. W. Norton.

Schenker, Heinrich. *Counterpoint, 2 Vols.* Rothgeb, John, & Thym, Jurgen, trans. 1986. (ISBN 0-02-873220-0). New York: Schirmer Books.

Schönberg, Arnold. *Preliminary Exercises in Counterpoint.* Stein, Leonard, ed. 1982. (ISBN 0-571-09275-6). Winchester, Mass.: Faber & Faber.

Searle, Humphrey. *Twentieth-Century Counterpoint: A Guide for Students.* Reprint of 1954 ed. 1986. (ISBN 0-88355-763-0). Westport, Conn.: Hyperion Press.

Westergaard, Peter. *Introduction to Tonal Theory.* 1976. (ISBN 0-393-09342-5). New York: W. W. Norton.

EAR TRAINING/SIGHTSINGING

Blombach, Ann K. *MacGAMUT, Intervals•Scales•Chords*. 1988. Mountain View, Calif.: Mayfield.

Carlsen, James C. *Melodic Perception: A Program for Self-Instruction*. 1965. (ISBN 0-07-009975-8). New York: McGraw-Hill.

Gregory, David. *Melodic Dictator* (Macintosh program). 1988. Ann Arbor, Mich.: University of Michigan Center for Performing Arts and Technology.

Ghezzo, Marta A. *Solfege, Ear Training, Rhythm, Dictation, & Music Theory: A Comprehensive Course*. 1980. (ISBN 0-8173-6403-X). University: University of Alabama Press.

Horacek, Leo, & Lefkoff, Gerald. *Programmed Ear Training*. 4 Vols. 1970. (texts & tapes). San Diego, Calif.: Harcourt Brace Jovanovich.

Kelly, Robert. *Aural & Visual Recognition: A Musical Ear Training Series*. 1972. (ISBN 0-252-00073-0). Champaign, Ill.: University of Illinois Press.

Olson, Robert G. *Music Dictation: A Stereo Taped Series*. 1970. (ISBN 0-534-00671-X). Belmont, Calif.: Wadsworth.

Trubitt, Allen R., & Hines, Robert S. *Ear Training & Sight-Singing: An Integrated Approach*. 1979. (ISBN 0-02-870810-5). New York: Schirmer Books.

Wittlich, Gary, & Humphries, Lee. *Ear Training: An Approach Through Music Literature*. 1974. (ISBN 0-15-518707-4). (records, tapes, or cassettes). San Diego, Calif.: Harcourt Brace Jovanovich.

Listen 2.0 (Interactive Ear Training Software for the Apple Macintosh). 1989. Menlo Park, Calif.: Resonate.

Note: As this book goes to press there are a number of computer programs available and more coming out all the time. You may wish to explore a number of programs available in this area published by Temporal Acuity Products, Inc., Bellevue, Wash., and CODA, Wenger Corp., Owatonna, Minn., for all types of computers.

FORM/ANALYSIS

Berry, Wallace. *Form in Music*, 2nd ed. 1986. (ISBN 0-13-329285-1). Englewood Cliffs, N.J.: Prentice-Hall.

Cook, Nicholas. *A Guide to Musical Analysis*. 1987. (ISBN 0-8076-1172-7). New York: George Braziller.

Cooper, Paul. *Perspectives in Music Theory: An Historical-Analytical Approach*. 1973. (ISBN 0-06-041368-9, HarpC.) New York: Harper & Row.

Dunsby, Jonathan, & Whittal, Arnold. *Musical Analysis*. 1987. (ISBN 0-300-03713-9). New Haven, Conn.: Yale University Press.

Epstein, David. *Beyond Orpheus: Studies in Musical Structure*. 1987. (ISBN 0-19-315150-2). Fairlawn, N.J.: Oxford University Press.

Forte, Allen, & Gilbert, Steven E. *Introduction to Schenkerian Analysis: Form & Content in Tonal Music*. 1982. (ISBN 0-393-95192-8). New York: W. W. Norton.

Green, Douglas M. *Form in Tonal Music: An Introduction to Analysis*, 2nd ed. 1979. (ISBN 0-03-020286-8). New York: Holt, Rinehart, & Winston.

Hutcheson, Jere T. *Musical Form & Analysis*. 2 Vols. (ISBN 0-8008-5454-3; 0-8008-5455-1). Boston: Taplinger.

Mason, Robert M. *Modern Methods of Music Analysis Using Computers*. 1985. (ISBN 0-9615669-0-6). Peterborough, N.H.: Schoolhouse Press.

Narmour, Eugene. *Beyond Schenkerism: The Need for Alternatives in Music Analysis*. 1980. (ISBN 0-226-56848-2, P893, Phoen). Chicago: University of Chicago Press.

Spencer, Peter, & Temko, Peter M. *A Practical Approach to the Study of Form in Music*. 1988. (ISBN 0-13-689050-4). Englewood Cliffs, N.J.: Prentice-Hall.

Wade, Graham. *The Shape of Music: An Introduction to Musical Form*. 1982. (ISBN 0-8052-8110-X). New York: Schocken Books.

Walton, Charles W. *Basic Forms in Music*. 1974. (ISBN 0-88284-010-X). Sherman Oaks, Calif.: Alfred Publishing.

Warfield, Gerald. *Layer Analysis: A Primer of Elementary Tonal Structures*. 1978. (ISBN 0-582-28069-9). New York: Longman.

White, John D. *The Analysis of Music*, 2nd ed. 1984. (ISBN 0-8108-1701-2). Metuchen, N.J.: Scarecrow Press.

GENERAL

Barra, Donald. *The Dynamic Performance: A Performer's Guide to Musical Expression & Interpretation*. 1983. (ISBN 13-221556-X). Englewood Cliffs, N.J.: Prentice-Hall.

Baur, John. *Music Theory Through Literature*. 2 Vols. 1985. (ISBN 0-13-607821-4; 0-13-607847-8). Englewood Cliffs, N.J.: Prentice-Hall.

Beach, David. *Aspects of Schenkerian Theory*. 1983. (ISBN 0-300-02803-2). New Haven, Conn.: Yale University Press.
Cogan, Robert. *New Images of Musical Sound*. 1984. (ISBN 0-674-61585-9). Cambridge, Mass.: Harvard University Press.
Cogan, Robert, & Escot, Pozzi. *Sonic Design: The Nature of Sound & Music*. 1976. Englewood Cliffs, N.J.: Prentice-Hall.
Fotine, Larry. *Contemporary Musician's Handbook & Dictionary*. 1984. (ISBN 0-933830-03-3). Sepulveda, Calif.: Poly Tone Press.
Helm, Eugene, & Luper, Albert T. *Words & Music: Form & Procedure in Theses, Dissertations, Research Papers, Book Reports, Programs, & Theses in Composition*. 1971. (ISBN 0-913574-00-7). Valley Forge, Pa.: European American Music.
Rahn, Jay. *A Theory for All Music: Problems & Solutions in the Analysis of Non-Western Forms*. 1983. (ISBN 0-8020-5538-9). Toronto: University of Toronto Press.
Reti, Rudolph R. *The Thematic Process in Music*. Reprint of 1951 ed. 1978. (ISBN 0-8371-9875-5, RETH). Westport, Conn.: Greenwood Press.
______. *Tonality, Atonality, Pantonality: A Study of Some Trends in Twentieth-Century Music*. 1978. Reprint of 1958 ed. (ISBN 0-313-20478-0, RETO). Westport, Conn.: Greenwood Press.
Schafer, R. Murray. *The Thinking Ear*. 1986. (C86-093409-8). Arcana Ed., PO Box 425, Sta. K., Toronto, Canada.
Toch, Ernst. *The Shaping Forces in Music: An Inquiry into the Nature of Harmony, Melody, Counterpoint, Form*. 1977. (ISBN 0-486-23346-4). Mineola, N.Y.: Dover Publications.

MUSICAL ANTHOLOGIES

Benjamin, Thomas E. *Music for Analysis: Examples from the Common Practice Period & the Twentieth Century*, 2nd ed. 1984. (ISBN 0-395-34225-2). Boston: Houghton Mifflin.
Berry, Wallace, & Chudacoff, Edward. *Eighteenth-Century Imitative Counterpoint: Music for Analysis*. 1969. (ISBN 0-13-246843-3). Englewood Cliffs, N.J.: Prentice-Hall.
Bockmon, Guy A., & Starr, William J. *Scored for Listening: A Guide to Music*, 2nd ed. 1972. (ISBN 0-15-579055-2, HC); records (ISBN 0-15-579056-0). San Diego, Calif.: Harcourt Brace Jovanovich.
Brandt, William; Corra, Arthur; Christ, William; DeLeone, Richard; & Winold, Allen. *The Comprehensive Study of Music*. New York: Harper & Row
Burkhart, Charles. *Anthology for Musical Analysis*, 3rd ed. 1979. (ISBN 0-03-018866-0). New York: Holt, Rinehart, & Winston.
Hardy, Gordon, & Fish, Arnold. *Music Literature: A Workbook for Analysis*. 2 Vols. 1966. (ISBN 0-06-042633-0, HarpC; 0-06-042634-9). New York: Harper & Row.
Kamien, Roger, ed. *The Norton Scores: An Anthology for Listening*, 4th ed. 2 Vols. 1984. (ISBN 0-393-95304-1; 0-393-95310-6). New York: W. W. Norton.
Melcher, Robert A.; Warch, Williard F.; & Mast, Paul B. *Music for Study*, 3rd ed. 1988. Englewood Cliffs, N.J.: Prentice-Hall.
Palisca, Calude V., ed. *Norton Anthology of Western Music*, 2nd ed. 2 Vols. 1988. (ISBN 0-393-95642-3; 0-393-95644-X). New York: W. W. Norton.
Ward-Steinmen, David, & Ward-Steinman, Susan L. *Comparative Anthology of Musical Forms*, 2 Vols. 1987. Reprint of 1976 Ed. (ISBN 0-8191-5600-0). Lanham, Md.: University Press of America.
Wennerstrom, Mary H. *Anthology of Musical Structure & Style*. 1983. (ISBN 0-13-038372-4). Englewood Cliffs, N.J.: Prentice-Hall.

MUSICAL NOTATION

Harder, Paul O. *Music Manuscript Techniques, A Programed Approach*, 2 Parts. 1984. (ISBN 0-205-07992-X [pt. 1], 0-205-07993-8 [pt. 2]). Boston: Allyn and Bacon.
Jarrett, Jack M. *Music Printer* (Apple IIe program) or *Music Printer Plus* (IBM program). 1987 & 1988. Bellevue, Wash.: Temporal Acuity Products, Inc.
Read, Gardner. *Music Notation*. 1979. (ISBN 0-8008-5453-5). Boston: Taplinger.
Warfield, Gerald. *How to Write Music Manuscript in Pencil*. 1977. (ISBN 0-679-30332-4). New York: Longman.

Notewriter II. (computer program for Macintosh). 1989. Half Moon Bay, Calif.: Passport Designs.

Note: As this text goes to press there are a number of notation programs available and more coming out all the time. You may wish to explore these more advanced programs: FINALE by Coda, *PROFESSIONAL COMPOSER* by Mark of the Unicorn, *MUSIC PUBLISHER* by Graphic Notes, *HB ENGRAVER* by HB Imaging (all Macintosh based) and *PERSONAL COMPOSER* by Jim Miller or *SCORE* by Passport Designs (IBM based.)

ORCHESTRATION

Adler, Samuel. *The Study of Orchestration*. 1982. (ISBN 0-393-95188-X). New York: W. W. Norton.

Blatter, Alfred. *Instrumentation-Orchestration*. 1980. (ISBN 0-582-28118-0). New York: Macmillan.

Burton, Steven D. *Orchestration*. 1982. (ISBN 0-13-639500-7). Englewood Cliffs, N.J.: Prentice-Hall.

Kennan, Kent, & Grantham, Donald. *The Technique of Orchestration*, 3rd ed. 1983. (ISBN 0-13-900308-8). Englewood Cliffs, N.J.: Prentice-Hall.

Polansky, Larry. *New Instrumentation & Orchestration: An Outline for Study*. 1986. (ISBN 0-945996-01-2). Oakland, Calif.: Frog Peak Music.

Read, Gardner. *Style & Orchestration*. 1979. (ISBN 0-02-872110-1). New York: Schirmer Books.

Please note that the many musical computer programs, based on both Apple and IBM systems and appearing all the time, may relate to one or more of the bibliographical areas above. Check with an instructor or musical computer listings for what is currently available.

index

Musical Examples

(Numbers refer to frames, except where page numbers are indicated (p. or pp.), which refer to examples used for Supplementary Assignments.)

index

Subjects

(Numbers refer to frames, except where page numbers are indicated (p. or pp.).)

NOTES

NOTES

NOTES

NOTES

NOTES

NOTES

NOTES

NOTES

NOTES

NOTES

NOTES

NOTES